Chemical
Deception

Chemical Deception

THE TOXIC THREAT TO HEALTH AND THE ENVIRONMENT

Marc Lappé, Ph.D.

PROFESSOR OF HEALTH POLICY AND ETHICS
UNIVERSITY OF ILLINOIS, COLLEGE OF MEDICINE CHICAGO

SIERRA CLUB BOOKS • SAN FRANCISCO

The Sierra Club, founded in 1892 by John Muir, has devoted itself to the study and protection of the earth's scenic and ecological resources — mountains, wetlands, woodlands, wild shores and rivers, deserts and plains. The publishing program of the Sierra Club offers books to the public as a nonprofit educational service in the hope that they may enlarge the public's understanding of the Club's basic concerns. The point of view expressed in each book, however, does not necessarily represent that of the Club. The Sierra Club has some sixty chapters coast to coast, in Canada, Hawaii, and Alaska. For information about how you may participate in its programs to preserve wilderness and the quality of life, please address inquiries to Sierra Club, 730 Polk Street, San Francisco, CA 94109.

Library of Congress Cataloging in Publication Data

Lappé, Marc.
    Chemical deception : the toxic threat to health and the
environment / Marc Lappé.
        p.   cm.
        "January 14, 1990."
        Includes bibliographical references and index.
        ISBN 0-87156-511-0
        1. Environmental health.   2. Toxicology.   3. Public health.
    I. Title.
    RA566.L35   1991
    610'.1 — dc20   90-9043
                                                                         CIP

Cover design by Paul Bacon

Production by Robin Rockey

Book design by Seventeenth Street Studios

Printed in the United States on acid-free paper containing a minimum of 50% recovered waste paper, of which at least 10% of the fiber content is post-consumer waste

10 9 8 7 6 5 4 3 2 1

For Don and Alice; may all our children grow up healthy

Contents

Acknowledgments

THIS BOOK COULD NOT HAVE BEEN WRITTEN WITHOUT THE GENEROUS offer of a three month sabbatical from the College of Medicine at the University of Illinois at Chicago.

Thanks also to Commonweal, that idyllic and resource-filled place by the sea in Bolinas, California and its staff—David and Nadine Parker, Asoka Thomas, and Jenepher Stowell—for their support. I am extremely grateful to Michael Lerner, a MacArthur Fellow and the president of Commonweal, for so generously offering the physical quarters that made work so delightful.

My very warm and heartfelt gratitude to Nichol Lovera, my wife and partner, who encouraged and supported me throughout this effort. Thanks also to the town of Bolinas and its support for our presence and work.

I also want to thank those who consented to be interviewed for parts of this book, notably Tom Talcott and Beverly Paigen, as well as staff in the Environmental Protection Agency and the California Department of Health Services.

A special thanks to Danny Moses, Erik Migdail, and Betty Berenson at Sierra Club Books for their special assistance in tracking this book from its genesis to its completion.

Preface

I WROTE THIS BOOK BECAUSE I AM CONCERNED ABOUT HOW TOXIC substances affect living things. Two spheres of concern — the personal and the global — define the dimensions of this book. To understand why chemicals may change all life on earth means understanding how such chemicals and their byproducts impact on individual lives.

Many scientists deny that synthetic chemicals could be responsible for much personal ill health or cancer; others reject that industrial pollution is responsible for the death of forests; and still others downplay the role of combustion engines or toxic emissions from factories as forces that are disturbing global climate or temperature. Knowledgeable physicians continue to prescribe medicines for women during pregnancy in the belief that the fetus is immune from adverse effects; others encourage women to put "biocompatible" breast prostheses in their bodies or to use birth control pills when they may be vulnerable to their adverse effects. Responsible public health officials continue to assure the public that the drinking water supply is safe, even as new evidence appears that toxic substances contaminate water supplies.

Modern-day scientists decry the public's gullibility in thinking that natural substances are somehow better than synthetic ones. Yet some of the scientists' pronouncements are deceptive. Respected researchers point to natural foods as the main source of most cancer-causing chemicals in our environment when it is primarily food processing or improper storage that causes most "natural" carcinogens. Others say that birth defects are simply part of our genetic legacy, or that cancer is simply an inevitable consequence of aging. Industrialists are increasingly downplaying the role of industrial sources in changing the climate. Some call the global warming trend an example of public "panic" and a "classic case of overreaction."[1] What is the truth here?

I wrote this book because I believe that a more complete story needs to be told. It is written from the perspective of a former public health official, and it has certain biases: public health protection takes priority over material goods or efficiency; particularly vulnerable members of society deserve special protection; and economic growth is not a fundamental good in and of itself. These values are often at odds with the needs of society to provide basic material goods to its members. Where the balance point between long-term safety and individual and collective prosperity is to be placed is a matter for public discussion. What makes risks "acceptable" is not dictated by facts alone. But the "facts" about what constitutes a "risk" worthy of public attention are a key element of the debate. It is these facts—facts that are often skewed by interpretative bias or simple misrepresentation—that form the myths addressed in this book.

The story of toxic contamination of the environment—and of the human response to chemical pollutants—is neither pretty nor simple. This book does not hide the details: I believe that a significant portion of the public would like to learn as much as possible about the personal and global risks of toxic substances. A survey of public attitudes released by the National Research Council in September, 1989, indicates that the public no longer wants or expects simple answers to the problems posed by exposure to toxic substances.[2] Nor does it want sensational or watered-down stories of environmental catastrophes. It wants the straight truth—how much we know, how much we don't, and how much we only guess at. Uncertainty, that slippery and bedeviling factor juggled by back-room risk assessors, must be brought into the open.

Before we can talk about "acceptable risk," we must understand the origins of risk-laden events. And the key to understanding human risks is to show how closely personal well-being is tied to wise use of our natural resources. Our folly in saturating the external environment with pollutants is matched by our excesses in exposing our internal milieu to unneeded drugs and chemical additives.

WHAT SHOULD WE WORRY ABOUT?

Are there really risks hidden in our daily exposure to commonplace substances? Should we focus our concern on the broader issues of global pollution? Don Lappé, my Utah-based cardiologist brother, once asked me: "What should I be worried about this week?"

My mind raced through the chemicals that I knew could cause health problems — pharmaceuticals he or his wife might have taken; chlorinated by-products and heavy metals in their drinking water; noxious gases in the rare Salt Lake City smog: aflatoxins in their peanut butter; diesel exhaust from their cars; polychlorinated biphenyls in the fish he had just eaten; preservatives in the delicatessen food we had just had for lunch; benzopyrene in last weekend's barbecued steak; and manganese, alcohol, and aldehydes in our beer.

After a quick review of this burgeoning list, I realized that his exposure to these chemicals was miniscule. His health, like that of a surprising number of Mormon Utah residents, was almost certainly way above the norm. (Cancer incidence among devout Mormons, who neither smoke nor drink, nor take any stimulants, is about *half* that of the rest of the country.)

I responded with what must have seemed a surprising bit of candor, "Well, actually, I don't know."

"Aren't you even going to try?" he asked.

"Well, to tell you what to worry about, I need to know what things bother you."

"Cancer," he replied simply. "Cancer worries me."

This information didn't make my task any easier. Lots of things can cause cancer, but most exposures to even known carcinogenic chemicals or radiation do not necessarily result in cancer for any given person. Cancer is an extremely complex phenomenon with many events interposed between exposure and the final malignancy. So I asked, "What kind of cancer?"

"The kind that kills you," he replied. (My brother tends to be somewhat laconic.)

"Most cancers don't kill you," I reminded him. "In fact, the most likely form of cancer you would get out here in Utah is skin cancer. And over 95 percent of common, nonpigmented skin cancers are curable. You don't have to worry about cancer."

"What about the pigmented kinds?" he asked. (Being a Johns Hopkins trained physician, Don knew that melanoma was a real killer.)

As I began to recite the statistics about the current epidemic of melanoma, I realized that there was a critical link between his activities and this highly malignant disorder. Not only did Don enjoy the sun (ultraviolet light is a major cause of melanoma), but he did so on vacations in which he was exposed for long periods of time. And then I had an insight.

"You know, Don," I said, "if you want to reduce your risk of getting skin cancer you really should recycle or better still, replace the chlorofluorocarbons in your air-conditioning systems."

"You're kidding!" he said incredulously.

"No, I'm not," I replied. "You know that refrigerants are destroying the ozone layer—and that's increasing the likelihood of lots of ultraviolet light exposure."

"I can't do anything about things like the ozone layer," he replied.

"Then maybe you *should* worry about cancer," I said.

"Oh, come on," he said, "I get an annual checkup, and we don't drink tap water."

"No, really, Don. Lots of things you're doing or thinking of doing with chemicals can affect your health. You just don't see the connections."

"No kidding," he said, with just a touch of sarcasm.

"Look," I said, "we've got to make sure that our kids aren't exposed to things now that may increase their cancer risk forty years from now. To do that, we've got to get involved with what's happening to the environment."

"That's your thing, isn't it?" he asked.

"Yes. If we take care of the planet, we'll be taking care of ourselves—and vice versa. If we do the things that we need to do to take good care of ourselves, we'll be taking care of the planet."

"Go on," he said, still skeptical, "give me an example."

Right then I realized how difficult it was to translate this idea into a single example. How could I describe how putting non-degradable silicones into the body was related to putting non-biodegradable plastics into the environment? Or that stimulating growth with hormones was akin to how we were causing eutrophication of our waterways and lakes? So I copped out. I said, "Nope, I'm going to have to write you a book."

Don smiled. "A whole book?"

"Yes, a whole book."

This is it, Don. I hope you like it.

Chemical Deception

CHAPTER ONE

Toxicological perspectives

WE ARE IN THE MIDST OF THE CHEMICAL REVOLUTION. IT IS ALMOST a given that the chemical industry and its allied fields of pharmaceutical and pesticide manufacture represent dominant forces that are shaping our world. However, the way chemical products impact on our lives is highly controversial. Some say that chemicals are the mainstays of modern existence, without which the good life would be impossible. Others point to the legacy of poisonings and environmental contamination and rue the day when chemical synthesis first became a reality.

Whatever perspective you take, it is clear that chemicals insinuate themselves into our lives. It behooves us to understand which are our friends and which our enemies—they are not simply going to disappear into the night. We have begun to realize that how chemicals are made, packaged, and discarded radically affects our lives. We have yet to learn how our own bodies, and that of the earth, cope with the chemicals we put into them.

We have good reason to suspect that something is wrong with our present system of controls. Even with tight regulation of all the steps in the manufacture, handling, labeling, transportation, and use of chemical products, we still have

1

major episodes of pollution and chemical contamination. Unwanted human exposure to toxic chemicals still occurs, often as a result of accident, unintentional releases, or mishandled waste. Even more toxic exposures occur because of error, fraud, or just plain folly in the production and use of potentially hazardous chemicals. We have encouraged the manufacture and release of chemicals that have harmed the biosphere. And we continue to use many products without appreciation of their subtle and not-so-subtle impacts on our health and that of the planet. It is time to understand some of these impacts.

This means that the by-products of the industrial revolution — and these include almost all of the toxic substances discussed in this book — must be scrutinized for their hidden effects on human health and environmental well-being. Nothing less than a science of planetary toxicology is needed to measure the results of chemical insults to the thin web of life on earth. Unfortunately, we have only studied this science on a small scale, usually limiting our examination of toxic effects to a few species closely related to ourselves. And we have barely begun our study of the human response to toxic chemicals.

THE SCIENCE OF TOXICOLOGY

The window into this world of real and imagined peril is through the science of toxicology. Sometimes called the study of poisons, toxicology offers the prospect of understanding the potential for harm in the real world and for avoiding those circumstances that can cause the most damage. Whole new sciences of behavioral toxicology, genetic toxicology, and neurotoxicology have emerged in the past twenty years as we chart the ever finer perturbations of the body that can be produced by even slight exposure to toxic substances.

However, our knowledge to date has not allowed us to say with certainty whether or not the symptoms seen in most large-scale human exposures to toxic substances (such as those among residents near toxic waste dumps) are attributable to toxic exposures, psychosomatic illness, or some other combination of reactions. That is, as a predictive science, toxicology has not lived up to its billing. It is true that toxicologists have proven instrumental in opening the world of chemicals and other hazardous substances to controlled study. They have been successful in studying the circumstances of occupational disease and outright poisonings. But until recently, toxicologists have confined their study to individual chemicals, not the witches' brew of toxicants common in many human exposure situations.

In populations known to be exposed to a plethora of toxic substances, like those at Love Canal, New York, gastrointestinal problems, unexplained rashes, miscarriages, neurobehavioral disorders in children, and neurological problems in adults comprise a common litany of nonspecific complaints. Such symptoms were not predicted by knowledge of the chemicals at issue. Yet, those who examined these residents, as well as others at similar toxic waste sites, are convinced that the symptoms are real. (Some of these investigations will be reviewed below.) Unfortunately, few if any studies of the effects of chemical wastes on human populations have been conducted. In the near future, the U.S. Agency for Toxic Substance Disease Registry will complete the first of many such studies, examining the health of populations exposed to common toxic substances like trichloroethylene and benzene.

What is needed now is a different perspective and a much broader scope of inquiry. Our own and the planet's survival may depend on making accurate predictions about the composite impacts of new chemicals and electromagnetic radiation on all living systems. Take, for example, the previously mentioned increase in exposure to ultraviolet light that is expected as a result of sunlight passing through our chemically fragmented ozone layer—the thin stratospheric shield that historically has separated life on earth from damaging radiation. Where will these powerful rays first impinge on living things? How will their effects be felt on ecosystems that depend on sunlight for their energy? How will humans, especially those whose skins are highly permeable to light, react? And how will ultraviolet light interact with the thousands of chemical contaminants that permeate the environment? Some chemicals become more toxic when their molecules are changed by ultraviolet light. Others interact synergistically with UV light energy.

Our survival may well depend on understanding these kinds of reactions. We need to learn what kind of adaptive mechanisms to radiation or chemicals life has inherited over the

3

millennia. Some of the first examinations of these issues should give us pause. We already know of some persons who develop cancer just months after exposure to certain wavelengths of ultraviolet light, and of other organisms whose immune systems are damaged by short, high-intensity exposures. But we know little about the reactions of higher animals and plants to the plethora of new chemicals we have loosed on an evolutionarily unprepared world.

For some this is an unimportant question. The major sources of toxicity are said to be "natural" not "synthetic" chemicals.[1] According to these scientists, life has lived with toxicants for millennia. Humans are no exception. Ever since wood was burned and food charred, people have exposed themselves to toxic chemicals. (Whether or not these exposures constituted natural selective forces that shaped our present ability—or lack thereof—to detoxify chemicals is discussed in Chapter 4.)

It is true that chemicals of any origin may be toxic or not depending on their interaction with living cells. It is erroneous to presume that "natural" automatically means "safe" (consider, for example, contaminated mussels or poisonous mushrooms). But focusing on such extreme reactions as poisonings can be misleading. Acute toxic reactions tell us little about which chemical agents comprise the true *agents provocateurs* to living systems, those that upset our cellular balance, disrupt nerve conduction, and/or cause genetic damage and cancer.

TOXIC EVOLUTION

Chemicals that kill outright without sparing any exposed life form are the stuff of science fiction. Most toxic chemicals produce a gradient of damage. That is, after exposure, some organisms die immediately while others are unaffected or perish so slowly that they live long enough to reproduce. Their survivors will in turn have some of the genes that affected the organism's resistance to the poisoning or its susceptibility to such chronic, long-term toxic effects as cancer. Only after generations of rigorous selection is it likely that sufficiently robust or resistant organisms come into being. Those that are genetically equipped to deal with novel chemicals in the environment are likely to survive any substantial intrusion of toxic substances.[2]

Such is the most optimistic scenario. Unfortunately, few organisms that have survived the onslaught of the chemical revolution have the genetic material to vouchsafe future generations. Only a very few genera, such as those filled with prolific microorganisms, have proven resilient in the face of toxic substances. It is almost certain that most of the myriad synthetic chemicals we are loosing into the environment will include some that are intrinsically more hazardous to life than are older, more "natural" chemicals. This will prove likely where scientists will introduce a new generation of highly toxic chemicals designed to overcome the resistance of weeds, pests, and microorganisms that have defied the first few generations of chemical poisons.

Neither we nor the plants and animals we most value in our biosphere have the genetic repertoire that would allow us to rapidly adapt to these extraordinarily rapid human-caused changes in our environment. While it is true that enormous amounts of human genetic variation exist, some of which blocks—and some of which abets—the toxicity of chemicals, no one person is in any broad sense "toxicologically robust." We have just not had time to adapt to the hordes of new chemicals we have put into the biosphere over the past century.

If evolutionary mechanisms are likely too slow to retard the impacts of our chemical onslaught, what then can we study to predict our response to such chemicals? One such venue is *pathology*—literally the science of suffering.

LESSONS IN PATHOLOGY

The cornerstone of pathology is the conviction that the cellular components of the body react in predictable and measurable ways to toxic insults. That is, when damage is found in a given tissue or organ, it reflects a failure of adaptation. The ultimate end point of adaptive failure is death of the organism. Another failure is cancer. Policymakers who would like to intervene effectively before these two eventualities must understand the body's defenses to chemical insults and to the progressive changes that lead to cancer.

Unfortunately, toxicologists have been extremely slow in appreciating the full sequence of pathology generated by most chemicals. They have been slower still in acknowledging that a wholly different risk-accounting system is needed to accommodate chemical carcinogenesis. According to University of Würzburg Professor Dietrich Henschler, " . . . conventional toxicologists hesitated for a long time before acknowledging that dose-response relationships in chemical carcinogenesis (where single doses applied over long periods accumulate almost without loss) differ in principle from the traditional system in that the classical threshold concept becomes invalid."[3]

We have thoroughly studied a bare handful of the millions of known chemicals, and only a tiny portion of the 60,000 to 80,000 that are currently in commerce. Some of what we have found is reassuring. Classic poisons are known to produce their toxic effects only after they have passed a certain level of concentration in the body. Such toxic substances are said to act above a critical threshold. This means that for the low levels of exposure that characterize most human exposure to environmental chemicals, little or no overt sign of poisoning is likely to be seen. But for some chemicals or elements with neurological or cancer-causing properties, no threshold for this poisoning may exist.

As an example, most of the chemicals that can cause cancer exert their toxic properties continuously over a long time, even when spread out at extremely low doses. These effects are insiduous and often inexorable. Many carcinogenic chemicals traverse the placenta and start a cancerous process in the fetus that only appears after adolescence. Almost all can produce genetic damage. When this damage occurs in the germ cells, toxic consequences can span generations.

Other chemicals produce latent damage, especially in the central nervous system, which only becomes manifest weeks or months after exposure. For many of these chemicals, little or no threshold is thought to exist. Some chemicals appear to react only minimally with living tissues, yet gradually provoke a smoldering immune reaction that can devastate the body. And substances that appear to be but chemical mimics of naturally occurring substances can have long-term deleterious consequences.

ASSESSING RISKS

What *are* the body's defenses to such toxicants?

Each organism commits a significant portion of its cellular repertoire to the recognition and elimination of chemical threats. The immune system, the skin, the liver, and the kidneys together comprise the major lines of defense against a chemically inhospitable world. In spite of this dramatic organic commitment to maintenance of a wholesome and balanced internal milieu, it is obvious that the body does not always adapt successfully to exposure to noxious environments, infectious organisms, or toxic substances, a point to be explored in Chapter 4.

To estimate the likelihood that harm will occur, researchers measure exposure characteristics and compute doses of chemicals entering the body, then compare the dosage with risk estimates. Usually these numbers come from animal studies. But, for some chemicals, such as benzene, enough human victims exist to plot the likelihood of effects such as leukemia and aplastic anemia against exposure and dose. These studies show that an increased risk of death from leukemia following benzene exposure extends on a continuous line down to and below the most common industrial levels.[4]

But for most of the chemicals of concern, the science of risk assessment is hamstrung by unknown interactive effects and by only indirectly predictive animal tests. For one thing, risk analysis has yet to devise a way of dealing with the multiplicity of chemical exposures that characterize almost every environmental assault. It is not uncommon for the list of toxic chemicals and metals at a Superfund site (the locale of a hazardous waste dump with a high potential for human harm) to exceed thirty different chemicals and a dozen or more metals, or for occupational exposure to be to fifty different chemicals over a lifetime of work at even a relatively simple worksite such as an electronics factory.

All of this is compounded by the existence of inadequately pretested drugs or chemicals for which no valid risk estimate was calculated. And some chemicals (notably early versions of birth control hormones) that appeared safe in the first hundred or two hundred exposed persons, have proved disastrous when a larger population was exposed. At least six episodes of mass toxic disasters or near disasters have accompanied the premature release of untested pharmaceutical products, and there have been many times that number of disasters involving industrial chemicals.[5] In many of the industrial cases, such as the toxic disaster at Minamata Bay in Japan where thousands of adults and children were poisoned with methylmercury, the damage did not become apparent until exposure was extensive. In the aftermath of such events, some scientists believe that at a minimum it behooves us to determine just how extensive our exposure to toxic chemicals has been.

EXPOSURE TO TOXICS

Sensitive assays have detected residues of over a hundred different foreign chemicals and metals in our tissues — compounds and substances that were virtually absent from the environments of our predecessors. It is perhaps surprising then that some researchers have maintained that toxic substances have always been part of the human legacy. Recent studies have cast these assumptions into a new light.

For a considerable period, toxicologists thought that a group of hazardous chemicals called dioxins (paired six-carbon benzene molecules with various numbers of chlorine atoms attached) could be formed in simple fires. The activities of our predecessors were thought to have generated these molecules. Dioxins, particularly the four-chlorine dioxins, such as TCDD or 2,3,7,8-tetrachlorodibenzodioxin, associated with herbicides used in the Vietnam War, were downgraded as potent toxicants because they were deemed to be the result of such prehistoric "natural" human activities as burning wood to cook or keep warm. This was an important idea since it suggested that humans had always lived with the residues of toxic substances. If this were true, then it was possible that we had arrived at some evolutionary accommodation to their presence.

A critical test would be to find some human remains that were old enough — and still had intact tissues for examination. By a fluke of climate, the ideal spot for preserving the dead was found in the exceptionally dry, high Andes desert of Chile. Researchers using the most exquisitely sensitive assays possible

8

examined the mummified remains of Chilean Indians who lived 2,700 to 2,800 years ago. The researchers found evanescent traces of some dioxins at the level of analytic detection — but none of the most toxic forms of dioxins or their molecular counterparts, the furans.[6] Their stunning conclusion: The presence of hazardous, chlorinated dioxins and furans in body tissues of modern humans is a contemporary problem, not an ancient one. Residues are most likely to result from current practices, such as the incineration of chlorine-containing chemical contaminants or other waste disposal activities. And we still do not know the health consequences to ourselves or our offspring from these potent molecules. (More about this in Chapter 6.)

Ideally, toxicological studies on animals in controlled laboratory environments should allow scientists to predict the consequences of exposures to chemicals such as dioxins. Guinea pigs with levels of the four-chlorine dioxin called TCDD in their tissues comparable to that of some humans (for example, the Vietnam veterans exposed to Agent Orange in Operation Ranch Hand) were found to do very poorly: some died, and others developed cancer. But humans appear strangely immune to the feared toxic effects of this chemical. No convincing evidence has been accumulated to date that shows overt signs of toxicity in dioxin-contaminated Vietnam veterans beyond a form of skin acne, although the evidence of certain rare tumors of the lymphatic system and body tissues (notably soft-tissue sarcoma) is strongly suggestive of a link to dioxin exposure. (More about this in Chapter 2.)

EPIDEMIOLOGICAL STUDIES

A tried and true way of beginning to understand the environmental factors that cause human cancer is to scrutinize studies on large populations exposed to different factors and to integrate these observations with clinical data.

These studies include so-called ecologic investigations in which the objective is to correlate patterns of exposure to specific substances in a given population with an outcome, such as cancer. These studies are particularly useful when populations are exposed to broad groups of contaminants (for example, in

9

water or air). Scandinavian observers used such an approach in uncovering an apparent relationship between exposure to broad classes of solvents or herbicides and coincident increases in observed tumor types. Under the leadership of Lennart Hardell, the Scandinavians found that workers with certain types of lymphoma appeared to be more likely to have had exposure to phenolic herbicides, pentachlorophenol, or other chlorinated phenols than were persons who did not have such tumors.[7] Hardell later extended his observations to soft-tissue sarcomas (a rare form of cancer affecting the muscular areas of the body) and colon cancer.[8]

Cohort studies are a form of investigation more limited in scope than are ecologic studies, but have the advantage of looking at more carefully defined groups of persons known or suspected to have been exposed to a hazardous agent. In studies of this kind, exposure may have begun before the investigation began (these are called *retrospective studies*); or the exposure in question may begin some time after the study is set up (*prospective studies*).[9]

An example of a successful retrospective cohort study was the sleuthing done on populations exposed to chlorinated water supplies from contaminated sources such as the Mississippi River. Researchers found that many members of such populations have higher rates of bladder, colon, and rectal cancer than do populations whose water supplies come from more pristine sources.[10]

A third type of study is known as a case–control study. Here a group of individuals who have had a disease (say, cancer) is compared to nondiseased persons, and the degree of exposure to a suspect causative agent is measured between both populations. In a matched case–control series, each affected individual is matched to one or more control individuals and then compared for exposure experience. Early attempts at piecing together ecologic correlations between water contamination and cancer rates generated ambiguous findings until case–control studies were done in the late 1970s.[11]

Similarly successful approaches to demonstrating a linkage between exposure to chemicals and cancer can be seen in the evolution of Hardell's work. As mentioned above, Hardell's initial observations were largely ecological in nature. But he followed up his initial observations of an apparent association of lymphomas with certain chemicals with a case-control study that matched individuals with this tumor against patients with other cancers and compared their exposure histories. When he controlled his studies in this way, Hardell found that exposure to organic solvents, as well as chlorophenols and phenoxy acids, was significantly more common among the cases than among the controls. This later work provided much stronger evidence that lymphoma could be linked to chemical exposure.[12] (Hardell's work provides a tantalizing link back to Vietnam veterans who were exposed to Agent Orange: Both the Swedish workers and the vets had a higher than expected incidence of soft-tissue sarcomas following their exposure to phenoxy herbicides, the backbone of Agent Orange.)

A final type of study begins with a single or small number of cases where there is, say, an unusual confluence of a rare tumor type and the use of a particular medication or exposure to particular hazardous substances. Such case studies are useful for triggering more intensive investigations. The discovery of a rare form of vaginal cancer in daughters of women who took diethylstilbestrol is a classic example. (See Chapter 7.)

Each form of epidemiological investigation has potential weak points. Selection bias, in which the population identified for study has unusual characteristics, can distort the interpretation of ecological studies. Not controlling for enough confounding variables is another problem. Sometimes when initial ecological studies are followed by more rigorous case-control studies, an apparent relationship between a chemical source and a particular cancer type disappears. This happened recently when patients with a type of tumor called mycosis fungoides were studied to determine if the previously identified occupational and chemical exposure correlates would hold up. No consistent relationships between employment or chemical exposures were found among cases with the tumor as compared to tumor-free matched controls.[13]

While it is important to recognize the need for caution in using these forms of epidemiological studies,[14] many investigators have uncovered dramatic and appreciable sources of human cancer through initial case studies and ecological observations. The original observations linking scrotal cancer to soot and liver cancer to birth control hormones (see Chapters 2 and 9, respectively) are classics in this regard. So, too, were the

11

discoveries of industrial-linked cancer in the dye, mining, rubber products, and woodworking industries.

SYNTHETIC CHEMICALS AND CANCER

Recently, studies using some or all of these designs have picked up new patterns of cancer associated with particular chemicals or have implicated synthetic substances in broader classes of cancer. Hardell's initial observations of soft-tissue sarcomas have been extended to agricultural and forestry workers,[15] as have his observations of tumors in the lymphatic system and in bone marrow (lymphomas and leukemias).[16]

Factors other than chemical exposure, though not considered in these studies, may also be involved in the genesis of leukemia. I recall an Iowan farmer, newly resident to Washington State, describing to me how common "cancer eye" was among his cattle back in Iowa. He wondered out loud if this tumor might present a hazard to farmers. He subsequently died of leukemia. Ironically, because he had moved before his tumor could be recorded in the Iowa Tumor Registry, his own cancer was not included in the two studies that subsequently linked leukemia with farming practices in Iowa.[17] Anecdotal reports of this kind lend some credence to the widely recognized linkage between viruses and leukemias in animals and humans. Thus, it is entirely plausible that a viral agent associated with farming activities confounds the apparent association of leukemia with agricultural chemicals. (More about this confounding principle in Chapters 2 and 10.)

BLADDER CANCER AS A CASE STUDY

As I will show in the next chapter, bladder cancer was among the first tumor types to be associated with employment and, hence, with synthetic chemical agents. And, as a result of recent studies, it is now possible to compute the actual amount of bladder cancer that can be attributed to such chemicals, over and against natural causes. If, as some would insist, bladder cancer is largely the result of dietary elements, then the proportion attributable to occupational exposure would be quite small.

This is especially so since a significant portion of bladder cancer (and all tumor types) may be hereditary, sporadic (the result of new mutations), or simply the result of indeterminate causes.

The most recent estimates for occupational factors in bladder cancer indicate that chemicals encountered in the workplace are a substantial cause of this tumor. As a result of systematic studies of 2,100 whites and 126 nonwhites compared to about twice that number of population controls, Debra T. Silverman of the National Cancer Institute and her colleagues found that men (particularly nonwhites) who worked in occupations such as auto working and painting had significantly elevated risks for bladder cancer.[18] A final calculation of all bladder cancers indicated that between 21 to 25 percent of the tumors occurring in whites and 27 percent of those in nonwhites could be attributed to occupational exposure to chemicals.

The overall significance of the Silverman work is that it points to a new constellation of chemicals that may be responsible for bladder cancer. In analyzing the occupational groups in which bladder cancer is now occurring in excess, Silverman and her associates have defined a new cadre of workers at risk for bladder cancer that differs significantly from those in the past. While excess rates among traditionally high-risk occupational groups such as leather and rubber workers have gone down, elevated bladder cancer rates for truck drivers and aluminum workers have now appeared for the first time.

A second group of still controversial studies has appeared in recent years that suggest a broad impact of occupational exposure on cancer in the population at large. These studies point to an as yet undefined linkage between parental occupation and childhood tumors. Workers in the aerospace industry, chemical, radio, and electronics areas all have had children with cancers in excess of predicted rates.[19]

CHEMICAL DISASTERS

Toxicology has provided an often distorted yardstick for predicting the consequences of the truly awesome exposures that have occurred after mass chemical disasters. Notable cases in which such exposures have occurred include explosions at at least eight different trichlorophenol plants in which hundreds of workers have been exposed to chlorinated chemicals, especially dioxins; the release of vinyl chloride from tank cars in a train derailment near MacGregor, Manitoba; and innumerable releases of refined petroleum products, most notably the *Torrey Canyon* spill and the *Exxon Valdez* spill in 1989.[20]

In some instances we have overestimated toxic effects almost as badly as we have underestimated them in others. Even as we await any evidence of the expected lethal toxicity of dioxin exposure to thousands of villagers in the region of Seveso, Italy, we are still counting the bodies from the chemical disaster in Bhopal, India.[21]

The Bhopal Catastrophe

Late one evening in early December 1984, at the Union Carbide chemical plant in Bhopal, India, something went seriously wrong with a reaction vessel designed to use methyl isocyanate (MIC), a precursor for the synthesis of a pesticide. Because of the failure of a cooling system, water entering the reactor caused an exothermic reaction: the reaction mixture overheated and exploded. Union Carbide claims that it was sabotage; the Indian government, that it was a foreseeable accident.[22]

Before the week was over, more than 2,000 people had died. Over the new few months, more than 1,000 other people were disabled by blindness and lung damage, and at least 8,000 others were injured.[23] Eventually, 3,500 people died as a result of their injuries. In February 1989, Union Carbide and the Indian government agreed to a $470 million settlement that was ordered by India's Supreme Court. But, more than two years later, the victims of the explosion have yet to receive any remuneration for their injuries or suffering. (Indian activists were outraged at the low amount and forced the court to stay its order.)

In spite of assurances that the 8,000 are only "injured" and not "disabled,"[24] the damage from the explosion at Bhopal may go much deeper. Preliminary clinical investigations and a recently completed animal modeling of this accident (discussed below) raise the ominous possibility that human contact with MIC should never have been allowed in the first place. That is, after the Bhopal tragedy, scientists at the National Institute of Health discovered that the data base for understanding

14

methyl isocyanate's long-term toxicity was flawed. Studies from Union Carbide were sequestered because of the pending litigation. Only *after* the accident were two studies initiated to test the toxicity of MIC. After a protracted delay of almost three years from inception, the results were reported: Methyl isocyanate was found to be a potent gene-damaging chemical and a potential carcinogen.[25]

To study its properties, researchers subjected standard cancer bioassay rats and mice to just two hours of exposure to MIC, an exposure that was "designed to approximate the exposure of survivors of the Bhopal incident."[26] (In fact, many persons had more—and others less—exposure.) One would think that MIC would have been thoroughly tested for the relevance of these very properties *before* it was marketed. (If it was, the records are part of the proprietary files of Union Carbide.)

In a break with tradition, the doses chosen were absurdly low by comparison to normal cancer tests in which lifelong exposure to maximally tolerated doses is the rule. Yet the results were still alarming.

Among the incidental findings were two disturbing facts: only the youngest animals could survive even two hours of exposure to the highest tested dose; and, between 35 and 40 percent of all the exposed animals had permanent lung damage when examined two years after the transient exposure. Translated into human terms, these data imply that as many as 70,000 to 80,000 of the 200,000 persons the Indian government believes to have been exposed to MIC may develop permanent lung disorders.

The most disturbing observation was the occurrence of cancer in the exposed animals. In male rats, in particular, certain tumors appeared in excessive numbers in a dose-related pattern that strongly suggests that methyl isocyanate caused them. In spite of the apparent significance of this observation to the survivors of the Bhopal explosion, the authors of the study stated that they could not tell if the observed increases were "relevant to those people exposed to MIC in Bhopal." They also added the caveat that "We caution that conclusions concerning the carcinogenic potential of MIC pertain only to the experimental conditions employed in this study."[27]

But, you might say, did not the research team *intentionally design* the study to be relevant to Bhopal? Given the immense sums of money involved in the subsequent litigation, the reluctance of the research team to go further in its conclusions is perhaps understandable—but hardly laudable. It is not ethically apparent why they chose to circumscribe their findings so severely that they could not be used in trial. At a minimum, the findings clearly point to the need for increased surveillance or medical monitoring of the population. Why did the authors not make even this seemingly innocuous recommendation?

The roots of this dilemma are embedded in two traditions in science: One is the belief that scientists must work within the lines of an "informed skepticism" that guarantees neutrality. The second is the requirement that conclusions regarding causation be postponed until overwhelmingly positive data, often linked to reproducible epidemiologic studies, are amassed. (For a long time, it was thought that scientists should only conduct studies that attempt to disprove a hypothesis, not establish its validity.)[28] The posture of scientists faced with data Bhopal-like contrasts markedly to the role of public health officials who must often warn or alert the public at a much lower level of certainty of risk.

The passivity of researchers and industrialists alike when it comes to extrapolating animal data to human risk contributes to a pattern of permissivity. All too often, it is still only after the fact of mass exposures, such as those at Bhopal, that studies surface that implicate chemicals in producing "unforeseen" harm.

THE BANALITY OF CHEMICAL EVIL

The immediate deleterious effects of some occupational poisons was made painfully clear to a generation of workers early in the industrial revolution who took the brunt of poorly managed production operations and frank neglect. (One specific case of industrial exposure is discussed below.) Now all of us face potential exposure to the by-products of the industrial and chemical revolutions through contaminated air, water, and earth. Having neither consented to nor participated in generating the resultant risks, many now ask what claims, if any, can we make on the chemical industry for future indemnification or retribution for past damage?

16

While these may appear to be purely legalistic questions, at root they turn on our system of values and beliefs about rights and duties in the free enterprise system. Nowhere is this conflict more evident than in the modern-day battle between the so-called "rights" of chemical manufacturers to produce, advertise, and sell their products in the public marketplace and the parallel "rights" of individuals to be assured of protection against injury and harm. The definitions of "safe," "acceptable risk," and "adequate warning" are malleable concepts that are as vulnerable to manipulation as are the public perceptions of the products themselves. The original assertions of industrial giants to *caveat emptor* and untrammeled liberty to manufacture goods in a marketplace economy has had to give way to a grudging recognition of public accountability to the consequences of mass manufacturing.

Global pollution may force us to reconsider the legal theory of strict liability that holds a manufacturer only responsible for adverse consequences of the *normal* use of the product. Will the law of liability slowly expand to include the consequences of releasing products into the environment? How will the public get the information that it needs to adequately address the issue of toxicity? Sometimes it is only the manufacture and perhaps one or two officials at a regulatory agency that have all of the "proprietary" information about a given product's toxicity profile. While regulatory bodies theoretically see all of the data that describe the toxicological properties of the chemicals that a manufacturer wishes to market, the reality is that often much of the needed information is sequestered in data files kept within the company's own offices.

As in the case of Union Carbide, the public's access to this material is often limited by agreements of confidentiality that regulatory agencies sign to assure the manufacturer that a "competitor" will not see the same data. This situation may mean that only one person in a bureaucracy may fully understand the risk-benefit equation for any given product. In my experience, this claim for secrecy is all too often a veil to assure that ambiguous or frankly compromising data will not reach the eyes of the public.[29] More commonly, relevant information about toxicity is simply not conveyed to those with a need to know.

The Glycol Ethers as a Case Study

A case in point concerns the glycol ethers, a highly toxic group of solvents and chemical intermediates still widely used in the paint and chemical industries. A human tragedy in 1933 with a related chemical should have flagged this group of chemicals for early attention, but it generated little notice among those who regulated the chemical industry.[30] In that year a drug company marketed an "elixir of sulfanilamide" to meet the heavy demand for an ingestible form of this early antibiotic. To make the complex sulfanilamide molecule soluble, the company dissolved it in the first chemical it could find that was plentiful, cheap and an excellent solvent: diethylene glycol. (Alcohol might have sufficed, but Prohibition assured that it was expensive and tightly controlled.) No animal testing was done.

Because of the use of the name "elixir," the public associated it with many other drug products that contained alcohol—and imbibed it along with the others as a dodge to avoid Prohibition. Before Prohibition was over, 108 people were dead, including the chemist who concocted the ingredients: he committed suicide.

These deaths should have provided ample early warning of the extreme toxicity of some of the glycol ethers. Industrial exposure to glycol ethers was linked to testicular damage, and neurological and blood abnormalities as early as 1938.[31] But regulatory agencies ignored these effects. It was not until 1979, when a new group of studies conducted under the auspices of the National Institute of Occupational Safety and Health (NIOSH) demonstrated that one such ether in particular (ethoxy ethanol) could cause reproductive damage—birth defects and sterility—at very low levels that other agencies took notice. In 1982, researchers showed that these ethers and related chemicals could harm developing fetuses at comparably low doses (measured in just a few milligrams for every 1,000 grams of the mother's body weight) and could cause death and injury to fetuses growing in the wombs of experimental animals.[32] Accordingly, NIOSH issued a Health Bulletin, alerting workplace operators to these hazards.

In August 1982, Richard A. Lemgen, a NIOSH official, met with the Occupational Safety and Health Administration (OSHA) director of health standards and urged him to ban the chemical altogether or, at a minimum, to provide more worker protection. According to the *Wall Street Journal* of June 26, 1984, Dow Chemical Company, a firm that manufactured large amounts of the ethers, subsequently reduced its own permissible exposure level to one-fortieth of the OSHA limit. Dow also sampled the air at several of its customers' plants and urged them to use better industrial hygiene practices. But neither Dow nor other major producers took more direct steps to reduce exposure, such as enclosing production operations, supplying adequate warning labels, or adding an odorant (such as the one in natural gas) that would give workers adequate notice of exposure.

Other companies, such as Shell Oil, designed warning labels that alerted workers to these reproductive hazards, but failed to require that the labels be used. In contrast, Union Carbide did require such labels to be used. The chemical facility of Du Pont de Nemours also labeled its products with warnings against reproductive hazards. The drums containing glycol ether used in-house were labeled with a warning that the chemical causes birth defects and damage to male reproductive organs. But when the drums left the premises, someone at Du Pont replaced the labels with ones that warned only "Avoid Contact with Eyes and Skin."[33]

Other companies appear to have engaged in similarly deceptive practices. Eastman Kodak reported its findings on another glycol ether to the EPA in 1983 but failed to mention the occurrence of malformations and dramatically smaller fetuses in exposed rats. The report indicated only "severe maternal toxicity," a finding the EPA related to decreased weight of the contents of the uterus.[34] These euphemisms hid the fact that fetuses had actually died in utero, while others were growth-retarded. The mothers were relatively unaffected.

In 1982, the California Hazard Evaluation System issued a Hazard Alert that warned all workers about the reproductive risks.[35] This alert has since been expanded and is now part of the materials every worker at risk for exposure to glycol ethers has a right to see.[36]

For many years, chemical companies and the U.S. Government had treated these highly toxic chemicals with blatant disregard for their toxic effects. In the 1960s and 70s, when the U.S. Navy dumped its spent paint remover at a landfill near

Hipps Road in Jacksonville, Florida, they unknowingly exposed dozens of nearby residents to toxic concentrations of glycol ether through their well water. Many of these residents later developed disabling neurological symptoms and complained of reproductive abnormalities and gastrointestinal illnesses. (The complex job of recreating exposures and piecing together medical files is still underway as of early 1992.) In spite of ample toxicological data that indicated health risks, local health officers did not shut down homeowners' private wells until 1983, four years after evidence of contamination was found and up to thirteen years from the date when their wells had first been exposed to glycol ethers.

These examples point out the discrepancies between known or observed health effects and consumer notification that such risks exist. Any such omissions greatly compound the likelihood of toxic encounters and raise major ethical issues about the social responsibility of the companies involved—points addressed in the material that follows.

CHAPTER TWO

A chronology of toxic encounters

HISTORICAL CONCERNS

I remember being slightly bemused when my Ph.D. advisor gave me a tattered and worn volume from 1775 entitled *Chirurgical Observations* by Sir Percival Pott[1] and suggested that I read it as part of my introduction to the modern science of experimental pathology. Pott was a public health advocate. In his chapter on "Cancer scroti," he graphically described the plight of chimney sweeps, still but boys, with malignant growths on their scrotums.[2] Pott noted that these poor wretches were often burned and bruised in the course of their work and commonly were poorly nourished—a device of their keepers that ensured the boys would remain sufficiently thin to fit down the chimneys that they swept out.

Pott also noted that the boys' personal hygiene was terrible, allowing soot to accumulate in the rugae (the folds in the skin that covers the scrotum) of their scrotal sacs. Pott had no doubt that he was witnessing an epidemic of cancer due to an environmental cause. To Pott the cause was clearly something associated with soot and he urged that the boys be protected from further exposure.

Almost seventy-five years passed before steps were taken to protect the chimney sweeps. In the mid-1800s, legislation was passed against using "climbing boys," and manual chimney cleaning was replaced by rules that required long brushes and other mechanical appliances. But as chimney sweep's cancer (as the scrotal skin tumors were called) became rarer,[3] another malady was discovered. This time the locale was shale works where oil-containing rocks were cooked and paraffin oils extracted.

In 1876, Joseph Bell, the Surgeon to the Royal Infirmary, reported on the occurrence of two cases of scrotal cancer in middle-aged men exposed to the shale oils.[4] Unfortunately, the lessons learned in England regarding the association between exposure to oils and naphtha extracted from petroleum failed to alert occupational physicians elsewhere to the dangers inherent in exposure to such oils. Not until 1983 was scrotal cancer recognized as a malignancy so clearly linked to occupational exposure as to be deemed an occupational "sentinel health event."[5] However, physician and hospital reporting of scrotal cancer cases remains so poor that the system of using these tumors to alert public health officials to cancer risks in the workplace has been unsuccessful.[6]

In the later 1800s and early part of this century, workers in the wool spinning industries in New England river towns began to develop scrotal cancers. In almost every instance, the tumors were associated with exposure to the mineral oils used to lubricate the spinning jennies.[7] The workers would commonly hold the jenny's spindle between their legs, saturating their pants with the carcinogenic oils. Because of the rich blood supply and extremely large surface area of the scrotal skin, the testes can easily absorb chemicals. Cutting oils in particular contain large amounts of N-nitroso compounds, chemicals with proven cancer-causing ability. Also because of this skin absorption, cancers elsewhere in the body also increased.

The move to commercialize the first synthetic chemicals outstripped concerns about their human — or environmental — effects. Within two decades of Friedrich Wöhler's epochal 1828 synthesis of urea from cyanic acid and ammonia (the first biological chemical made in a laboratory), organic chemistry flourished on a grand scale. Dyeworks, a whole industry pro-

phetically based on coal tar derivatives, sprang up throughout Germany. In 1856, W. H. Perkin made the first aniline
dye, which produced a wildly popular shade of purple known
as mauve. Forty years later, L. Rehn reported incidents of
unexplained forms of cancer in this industry: Dyestuff workers had become the first victims of synthetic chemical–caused
cancer.[8]

In fact, bladder cancer eventually affected as many as half
the men working in some dye-making jobs.[9] From a chemical perspective, such occurrence was predictable, if only vaguely
perceived at the time. Dyes interact with the proteins and other
components of living tissues. This observation led Otto and
Emil Fischer to design dyes that stained living cells, thus making the field of histopathology possible. Unfortunately, these
same interactions with biological molecules are what give so
many dyes their carcinogenic activity.

Over the first few decades of the twentieth century, the list
of suspected and proven chemical carcinogens grew slowly.
At the turn of the century, cancer-causing occupations were
thought to be limited to tar workers and chimney sweeps.
Thereafter, nickel refining and dye-working were added. By
1928, a French and Italian team clearly linked benzene exposure
to leukemia.[10] By 1930, work with chromium compounds was
added to the list of activities suspected of causing human cancer.
In the next decade, aniline and auramine dyes as well as ben-
zidine were clearly implicated as human carcinogens. Then,
between 1940 and 1950, arsenic, asbestos, and 2–napthylamine
were added to the list of suspected human carcinogens, along
with hematite mining and isopropyl alcohol production. Between 1950 and 1970, 4-aminobipheynyl and mustard gas were
found to be carcinogenic, and the activities of manufacturing
rubber boots, shoes, and furniture products were found to be
associated with higher-than-expected cancer rates. In 1962,
vinyl chloride was linked to a rare tumor of the liver (angiosarcoma) and brain tumors such as gliomas and schwannomas.
Surprisingly, in the next decade, only bis-chloromethyl ether
was added to the list of clearly identified human carcinogens.
By the 1980s, sufficient evidence was available to show carcinogenicity for twenty-eight chemicals and five industrial
processes.[11]

BENZOPYRENE AS A CASE STUDY

In spite of a century-long suspicion that soots and tars were capable of producing cancer, it was not until 1915 that two Japanese workers, K. Ichikawa and K. Yamagiwa, succeeded in producing cancer.[12] Their painstaking labors entailed daily applications of tar to rabbit ears for more than two years. On one cold winter day in 1915, Yamagiwa recorded in his diary, "Two years work, cancer is produced."

It took British researcher E. L. Kennaway another seven years to duplicate these findings with hydrocarbon extracts from tar,[13] and fellow workers J. W. Cook, C. I. Hewitt, and I. Hieger another eight to isolate the major cancer-producing chemical in coal tar, benzo(a)pyrene.[14] Today, this chemical is recognized as perhaps the most ubiquitous carcinogenic agent in the human environment.

Our inability to assimilate these early lessons into our daily lives is still apparent. Cigarette smoke, a major source of benzo(a)pyrene, is the clearest example. More than 40 million Americans still smoke. And according to such well-known cancer researchers as Cesare Maltoni and Irving Selikoff, the incidence of cancer in the United States has been increasing at the rate of about 1 percent a year for the past thirty years.[15] The causes of this increase are hotly debated. Some believe that all of the increase is due to cigarette smoking and lung cancer, while others believe the increase involves a spectrum of cancers. Perhaps the best way to resolve this dispute is to look at cancer rates after eliminating the two cancer types that we know are undergoing dramatic changes, namely, lung cancer (which is still increasing annually in incidence, especially in women) and stomach cancer (which has fallen dramatically in the past two decades). Having done this, the cancer rates contributed by the remaining cancers are still going up at a slow but constant rate, with most of that increase occurring in men.[16] (More about this in Chapter 10.)

Places exist where environmental agents other than cigarette smoke are the major causes of lung cancer. In Xuanwei County in China, the overall rate of lung cancer mortality is more than five times the average of the country as a whole, and almost ten times the average of Yuannan Province, of which it is a part. In Xuanwei, high-risk areas have been identified in which the cancer rate per 100,000 population exceeds 118 for males and 125 for females, compared to rates of 4.3 and 1.5, respectively, for the rest of the province.[17]

One of the remarkable epidemiologic features of this observation was the inversion of the usual male predominance in lung cancer statistics worldwide. Chinese scientists who reviewed the circumstances discovered that in this farming region, local residents commonly burned fuel in shallow grates or hearths without chimneys. Most importantly, it was the women who tended these fires and prepared food. In the high-risk areas, scientists found that families commonly relied on a smoky, benzo(a)pyrene-rich coal for fuel, while in lower-risk areas only charcoal or smokeless coal were used.

In a series of studies reminiscent of the history of Western efforts to discern the causes of soot cancer, the Chinese extracted soot from the high-risk area and demonstrated its ability to induce cancer in mice and demonstrated the existence of genetic damage in animals and cells treated with extracts of soot.[18] Yet, to date, no government policies regulating the availability of carcinogenic coal or setting environmental standards for benzopyrene exist in China.

LESSONS IN CANCER FORMATION

The lessons of these observations have become clear to me in stages. Pott did not know that the scrotum is a unique site for the absorption of chemicals through the skin. Also, since benzo(a)pyrene is a potent agent that suppresses the activities of the immune system, whatever defenses the chimney sweeps might have had against cancer were likely quashed even as the first colonies of tumor cells were growing.

The Chinese who developed such a high incidence of lung cancer were similarly exposed to systemic benzo(a)pyrene from smoky coal. In addition to possible immunosuppressive effects, the smoky coal also contributed sulfur dioxide and other lung irritants as well as particulates that absorbed the cancer-causing chemicals. (Lung cancer in animals could not be produced by cigarette smoke until smoke condensates were allowed to adhere to hematite, an iron particle that carried the carcinogens deep within the lung.) Risk estimates for benzo(a)pyrene as a human carcinogen still often neglect these critical components of the carcinogenic mixture.

Pott's data also pointed to another overlooked risk factor. Childhood or even fetal exposure to carcinogens can amplify the noxious effect of certain chemicals. Nature has generally ensured that young people do not get cancer. (Cancers that do occur are either genetic, such as retinoblastoma and Wilm's tumor of the kidney, or viral, such as a few forms of lymphoma and leukemia.) Natural selection tends to make cancer a disease of old age, postponing the appearance of life-threatening lesions until after menopause in women and old age in men. Almost all adult cancers show a propensity to become increasingly common with age.

Public policies that drastically and preferentially limit exposure of fetuses and children to known carcinogens are still few and far between. (A notable exception was the decision to remove from children's pajamas a fire retardant called Tris that was structurally related to DBCP, a known mutagen and probable carcinogen. See Chapter 3.) Equally aggressive policies to limit adult exposure to environmental carcinogens have been similarly tardy. Only in the 1980s did we begin to recommend policies to significantly limit worker exposure to benzene, a known human leukemogen.

At least part of the problem rests with the apparent disparity with the long history of cancers in the workplace and the successful demonstrations of their association with particular chemicals, and the unsuccessful demonstration of associations of apparently real "clusters" of cancer cases among the general populace with any known environmental agent. This rift in our knowledge base, between real and meaningful causal chains linking occupational chemicals to cancer versus virtually absent causal chains between population-wide cancer clusters and any outside agency, is certainly mystifying. In more than a hundred different leukemia clusters, epidemiologists (scientists trained to study diseases of populations) were unsuccessful in tracking a reasonable cause. So unsuccessful has the "cluster buster" model of epidemiology been that, in the early 1980s the Centers for Disease Control formally got out of the hunt for causes of groups of human cancers. In the case of Woburn, Massachusetts, this move appears to have been premature.

THE WOBURN CLUSTER MYSTERY

Between 1970 and 1982, in Woburn, an old industrial, leather-working, and mill town in central New England, first one and eventually twenty cases of leukemia in children were found — some eleven more than expected by chance — in a clear-cut cluster. I was one of the scientifically trained people brought in to examine the circumstances of this event. Not surprisingly, since more than 50,000 water districts nationwide have been found to contain significant amounts of industrial contaminants, Woburn's water system was found to be heavily contaminated with chlorinated solvents used in many different industries. These solvents, particularly one called trichloroethylene or TCE for short, were eventually shown to occur in wells used disproportionately by the townspeople whose children developed leukemia. What made the Woburn conditions so provocative was the simultaneous exposure of the affected residents to other chlorinated solvents and benzene, a known leukemia-causing chemical; and the fact that *all* the leukemic children had the opportunity to be exposed in utero.

A detailed epidemiological study by the Harvard School of Public Health researchers further demonstrated an association with two wells, called wells G and H, and the leukemia families.[19] These families relied on wells G and H proportionately more than did other families in town — and these wells and not the others were contaminated with chlorinated solvents. Some critics of this study have pointed out that the leukemias have continued to occur even after the wells were closed. Others noted that since the cluster of cancer deaths centered on the eastern half of the town, *anything* found predominantly in that part of town would perforce have "statistical" association with the cancer cluster.[20]

In the case of the Woburn families, the most provocative finding was that each of the mothers who had a child who later developed leukemia drank water from wells G and H at some point during their pregnancies. But even this observation provided only a tantalizing clue about what might have triggered the leukemogenic event. That is, what appeared to be a reasonable explanation for the cancer events might just as well have been a fluke of confounding circumstances. The Harvard team concluded that, at best, the water-use pattern explained only four or six of the leukemia cases seen. So the causal net here, as elsewhere, was found to be riddled with large holes through which the genie of causation might very well have escaped.

CANCER LATENCY

Why haven't we been able to trace even dramatic cancer clusters in the natural environment to suspected chemicals? For one thing, the event that probably instigates such cancers is likely to have occurred years if not decades before the tumors make their first appearance. In Nagasaki, Japan, for instance, researchers have recently seen the first signs of an upswing of skin cancers in persons exposed to the nuclear radiation from the atomic blast in August, 1945—an interval of over *40 years!*[21]

This observation underscores an important reality: many of the chemicals of greatest public concern have long (albeit not this long) latency periods before their effects become manifest. Part of the reason for this hiatus between exposure and appearance is the commonly weak exposures to chemical carcinogens that characterize low-dose carcinogenesis. People in the typical environments of urban homes or dwellings might receive doses of suspected carcinogens that are tens or hundreds of times lower than those received by their occupational counterparts. Since workers who develop leukemia after occupational exposure commonly show latencies of eight to fifteen years or more, people who receive lower exposures might not develop tumors for twenty or more years.

This principle is illustrated by classic animal cancer studies. When mice are exposed to a typical carcinogen, and the dose of carcinogen is dropped lower and lower, the interval before the first skin tumor appears gets progressively longer. This phenomenon, called tumor latency, is of such importance that I have devoted part of a chapter to it (see Chapter 5).

Does this mean that all human epidemiology studies are doomed to fail? Not at all. Few if any studies incorporate *cofactors* into their analysis that might shorten the latency between the carcinogenic insult and the tumor's first appearance. One of these cofactors is immune competence. My own work has shown that lowering the immunologic competence of test animals can reduce the time of appearance of tumors compared to immunologically intact animals.[22] This helps explain why patients with AIDS, whose immune systems are all but ineffectual, have developed more tumors (especially Kaposi's Sarcoma) at a younger age than have their immunologically normal peers. Some of these tumors are also remarkable for their aggressiveness in AIDS patients, penetrating normal tissues much more avidly than do tumors in persons whose immune systems still function effectively.

POLICY IMPLICATIONS

The lessons of these studies need also to be put into a policy framework. Immunosuppressing toxic substances can indirectly increase cancer risk, even if they do not cause cancer themselves. The corollary of this realization is clear: if you know that you are immunologically impaired — as are virtually all persons who test positive for the AIDS virus — avoid carcinogenic insults at all costs. For persons who are immunologically less competent than normal because of the immaturity of their immune systems or susceptible for genetic reasons, special protection against toxic exposures also appears particularly important.

A further confounding variable has to do with the probabilistic nature of the carcinogenic insult itself. Not everyone who receives even massive doses of known carcinogens will develop cancer. Each of us knows of heavy smokers who died in their sleep of old age (and perhaps even more who died horrible deaths from emphysema or lung cancer). Even in cancer bioassays, in which scientists expose genetically identical rodents to near lethal concentrations of carcinogenic chemicals, not every animal develops cancer within its lifetime.

We cannot yet predict which of a hundred genetically identical animals exposed to heavy doses of a known carcinogen will, in fact, develop cancer or when the first tumors will appear. Part of the unpredictability of the carcinogenic process and the intractability of many animal (and human) hosts to the actions of known carcinogens can be traced to a number of factors: random distribution of cancer-causing molecules; delivery of the carcinogen to sensitive target tissues; concomitant stimulation or insult to the affected tissue; dietary status; immunological strength; and genetic resistance.

Today, as many more chemicals become implicated as carcinogens or serious hazards to human health, it is clear that a vital step has been missed in the process by which we permit the mass marketing of products with the potential to interact with our bodies. We neglect the indirect toxicity of chemicals and their likely interactions with other substances that might alter their effective toxicity. We make a similar mistake with our assessments of environmental agents. We often fail to examine the possibility that chemicals might cause *future* harm to people or the biosphere—before these products are allowed into the marketplace.

CHLOROFLUOROCARBONS AND OZONE DEPLETION

The chlorofluorocarbons (CFCs) are a prime example of such an omission. Here the need to perfect a nearly fireproof and seemingly nontoxic (to living systems) molecule led to the development of a group of molecules by Du Pont Corporation that incorporated both fluorine and chlorine atoms on a two-carbon backbone.

The CFCs served as nearly indestructible molecules that could be used as degreasers, heat exchangers, and general solvents with little apparent danger. They appeared to be the perfect solution to a chemical engineering problem.

What went awry? The major flaw was in failing to perceive their environmental fate. Was it knowable thirty years ago when Du Pont first made the CFCs 11, 12, and 113 (under their trade name Freon) that these molecules would interact with ultraviolet light to liberate ozone-destroying chlorine?

Perhaps not then, but certainly by the early 1970s. In December 1973, Sherry Rowland of the University of California at Irvine deciphered what any fourth-year chemistry student could have found in writing the equations for the chemical reaction of ozone to CFC-released chlorine to produce oxygen and chlorine monoxide: $Cl^- + O_3 \rightarrow ClO + O_2$. In a second series of reactions, chlorine monoxide breaks down to release oxygen and more free chlorine atoms. In this way, a single chlorine atom can destroy 100,000 ozone molecules before finally dispersing.

Still more potent depleters of the ozone layer — carbon tetrachloride and methyl chloroform — could also have been predicted to be chlorine releasers in the upper atmosphere. And each has been produced in the thousands of metric tons each year.

The failure to consider these reactions has led to the destruction of part of the ozone layer. (Each of these ozone depleters has also been found to contribute to global warming. More on this in Chapter 3.) An equally serious omission that is just becoming evident was the assumption that the Freon class of molecules would be so nonreactive with other biological molecules that for all intents and purposes they would be nontoxic.

By the early 1980s it became clear that the presumption that all of the chlorofluorocarbons lacked biological toxicity was erroneous. Like other chlorinated solvents, CFCs have a special toxicity for the heart muscle and can induce narcosis and central nervous system depression. Some of them have proven positive in recent reassessments of their cancer-producing capacities.

THE MYTH OF NONREACTIVITY

At the core of this error was the deceptive belief that virtual chemical inertness ensures harmlessness. In the 1950s, a similar emphasis on nonreactivity contributed to the expansive use of plastics. By making long chains of otherwise highly reactive chemicals, chemists in the mid-1900s were able to make plastics with almost any property they chose. This process (called polymerization) worked fine if all the reactive molecules (monomers) were trapped in the polymerized chains. This has not always proved possible. Polystyrene, ABS (acrylonitrile, butadiene, and styrene), polyethylene, polybutylene, and polyvinyl chloride (PVC) were touted as nonreactive plastics ideally suited for carrying beverages, wrapping food, and transporting water. Each has proven to pose unforeseen problems in their early formulations. For example, alcohol carried in acrylonitrile bottles was found to extract residues of carcinogenic monomers still present in the plastic, leading to the hasty recall of all alcohol-containing plastic bottles. Other plastic products have proved permeable to chemicals that were supposed to stay *outside* their walls. Plastic pipes made of polyethylene or polybutylene are suspected of allowing solvents or gasoline constituents such as benzene to cross their walls, thereby contaminating the water carried inside without breaks in the pipe walls.[23]

As I will show for other chemicals, the assumption of "nonreactivity" has proved to be a dangerous misconception. For one thing, the highly reactive ingredients that are used in making these so-called inert substances often remain as residues in the finished product. For early versions of PVC pipe, for instance, a high residual level of the carcinogenic monomer vinyl chloride almost spelled the end of its possible usefulness.[24] Later versions, which were reinforced by adding extra chlorine molecules (CPVC pipe), were contaminated by the "secret" process that added chloroform and carbon tetrachloride to the pipe. These molecules only showed up after the state of California measured the extractability of possible toxic molecules into drinking water from plastic pipes. The major producer of the pipe belatedly changed the formulation process to reduce or eliminate these potential carcinogens. But even when polymerization is perfect and little or no residual chemical monomers remain, nontoxicity cannot be assured. Living things react with often unanticipated vigor to what initially appear to be nonreactive chemicals.

Other supposedly nonreactive molecules include the silicones, long-chain polymers of silicone oxide bracketed with methyl groups. Like the plastics used in the food industry, silicones were initially not completely polymerized. In some cases, as we will see in Chapter 8, free silica was intentionally added to give different properties to the silicone gel, a possibly fatal chemical error. The silicone molecule, like its silicon oxide precursor, appears to share the property of eliciting an insidious, chronic inflammatory reaction. In certain persons this reaction appears to be a precursor of a still more disruptive reaction: a smoldering disease process in which cells of the immune system attack the body's own tissues.

The rest of this book is about the other errors we are still making in generating new chemicals for mass production or consumption. We still operate with the belief that by merely knowing the full chemical structure and the immediate interactions of a product we can predict that product's ultimate fate in the environment or in our bodies. All too often, in the synthesis of chemicals tailor-made for one function we failed to consider other chemicals with which they might interact. And individuals vary—sometimes enormously—in their capacity to break down or utilize potentially toxic molecules. For some persons, the very act of breaking the molecule down during metabolism converts a previously harmless molecule into a potent toxin. (More on this in Chapter 4.) Nor have we learned how to factor into our equations the long-term fate of molecules released into the environment. (See Chapter 12.)

Living things can react with often unanticipated vigor to what initially appear to be virtually nonreactive chemicals. This belated realization has led to a generation of failed medical devices. Often these plastic or titanium-based products appeared to be tissue compatible in the short run, only to cause massive blood clots or chronic tissue reactions a few years later. Other products, many based on silicone, were implanted into the body with the expectation that they would prove innocuous. Gold salts, which are based on a nonreactive elemental core, have been used in treating arthritis because of their remarkable, albeit as yet inadequately explained, anti-inflammatory activity. Other supposedly biocompatible or nontoxic molecules, including synthetic versions of naturally occurring hormones, silicones, solvents, and chemical degreasing agents, have been introduced, only to be recalled or reevaluated when unexpected toxic reactions flared.

Perhaps the most surprising hubris is that even when we *precisely* duplicate the atomic structure of a natural chemical, as we did in 1938 with George Corner's first synthesis of a steroid (progesterone), we are not assured of any greater wisdom in its use than if we fabricated an altogether alien mimic. Excessive doses of common hormones can produce serious toxic reactions. As I will show, even synthetic chemicals that are near perfect analogs to their natural counterparts (as was the case for synthetic estrogens such as diethylstilbestrol or the semi-synthetic estrogens in birth control pills) can seriously disrupt bodily functions or cause cancer. (See Chapter 9.)

What we apparently failed to factor into our chemical knowledge base was a satisfactory model of biological inertness: It is precisely because of their nondegradability that many complex chemicals accumulate inexorably in body tissues, causing smoldering chemical contamination with as yet poorly charted consequences. Some of these same chemicals and fluids — particularly the silicones — serve as a seemingly innocuous residue, waiting for the organism to begin what can become an unstoppable reaction to their presence. Other chemicals, like the polychlorinated biphenyls (PCBs), persist in body tissues indefinitely, stored away in fat cells. When these cells are mobilized during starvation, lactation, or just plain dieting, PCBs can be released en masse with visible toxic consequences. Their very inertness assures that they will persist, and because they are difficult to break down, they concentrate in animals high up on the food chain. This has proven especially problematic for DDT and its metabolite, DDE.

Could these toxic effects have been foreseen? Or once having been observed, could we have mitigated their consequences earlier? These questions are easier to answer in hindsight than with the kind of predictive skills we have come to expect of our best scientists. We need a "long look" at the molecular future. The first step is to chart the extent to which the planet — and our bodies — are contaminated with potentially hazardous chemicals.

CHAPTER THREE

Myth 1:

The problem is localized

THE EXTENT OF CHEMICAL CONTAMINATION

The rate of production of new chemicals continues to outstrip our ability to anticipate their adverse effects. In her prophetic book, *Silent Spring,* Rachel Carson anguished that the chemical industry would bury us under an untested and potentially calamitous avalanche of toxic contaminants.[1] Since then, toxic substances have been the major focal point of the environmental anxiety of a generation of Americans. The first Earth Day, held in April 1970, focused public attention on the diminishing natural resources of the planet and the depredations of its wildlife from overuse of toxic chemicals such as DDT and PCBs. In 1976, partly in response to revelations about widespread environmental contamination with PCBs, the U.S. Congress passed the Toxic Substances Control Act; the Green party in Europe began to mobilize; and Earth Day took on a political

35

tone. Gas masks replaced laurel wreaths, and mothers expressed disbelief at discovering that their breast milk was contaminated with PCBs. By the 1980s, concern about a toxic planet was becoming a major feature of the daily news stories.

Yet, even where production of chemicals such as PCBs had been halted out of concern for the public welfare, the state and the planet were left with a staggering toxic legacy. By 1972, 560 million kilograms (1,232 million pounds) of PCBs had been manufactured, with half of that coming from the United States alone. By the end of 1977, almost two-thirds of all PCBs were still in commerce, a year after the Toxic Substance Control Act called for a halt in their production.[2] Highly regarded researchers declared that it is "prudent" to consider any exposure to PCBs as undesirable.[3] Yet, no reliable, widely available method exists to safely destroy the remaining 748 million pounds still in the environment.[4]

By the end of the 1980s, hundreds of tons of other toxic chemicals were still not inactivated or destroyed. And there have been nearly 3,000 new chemicals produced annually, far surpassing the nation's ability to test the substances for any cancer-producing capacity.[5] By 1990, only about 2,000 chemicals were tested in animals for carcinogenicity. And of those tested as of this writing, about half were found to be positive.[6]

As of 1989, some 70,000 different chemicals were in commerce, and their volume was at an all-time high. The rate of increase in new chemicals, which was as high as 20 percent a year in 1984, was still growing at 5 percent a year. Considering both organic and inorganic chemicals, the total number of pounds of chemicals produced in 1988 was *609.55 billion,* of which perhaps 1 to 5 percent represent the most toxic core. According to *Chemical and Engineering News,* the total output in 1989 of the fifty major chemicals has been well above the annual average set for the past decade.[7] Because many of these chemicals are both profitable and hazardous, this is good news for the chemical industry, but bad news for the environment.

THE PROBLEM OF HAZARDOUS WASTE

Today, more than a hundred *billion* pounds of hazardous waste are generated annually in the United States. Enormous volumes of other chemicals are discharged directly into the air and water. In 1989, the Environmental Protection Agency (EPA) disclosed that 22.5 billion pounds of hazardous substances had been released into the environment two years earlier, a figure that the agency itself declared to be "startling and unacceptably high."[8]

In the past thirty years, it has been estimated that more than *750 million tons* of wastes from this chemical production have been dumped in 30,000 to 50,000 designated hazardous waste sites across the United States.[9] EPA has estimated that as many as 90,000 of the combined land disposal and hazardous waste sites it knows of are contaminating surface and ground waters with hazardous chemicals. The good news is that 80 percent will close within twenty years. The bad news is that this still leaves 20 percent of the sites to present a legacy of pollution to generations to come.[10]

By October 1984, the EPA had identified almost 19,000 "uncontrolled" hazardous waste sites where permits or other regulatory controls were absent.[11] Many other as yet undiscovered sites are illegal or abandoned. Some are close to populated areas. A disturbingly high proportion are adjacent to the poorest neighborhoods. The existence of new, more stringent controls and high fines has not stopped the problem. An indeterminate amount of toxic waste is still being dumped illegally in land fills and other unsecured sites. It was in part to stem the toxic tide of pollutants from such activities that the U.S. Congress passed legislation to control and clean up hazardous sites.

Superfund Sites

All hazardous waste sites pose a pollution problem and each poses a different potential for human harm through contamination of air, soil, and/or water with toxic chemicals. The worst are classified as "Superfund Sites," named after the enabling legislation that provides public funds for cleaning up the sites that pose the greatest risk to public health.[12] Since 1980–81, when the EPA first established its original list of 538 Superfund Sites, the number has already doubled. At the end of 1990, 131 sites were deemed to pose a clear and present danger to human health.[13] Of these, only a handful had been fully evaluated, and an even smaller number (some 33 by the end of 1990) had been secured and cleaned up.

A new site added to the list is the Union Chemical Plant site in Hope, Maine, a township where I have been serving since 1985 as an advisor on toxic substances to the surrounding community. This site is typical of many others, having been the repository of more than 20,000 55-gallon drums of hazardous wastes, numerous "accidental" spills of waste chemicals, and the location of an incinerator that indiscriminantly burned mixtures of oils, toxic industrial by-products, and hazardous solvents. During the winter, this witches' brew of chemicals was often used as a heating fuel for the facility.

The history of this site shows that a few prescient scientists foresaw the calamities that lay ahead. In 1978, when Union Chemical Company first proposed using the site of a stately old church on Route 17 near Hope, Maine, for hazardous waste, the community was incredulous. What possible reason could anyone have to use a lovely rural community and its historic church as a repository for foul and dangerous chemicals? According to research scientist Beverly Paigen, an epidemiologist retained by the community at the time, the community was originally dumbfounded that any regulatory agency would permit the siting of a hazardous waste site in their backyard. Paigen helped them demonstrate that Fish Pond, a major water source, only a hundred yards away from the edge of the property stood in the path of any plume of contaminants.[14] But the community was small, without much political power, and the pressures of industry and the new owner of the site prevailed. In 1984, the EPA granted a permit to allow the storage and later the incineration of hazardous wastes right in the backyard of the church.

What makes this site uniquely hopeful (no pun intended) is that it is the first place in the United States where an agreement was reached with the principal responsible parties (some 425 strong) to provide funds to begin to abate the hazards posed by plumes of subsoil wastes emanating from the plant and by the toxic residuals of the burning operation. A research team found the site itself to be heavily contaminated with solvents and highly toxic by-products of the incineration operations, making it uninhabitable for the foreseeable future. As of 1991, most of these hazardous chemicals have not yet left the site to contaminate soil and pond sediments in the community. A cleanup operation, in the planning stages for five years, is slated to begin in the early 1990s. But this pending "solution" has not erased the years of pervasive and gut-wrenching anxiety that the lives of the families living near the site and those of their children have been irrevocably damaged by the unmeasured by-products of years of burning and contaminated well water.

It was partly to allay these fears that I was asked to come in to serve as an intermediary, explaining chemical properties and the risks posed by the as yet low amounts of environmental pollutants measured near families' homes or in their wells. This site may be one of the few where any further problems have been nipped in the bud, but elsewhere the analysis of the problem is less sanguine.

Higher than expected numbers of four cancers—bladder, stomach, large intestine, and rectum—have been consistently seen among populations that live in proximity to hazardous waste sites.[15] (Not coincidentally, these are the same organs where increased cancer rates have been recorded in populations drinking heavily chlorinated water: see Chapter 9.) Although some scientists are chary in assigning a direct causal link between the chemicals at hazardous waste sites and these excess cancers,[16] any extra cancers in a population are disturbing and point to the urgent need for additional study.

THE PROBLEM OF PESTICIDES

Hazardous waste sites are not the only vehicle for exposing the human population to potential hazardous substances. Each year, more than 2 billion pounds of pesticides are used on our food crops. A commonly used estimate is that less than 1 percent of these often highly toxic chemicals actually reaches a "pest," but no one really knows. What is unequivocally known is that virtually all of the nonbiodegraded residue enters the soil, air, and water supplies, with some fraction contaminating the food chain. At the end of the food chain, creatures (including us) absorb and retain pesticide residues, concentrating the most persistent ones in our fat. Later, as mothers nurse their infants or fathers come home in dusty clothes, pesticides can be released and passed along to children, posing indeterminate risks to their health and well-being.

Newly discovered clusters of cancers among farmworker children at places like McFarland and Earlihart, California, point ominous fingers back toward the tremendous variety of pesticides and crop protectants (including arsenic-containing herbicides) that had been used over the past two decades. Many advocates of better farmworker protection programs, such as Ralph Abascal, general counsel of California Rural Legal Assistance, believe strongly that pesticide registration and usage patterns have consistently put crop protection above human protection.[17] He may be right.

A pattern of excess cancers among farmers themselves has been building over the past twenty years, without any single chemical or group of pesticides being clearly implicated.[18] That pesticides as a group *are* implicated in cancer deaths is strongly suggested by recent epidemiological studies. A group of researchers who examined the death records of people who lived in rural counties throughout the United States discovered that those who died of certain cancers were more commonly found among pesticide users than among groups of workers in other industries or with other demographic identifiers. When compared with other industrial activities, residence, family income, country of origin, or educational level, this research team found that use of agricultural chemicals was the best predictor of who would die from certain cancers. In keeping with other work (see studies cited in Chapter 1, ref. 12), herbicide usage strongly predicted deaths among white males from genital, lymphatic, and digestive cancer; while insecticides had a strong positive relationship to respiratory cancer.[19] The jury is still out regarding the collective impact of all the pesticides in commerce, but there are specific pesticides that have wreaked a clear-cut pattern of human health damage in exposed populations.

DBCP Contamination

In 1976, as a result of casual locker-room conversations, and the prodding of a visiting film crew, pesticide workers at the Occidental Petroleum facility in Lathrop, California, discovered that a large number of them had been unable to conceive children. Researchers who pursued this tantalizing puzzle found that 35 of the 114 men examined had abnormal sperm counts. Careful analysis of tissue biopsies from their testes revealed even more alarming news: 15 of the men had no detectable sperm-production capabilities.

When the occupational health specialists examining this group studied the workplace, they found one common denominator for all of the most severely affected men. All worked in or around a soil sterilant and nematode poison called 1,2-dibromo-3-chloropropane or DBCP for short.[20] A small number of the men eventually recovered their ability to produce sperm.[21] The remainder stayed "azoospermic," a medical euphemism for being completely incapable of producing sperm. Further research revealed that in spite of the fact that DBCP had been shown in 1961 to be capable of producing atrophy of the testis,[22] this knowledge was not incorporated into industrial safety practices or warning sheets. In 1978, seventeen years after its sterilizing capacity became known, the chemical was banned outright in California. A year later, the federal government banned all interstate commerce in DBCP. (This did not stop its major producers—Dow Chemical and Shell Oil— from continuing their sales of DBCP formulations abroad.) In 1983, a San Francisco jury awarded 6 U.S. workers $5 million for their DBCP-related fertility impairment: a lawsuit for 82 Costa Rican workers alleging similar infirmities is now pending before a Texas court.

But, in a pattern that has become the hallmark of the last two decades, what was originally an occupational problem has become a population-wide one. In the late 1970s and 1980s, DBCP became the most widespread pesticide contaminant of water in southwestern agricultural states. California wineries, which were supposed to have stopped use of this potent nematocide in 1978, began to find DBCP-contaminated grapes in 1979. That year one such winery, the Delicato Vineyards, found that it had 50 million gallons of DBCP-contaminated wine on its hands. As a result of a worried (but unauthorized) call from its chief plant operator, the California Department of Health Services learned about the presence of this outlawed chemical.

In an unprecedented move, then Deputy Director for Public Health, Donald Lyman, M.D., overrode the objections of his own Food and Drug Branch and permitted the winery to dilute the 50 million gallons of DBCP-tainted wine with uncontaminated wine to bring the DBCP concentration to an "acceptable" level.[23] As a result, in the early 1980s, an indeterminate number of Americans drank a little DBCP with their Green Hungarian varietal wines concocted from Delicato's brew.

Thereafter, first one small community in the immediate area of the plant and then whole clusters of townships up and down California's Central Valley began to report that their drinking water was contaminated with DBCP. Lawsuits were quietly settled out of court enabling the manufacturers of this potent and persistent chemical to keep a low profile.

The first case of a citizen (a policeman in Fresno, Calif.) who experienced the same form of azoospermia as had the Lathrop workers — and whose well water had been contaminated with DBCP since he was a child — went to court in 1985. Evidence was presented to show that adolescent animals are exquisitely sensitive to the sterilizing effects of DBCP and that the policeman's exposure was sufficient to cause his sterility (he swam in, showered with, and drank copious quantities of DBCP-contaminated water). By extraordinary legal maneuvering, the defense was able to get key testimony about the equivalence of this exposure to those of the Lathrop workers quashed, and the jury had to find in favor of the defendants. And while no evidence has yet surfaced that the fertility of DBCP-exposed populations in California's Central Valley has been impaired en masse,[24] by anyone's estimation the valley's populace has had a close brush with disaster.

THE HAZARD ALERT SYSTEM

Prompted by the DBCP episode, the state legislature in California passed legislation in 1977 to create a repository of information on commercially used chemicals to assure that available information about the toxic effects of exposures would be expeditiously transmitted to appropriate state or federal agencies.[25] I set up this group in 1979, under the rubric of HALTS, the Hazard Alert System.

One of the first tasks of HALTS was to identify the chemicals of greatest concern for Californians — and by inference for the United States generally. Our research showed that the mass production of toxic chemicals and other substances was proceeding at an accelerating rate. By 1980, we had found that more than 30,000 chemicals were being produced in quantities that exceeded 1 metric ton per year.[26] Of course, what matters for the health of the general public is not how much of a given chemical is produced, but whether the chemical is harmful in its final form. As we have seen, many plastics like PVC or ABS are, in fact, composed of carcinogens. But in their polymerized state the chemicals pose little or no danger — unless they are re-created when degraded or if a free monomer (the individual molecule of the polymer chain) is left in the plastic during production.

Of course, the workers who assemble or synthesize these benign products from their hazardous precursors are almost always at risk of adverse effects unless they are fully insulated from exposure to the carcinogen in question. The group of precursor molecules for chlorinated plastics includes chlorinated solvents. Among these, we singled out a related compound, trichloroethylene (TCE), a widely used degreasing agent, for particular attention. In 1976, studies had shown TCE to be carcinogenic in animals,[27] and we wanted to ensure that workers would not be unnecessarily exposed. We also discovered that TCE could cause neurological problems following exposure from levels in the workplace that were below those currently permitted. Consequently, in 1980 we recommended lowering the permissible exposure to TCE by 90 percent (from 100 ppb to 10 ppb). Two years later, a compromise level of 25 parts per billion (ppb) was set in California, a precedent that was followed in 1989 with a lowering of the federal standard to 50 ppb. Workers are now substantially better protected from the neurological effects of exposure to this solvent.

PUBLIC EXPOSURE TO TOXIC SUBSTANCES

For the rest of us, the issue of toxics-induced diseases turns on the likelihood of exposure to a harmful chemical. Some estimates that put the number of people exposed to toxic substances at home or in the workplace at more than 20 million.[28] Much of this exposure is to simple solvents, such as TCE or 1,1,1-trichloroethane, which find their way into a plethora of household and industrial products from "white-out" correction fluids to degreasing agents.

In spite of the great opportunity for exposure, reported toxic events are rare from contact with most consumer products (pesticides, correction fluid, and glues are notable exceptions). However, public exposure from airborne contaminants released from incineration or atmospheric dumping of chemicals is a different story. According to the 1987 EPA Inventory of Toxic Substances Released into the Environment, in 1986 more than 7 billion pounds of toxic by-products were emitted into the air, land, and water by 19,278 different companies. Many of these substances, notably benzo(a)pyrene and dioxins, pose substantial risks to persons who receive high exposures. In certain communities, notably Los Angeles, benzo(a)pyrene exposure can exceed recommended limits on a significant portion of the days of the year. Such air pollution can increase the likelihood of cancer, as suggested by studies that demonstrate heightened risks of lung cancer in persons living in high contamination areas.[29]

In spite of the likelihood that most of the significant toxic risks stem from airborne emissions, the public associates the highest risk to well-being from land-based waste sites. According to a Roper Organization survey conducted in the spring of 1989, more than 60 percent of the public views active and abandoned hazardous waste sites as comprising "very serious" environmental risks.[30] The EPA, for its part, believes that such sites pose only marginal risks, and then only to a small minority of the population. In 1989, the EPA ranked problems such as global warming and ozone depletion much higher than hazardous wastes, and downgraded risks from toxic substances emanating from waste sites in favor of those from radon and asbestos.[31]

In the comments accompanying the report of this survey, EPA official Frederick W. Allen contrasted his agency's views with those of the public by observing that: "The most obvious reason [for the discrepancies] is that the general public simply does not have all the information that was available to this task force of experts. . . . People often overestimate the frequency and seriousness of dramatic, sensational, dreaded well-publicized causes of death and underestimate the risks from more familiar, accepted causes that claim lives one by one."[32] But does the public really misjudge chemical risks? Some of the questions that both sides agree need answering are discussed below.

CHEMICAL CAUSES OF CANCER

How many of these chemicals represent potential threats to human health depends on five interrelated factors: (1) Is significant human exposure likely? (2) Did exposure occur in a manner likely to deliver a toxic dose? (3) Was the dose received sufficient to cause the adverse health effect in question? (4) Was the exposed person especially vulnerable to the effect in question? (5) Were potentially conflicting causes of the same effect excluded?

From the public's point of view, these questions take on a particular urgency when someone appears to have been hurt by exposure to toxic substances. The urgency stems from the understandable fear that the exposure might be general, that family members might be at risk. But, from my own experience in lawsuits involving exposure to toxic substances (termed "toxic torts"), these major cases are often extraordinarily difficult to resolve.

The central legal question is commonly the one that scientists are often only able to answer after years of study, namely, did chemical X *cause* disease Y. The core problem for the plaintiff's lawyers is establishing the existence of a causal link, often in the face of incomplete data.

Leukemia as a Case Study

Benzene is a case in point. In spite of the fact that 11.67 billion pounds of this chemical entered commerce in 1989,[33] an amount more than sufficient to cause leukemia in everyone in the United States given long enough exposure, no one claims that all cases of leukemia are caused by benzene exposure. This is because leukemia has other causes and because only a small percentage of the benzene reaches the public in a form where exposure occurs. For example, most benzene is sequestered in products such as gasoline or kerosene where its use results in its destruction (through combustion). Other benzene molecules are used in chemical reactions in the synthesis of other organic chemicals.

Nonetheless, significant emissions of benzene occur from industrial activities and represent a potential threat to human health in the United States. The EPA has identified twelve major industry activities or groups that are responsible for most of these emissions, and in 1979 selected five of these groups for regulation. However, four years later, the EPA had still not set standards to protect the public from any of the twelve sources of exposure. In July 1983, the EPA was called before a congressional panel to explain why it had not set standards to protect the public from emissions in gasoline vapors. At the same time, the Natural Resources Defense Council and the Environmental Defense Fund filed suit in the U.S. District Court in the District of Columbia to enjoin the EPA to issue standards for all of the twelve categories identified in 1979.

In a partial response to the lawsuit, the EPA announced on December 16, 1983, that it intended to issue final standards for fugitive emissions (from gasoline pumping operations); propose standards for coke by-product recovery plants; and that it intended to withdraw proposed standards for the remaining categories. In rejecting these areas of potential regulations, the EPA asserted that the risks posed by these activities were "insignificant," even though they constituted levels that in any other setting would be considered excessive (for example, 3.6 cases of cancer per 10,000 persons exposed to benzene from storage facilities; 7.6 cases per 100,000 from maleic anhydride; and 1.4 per 100,000 from ethylbenzene/styrene).[34]

Subsequently, the EPA issued strict standards for controlling benzene from gasoline sources (1984), but has only recently (1991) issued more stringent requirements for benzene emissions from these other sources. This ambivalence means that we have continued to permit emissions that have exposed the public to significant risks from benzene exposure. In fact, most people who live in urban areas are constantly exposed to levels of benzene in the range of 6–91 $\mu g \neq m^3$ with as yet unquantified ill effects, such as the leukemias linked to higher workplace exposures.[35]

A recent case of a young man who developed a form of leukemia called acute myelocytic leukemia (a form of leukemia that has been linked to benzene since 1928) is a classic example of the difficulties entailed in demonstrating cause-and-effect linkages between toxic exposures and human illness.

When I first inquired about the circumstances of the young man who developed this form of leukemia, I asked about his occupation, thinking that since he had developed a chemically induced leukemia, that was where most of his exposure was likely to have occurred. It turned out that he did have significant opportunity to have been exposed to benzene: He was employed by a car dealership when he was only 16 and then by two service stations. My first thought was that he might well have been exposed to benzene while working at these jobs since benzene is found in gasoline (around 1 percent) and is a common component of many solvents and degreasing agents. His work had entailed using a solvent for cleaning the floor of the auto shop, but the solvent in question was supposedly free of benzene. I suggested that the solvent be tested for benzene. The tests came back positive: in fact, there was up to 500 ppm of benzene in the solvent.

But was he exposed to enough of the benzene in the course of his workday to account for his leukemia? Further inquiry revealed that his job entailed wet mopping the floor with an open 2-gallon pail of solvent. This would have exposed him to evaporating benzene fumes, and since he almost always got his tennis shoes and socks soaked by the solvent mixture, he was also at risk for absorbing benzene through the skin. A simple calculation of the effective dose of benzene he could have received from his occupational exposure put him above the recommended standard at the time of his exposure (in 1977), namely, 1 ppm for a day's work.

Did these observations demonstrate that his leukemia had been *caused* by the solvent? Not in and of themselves. It was also important to rule in or out any other exposures that might have contributed to his "dose" of benzene. He had also worked on his car on weekends — and he used a cup of gasoline to wash the car parts. Some of the solvents and lubricants that he used also contained benzene. And, like most of us, he often filled his own car tank with gasoline, a procedure that causes short-lived exposure to as much as 50 ppm of benzene for a few seconds.

The key legal question was to identify which of these exposures was the *major* contributing factor — and to what extent any of the other exposures were "substantial contributing causes" of his leukemia. Simple calculations using the principles of industrial hygiene pointed to the wet-mopping operation.

Now the remaining problem was establishing that the exposure was of sufficient duration and that a reasonable interval had elapsed between his exposure and the appearance of the cancer to satisfy the conditions of full dosage (usually measured in part-per-million years) of a carcinogen and the latency between exposure and the appearance of the cancer. Here there appeared to be a possible problem: the young man's exposure had taken place only over a two-year period of employment — and he had worked for only about two hours a day on his job of wet mopping. The leukemia itself appeared four years after he finished work at this job, an interval that is shorter than the norm of ten to fifteen years for previously demonstrated associations between benzene exposure and leukemia incidence.

What might have contributed to this apparent enhancement of the carcinogenicity of the benzene? Part of the answer lay within the composition of the solvent itself. I reviewed the literature on solvent mixtures and discovered that in the 1950s, analogous solvent mixtures had been tested in animals and found to accelerate the formation of tumors.[36] This observation suggested that any carcinogenic insult from benzene might be aided and abetted by the concomitant exposure to other chemicals in the solvent mixture.

The second factor was the young man's age. He was only 16 when he started working at the auto sales and repair business. It has been a long-established principle of chemical carcinogenesis that young or adolescent animals are more susceptible to tumor development than are adults receiving comparable doses. This observation is in part attributable to the higher rates of cell division common in younger animals who are undergoing rapid growth. Rapidly dividing cells are also more vulnerable to interaction with chemicals such as benzene that form reactive molecules that bind tightly with DNA.

An investigation of the young man's medical records also revealed another suggestive observation. He had a long history as a child of swollen lymph nodes. But the fact that the nodes regressed — and that he had had a normal blood picture prior to his employment — indicated that the nodes were not themselves indications of a preleukemic state.

A remaining question was to ask if anyone else exposed to a comparable mixture of solvents also developed leukemia. For this analysis, one has to rely on epidemiological data from other work sites where a naptha-like solvent (similar to the one used here) was commonly used. I knew that, until recently when

latex paints largely replaced oil-based ones, painters had relied heavily on such solvents for diluting their paints and cleaning their brushes. A survey of the literature revealed a study
done in Sweden that strongly associated exposure to such solvents, again containing only a small amount of benzene, to a
high risk of leukemia.[37]

So, in this case, the evidence available appeared to point
toward benzene exposure *with* other solvents as a reasonable
explanation for this person's leukemia. Unfortunately, the judge
ruled against allowing the jury to consider the contribution
of other solvents into evidence. After two days of often-heated
deliberation, the jury ruled against the plaintiff.[38]

GLOBAL WARMING AND TOXIC SUBSTANCES

While the public continues to be fascinated with local stories
about toxic wastes or chemical exposures such as these, the
EPA has identified global warming as the principal cause for
alarm in the world's encounter with chemicals.[39] The EPA's
focus on the health effects of a possible global warming and
the public's concern about toxic wastes may not be as divergent as appears at first blush. Global warming is a striking consequence of the industrial age. Researchers estimate through
computer simulations that the global temperature will increase
between 1.5° and 4.5° Celsius (3° to 8°F) over the next seventy-five years. The likely impact on life on earth will be enormous, considering that the world's temperature has increased
only 4°C since the last Ice Age some 20,000 to 25,000 years
ago. We are talking here about *rapid* change, the kind that living
organisms are ill prepared to anticipate. As the world's temperature rises, the ability of slow-moving organisms — in particular, plant life — to keep up with changes in their habitat
through seed dispersal or migration will likely be stressed to
the limit. Those that can't keep pace will become extinct.

The causes of global warming, while complex, point to
several sources. First and foremost, global warming is basi-
cally a result of the shifting characteristics of the earth's atmosphere. Overall, about 20 percent of the sun's energy is
absorbed by the atmosphere, 50 percent warms the earth's surface, and the remaining 30 percent is reflected back into space.

It is this reflected energy that is undergoing the most radical shift. Water vapor and carbon dioxide are the principal chemical heat shields. Most commentators believe that the global warming we are seeing is the result of the dramatic increase in carbon dioxide, from 280 to 350 ppm since the Industrial Revolution. Less well characterized is an equally dramatic contribution of synthetic gases, particularly the chlorofluorocarbons (CFCs). Molecule for molecule, CFCs (such as Freons 11, 12, and 113) are almost 10,000 times *more* effective in contributing to global warming than is carbon dioxide.

At their present rate of production, CFCs are predicted to contribute fully half as much to global warming by the year 2030 as does carbon dioxide.[40] At least forty-four countries appeared to recognize the gravity of this impact when they met in Montreal in 1988. The signatories of the Montreal Protocol on Substances that Deplete the Ozone Layer agreed to reduce CFC production by 50 percent by the year 2000. In a meeting in Helsinki in May 1989, the European Community proposed an even more aggressive stand, calling for a 50 percent reduction in output by 1991 or 1992, and a 95 percent slash five years later. In June 1990, an agreement was reached to halt CFC production globally by the year 2010.

Other chemical sources that contribute to global warming include nitrous oxide (a by-product of combustion engines), and methane. The final gas involved (accounting for about 10 percent of global warming) is ozone—but ozone in the lower levels of the atmosphere (the troposphere). Thus CFCs not only deplete *stratospheric* ozone at a dramatic rate, they participate in reactions that lead to its increase in the lower atmosphere where they help trap radiant heat and contribute to smog formation. In the hotter climate expected as a result of the greenhouse effect, the health consequences of smog (bronchitis, asthma, and emphysema) are all likely to be exaggerated.[41]

THE OZONE LAYER

A more insidious effect of the depletion of stratospheric ozone is the consequent increase in the amount of ultraviolet (UV) light reaching the earth. The Ozone Trends Panel of the U.S. National Aeronautics and Space Administration has concluded that the earth's protective ozone concentration has decreased an average of about 2.0 percent over the past twenty years, largely as a result of interaction with CFCs.[42] As we saw in Chapter 2, the chemical interaction of CFCs with ozone results in the breakdown of ozone into smaller molecules and the coincidental release of more chlorine, which perpetuates the cycle of destruction.

The sun emits a full spectrum of potentially damaging UV light. But, it is mainly the longer wavelengths of ultraviolet light that readily penetrate the stratospheric ozone, along with smaller amounts of the next-longest wavelength. However, when that ozone is depleted — even only modestly — the protective shield against penetration of the shorter-wavelength UV light thins, and dramatically more of this life-damaging wavelength penetrates to earth.

It is not difficult to see why UV light is potentially so damaging to living systems. Ultraviolet light is the most "energetic" light within the spectrum of visible and near-visible light (insects can see much further into the ultraviolet range than can humans). The ultraviolet spectrum begins where the X-ray spectrum leaves off. At its lowest end (the shortest wavelengths), UV light packs a real wallop to biological molecules. Deoxyribonucleic acid (DNA, the genetic material) absorbs light within a narrow set of bands in the ultraviolet spectrum. As a result, much of the energy contained within the light is released directly into the DNA molecule. Disruptions and open breaks are often the consequence, followed by so-called unscheduled DNA synthesis. This new burst of DNA production is thought to represent a repair response.

For most of us, this repair system corrects some or all of the UV-inflicted DNA damage. We each have enzymatic systems in our cellular nuclei that can find the break, snip off the loose ends, and neatly restitch the missing length of a DNA strand so that it exactly complements the intact chain. However, for some persons, notably those with the class of genetic defects known as xeroderma pigmentosum (XP), these enzyme "repair kits" are defective. In some persons with this disorder, even a *single* exposure to high-energy UV light can set in motion a series of genetic errors that lead to skin cancer.[43] The most lethal form of skin cancer, melanoma, is unfortunately also increased among these persons. Even XP children as young as 3–5 years old have developed malignant skin tumors after exposure to sunlight.[44]

The reaction of such XP children to UV light demonstrates in a highly exaggerated form the response of normal skin to sunlight. Following UV-mediated genetic damage, skin cancer can result in even the most genetically "normal" persons. This is especially true for light-skinned Caucasians. And skin tumors have been increasing dramatically in the United States in the past two decades, with more than 400,000 new cases being diagnosed annually.[45] According to skin cancer researcher Margaret Kripke of the University of Texas M.D. Anderson Cancer Center, this upward trend "is probably due at least in part to the increasing exposure of our population to both natural and artificial sources of UV radiation."[46] The current depletion of the ozone layer has greatly exacerbated this trend, particularly as some of these tumors are also linked to chemical contaminants such as benzo(a)pyrene, which are also increasing. The best estimates are that for every 1 percent depletion in the ozone layer, the rate of nonmelanoma skin tumors will increase by 2 percent.[47] According to the EPA, the present rate of ozone depletion will result over the next 50 years in 12 million Americans developing skin cancer; 200,000 will die.

Melanoma as a Case Study

Of the skin tumors linked to UV radiation the most malignant is melanoma. (Unlike other skin tumors such as basal cell or squamous cell carcinomas, which have a cure rate of 90 to 95 percent, fewer than one-third of malignant melanoma patients typically survive five years.) The linkage to UV light is reinforced by the observation of the previously cited increase of melanoma in xeroderma pigmentosum patients. Laboratory studies have also shown that UV wavelength radiation affects the formation and accelerates the growth of these tumors. The most dramatic new finding is that in experimental animals, UV light can suppress the immune system, acting first locally in the skin and then producing a long-lasting immune impairment in the body as a whole.[48] This immune suppression may lift a second protective shield to melanoma formation, that of the immune surveillance system. These effects singly and together combine to put the central focus of concern on the ozone layer.

The evidence linking environmental factors to melanoma occurrence is thus extremely strong. For one thing, melanoma has been increasing fastest in those countries where significant numbers of fair-skinned individuals have high solar exposure. For example, between 1968 and 1988, the incidence of melanoma has increased an average of 7.5 percent per year in countries such as the United States and New Zealand, predominantly in people who reside closest to the equator, demonstrating a strong geographic gradient.[49] While many factors point to sunlight (especially UV light) as the principal cause, the evidence also points to additional environmental factors that contribute to melanoma's increasing incidence.

One clue for this likelihood is that melanoma preferentially strikes the young. (One-third of all patients are under age 40 at the time of diagnosis.)[50] But it also concentrates selectively in some families, suggesting that constitutional and genetic factors also play a role in melanoma's genesis.

At the close of a 1987 conference on this tumor, the conference coconvenors noted that "Malignant melanoma has now become a major international health problem, affecting all nations with increasing incidence and mortality. It may be epidemic in the Western world and of increasing importance in the Eastern countries."[51] While new cases of malignant melanoma are recorded at a rate of only 0.02 cases per 100,000 persons per year in Osaka, Japan, the case rate has reached 6.3 to 6.5 per 100,000 persons per year in the United States and 15.2 to 19.1 cases per 100,000 persons per year among inhabitants of New South Wales, Australia.[52]

Contribution of Other Factors to Melanoma. Recent analyses of so-called cancer clusters of malignant melanoma and its precursors underscore the likelihood that factors other than ultraviolet light play a significant role in the melanoma genesis. In 1977, the first nineteen of what were to become more than two dozen cases of malignant melanoma were reported among the workers at the Lawrence Livermore Laboratories in Livermore, California. A team of scientists led by Dr. Don Austin investigated the existence of a possible cluster. Once they confirmed the presence of an unusually high incidence of cancer at the laboratory (as compared to matched controls among Livermore residents), the team examined the contribution of work-related factors that could account for its occurrence.

The team found that five types of work experience at the laboratory were heavily overrepresented among the workers who had developed melanomas: a job that took the worker to a classified site (known as Site 300) where nuclear detonators were exploded; being employed as a chemist; being on-site at the detonation of nuclear weapons in the U.S. West or the Pacific; handling radioactive materials; and being exposed to photographic chemicals possibly including radioactive emulsions. These experiences accounted for virtually all of the excess risk of melanoma according to Dr. Austin,[53] a conclusion hotly disputed by the laboratory. But when the laboratory followed up Austin's report by asking another institution to redo the study—it found the same five activities to be overrepresented among the melanoma cases. And both studies strongly implicate one or more common factors in the five job activities: one is excess exposure to radiation; another is chemical exposure (which chemicals—and how much and what form of radiation—remain unknown at the present).

Geographic Melanoma "Hot Spots"

The possible existence of "hot spots" for melanoma is revealed by cancer maps first released by the National Cancer Institute in 1975.[54]

The map for melanoma in the United States dramatically illustrates the role of *latitude* in the United States in determining the geographic distribution of melanoma. It is evident that melanoma becomes progressively more common as we approach the equator. With the exception of a few counties in southern Illinois and northern Kentucky, virtually all of the high melanoma risk areas for both men and women are found below the Mason-Dixon line. (It is noteworthy that the counties *above* the Mason-Dixon line that have elevated risks for women include heavily industrialized communities that take their chlorinated drinking water supplies from polluted waterways or are farming communities that are heavily exposed to pesticides.)

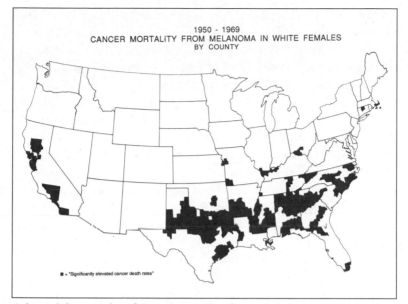

Adapted from *Atlas of Cancer Mortality for United States Counties 1950–1969,* T. J. Mason, et al., eds., Department of Health, Education and Welfare

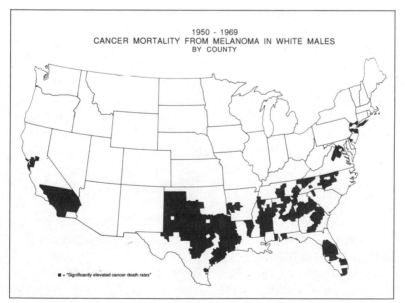

Adapted from *Atlas of Cancer Mortality for United States Counties 1950–1969,* T. J. Mason, et al., eds., Department of Health, Education and Welfare

The equatorial gradient for melanoma generally holds true around the world. The province of Queensland, Australia, with most of its population between latitudes 20° and 27°S, has the highest rate in the world: 286 cases per 100,000 among men and 298 per 100,000 among women. By comparison, New Zealanders who live below 27°S (further from the equator) have an incidence rate of 188 per 100,000.[55] Similar data exist for Scandinavian countries and for Scotland, England, and Wales, with the highest rates appearing in southern England, and the lowest in Lapland.

Data like these made it patently obvious to some scientists that some factor related to sunlight was causally linked to melanoma. Also, since significantly more men than women develop melanoma in the United States, as well as in New Zealand and Japan,[56] outdoor activity related to solar exposure fit the data to a "T".

Confounding Factors.   But, as we will see for almost all environmentally associated "causes," a simple model is not always the most satisfactory. For melanoma, it is evident that *intermittently* sun-exposed areas of the body (such as the chest or back in men and the lower legs in women) have shown the most rapidly increasing incidence and mortality rates,[57] suggesting that "bursts" of high-intensity exposure may be more significant for melanoma than is the continuous, chronic exposure to sunlight that accounts for the majority of other skin tumors. Also, paradoxically, melanoma can occur on the soles of the feet and the buttocks, areas that are rarely if ever exposed to the sun.

These observations suggest that some systemic element may be activated by sunlight to provoke pigmented cells to become malignant. Alternatively, the highly migratory pigmented cells themselves may move from their original, high-intensity exposure sites to the more remote regions of the body that eventually develop melanomas. The fact that ultraviolet light can suppress the body's immunity, perhaps system-wide, could also explain this finding.

Also, since UV exposure has been shown to knock out significant portions of the immune system in experimental animals, it may set the stage for the emergence of especially "antigenic" or chemically dissonant tumors as the normal surveillance mechanism is disabled. My own view is that while all of the above factors come into play, the most plausible explanation is that UV light activates carcinogens in the body which then circulate to distant sites to produce their genetic damage.

The evidence for this hypothesis, while still circumstantial, is intriguing. Japanese research has specifically implicated certain chemicals found in polluted industrial areas in the genesis of pigmented tumors such as melanoma. One particularly provocative environmental study of this kind was conducted by a team of eight Japanese researchers.[58] Like many other marine scientists, members of this team had noticed a distressing new phenomenon in estuaries and bays close to industrial centers: fish, especially those that live in the shallow water, were showing up with pigmented skin tumors and other cancers that had not been noted before. To these scientists, such tumors serve as environmental "sentinels" that herald more widespread cancer and potential human disease.

Previous work had shown that marine catfish,[59] and gulf croakers, freshwater drum, and brown bullhead[60] had all developed novel and sometimes life-threatening tumors in polluted waterways or oceanic areas. The U.S. studies of the drum and bullhead species are particularly tantalizing: they showed that fish in the Niagara River (in the same catchment area as Love Canal) had unusual tumor types in polluted stretches of this waterway (which drains the Great Lakes).[61]

The Japanese team investigated a melanoma-like tumor in two species of fish: croakers (*Nibea mitsukurii*) and sea catfish (*Plotosus anguillaris*), both bottom feeders that live in shallow water in the coastal regions of much of Japan. Their findings were remarkable on two counts: first, they linked the annual occurrence of melanoma-like skin tumors to the presence of effluents of specific chemical industries; and, second, they demonstrated that the seawater in which the most severely affected fish lived contained highly potent mutagens. The team refined their investigation by showing that they could induce identical tumors in catfish by exposing them to chemicals extracted from the waste water obtained from a factory in the highest risk area.[62]

The researchers believe that the tumors stemmed from the fish's exposure to such environmental pollutants as nifurpirinol,

N-methyl-N'-nitro-N-nitrosoguandidine and 7,12-dimethyl-benzanthracene. (The last two chemicals are members of a class of substances we will see more of in this book: the *N-nitroso* compounds and the *polycyclic aromatic hydrocarbons*.) Convincing environmental data came only after the Japanese conducted cleanup operations — once the contaminated river sediments at one high-incident site were removed, the incidence of tumors in the fish fell dramatically even as UV exposure persisted.

Other studies have shown that animals only develop full-blown pigmented tumors when two factors are present: a chemical carcinogen *and* ultraviolet light. Since UV light can penetrate the ocean to depths of 20 to 30 meters in clear water — and up to 5 meters in even the more turbid waters close to shore[63] — the coastal fish studies of the Japanese and others may invoke a chemical-UV link. Some research has, in fact, been done on the effect of combinations of chemicals (such as poly-chlorinated biphenyls) and UV light on skin cancer and mela-noma.[64] In support of the view that UV light "photoactivates" chemicals to become potent mutagens and carcinogens, recent research has shown that many potent chemical carcinogens can be activated by light in the near-UV spectrum.[65]

Policy Implications

The number of studies demonstrating photoactivation is by now sufficient to suggest that this is a general phenomenon. Many diverse chemicals have been shown to be activated by UV light to become active mutagens and carcinogens.[66] These findings suggest that the global consequences of permitting more UV light to enter the biosphere may be much more far-reaching than previously considered. Up until now, only the immediate effects of UV light on skin carcinogenesis have generally been considered in making policy determinations about the "ozone hole." But if UV light serves as a catalyst for generating highly dangerous mutagens from otherwise relatively benign precursors, its effects on life on earth may be even more catastrophic than previously envisioned.

From the material presented above, it is evident that much more far-reaching policies are needed to anticipate the effects of an inevitable increase in the amount of UV light impinging on the global ecosystem. These policies might properly include the development of stringent regulations on chemicals that can be photoactivated; the diminution of the presence of such chemicals in urban smog; and the frank prohibition of the manufacture not only of the chlorofluorocarbons that contribute to the ozone hole but also of chemicals such as the heterocyclic and aromatic amines that become the most potent mutagens after contact with UV radiation. These preemptive policies are particularly apt in the face of mounting evidence that increasing amounts of UV radiation are almost certainly going to occur over the next few decades.

THE COMPLEXITY OF ENVIRONMENTAL EXPOSURE

For the rest of us, there is the question of whether the trace exposures we experience daily to chemicals like benzene constitute a cancer hazard. The EPA finally concurred in benzene's case. At the end of August 1989, it ordered emissions of industrial sources to be cut by 90 percent. Resolving this question for other chemicals is complex, not least of all because of the difficulty in moving from the unusual and often exaggerated exposures in occupational settings to the low level of exposures typical for most communities. The root of this dilemma can be found in the origins of toxicology and its dependence on knowledge gleaned from animal studies or heavily exposed worker populations. That is, the very idea that environmental levels (commonly measured in parts per billion) of chemicals could influence human health derived from studies of much more heavily exposed workers for whom often severe and acute illness was documented. One of the core issues is that of extrapolation — to what extent can effects seen at high doses be expected at much lower ones? Another is the question of whether and how such low doses produce health effects.

At least part of the misperception generated by often vested interests that low doses of carcinogenic chemicals "can't possibly" hurt anyone[67] is due to a misconception of the rationale for testing chemicals at high doses in animal populations. When chemicals suspected of having carcinogenic activity are put into cancer bioassay tests, it is common practice to use doses that are near the levels at which overt toxicity is likely to occur (the so-called MTD or maximally tolerated dose) and then to range downward in usually two successive steps to intermediate and lower doses. Still, the lowest dose tested is often hundreds if not thousands of times higher than are likely environmental exposures. The reason for such high-dose studies is to ensure that a carcinogenic effect will be seen if it is there. (Were lower doses used, thousands of animals would often be required to reveal carcinogenicity.)

When a carcinogenic effect is observed, it is commonly seen only in the higher dosed animals. Often the "low" dose group is free of any overt signs of malignancy. But this does not mean that people or even other animals who receive this lower dose, or even less of the chemical, will be free of cancer risk. Rather, it means that for the limited number of animals tested, carcinogenic effects were not seen within the duration of the experiment. Also, as doses of cancer-causing substances are lowered, the likelihood that any one individual will get cancer goes down proportionately. Concurrently, the *latency* between the initial exposures to the carcinogen and the final appearance of a cancer will grow increasingly longer. (A fuller discussion of latency appears in Chapter 5.) Thus, the adage among pathologists that I studied under was that if people lived long enough, it was inevitable that they would get cancer. What prevents universal confirmation of this adage, according to pathology pundits, is that most of us die of other causes before we have time to develop cancer.

This concept rests on the belief that the latency for most tumors is sufficiently protracted so that only a small percentage of persons get cancer in their lifetime. However, with the advent of antibiotics and effective interventions for cardiovascular diseases, the cancer incidence statistic is inevitably going to shift upward. Thus, it is increasingly urgent to define the circumstances and events that commonly bring people into contact with substances that may trigger the carcinogenic process or one of its stages. Equally important is defining just how the body deals with these toxic substances and how those interactions lead to enhanced risks of cancers appearing within our lifetimes.

It should be clear by now that toxic problems and cancer

are neither solely individual problems nor ones limited to small areas of unusual dietary habits or geology. The global reach of toxicity is made apparent by the ubiquity of air and water contamination and the occurrence of previously unrecorded cancers in fish and animals. The present epidemic of melanoma in humans serves as a clear indicator of our vulnerability to environmental cancer. Its worldwide scope raises serious questions about our ability to control the environmental causes of cancer, and our bodily defenses against it.

CHAPTER FOUR

Myth 2:

The body's defenses are adequate

WE WOULD ALL LIKE TO BELIEVE THAT THE BODY KNOWS HOW to defend itself against the onslaught of chemical toxicants. Were this true it would add much needed symmetry to a world infused with toxic chemicals. That is, what we create we can destroy. It is true that the body does *attempt* to break down most of the chemicals that it encounters. But the consequences of this effort are not always salubrious. Sometimes the end result is a *more* toxic chemical, rather than a detoxified one. To understand this paradox, it is critical to first understand what makes chemicals toxic.

WHAT MAKES A POISON?

Why . . . should I marvel or let myself be frightened because one part is poison, and despise the other part too? . . . Who despises poison, knows what is in the poison.

All things are poisons: there is none which is not a poison. The right dose differentiates a poison and a remedy.

He who strikes the middle, receives no poison. . . . If you wish justly to explain each poison, what is there that is not poison? All things are poison, and nothing is without poison, the Dose alone makes a thing not a poison.

Paracelsus

The answer supplied by the Swiss physician Paracelsus (1493–1541) almost five hundred years ago is that it is the *dose* of each substance that determines its toxicity. This common aphorism, repeated on the title page of the classic treatise on toxicology, L. Casarett and J. Doull's *Toxicology, The Science of Poisons* (New York: Macmillan, 1986) takes Paracelsus's words out of context. Casarett and Doull ignore two salient points: first, that Paracelsus believed that biological effects of substances were to be expected at *both* ends of the dosage spectrum: at high doses, a substance might produce toxic effects, while at low doses, the same substance might prove to be a "remedy," perhaps by stimulating the body's defenses. (This theme will be explored in Chapter 6.) Second, that the effective toxicity of any chemical is determined by the body's *reaction* to a potentially toxic substance, not merely to the dose.

The body's internal defenses engage most chemical invaders in a series of reactions that change the form of the invading molecule into one that is more readily excreted. What we generally call "detoxification reactions" are in reality a complex mix of enzyme-mediated steps. These reactions sometimes *heighten* or even *create* toxic molecules from an initially relatively benign starting chemical as the molecules are passed down enzymatic reaction chains that change the chemical from one form to another. This process, called *biotransformation,* needs elucidation if we are to understand how the body handles toxic substances.

DETOXIFICATION MECHANISMS

To the extent that detoxification reactions both heighten and lessen the toxicity of different molecules, the notion of an effective detoxification system is a misnomer. Many toxic molecules acquire their most harmful characteristics precisely *because* the body attempts to detoxify them. Eventually, however, all but the most chemically intransigent molecules are excreted through two general processes. One set of reactions renders the starting chemical more soluble, and the second links it up to a carrier molecule (a process called *conjugation*) for eventual excretion or elimination.

The chemical processes that detoxify molecules rely on enzymes (precisely folded proteins that can recognize and attach to specific sites on molecules). In the first set of reactions, these enzymes serve as a kind of scaffolding that enhances the body's ability to attach smaller molecules to the target one. Many of these molecules like the OH group make the potentially toxic substance more soluble, thereby facilitating its eventual dissolution in the blood and urine. The common chemical reactions of oxidation, reduction, and hydrolysis (addition of water atoms) occur during this phase.

When the body is exposed to some certain highly reactive toxic substances, these steps may not be taken in time to prevent toxic interactions from occurring. For such molecules, the first contact with an organ system can sometimes be the chemical's last. This appears to be the case for chemicals such as formaldehyde. Formaldehyde binds so avidly with the first molecules it encounters that it is called a direct-acting toxicant. For example, after contacting the mucosal cells that line the nasal passages or the lungs, formaldehyde binds tightly to the cellular proteins and DNA and produces local damage. (This is especially problematic because many "front-line" organs such as the nose and lungs are deficient in detoxifying ability.) In mice and rats, where nose breathing is obligatory, the nasal lining has a much less efficient detoxifying system than does the liver.[1] Humans not only have much less surface area in their noses, but after smelling the irritating vapors can breathe through their mouths. These differences may explain why inhalation of formaldehyde by certain strains of rats leads to the formation of tumors of the nasal passages and pharynx (so-called nasopharyngeal carcinomas) while such tumors remain rare in formaldehyde-exposed humans.

BIOTRANSFORMATION

Some chemicals begin life as relatively nontoxic molecules. For example, carcinogens such as benzo(*a*)pyrene, aflatoxins, and

2-acetylaminofluorene (AAF) begin their lives in the body as relatively innocuous chemicals. Their interaction with the body's defense system leads to a kind of Dr. Jekyll/Mr. Hyde transformation that produces highly toxic intermediates. If the route of exposure is the skin (dermal absorption) or the lungs (inhalation exposure), the chemical is taken up in the general circulation, along the way triggering enzymatic reactions that change the molecule into its active forms.

If it is ingested, the chemical is likely to go first to the liver before entering the general circulation. This allows chemicals that are taken in with food to be efficiently broken down before contacting other tissues. After being swallowed and passing through the stomach, an ingested chemical passes through the walls of the small intestine into the portal circulation that takes it directly to the liver. Here special enzymes in cellular subparticles, called *microsomal* enzymes, begin the conversion process.[2]

What sets these liver enzyme systems apart from other systems in the body is that they can spring into action from a very low level of activity after only transient exposures to certain chemicals. This enhancement or "hyping" of enzymatic activity is known as induction. In the case of toxic molecules, which are readily broken down by induced enzymes, having a ready-made system leap into action is a blessing. But for those molecules whose toxic activity appears only *after* interacting with enzymes, induction of the microsomal enzyme system can be a curse. In this case, a preset high level of microsomal enzyme activity can lead to the appearance of hordes of fully activated toxic molecules springing like Athena from the shoulders of Zeus.

Benzene as a Case Study

This undercutting of the body's effectiveness in detoxifying toxicants is most apparent in the case of benzene. Here, one of these enzyme systems (the P-448 group) works on the benzene molecule to convert it into a more reactive molecule. The critical enzyme adds an oxygen group to the benzene molecule that bridges two carbons, creating an *epoxide* (epoxides are thought to be one of the major chemical forms that most carcinogens assume in carrying out their gene-damaging or protein-binding activities). Epoxides are extremely reactive.

In benzene's case, the epoxide rapidly interacts with other organic molecules or rearranges with freely available water molecules to form phenol or other molecules.[3]

The importance of these conversion steps is that it is these new, intermediate chemicals—and *not* the starting chemical itself—that are thought to carry out the reactions that cause damage in the body. Should the body simultaneously be exposed to drugs (such as certain antimalarials) that further activate the microsomal system, the benzene molecule can be opened up to form muconic acid, a still more potent chromosome-damaging chemical. Conversely, if it is exposed to a molecule like toluene which competes with benzene for reaction sites, fewer toxic benzene intermediates may be formed.

As with virtually all toxic chemicals, what constitutes a "toxic" interaction with a cell is determined by how avidly and tightly the molecule binds with key cellular constituents. With benzene, the tight cellular binding of its metabolites takes place among cells in the bone marrow. There it binds to certain cellular proteins and, most importantly, to the DNA in the cell's nucleus, leading to chromosome breaks and rearrangements and cell death.[4]

As benzene toxicity progresses, it commonly causes vague symptoms of headache, fatigue, and loss of appetite and then more subtle damage of the blood-forming elements in the bone marrow. There, exposure to benzene metabolites can kill cells, leading to cellular loss and to a breakdown in the ability of the marrow to produce normal cells. Weeks or months after initial exposure to relatively high levels of benzene,[5] the loss of white blood cells may become noticeable, resulting in a depressed white blood cell count known as leukopenia. In some persons this depletion progresses to an aplastic anemia, which can be fatal. Another end point of benzene's toxicity is leukemia, most commonly the form known as acute myelogenous leukemia or AML.[6]

Morte la Difference. One of the central observations about benzene toxicity in humans is the extreme variability of responses to similarly exposed people. In one instance, a husband/wife team, who used pure benzene in making Pliofilm plastic and therefore had almost identical exposures, showed entirely different reactions: the wife developed aplastic anemia and died, while the husband had virtually no reaction at all. Stories of this kind underscore the existence of major differences due to sex, physiognomy, genetics, and body makeup in the way toxic substances are handled.

The toxic effects of any given chemical depends on its metabolism in the body — and this metabolism may differ from person to person. Some of the common genetically determined variants of metabolism that affect toxicity are shown in Table 4-1.

Some of these genes, notably the one called AHH (for aryl hydrocarbon hydroxylase), determine the body's response to certain polyaromatic (multiringed) hydrocarbons. And many of these hydrocarbons induce the enzymes that activate them into their carcinogenic form (the so-called proximal carcinogen). Animals or persons who are deficient in this gene-modulated activity are less well equipped to metabolize polycyclic hydrocarbon carcinogens. Depending on the molecule in question, this deficiency may make them paradoxically *less* vulnerable to the carcinogenic effects of these molecules that become more toxic as they are metabolized. That is, a weak enzyme system may produce fewer of the activated molecules that produce cancer.

The likelihood that some workers may be more susceptible to the carcinogenic effects of occupationally encountered carcinogens should clearly be a factor in setting health policy decisions about their exposure to certain chemicals. For instance, the AHH system varies fortyfold among people. Those that have high activities are presumably at much higher risk for developing lung cancer than are those who have lower activities.[7] These predictions appear to hold for strains of mice that have AHH variants — but only at high doses of carcinogens.

The opposite problem exists for workers at risk for bladder cancer. In this instance, a liver enzyme (known as N-acetyl transferase) appears to be linked with the ability to safely metabolize certain substances that can produce cancer in the bladder. So-called slow acetylators — roughly half of any working population — are at higher risk of developing tumors (especially urinary bladder cancer) — following exposure to N-nitrosamine carcinogens than are the faster metabolizers. (Fast acetylators, though, are more prone to develop colon cancer.) This last group is able to clear many offending chemicals from the body more quickly than are slow acetylators.[8] Under conditions where the

Genetic Disorder	Nature of Susceptibility	Chemical Hazards
Acetylation: slow acetylators	Bladder cancer	Nitrosamines
Aldehyde dehydrogenase deficiency	Central nervous system symptoms and flushing	Alcohol
Alpha-1 antitrypsin deficiency	Chronic lung disease	Silica; dusts in air
Aminolevulinic acid dehydratase deficiency	Anemia; nerve damage	Lead
Aryl hydrocarbon hydroxylase inducibility	Acute childhood leukemia	Unknown
Benzo(a)pyrene hydroxylase inducibility	Cigarette-induced bronchogenic carcinoma	Benzo(a)pyrene
Debrisoquine hydroxylase variants	Lung and bladder cancer	Unknown
Glucose-6 phosphate variants	Red blood cell damage	Carbon monoxide
Oxalate metabolism abnormal	Reproductive damage	Ethylene glycol
Oxygenases: high inducibility of P-450 mono-oxygenases	Increased risk of cancer	Benzo(a)pyrene; PAHs (polycyclic aromatic hydrocarbons)
Paraoxanase deficiency	Risk of pesticide poisoning	Malathion; parathion

Table 4-1. Common Genetic Disorders Predisposing Humans to Susceptibility to Toxic Substances

carcinogenic chemical requires activation, the predicted vulnerability of slow acetylators to chemical carcinogenesis can be reversed. In these circumstances, fast acetylators would be at higher risk than slow ones.[9] For key carcinogenic chemicals such as AAF (2-acetylaminofluorene), researchers have found significant variation among persons in these and related liver enzymes, suggesting that in the future it may be desirable to link policy decisions to an understanding of the risk spectrum.[10] Ethical problems abound in any such decision, since possession of certain "high risk" genes does not in itself make a person sick—or diminish that person's intrinsic rights.[11]

Human variability also plays a critical role in determining who gets hurt from molecules with toxic properties other than cancer. In the instance of drug toxicity, a major source of variation in response to standard prescription products is genetic.[12] In the United Kingdom, some 1,717 reports of fatal drug mishaps were reported between 1964 and 1980—and about a hundred times that number occurred in the United States.[13] Many fatal drug reactions are attributable to human differences in drug metabolism or excretion. The debrisoquine hydroxylase system is one such example. To fully appreciate the complexities by which the body interacts with toxic substances, we must focus on the epicenter for detoxification activity, the liver.

THE LIVER AS A MODEL

Your liver weights about 3 pounds and conducts three major activities in addition to its role in detoxifying chemicals taken into the body. It is a synthesizer of several of the key blood proteins (for example, albumin and alpha globulins); it maintains critical balances of key hormones in the body through its metabolic activities; and it scavenges bacteria from the blood stream.

The liver's principal evolutionary role can be visualized as a cellular net for filtering out potentially harmful substances and preparing them for eventual elimination. Human liver cells, known as hepatocytes, are particularly efficient at absorbing and detoxifying certain potentially hazardous molecules.[14] These cells use a rich set of detoxifying enzymes to facilitate the metabolic conversion of toxic chemicals. One path, as we have already seen, leads to binding the toxics with special carrier molecules—in effect keeping them at arm's length from any further interaction with the body's cellular constituents—as it prepares the molecules for excretion. Another leads to solubilization.

For all but those few chemicals that become more dangerous through the process of metabolism, the liver is a literal lifesaver — converting toxic chemicals into alcohols or mild acids or linking the toxic chemicals to a kind of shuttle molecule called glutathione that can be readily excreted. The liver is so effective in performing this last function (called conjugation) that surgeons have devised simple but ingenious means of rescuing persons in comatose states caused by the buildup of toxic residues in the blood. They do so by passing the contaminated blood of the patient over small pieces of liver tissue that then detoxify the harmful constituents.[15] Other researchers have devised hollow fibers to approximate the labyrinth of vessels that course through the liver. By distributing liver enzymes critical to the conjugation of toxins to glutathione on the outside of these permeable tubes and running the toxic substance–containing blood through them, they have successfully shown that it is possible to detoxify chemically contaminated blood.[16]

The liver's detoxification system is likely responsible for the lack of potent carcinogenicity in humans of several naturally occurring molecules as well (see Chapter 10). Aflatoxins, a group of extremely toxic substances produced by molds, can be rendered relatively harmless by interaction with the liver's stores of glutathione. One factor determining aflatoxin toxicity is thus the amount of available glutathione. A well-nourished American is probably considerably better off in this regard than are relatively poorly nourished African populations who have the highest exposures to aflatoxins. The extent to which a given animal or individual is capable of doing such binding generally determines how poisonous or, in this case, carcinogenic a given amount of an aflatoxin will be.

For instance, mice are extremely resistant to the kind of cancer caused by mold aflatoxins (particularly aflatoxin B1) compared to most other species tested. Their livers are much more richly endowed with the enzymes needed to excrete aflatoxin (through binding the activated form of the molecule to glutathione) compared to any other species tested.[17] Of great interest (and discussed at more length in Chapter 10) is the fact that these enzymes can be stimulated by certain dietary factors. A sulfur-containing plant substance called eugenol has been found to enhance the detoxifying enzymes used by the liver and thereby to reduce the likelihood that dietary exposure to aflatoxins and related substances will be carcinogenic.[18] When you consider that the mouse has evolved in close proximity to human habitations and agricultural activities, and is a habitué of grainaries and corn bins from which it almost certainly pilfered aflatoxin-contaminated grains over the last few thousand years, the finding of a rich detoxifying system makes sense.

The Glutathione Story

Of great concern is the observation that short intense exposures to high concentrations of toxic chemicals can dramatically deplete the liver's supply of glutathione. For example, depletion of up to 95 percent of residual glutathione was observed in rats exposed to a short high-level burst of ethylene oxide.[19] Such an exposure mimics those that were once common for nurses in hospital sterilizing operations that used ethylene oxide to decontaminate plastic hospital supplies or surgical equipment. On opening the sterilizer door, nurses were commonly exposed to short high-level concentrations (up to several hundred parts per million) of ethylene oxide vapors.

If these exposures depleted liver reserves of glutathione, and if a nurse were simultaneously exposed to another toxic chemical (such as a chlorinated solvent or more ethylene oxide itself), it is possible that what might otherwise be an innocuous encounter could lead to chromosomal breakage and possibly serious organ damage or cancer. This is because a glutathione-depleted liver is less able to detoxify and excrete certain carcinogenic chemicals than is a liver with its stores of glutathione intact.[20] In fact, studies have shown dramatic evidence of chromosome breakage in sterilizer operators.[21]

Other chemicals deplete the liver of its primary sources of the enzymes needed to detoxify toxic molecules. Certain highly carcinogenic molecules such as AAF can deplete the P-450 enzyme system associated with the covering of the cell nucleus to virtually zero. Antioxidants in the diet, such as butylated hydroxytoluene (BHT), can protect the liver from such depletion.[22] Other dietary additives commonly touted for their protective effects, such as ascorbic acid (vitamin C), not only can deplete glutathione reserves when given at high doses, but tend to induce the enzyme systems that convert precarcinogens into their active forms.[23] Put into practical terms, these observations mean that it is *not* necessarily a good idea to take the massive amounts of vitamin C recommended by some scientists if you want to maximize your ability to combat toxic substances.

A logical extension of this observation is to inquire about other circumstances that might deplete glutathione. Simply taking therapeutic doses of the aspirin-substitute acetaminophen (for example, Tylenol) can make modest inroads on the stores of this key molecule.[24] This is not to imply that you are vulnerable to toxic insults after a few Tylenol tablets. In most persons, new glutathione is readily synthesized within hours after it is depleted. Only in severely ill patients or other compromised persons would such use be contraindicated. A notable exception would be anyone who had been given ether anesthesia, since animal studies suggest that even small doses of ether greatly exacerbate the toxicity of acetaminophen.[25]

Another circumstance in which resistance to toxic injury is potentially impaired is stress, in particular physical injury. Animals subjected to controlled surgical stress (such as tying off an artery to a limb) become glutathione depleted and, more critically, vulnerable to toxic effects from exposures to chemicals at usually nontoxic doses.[26]

A final factor that can determine the effective toxicity of a given exposure is the age of the person exposed. What for a young adult is a nontoxic dose can be a toxic one for an elderly person or for an infant. The glycol ethers, for instance, are more toxic in older animals than in young ones, largely because of the reduced ability of the liver in older animals to detoxify them.[27] The very young infant, or the fetus in utero, is also often at higher risk of damage from chemical insults because of the immaturity of the liver's detoxifying system.[28] (This vulnerability is the subject of Chapter 7.)

Liver Damage

The liver itself is subject to damage and disease. For the purposes of this book, we are concerned most about those disorders that are mediated by chemicals. There are at least 150 drugs in our pharmacopoeia that can produce serious liver damage. Many of them are hepatotoxic at doses that are close to the therapeutic range.[29] Because it is at the epicenter of detoxification reactions in the body, it is tempting to hypothesize that the liver would be among the organs most resistant to the injurious actions of most chemicals. While for many chemicals this is true, for others exactly the opposite holds true.

By virtue of its attempts at detoxification, the liver can convert some chemicals into more toxic intermediates right in the liver itself. In this sense, the liver can be a self-intoxicating organ. A sick liver is also one that is subject to chemical injury. In diseases of the gall bladder where bile secretion is impaired, or in other circumstances in which bilirubin and related chemicals are increased (as occurs in premature infants), researchers have found that the liver may be unusually susceptible to chemical injury.[30]

This toxicity can take three forms: those that lead to the development of a "fatty" liver, a necrotic liver, or liver cancer. A fatty liver, as unappealing as that sobriquet is, is an all too common response to chronic overuse of alcohol. Alcohol, or more particularly its metabolites, interferes with the rate at which certain fatty substances in the blood (triglycerides) break down in the liver. Other chemicals, such as carbon tetrachloride, phosphorus, and orotic acid, also interfere with the synthesis of proteins that are integral to the process by which triglycerides are kept in balance in the blood.[31]

Liver cirrhosis, an end point of alcohol intoxication or poisoning with certain molds, carries a particularly grave prognosis. A healthy liver is necessary for survival—an alcoholic with a cirrhotic liver may live for only four years from the date of the diagnosis.

Hepatic necrosis, a serious, life-threatening condition, is usually rare. In order for necrosis to occur, some kind of metabolic activation and interaction of chemicals with the DNA of the liver cells is necessary.[32] Luckily, most of the cells in the liver are in a "resting" state, neither making DNA nor dividing actively. In practice, this means that for most species—and most people—liver necrosis is rare.

The critical status of the liver means that it is often the last organ to be sacrificed when the body is under stress. Even when the liver is in a person assailed by malnutrition or starvation, the liver itself is largely unscathed.[33] This means that anytime reports appear of cells dying in the liver, something extremely unusual is likely to be happening. Just such an event presented itself when outbreaks of liver necrosis and cancer were reported in a mink colony in Argentina. Investigators studied the possible causes of these two interrelated phenomena for several years. On examination of all of the possible environmental sources of toxic chemicals, they discovered that the minks' food was contaminated with large amounts of dimethylnitrosamine, a potent carcinogen. The minks themselves were genetically handicapped in their liver enzyme repertoire, which impaired their ability to detoxify this toxic amine.[34]

Further review of the minks' diet revealed that the source of the nitrosamine was from nitrites that had been added to their feed as a preservative. Since nitrites are a common preservative for many of our own foods (hot dogs, bologna, and so on), and nitrosamines form readily from them under some acid conditions in the stomach, it behooves us to take this lesson seriously: Avoid nitrite-preserved foods. This is especially important since it is not yet known to what extent our own genetic variability may leave some persons vulnerable to nitrosamine formation.

Metallothionein Protection

A critical area in which the liver affords dramatic protection is in the domain of metal toxicity. Cadmium and lead are some of the so-called "heavy" metals that produce profound neurological toxicity and bone marrow damage at extremely low concentrations. For many years it has been known that prior exposure of animals to zinc greatly reduces this toxicity. The major factor responsible for this protective effect has now been isolated: it is a liver-made protein called metallothionein. Metallothionein increases dramatically after exposure to zinc, and it continues to be produced at high rates for a day or so after the zinc stimulus has waned. The presence of metallothinonein within liver cells serves as a molecular sponge for cadmium atoms or other toxic heavy metals,[35] binding them tightly and allowing the body to excrete them without significant toxic consequences.[36]

Liver Cancer

Liver cancer is a focal point of two of the chapters in this book: those that deal with diet and with estrogens (Chapters

9 and 10). The occurrence of cancer in this otherwise well-protected organ is significant on at least two counts: (1) liver tumors are almost always fatal, and (2), they reflect the failure of adaptation of the liver's detoxifying system.

The general features of liver carcinogenesis are now fairly well understood: the first step entails the rapid activation of a chemical into a proximal carcinogen within the liver itself. The second involves an interaction between these chemical intermediates and the liver cells' genetic material. This leads to many different point mutations and chromosomal breaks and rearrangements. Occasionally, these mutations occur at sites that activate latent "oncogenes" that change the cell's surface and free it from growth inhibitors.

The third and final step is more prolonged than are the other two. Here, other environmental or exogenous factors—indeed, any event that leads to liver damage and regeneration—promote or accelerate the outgrowth of the changed or initiated cells. (Many researchers believe that this is how estrogens accelerate liver cancer.) During this phase, some factor or factors is thought to selectively prod the initiated cells into dividing more quickly.[37]

As we will see in Chapter 10, liver cancer in humans is now thought to be the result of complex interactions among viruses, diet, and chemical agents—some "natural" and some from the synthetic environment. Numerous studies implicate dietary protein as a major component in the carcinogenicity of chemicals. In many instances, *lowering* the diet's protein content appears to *increase* the carcinogenic effect of exposure to chemicals capable of producing liver cancer. (We have already seen that this is true, for instance, for aflatoxins, a point discussed at more length in Chapter 10.)

This enhanced carcinogenic effect of marginal dietary restriction is thought to be due to impairment of the liver's detoxification ability, leaving more unmetabolized intermediates around to bind with DNA or other molecules and start the carcinogenic process. (This phenomenon is analogous to the enhanced carcinogenicity of nitrosoamines seen in minks.) At the extreme, prolonged restriction of caloric intake can reduce the number of tumors in carcinogen-exposed animals. No simple answers appear forthcoming. From recent animal studies it is evident that a complex interplay exists between diet, viruses, and chemicals.

Viral Infection and Detoxification

When I was a graduate student in the late 1960s in the Pathology Department of the University of Pennsylvania, one of the attractions of the site was the close proximity of beautiful farm country in Bucks County. The countryside also held an attraction to some of the other pathology students: it was richly populated by woodchucks. A surprising number of fellow students, in fact, chose to study woodchucks for their thesis topics. At the time, I thought they were going pretty far afield for a relevant thesis or research topic. I could not have been more wrong.

Woodchucks are one of the few, if not only, animals that are sometimes naturally infected with a liver virus analogous to human hepatitis viruses. Careful study of these rodents has not only helped elucidate the origins of chronic hepatitis infectious states but has begun to clarify the interaction of these viruses with the liver. In 1987, researchers found that virally infected woodchucks were more likely to metabolize potential carcinogens into their active final form than were uninfected controls.[38] Put in simple terms, these data showed for the first time that viral infections could change the way the body interacts with toxic substances. (As we will see in Chapter 10, these data also suggest that Africans for whom chronic hepatitis B virus infection is a common reality may be much more vulnerable to chemicals that can cause cancer than are uninfected persons.)

Such complex reactions among different factors in the environment make it clear that simple "risk assessments" based on examining the actions of single chemicals fall far short of predicting whose detoxification system will and whose will not deal adequately with a given toxic substance. None of us are evolutionarily prepared to meet the entire chemical universe. Some of us are better equipped than others. And a significant number of the world's citizens are severely handicapped by the presence of other factors in their environment that compromise their ability to deal effectively with such chemicals.

One of the most common misconceptions about the impact of toxic substances is that we are only vulnerable to an effect from exposure to hazardous chemicals after they have reached some critical threshold. This maxim may be generally valid for simple molecules such as salt or sugar, but, as we have seen for almost all carcinogens, lowering the dose of a given chemical does not eliminate the possibility of adverse consequences. And, as we will see in the next chapter, some toxic substances continue to have effects for a considerable time after initial exposure, long after all traces of the original molecule have left the body.

CHAPTER FIVE

Myth 3:

Toxic effects not seen immediately will not occur

THE IDEA THAT TOXIC SUBSTANCES CAN ONLY DAMAGE THE BODY while they are present is an adage that can still be found in modern toxicological thinking. While it is understandable why so many scientists believe that toxic effects occur only in the period immediately after exposure and pass with the excretion of the offending molecule, it is now clear that many substances leave their mark on the body's tissues for weeks, months, or even years after they have been metabolized and excreted.

Few if any epidemiological studies have followed human populations for the thirty or more years commonly needed to observe fully the effects of exposure to carcinogens. (Recall that skin tumors in Nagasaki occurred some forty years after radiation exposure.) In part, these oversights can be explained by the lack of patience and sheer perseverance needed to follow people or experimental animals for long periods. On a larger scale, the failure to detect hidden, long-term effects stemming from chemical or radiation exposures reflects a cultural bias that seeks short-term answers to complex problems. This tendency has had particularly severe consequences in the area of public health regulation where governmental agencies have ignored the latent effects generated by toxic substances.

THE DELAYED EFFECTS OF TOXIC SUBSTANCES

Federally mandated toxicity testing has hinged on the original belief that toxic effects would be observed early on if at all. This viewpoint has meant that regulatory bodies for a long while overlooked whole categories of delayed tissue damage. A case in point is the recommended screening for nerve tissue toxicity. Testing measures have consistently failed to identify a potential for delayed neurotoxic effects because they focused on observations linked to acute exposures.[1] (More about this below.)

Some toxic chemicals *only* exhibit delayed effects as well. For instance, cattle that eat *Senecio* plants (for example, tansy, ragwort, or threadleaf groundsel) that contain pyrrolizidine as a toxic contaminant may be well for several weeks after ingesting the plants, only to succumb months later to a form of alkaloidosis.[2] This condition, which affects humans who eat such plants as well, is characterized by a delayed form of chronic pulmonary hypertension that leads to enlargement of the right side of the heart and, in severely affected individuals, eventual heart failure.[3] Similar delayed effects have been observed in people who ingest poisonous mushrooms. The initial symptoms after ingestion of members of the *Amanita* genus (in particular, *Amanita verna,* the destroying angel, and *Amanita phalloides,* the death cap mushroom) are nausea, vomiting, cramps, and diarrhea, which usually lead to a fever and to fluid imbalances. Thereafter, the symptoms may appear to abate, until liver necrosis occurs four to five days later. Death is usually the result of liver failure coupled with deterioration of the heart muscle.

The most significant effects of exposure to many industrial and environmental chemicals may also be delayed. This important fact is underscored by the observation that many of the most protracted effects, particularly those that affect the nervous system, are irreversible.

79

DELAYED NEUROTOXICITY:
OUT OF SIGHT, OUT OF MIND?

Delayed effects on central nervous system functions following chemical exposures can be grouped into two general kinds:
those that are related to a hydrocarbon solvent exposure and
those that are linked to exposure to organophosphorous esters.

Solvent-Related Neurotoxicity as a Case Study

The managers of a steel plant decided to reactivate a 30,000-
gallon closed container that had been used to store waste oils.
The tank had not been in use for ten years prior to this decision—and it had been vented to the open air for at least two
weeks before a team of three workers was sent in to clean it
out. A welder and two helpers entered the tank without it being tested for residual gases or fumes (this was considered unnecessary given the duration of down time and venting). After
working for less than ten minutes at removing some gooey
sludge at the bottom of the tank and welding a flange to the
tank's side, the welder became confused and sought help. He
was taken to a first aid station at the plant premises. The other
two workers continued to work. Soon they, too, became dis-
oriented and confused. All three were taken to a local emergency room, and one worker was hospitalized.

Three months later, the workers were seen at the Occupational Medicine Clinic in Pittsburgh. All three showed damage
to their vestibular systems (associated with balance), and all
had varying degrees of impairment of their ability to think.[4]
The authors of this report remarked on the duration of the
disabilities—the workers were *still* impaired a year and a half
after this transient incident. A year after the exposures, two
of the workers would still consistently omit or distort information about details in images they had just seen, suggesting
that the men could still not process visual information rapidly.
One worker was found to be clinically depressed, and all three
had experienced loss of self-esteem, insomnia, and depression.
The research team concluded that the workers had experienced
"a mild central cognitive damage of a pattern well described after
exposures to organic solvents" and that "the disease persisted

much longer than would be generally expected from a short-term exposure."

Among the candidate neurotoxins that could produce such long-term effects are tetrachloroethylene, trichloroethane, and certain short-chain aliphatic hydrocarbons. The key ethical question is whether the "surprising" finding made by the authors in the above study (dated 1989) should have been so surprising. In fact, first in 1955 and again in 1961, studies appeared that clearly documented the ability of such chlorinated solvents to produce profound neurological effects at commonly encountered occupational exposures.

The 1955 study, by Swiss researcher E. Grandjean, showed that workers who were exposed to levels of trichloroethylene considerably below the current occupational permissible level (set at 200 ppm) experienced neurological impairment. At levels as low as 10 ppm or, more commonly, at 40 to 80 ppm in the air, trichloroethylene exposure led to loss of memory, slowing of intellectual processes, sleep disorders, disorientation, and emotional instability.[5]

As a result of these observations, Grandjean recommended that exposures to trichloroethylene be kept below 40 ppm. Grandjean's observation that long-term neurological impairments can result after exposure to chlorinated solvents was only belatedly recognized by U.S. regulatory bodies. By 1985, it was evident that an acute, high-level exposure to trichloroethylene could produce permanent damage.[6] However, while the standard was lowered in 1963 to 100 ppm (from 200 ppm), no reduction even approaching Grandjean's recommended level occurred until January 1989, when the National Institute of Occupational Safety and Health recommended that the level be set at 50 ppm.

Long-term neurologic and systemic effects of other chlorinated solvents were also known to industry. In 1961, researchers at the Dow Chemical Company in Midland, Michigan, reported that exposure to a short burst of a high concentration of vapors from a solvent mixture could produce protracted effects.[7] The Dow report cited the case of a 21-year-old man who had lost consciousness while cleaning steps with a mixture of tetrachloroethylene and a solvent mixture known as Stoddard solvent. Although the man was brought around in a hospital, his apparent complete and uneventful recovery was short-lived. Nine days after his exposure, his liver function became abnormal. Sixteen days after exposure, he suddenly began to exhale tetrachloroethylene again.

The authors conclude that the patient's clinical course and the studies they performed underscore two points: first, that an apparently short-lived ("acute") exposure to tetrachloroethylene could be a chronic one from the body's point of view because of the compound's slow excretion rate. Second, liver function can become abnormal and remain so beginning two to three weeks after a high-level exposure. The significance of these findings turns on the observation that it is possible to have a protracted insult (measured in weeks) from only a few minutes of exposure.

In spite of these provocative studies on widely used industrial solvents, research into the delayed and long-term effects of chemical exposures tended to concentrate on a group of six-carbon solvents: hexane, methyl n-butyl ketone, and hexane-2,5-dione (the chemical to which the first two agents are metabolized), or on carbon disulfide and triorthocresyl phosphate (TOCP). First in Japan and Italy, and later in the United States, researchers found that workers who used solvents to glue shoe soles or clean printed fabrics experienced a chronic and often irreversible form of nerve damage. Japanese studies of sandal makers exposed to hexane in glues showed that protracted exposure to this solvent led to chronic damage to the motor and sensory nerves of the legs and arms — a so-called polyneuropathy — and severe muscle weakness.[8] Some of the affected workers experienced loss of appetite, blurred vision, cold sensations in their limbs, fatigue, headache, and weight loss. The neurological symptoms lasted for years.

Solvent overexposures were probably more common during the 1960s and 1970s than the meager reports in the literature suggest. For example, consider a typical operation that used solvents to clean brocade sashes. A petroleum solvent was used in a small, poorly ventilated workroom. Workers would place a dirty sash on a table and scrub it with a brush dipped in the solvent. They commonly performed this repetitive task for up to twelve hours a day. A 16-year-old boy who had worked there for five months began to lose his appetite and muscular strength.[9] Two months later he had to quit the job because he had great difficulty walking. He entered a hospital two months later, showing muscle atrophy in his forearms and beneath the mid-thighs. His reflexes in the lower limbs were diminished or absent. Such symptoms are classic signs of a form of delayed neurotoxicity called polyneuropathy.

Other research has linked a tendency to develop focal epilepsy to exposure to organic solvents.[10] But until such studies demonstrated a direct toxic effect of some solvents on the brain, no one gave much credence to the likelihood that some individuals could experience profound neurological effects that would persist years after all of the solvents had been metabolized and excreted from the body. Until the 1980s, very few studies (Scandinavia is an exception) focused on the early signs of chronic neurological dysfunction that might have alerted regulatory agencies to the delayed consequences of exposure to solvents.[11] These early signs include decreased hearing acuity, memory disturbances, altered color perception, impaired verbal ability, and defective psychomotor function.

I recently had an opportunity to review the case histories of ten workers who had an average of seven years of exposure to chlorinated solvents while working at a telephone assembly plant in Albuquerque, New Mexico. After being evaluated by a team of neuropsychiatrists and psychologists, nine of the ten were found to have pronounced difficulties in remembering facts and organizing their lives around daily activities. All nine (whose average age was less than 45) had a form of presenile dementia that would normally not be seen except in Alzheimer's disease patients. For example, one worker could not remember when she had gotten married, even though it was only a year and a half before her interview. Another worker's daughter had to post on the refrigerator what her mother was supposed to fix for her meals—three times a day. These seemingly trivial deficits in memory (of course, most of us forget at times what we went to the market to buy) proved to be the tip of an iceberg of pervasive central nervous system damage of a much larger cohort. When the psychiatric team examined 159 of the workers and 117 controls, evidence of profound neurological damage was uncovered in virtually all of those who had worked at the plant for five years or longer.[12]

All of the affected individuals experienced some form of dementia, clinical depression, insomnia, or had evidence of profound central nervous system damage. On careful, controlled testing, the workers were found to have lost varying degrees of their ability to concentrate, to organize their visual space, to remember things that had recently occurred (short-term memory loss), and to coordinate their hand and finger movements when compared to the control group. The team concluded that they were witnessing a long-term and possibly permanent consequence of the workers' daily exposure to a constellation of solvent chemicals.[13] Tragically, the impairments in the exposed women had persisted for up to fifteen years since the cessation of their employment, and the researchers concluded that there was little likelihood of full recovery for most of them.

Most scientists would recognize these symptoms as the hallmark signs of a syndrome of toxic encephalopathy, an almost always irreversible neurobehavioral constellation of problems caused by excessive exposure to certain organic solvents. This syndrome is variously named psycho-organic syndrome, chronic encephalopathy, presenile dementia, organic brain syndrome, painters' syndrome, or neurasthenic syndrome.[14] Its earliest manifestations are tiredness, irritability, depression, and episodes of anxiety. (When workers at the telephone assembly plant complained of these symptoms, they were told to stop malingering, that these were merely "female problems.")

In spite of the seriousness of this syndrome, there remains much controversy surrounding its appropriate definition and occurrence — contributing to the delays in lowering permissible exposures to the putative causative agents. As one review team commented, "Although it is clear that toxic encephalopathy may occur in individuals heavily exposed to some solvents over a period of months to years, the exact exposure levels that lead to irreversible neuro-behavioural changes remain to be determined."[15]

Organophosphorus-Related Neurotoxicity

The second form of delayed neurotoxicity is caused by exposure to a group of phosphorus-containing chemicals. The most unusual episode involving neurotoxicity from ingesting one of the chemicals in this group occurred during Prohibition in the United States. In 1930, literally thousands of unsuspecting people took a popular remedy called Ginger Jake, believing it could cure menstrual disorders, prevent respiratory infections, and aid digestion. The fact that it contained appreciable amounts of alcohol as well as ginger flavoring undoubtedly contributed to its appeal. (Bootleggers diluted the required amount of ginger with castor oil or molasses to make a potable drink.) Unfortunately, in 1930, one bootlegger used a furniture finisher called Lyndol when castor oil became too expensive and unknowingly contaminated several batches of this ersatz drink with TOCP. Those who consumed this adulterated version of Ginger Jake developed varying degrees of polyneuritis and paralysis. Typically, an inebriant would recuperate, only to experience calf pains one to three weeks after ingestion and have the pains progress to weakness and paralysis days or weeks later. Estimates of the number of people affected in the Southeastern part of the United States range as high as 100,000, with 4,837 cases being documented.[16] The TOCP-adulterated elixir caused such a characteristic and widespread disturbance in natural gait and coordination in the South as to stimulate the production of twelve commercial recordings such as "The Jake Walk Blues" and "The Jake Leg Blues."[17] Many of the victims of this tragedy still exhibit paralysis almost fifty years later.[18]

Triorothocresyl phosphate (TOCP) serves as a prototype chemical for others that produce delayed neurotoxicity. As early as 1899, tuberculosis patients who were treated with a related compound called phosphocreosote developed delayed neuropathies.[19] When hens (but, strangely, not other animals) are exposed to TOCP, they develop the same ataxia and lack of coordination as did the ginger inebriants during Prohibition. This led to the use of chickens as test hosts for screening pesticides for delayed effects.[20]

Tragically, the attention focused on TOCP during the past forty years has not protected other populations around the world from being poisoned by cooking oils adulterated by this insidious, and highly poisonous, chemical. In the late 1970s in Sri Lanka and twenty years earlier in Morocco, thousands of families were poisoned by TOCP-contaminated cooking oils.[21]

Other highly toxic organophosphorus compounds have been developed since World War II. Because of their ability to interact with biological molecules and inhibit their function, organophosphorus esters have been extensively tested as biological poisons. Since the late 1940s, more than 500,000 different organophosphate chemicals have been screened for possible effectiveness in killing insects, worms, fungi, and weeds.[22] Of this vast array of potential agents, some 200 have found their way into commercial use.[23]

Approximately eighty organophosphate (OP) pesticides are currently registered by the U.S. Office of Pesticides of the Environmental Protection Agency. All share the common ability to inhibit the enzyme acetylcholinesterase, a key molecule needed to permit the regeneration of acetylcholine at neuromuscular junctions and thereby control nerve to muscle transmission. People who are poisoned by OP pesticides commonly have low blood levels of acetylcholinesterase, and exhibit signs of chronic stimulation of certain muscle groups such as tearing, salivation, stomach and intestinal cramps, vomiting, diarrhea, and pinpoint pupils.

It is this remarkably specific activity that gives the oganophosphorus esters their potent acute toxicity. That is, the direct neurotoxicity of these compounds which makes them such effective insecticides, is the same property that makes them effective nerve gases that can kill soldiers after exposure to only a few drops. In fact, when this group of chemicals was first discovered by Gerhard Schrader at the IG Farbenenindustrie plant in Germany in 1928, he turned the invention over to the military, which went on to make sarin and tabun — still among the most poisonous nerve gases known.

Many organophosphorus compounds also have the ability to damage nerves directly. Unlike the inhibitory effects on acetylcholinesterase, these effects are largely irreversible — and delayed. Typically, after exposure to an organophosphorus ester pesticide, six to twenty-one days may elapse before any observable signs show up of motor nerve damage. In 1953, the first reported episode of poisoning involved two British chemists who were working with an experimental insecticide called Mipafox. Two to three weeks after appearing to recover from an acute poisoning, both men developed weakness and a lack of coordination in their lower limbs. One recovered while the other developed complete paralysis and muscular wasting of his legs.[24] (A so-called intermediate syndrome has been recently described in which workers who have been heavily exposed to organophosphorus pesticides develop less severe manifestations of poisoning one to four days later.)[25]

Other studies have shown that the central nervous system can also be affected by organophosphorus compounds. Many of the most important nerve tracts in the brain stem and spinal cord undergo degeneration in experimental animals exposed to one of these compounds (triothotolyl phosphate),[26] suggesting that human poisoning with the related compound triothocresyl phosphate (TOCP) may have much more profound and irreversible damaging effects than was previously appreciated.

Organophosphorus pesticides also undergo chemical changes as they age on the shelf (or in the environment), which makes them more poisonous. One reaction that occurs spontaneously is a change that creates a dangerous chemical called thioalkyl phosphoryl that has insidious toxicity for mammals. As a contaminant, it can produce dramatic short-term and long-term toxicity beyond the expected range of toxic effects of its parent molecule. Even though widely known to the scientific community, these common contaminants have only recently been studied,[27] while their less toxic progenitors can still be registered.

In spite of the common knowledge that delayed effects are among the expected consequences of exposure to organophosphorus compounds, the safety testing of possible delayed neurotoxic effects from exposure to the organophosphorus pesticides has a dismal track record. In 1976 and twice during 1983, the National Institute for Occupational Safety and Health (NIOSH) was called in to assess the possibility that workers had experienced a delayed effect from exposure to three organophosphorus pesticides: leptophos, fenthion, and isofenphos. Inexplicably, the human neurotoxicity observed in the workers exposed to either of the first two pesticides was the *first indication* that these chemicals could cause delayed neurotoxicity. Leptophos was manufactured in Texas from 1971 to 1976. Health problems were evident in workers beginning in 1974. By 1975, a medical consultant to the company identified twelve workers with serious neurological problems. Four were mistakenly diagnosed as having multiple sclerosis; two with psychiatric disorders; and three others with inflammatory processes. In 1976, when NIOSH investigated the plant, it concluded that all the workers had delayed neurotoxicity. But, despite frank evidence of organophosphate poisoning, the investigators failed to alert the scientific community to the delayed dangers of leptophos, claiming that they could not distinguish the observed effects from those produced by a non-organophosphate, h-hexane.[28]

In 1981, a researcher who reviewed the toxicological summaries of 248 organophosphorus esters in commerce concluded that as many as 113 of them showed evidence of delayed neurotoxicity.[29] But as Yale University researcher Martin Cherniack has pointed out, we currently lack a standardized reference test for neurotoxicity and a consistent protocol for testing suspect substances.[30] Chemicals with dramatic and clear-cut evidence of neurotoxicity (including human exposure events) are still marketed and promoted widely, particularly in the Third World. An archetypal example is leptophos, the pesticide responsible for the Texas worker injuries. After the NIOSH study of human exposure was under way, the manufacturer withdrew its U.S. registration application as if sensing that the writing was already on the wall. But it continued to sell leptophos abroad. According to Cherniack, more than 17 million pounds of leptophos were marketed in more than fifty foreign countries between 1971 and 1976, *despite* further neurotoxicity findings in the United States. This has caused numerous episodes of human and animal intoxication, including one disaster in which about 1,300 water buffalo were poisoned and died of a paralytic disorder in Egypt in 1971.

It is apparent from these findings that delayed toxicity safety thresholds for organophosphorus ester–based pesticides generally are poorly used in protecting both workers and the public at large. Hopefully, some new proposed approaches for assessing nervous system toxicity will reduce the likelihood of further worker tragedies like those in Texas.[31]

Delayed Neurotoxicity: The Case of William O.

When I directed the Hazard Alert System (later to become the Hazard Evaluation System), I asked my scientific team to evaluate the herbicide 2,4-dichlorophenoxyacetic acid and its salts (2,4-D) for possible neurological and other previously unrecognized toxic effects. My team, headed by Jon Rosenberg, M.D., a pharmacology-trained physician, concluded, on the basis of human exposure data from persons who had absorbed or ingested large quantities of this chemical, that 2,4-D could produce a form of delayed neurotoxicity—polyneuropathy. The head of our advisory group, M. Donald Whorton, M.D., discouraged our release of this report, asserting that the likelihood of workers experiencing the kind of neurological damage we predicted was extremely remote.

Just a few weeks later, we learned of a crew of forest workers in Oregon that had been using an herbicide formulation (Tordon) which contained 2,4-D. Because of a recent ban on aerial application, they were using hand sprayers. William O., one of the workers, had become drenched with the spray—and had accidentally sprayed himself in the face, drinking a few milliliters of the spray formulation. Some three weeks later, this worker began to lose muscular strength in his upper body, and he subsequently developed the unsteady gait that is the signature of delayed neurotoxicity. The physician for the Department of Food and Agriculture who reviewed his case, Peter Kurtz, M.D., diagnosed it (without seeing the patient) as a form of Guillain Barré syndrome—and exonerated the herbicide. Our team, along with a neurologist, evaluated the worker a month after his reported illness started, and found 2,4-D still being excreted in his urine. To us the case was straightforward: the worker had experienced a form of delayed neurotoxicity.

Again our advisory group declined to allow us to publish a Hazard Alert, claiming that the results were inconclusive. I released the Alert to a reporter from the *Los Angeles Times* who had called to question us about the case. I was asked to retract it by members of the advisory committee. Later, I learned that Dr. Whorton's private company, Environmental Health Associates and the Stanford Research Institute (SRI International) had been under contract by the National Forest Products Association to write reports on the safety of phenoxy herbicides, especially 2,4-D and its congener, 2,4,5-T. The Environmental Health Associates report—coauthored by Whorton—concluded that "data from valid scientific inquiries appear to support the safety of continued use of this herbicide when used as directed."[32] While technically true, this conclusion perpetuated the deception that the chemical *itself* was safe. Since no one can ensure that workers and consumers will always handle 2,4-D "safely," hiding this side effect prevents the medical profession from dealing effectively with poisonings.

The case of William O. and the delayed neurotoxicity reports identified above point to an unresolved dilemma in toxicity testing. While we know a great deal about the short-term effects of chemicals, we have somehow failed to take into account long-term effects of short-lived exposures. What we need now is to recognize that many toxic substances have delayed effects and to identify suitable assays to quantitate and identify them. Most importantly, we need to pinpoint the high-risk chemicals with such effects and design safe methods for their use or, better yet, find alternatives that lack this "time bomb" effect.

TUMOR LATENCY

The most dramatic and least well understood delayed phenomenon occurs in the induction of cancer. Chemical or radiation exposures occurring years before may set in motion reactions that lead to overt malignancy, without any forewarning. Understanding how this might happen calls for a review of the phenomenon of tumor latency.

Findings presented in a recent issue of the *New England Journal of Medicine* graphically illustrate the delayed consequences of even low-level exposure to potential carcinogens.[33] In the first half of this century, medical dogma held that, in some infants, a bulging gland called the thymus just under the rib cage represented a pathologic manifestation that could portend death. Called status thymicolymphaticus, this *perfectly normal anatomical situation* was treated aggressively as a pathological condition. Without understanding the function of what we now recognize as a central gland in the body's immunologic defense system, some surgeons removed the thymus entirely while other physicians used X rays to shrink its "abnormally" increased size.

A look at the surviving population some thirty to thirty-six years later showed that by the age of 36, the irradiated women had almost four times the rate of breast cancer as did age-matched controls. (Male infants were not studied.) As with the tumors that appeared many years after the atomic bombing of Hiroshima and Nagasaki, the breast tumors began to appear only twenty-five years or more *after* the radiation took place. In the instance of the status thymicolymphaticus infants who were irradiated in infancy (usually before the age of 6 months), the first tumor appeared twenty-eight years after exposure.

These findings underscore the recent realization that the thyroid, lungs, bone marrow, and mammary glands are among the tissues with the highest susceptibility to radiation carcinogenesis.[34] And if tumors in these tissues have such long latencies, it is likely that there will be still more excess cancers at these tissue sites among the A-bomb survivors from Nagasaki and Hiroshima.

Two complementary explanations are possible for the delayed effect seen in radiation-induced breast cancer: one, favored by the authors of the *New England Journal* article, holds that the radiation initiated clones of premalignant cells in greater numbers in the exposed girls than would occur normally. These cells lie fallow until they are flushed out by the surge of estrogen that accompanies puberty and later sexual maturation. The second explanation points to the central role of the thymus in mediating immune functions and suggests that direct destruction of this gland dampened the normal function of portions of the immune system that recognize and destroy incipient tumor cells—called the immune surveillance system. In this latter model, the hypothesized immune depression that would accompany radiation of the thymus would be tantamount to the lowering of a dam, permitting the early arrival of a flood of tumor cells that would otherwise have been held in abeyance by active immune surveillance cells.

The absence of such an early surge of tumors—recall that it was twenty-eight years after irradiation before the first tumor appeared—does not necessarily invalidate this idea. My own work has shown that immune surveillance may only operate during the period when incipient tumor cells are rapidly dividing in their early, premalignant stages.[35] Once malignancy has supervened, little or no effective spontaneous surveillance appears to occur. In the case of the breast tumors developing after irradiation, it is plausible that surveillance operated more effectively in the nonirradiated women after puberty than it did in the irradiated ones.

In my own view, it is likely that both factors came into play in these unfortunate victims of medical ignorance. The iatrogenic tumors that resulted were directly caused by the radiation—and they were facilitated by secondary effects on the immunosurveillance system. (A similar effect of immune suppression in facilitating the occurrence of virally induced tumors has been seen in experimental animals.)[36]

This view ignores many other potentially salient factors that affect the latency of breast tumor in susceptible hosts—including diet, pregnancy, the age of bearing a first child, and lactation. (Even the mother's diet during pregnancy can affect when and if malignant tumors appear in animals.[37]) Still less well appreciated factors can also come into play. One of the least well understood factors is the regulation of the circadian or daily rhythms of hormone levels. If, for example, the cyclical rise and fall of hormones such as melatonin is interrupted by removing the pineal gland and artificially replacing this chemical, the latency of chemically induced breast tumors in animals is greatly increased.[38] Conversely, one could argue, irradiation of the thymus could stimulate the pineal (distantly located in the radiation field) and produce more melatonin.

Other hormones can profoundly influence the latency of tumors. Levels of circulating estrogens can dramatically influence the occurrence of tumors in the liver. Liver tumors can also be influenced by the thyroid gland, a central endocrine organ that regulates metabolic activity in the body. In hypothyroid rats (those with underactive thyroid glands), the ability of aflatoxin to produce liver tumors is much delayed. Tumor incidences were lower and the time before tumors appeared was significantly longer in hypothyroid as compared to euthyroid (normal glandular activity) controls.[39]

The existence of often protracted latencies in tumor development can also delay awareness of workplace carcinogenesis. Vinyl chloride monomer (the key ingredient in polyvinyl chloride plastics) is a classic example of an agent whose carcinogenicity was signaled by a long-latency tumor (angiosarcoma of the liver). By 1977, NIOSH had identified sixty-four cases of angiosarcoma among vinyl chloride polymerization workers. The average latency from first exposure to tumor appearance was twenty-one years. Most of these workers had heavy exposure to vinyl chloride monomer.[40] But even this seemingly dramatic effect has been disputed by industry since fewer tumors than predicted from animal carcinogenicity tests were seen initially among workplace populations. The missing link is tumor latency: highly exposed workers have shorter latencies; those with lower exposures may simply not have had time to develop cancer. This likelihood now appears true.

Only recently has the full extent of tumorigenesis in such workers come to light. Among 5,498 British men who worked at least one year between 1940 and 1984 in the vinyl chloride industry, fully seven died because of angiosarcoma, and an additional four died from another form of primary liver cancer. The average latency was twenty-five years.[41] Since the expected liver tumor mortality rates among males is in the order of 5 and 12 per 100,000,[42] these findings suggest that the relative risk of dying from liver cancer among British vinyl chloride workers was approximately twenty times higher than expected.

Protracted tumor latencies can also obscure the compound effects of exposure to multiple factors that can increase cancer risk. Fire fighters are a prime example. Many industrial hygienists have long expected fire fighters to have high cancer rates since many of the chemicals that are released during a fire are highly carcinogenic. But until retired fire fighters were examined, a high occurrence of certain tumors (bladder, colon, and brain) as causes of death among this population had gone unrecognized.[43]

A similar pattern emerged in studies of granite workers. A high lung cancer mortality independent of smoking was observed, but only among workers who had been exposed to granitic dusts some fifteen to thirty-five years before the cancer appeared.[44]

CANCER LATENCY: WAITING
FOR THE OTHER SHOE TO FALL

It is now axiomatic among those who study carcinogenesis that the dose of a given carcinogenic stimulus determines not only the amount of tumors but the time of their occurrence.[45] As dosages fall, tumors tend to take longer and longer to appear. The converse is also true. With high doses of a carcinogen, the latency (or "time to tumor") is often compressed. This systematic relationship, where dose is inversely related to latency, can be seen in the data from virtually all of the standard cancer bioassays conducted by the National Toxicology Program.

This simplified picture of latency and its relation to chemical carcinogenesis can lead to overgeneralizations regarding hypothesized cause-and-effect relationships. For instance, in the case of the benzene-exposed worker discussed in Chapter 3, the time between when he started work and his diagnoses of leukemia was only four years, while typical latencies for benzene-associated leukemias are commonly ten years or longer. (In the largest study of this kind, conducted among some 28,460 benzene-exposed workers in China, the average tumor latency was 11.4 years.[46])

In the case of the U.S. worker, such a short latency would ordinarily suggest a very high exposure to benzene. But among the chemicals to which he was exposed were agents with "promoting" or tumor-accelerating properties that could have shortened his tumor latency. (Recall that his work entailed heavy exposure to a broad constellation of chemicals in petroleum naptha, some of which have been associated with promoting tumors in experimental animals.) Drugs can also interact with benzene to enhance its leukemogenicity. One such agent, an antimalarial drug called praziquantel, dramatically increases benzene's chromosome-breaking activity. It apparently does so by shifting the preponderance of the metabolic by-products of benzene toward muconic acid and aldehyde, two of the more potent chromosome-breaking agents.[47] Such an effect could also explain the results. Ironically, the final resolution of what caused his cancer will be made in a courtroom rather than in the halls of academe.

What is clear is that many factors can interact to shorten tumor latency. We have some understanding of the effects of hormones and immunologic strength. But there is much we do not understand. For instance, at each of three identical dose levels, carcinogen-treated mice housed in polycarbonate cages develop skin tumors much earlier than do their genetically identical littermates housed in conventional stainless steel cages.[48] Since polycarbonate itself is presumed to be virtually chemically inert, such factors as lighting, heat retention, or even air circulation may have come into play in creating the conditions that led to the acceleration of tumor growth.

Experimental studies in which mice were subjected to low environmental temperatures (albeit lower than might be encountered in heat-conducting stainless steel cages) show that cold environments tend to increase tumor latency.[49] Data of this kind suggest that subtle environmental factors can influence the genesis of tumors to a much stronger degree than we previously believed.

These findings demonstrate that toxic effects may not only appear after a period of quiescence, but that many chemicals can exert heightened toxic effects by their interactions. It is incumbent on any agency looking at the long-term implications of the broad-scale environmental changes we have set in motion to consider the latent properties of exposures, particularly the cataracts and skin tumors that may occur long after exposure to ultraviolet radiation,[50] as well as the possibility of interactive effects.

All of these effects cannot be predicted on the basis of classic toxicological principles that rely on simple dose–response relationships. This is true in part because of *synergistic* effects of some chemicals taken in combination (for example, the concurrent exposure to sulfur oxide and particulates in the air is more noxious than would be predicted by a simple additive effect of their toxicities). It is also possible that many substances that are considered to act adversely on the organism only after they have reached a certain threshold may actually have effects below threshold levels. It is these effects which may remain hidden for months or years. Still other chemicals may appear to acquire new properties as their effective dose is diminished. It is of obvious importance to know these consequences if the full gamut of toxic consequences following environmental exposure are to be anticipated.

CHAPTER SIX

Myth 4:

All effects of toxics disappear as doses diminish

ONE OF THE WAYS WE GET INTO TROUBLE IS WHEN WE FAIL TO factor into our policies the full range of toxicity and biological activity of the chemicals we introduce into our bodies and into the ecosystem. Understanding the breadth and depth of toxic reactions requires going beyond the simple maxims of popularized toxicology. As noted already, the central dogma of toxicology that the "dose makes the poison" can be seriously misleading.

The dose-dependency dictum implies a diminishing gradient of toxicity and effects as one moves from high to ultralow doses of a given chemical. One of the least well understood aspects of this relationship is the "slope" of this gradient. Just where do toxic properties leave off and benign responses begin? Is it possible that new properties of toxic chemicals emerge as doses are reduced? Can high doses of certain chemicals trigger defensive reactions while low ones "slip through" to escape detection? Epidemiologists and researchers are uncovering more and more circumstances in which animals and people manifest symptoms at doses below those that had previously been thought necessary to produce toxic effects.[1] Even more un-settling, some substances seem to acquire different properties at low doses than they had at high ones. Some of these new properties include the ability of low doses of contaminants of organophosphorous pesticides to *stimulate* parts of the immune system that high doses suppress.[2] Selenium, normally a cancer protective element, can *enhance* carcinogenesis when the dose is changed.[3] And chromate, a caustic salt at high doses, ac-quires allergic properties when diluted to infinitesimally low concentrations.[4]

These provocative, but still ungeneralized observations, sug-gest the need for research to understand the mechanisms by which certain substances produce unforeseen toxic effects. Such studies would prove invaluable to assess the risks to the pub-lic of contaminated groundwater or air. Such episodes of air and/or water contamination have involved benzene, chlorinated solvents, and heavy metals in the parts per billion range.[5] These levels are substantially below those that cause documentable problems in the workplace, but many persons exposed to low-level contaminants nonetheless report adverse effects.[6] As a result, scientists are eager to resolve this question of toxicity at low doses. Obviously, the exposed people would like this question to be resolved as well. Unfortunately, the forum in which the early debates have taken place has been the court-room, where it is extremely difficult to discern the kernels of truth behind often extreme claims from both sides.

LOW-DOSE CANCER

A central issue in many disputes involving low-level water con-tamination is whether or not exposed citizens face any increased risk of cancer. For this eventuality to be possible, there must be some mechanism by which small numbers of molecules of a putative carcinogen can interact with cells and leave a legacy of cancerous changes. One such possibility is for a potent toxic molecule to interact with a cell's DNA to produce long-lasting, heritable damage. And one form of such damage would be the capacity of affected cells to escape normal regulatory controls. Should these affected cells be perpetuated as the affected cell population grows, the stage may be set for the appearance of cancer. In theory, a cancerous cell population can be produced by even a single encounter with an active chemical.

Most (but not all) experimental observations of highly carcinogenic toxic chemicals such as 2-acetylaminofluorene (AAF) or ionizing radiation suggest that these agents continue to have biological effects down to very, very low doses. The possibility that even trace exposures—down to a few or even one molecule per cell—can contribute to the heritable change that leads to cancer is suggested by six independent lines of evidence:

1. Most malignanices can be traced back to a single cell of origin.

2. Visible and chemical changes in the tumor cells remain constant as the cells divide, suggesting that they are based on inherited changes.

3. Specific genetic changes at identified locations on the chromosomes (including the sites for the so-called oncgenes) are now well established.

4. Agents that have high cancer-producing ability are usually also potent gene-damaging agents (and vice versa).

5. A dose-response relationship exists (even at very low doses) between the amount of the chemical and the number of cells that can be transformed into tumor-producing colonies in tissue culture.

6. A straight line, dose-incidence relationship exists (again even at low doses) between the amount of chemical and the number of tumors an exposed animal develops.[7]

Of course, exceptions to these observations abound. The only true large-scale test of the no-threshold theory provided good evidence that some carcinogens continue to act at very low doses. It also provided a suggestion that for one organ in the body, the bladder, there might be a threshold for carcinogenic activity.[8] But this reaction can be explained by the unique anatomical location and function of the bladder. Since it is at the end of the excretory pathway, it is possible that at low doses, no carcinogen could reach this organ. The liver, the primary site of metabolism, would receive continuous exposure down to the lowest doses. It showed no threshold.

Studies on radiation-induced cancers suggest that the bladder cancer story may be the exception to the rule. Most animal and human studies with radiation show a continuous dose-response relationship down to the lowest doses tested.[9] This is particularly true when the experimental conditions can be tightly controlled, as in tissue culture. Some experiments even show lower doses of ionizing radiation producing *more* than the expected number of tumors in some instances.[10] At high doses, there is evidence from other studies that the incidence of tumors begins to fall off as the dose is increased, suggesting an interference effect of high-energy radiation exposure.[11]

The most provocative human data comes from situations in which radiation was mistakenly given in the false belief that X rays or fluoroscopic treatments would benefit patients with diseases as diverse as ringworm of the scalp or inflammation of the breast. Further radiation data also exists as a result of diagnostic tests using thorotrast as a radioopaque dye and from the tragic exposures that occurred at Hiroshima and Nagasaki.[12]

In the first instances, the calibration of the machinery that delivered the X radiation or fluoroscopy has permitted an accurate re-creation of the actual tissue dose to the organ in question. Results show a clear near-linear pattern of radiation received and tumors produced. In the second, while we must still make assumptions about dosages, women who were at known distances from the epicenter have developed breast cancer (after five to twenty-five years) as predicted. These data together strongly suggest that no threshold for radiation carcinogenesis exists.

The overall conclusion—and the policy adopted by virtually every regulatory agency—has been to accept the likelihood that most carcinogenic agents including radiation exert their effects down to the lowest doses encountered.[13] In other words, carcinogens act without a threshold. Thus, we can rationally assume that even very low exposures to carcinogenic chemicals (for example, from contaminated drinking water) place persons at risk of cancer. The *magnitude* of this risk will always be related to how long—and how much of—the putative carcinogen has been received. With very low doses, very low incidences will be expected and any tumors may take exceptionally long times to appear after exposure. This protracted latency (see previous chapter) makes it difficult to award damages to persons who are known to have been exposed to carcinogenic insults at low doses. For many, if not most of them, the likelihood that a tumor will appear in their lifetime is only slightly above the population norm. Yet, such exposed persons have clearly been put at risk from the uninvited exposure. How the courts should handle such exposures is a burgeoning issue in the field of toxic torts. In this field of law, lawsuits are often filed alleging future harms from carcinogenic exposures that are extremely difficult to quantitate.

Resolving such difficulties is compounded by the uncertainty surrounding the proper classification of a given chemical. Most suspect chemicals are categorized by often ambiguous terms such as potential, possible, probable, or proven human carcinogenic. These phrases embrace a spectrum of categories into which federal regulatory agencies such as the Environmental Protection Agency (EPA) or the Occupational Safety and Health Administration (OSHA) place most chemical agents based on the weight of animal and human epidemiologic data.

ETHICAL CONSIDERATIONS:
TRICHLOROETHYLENE AS AN EXAMPLE

Sometimes, as with the chlorinated solvent trichloroethylene (TCE), one agency will adopt a more restrictive category than another. In January 1989, the National Institute of Occupational Safety and Health reversed a decade of decisions by declaring that it was premature to classify TCE as a carcinogen, although the EPA continued to treat it as if it were. The issue in part turns on interpretation of scientific studies (what constitutes a "valid" carcinogenesis experiment) and politics (what consequences might result from classifying a chemical like TCE that has contaminated scores of aquifers and thousands of workers).

In the instance of TCE, it is my view that the evidence is more than sufficient to warrant treating it as if it were a human carcinogen. But whether its carcinogenic activity is predominantly "promotive" (in that it pushes other tumors along) or "complete" (in that it both starts and promotes tumors on its own) is still a matter of serious debate. The industry view (and that of some academic scientists) is that there is insufficient evidence to link TCE with human cancer risk.[14]

Regulating a chemical *as if it were a carcinogen* when there is only limited evidence for carcinogenicity based on animal studies and no conclusive human epidemiological data is clearly more problematic than if there is clear evidence of animal carcinogenicity and suggestive human epidemiological data. From an ethical perspective one could consider the consequences of adopting either the regulate-as-if-carcinogen policy or of adopting a less stringent position (that is, await further human data).

The circumstances in which these polar positions would apply most vividly would be in instances where exposure has been transient, low level, or both. An error in which we treated TCE as if it were noncarcinogenic might put only a few persons at real risk of cancer, while the decision to treat it as if it were one would put burdensome cleanup costs on industries that used the chemical in the past, and any that contemplate reintroducing the chemical in the future.

Toxicological principles could be invoked to support either position: from what we know based on animal studies, the low doses encountered in the environment would be relatively unlikely to produce tumors in a human lifetime, *even if* TCE were a carcinogen. (This position was adopted by the defense in a lawsuit involving citizens in Dowagiac, Michigan, who had drunk water with about 12 parts per million of TCE over a six- to twelve-year period. Calculation of their likelihood of getting cancer from such an exposure generated a statistic of 188×10^{-5}, or just under 2 in 1,000.)

Clearly, this is a low risk. But are low risks to an involuntary exposure *morally* the same as those that are knowingly undertaken? Had this risk been encountered in the workplace, it would have initiated a major regulatory action. But at Dowagiac, the Michigan court required that it be shown that it was "more likely than not" that an exposed individual would get cancer. (A risk of 2 in 1,000 is certainly not 51 percent.) This test puts an undue burden on any litigant since no chemical (with the possible exception of some bladder carcinogens) has ever produced cancer in more than half the exposed population.

What is also left out of equations of this sort is the likelihood that agents such as TCE, which have some carcinogenic activity, might interact with other low-level carcinogens or carry other toxicological risks as well. These risks may be potentiated or magnified by some of the mechanisms previously discussed.

For instance, as we saw in Chapter 4, any drug or other toxic substance that affected the liver's enzyme system could also enhance TCE's toxicity. Or if one of TCE's cancer-causing metabolites were passed through the placenta, it could have entirely different and more potent carcinogenic effects in the fetus than in the adult. (Only mature animals were used in the studies.)

This latter event was documented at Dowagiac, where a concerned pregnant mother had her newborn's cord blood tested, and trichloroacetic acid was found. (Trichloroacetic acid causes cancer in animals.[15]) To date, no one has told her of the possibility that her son was exposed to a carcinogen, although that is precisely why she had her child's cord blood tested.[16] Disclosure of unknown carcinogenic risks raises ethical questions of its own. Balancing the stresses of hearing "cancer" against the benefits of respecting autonomy poses a knotty problem.

THE EFFECTS OF LOW DOSES OF CHEMICALS

These observations make it imperative to have as full an understanding as possible of what may occur to persons exposed to low doses or mixes of environmental chemicals. While it is almost axiomatic that at sufficiently low doses all biological effects of individual chemicals attenuate, the examples in the introduction to this chapter suggest that toxicology in the real world of multiple and simultaneous exposures is infinitely more complex. At low doses certain chemicals can interact synergistically to enhance each other's toxicity.[17] Extremely low doses of elements such as selenium or heavy metals such as cadmium can dramatically activate defensive proteins such as metallothioneins. And pharmaceutical scientists are familiar with the so-called bimodal curve of response for many drugs (where an effect that occurs at a high dose disappears at midrange, while another appears again when low doses are tested).[18]

Three broad areas of research in toxicology bear on these questions of low-dose phenomena: these areas involve (1) ultra-toxic chemicals, (2) paradoxical effects of microdoses, and (3) biological vigor-enhancing effects of low doses. The first area is straightforward: some toxins are so powerful that even astonishingly small doses can have noxious effects. The second focuses on microdoses of substances that may have curative properties. The third is called *hormesis,* which is a controversial phenomenon in which certain toxic chemicals and ionizing radiation acquire life-prolonging properties at low levels of exposure. But before we can use toxic chemicals wisely, it behooves us to understand these properties.

The Powerful Toxins

It is desirable first to define what is meant by "extremely low doses." Table 6-1 gives the units of measurement used in this chapter.

Unit	Proportion of Gram*	Symbol
Milligram	1/1,000	mg
Microgram	1/1,000,000	µg
Nanogram	1/1,000,000,000	ng
Picogram	1/1,000,000,000,000	pg

*A gram is 1/1,000 of a kilogram (2.2 lbs) or about the weight of a penny. For comparison sake, one of the most toxic chemicals on a milligram/kilogram basis is the nerve gas known as soman that can kill a human at a dose of only 0.01 mg/kg or 10 µg/kg. (For a grown man weighing 70 kg, this equates to about 0.7 mg or less than a thousandth of a gram.)

Table 6-1. Metric units of measurement

Keep in mind that many chemicals can have effects when given in small amounts (measured in parts of a gram), but the actual number of molecules may be smaller for some chemicals than for others, even when the same absolute mass (commonly called its weight) of the chemical is administered. In fact, the number of molecules in any given mass of a chemical is inversely proportional to its molecular weight: the larger the molecule, the smaller the number of molecules in any given unit of weight.[19] This idea begins to make sense if you visualize two bags of the same weight filled with large or small marbles. For any given bag, the number of marbles available to "hit" an opponent's target depends on the marbles' size. In a similar way, the most toxic molecules in nature as measured by their effective dose (say in mg per kg) are found among the largest ones. This is so because a given weight of a large molecule will contain fewer molecules than the same weight of a smaller one.

Among the most toxic large molecular weight poisons are those produced by bacteria. Most notable among these are three genera: *Pasteurella,* which includes bacteria responsible for the Black Death (the plague that decimated Europe in the fourteenth century); *Clostridia,* including the bacteria responsible for food poisoning; and *Shigella,* a group including the bacteria responsible for dysentery in countries with poor hygiene.

Toxins from the *Pasteurella* group of microorganisms are particularly potent liver toxins. Doses as low as 15.6 nanograms (ng) of one *Pasteurella* toxin will cause severe liver damage and growth suppression in rats; about twice that dose is fatal, causing severe liver necrosis.[20]

One of the most potent bacterial toxins, a contaminant of soils, is the tetanus toxin. Any medical student who has heard stories of lockjaw and the profound paralysis that sets in after wound contamination has been duly impressed with the effects of this toxin. What few of us remember is that the toxin that causes the poisoning can act on cells at concentrations as low as 1 picomole (that is, one *trillionth* of its molecular weight in grams.)[21] Such a miniscule dose still leaves more than 6×10^{11} molecules to do cellular damage. This means that anywhere from 100 to 1,000 molecules of toxin per cell are available to work on any given target organ. Other toxins require less than 100 molecules per cell to kill. For example, a disease-causing relative of our native intestinal bacterium, *Escherichia coli,* has been shown under experimental conditions to be effective in doses as low as 5 to 20 molecules of toxin per cell.[22]

Still more potent bacterial toxins exist, notably those derived from the *Pseudomonas* and *Corynebacterium* organisms. These toxins can kill cells with a dose as low as one molecule per cell. (This feature has made them candidates for a remarkable new form of cancer therapy called targeted toxin therapy in which the toxin is linked to an antibody that homes in on cancer cells.[23])

Plant toxins are also effective at extremely low doses. The classic such poison, known as ricin, consists of two parts: A and B. When combined, these two chains form a molecule that can be lethal to individual cells at levels of one molecule.[24] Again the liver is the major site of action, concentrating almost half of an injected dose.[25]

As with the *Pseudomonas and Corynebacterium* toxins, researchers have recently capitalized on this remarkable toxicity by combining ricin toxin from chain A with special antibody molecules that are targeted to tumor cells.[26] Similar initial success from this promising approach has been obtained from a toxin isolated from the plant *Saponaria officinalis*[27] and from the *Pasteurella* bacterium.[28]

Axioms of Low-Dose Toxicity

An axiom of low-dose toxicity is that substances that produce toxicity through overt damage at high doses may have more subtle effects at lower doses. For instance, exposure to the neurotoxic chlorinated pesticide dieldrin at very low doses (between 0.5 and 4.5 milligrams per kilogram) will produce behavioral problems in rats without visible evidence of damage to nerve cells.[29] Similar findings have been made for a metabolite of TCE called chloral. Chloral (known from 1920s and 1930s gangster movies as the ubiquitous knockout drops) is a powerful adult hypnotic (sleep inducer). At amounts likely to be ingested by drinking TCE-contaminated water (for example, where TCE is found at concentrations of 200 parts per billion), it is unlikely that adults would experience a narcotic effect. But children might show problems in learning or memory loss.[30] These more subtle signs of neurotoxicity are a particularly important consideration when children or infants are exposed to low doses of neurotoxic chemicals or drugs whether through drinking contaminated water or exposure to powders, soaps, or other seemingly "benign" nostrums.

This lesson was lost on clinicians who rushed to use antiseptic chemicals to shore up the faltering antibiotic control of bacterial infections in newborns. When epidemics of staphylococcus occurred in nurseries in the late 1950s and early 1960s, many pediatricians turned to a bacteria-killing chemical called hexachlorophene. Beginning in 1961, hospitals used talcum powders and bath soaps containing hexachlorophene in the mistaken belief that it would safely protect particularly vulnerable premature and newborn infants from staph.[31] (Ironically, bathing infants with hexachlorophene did nothing to control life-threatening infections but merely changed the kinds of dangerous bacteria growing on their skin.) What clinicians did not consider was the unique permeability of newborn skin to fat-soluble chemicals and the exquisite vulnerability of the developing nervous system to damage.[32] The result: an epidemic of brain irritability and central nervous system damage. In 1972, hundreds of French infants powdered with hexachlorophene-containing talc developed neurological signs of poisoning and thirty died.[33]

Since hexachlorophene was an over-the-counter remedy developed and marketed in the 1950s, it was exempt from normal FDA submissions regarding safety and efficacy. Whatever data pharmaceutical firms had accumulated regarding hexachlorophene's toxicity were buried in corporate files. Unfortunately, it was not until 1971 that the FDA issued its first warning about the chemical—nonprescription use was banned a year later.[34]

In fact, neurotoxicity from hexachlorophene was reported as early as 1959.[35] Ironically, animal studies could have readily demonstrated neurotoxicity from hexachlorophene—but most were not done until *after* the FDA's action.[36] Hexachlorophene soaps were sporadically used through the 1970s as a prescription drug without clear-cut warnings that use in children could produce permanent brain damage. Only in the late 1970s and early 1980s did researchers conclude categorically that hexachlorophene use was contraindicated for young infants.[37]

Lead is a third major example of a substance that was known to be poisonous to children in the 1920s and 1930s but has only recently been recognized as affecting the central nervous system of children at extremely low doses.[38] Based on the pioneering work of Herbert Needleman of the University of

Pittsburgh, we now know that lead commonly enters the bodies of young inner-city children at doses that can produce measurable deficits in school performance, intelligence (as measured by IQ tests), and behavioral skills.[39] Data from the Center for Disease Control's (CDC's) Second National Health and Nutrition Examination Survey (NHANES II) indicate that 3 to 4 million children age 6 months to 5 years are exposed to environmental lead via food, water and eating contaminated paint chips or dirt (pica) at concentrations sufficient to raise blood lead levels above the critical level of 15 micrograms per 100 milliliters. An additional 6 to 12 million are at risk from breathing atmospheric lead, according to Barry Johnnson, assistant administrator of the Agency for Toxic Substances Disease Registry.[40]

Even more toxic effects of lead can be expected from organic lead compounds such as those added to gasoline as antiknock compounds. Tetraethyl lead and, more recently, triethyl lead (lead atoms with four and three ethyl groups, respectively) have been shown to be extremely toxic to animals' developing nervous systems. As little as 3 or 6 milligrams per kilogram of triethyl lead injected into newborn rats impairs their ability to smell and suckle normally.[41] (A paradoxical effect of low-level lead exposure on developing rats is discussed below in "Hormesis.")

Industrial chemicals such as the glycol ethers are also highly toxic when administered to test animals at low doses relative to the doses needed for lethality. A single oral dose of 160 milligrams per kilogram of ethylene glycol methyl ether given to pregnant rats at the midpoint of their gestation causes a wide range of birth defects in the offspring.[42] Male rats are also at risk from glycol ether exposure.[43] (It was data such as this that prompted the California Hazard Evaluation System to issue the previously mentioned emergency warning about glycol ethers.[44])

At slightly higher levels, glycol ethers are toxic for developing sperm. But still more highly toxic for sperm production is the chemical gossypol. Gossypol has been tried as a male contraceptive by the Chinese, but animal studies conducted in this country show that there is an extraordinarily fine line separating the sperm-toxic dose with one that causes damage to the whole animal.[45] Data like these indicate that even highly specific and useful chemicals are likely to be dangerous when they have a narrow range of therapeutic efficacy versus toxicity.

A final category of high-potency toxins are those found in fungi or molds. In addition to the well-known toxicity of deadly nightshade and mushrooms, molds can produce especially toxic by-products such as the T-2 group of trichothecene poisons. (Thought to be responsible for the still unproven health effects of "yellow rain," this group of poisons is produced by mold that grows on pollen in bee feces.) Actually, the mold toxins (see Chapter 10) may be the major causes of cancer in some areas of the world. In fact, the esophagus has recently been identified as a location for the carcinogenic effects of a group of trichothecene toxins found in moldy corn.[46] Most interestingly, these toxins were isolated from Linxian, the same province in China previously cited for its high rate of lung cancer.

CORPORATE RESPONSIBILITY

In many examples of "low-level" environmental contamination, some companies and corporations were found to have surreptitiously placed hazardous chemicals into aquifers, waste dumps, or sewers or added them to products sold commercially. The contamination of the James River near Hopewell, Virginia, with kepone in the 1960s by the Life Sciences Products company;[47] the dumping of TCE at the Woburn site by W. R. Grace;[48] and the addition of a "secret" antiknock ingredient called ethyl (tetraethyl lead) to gasoline are but three such instances I have reviewed.[49]

These observations are potentially important because kepone, TCE, lead, and benzene are representative of the major groups of environmental contaminants at many Superfund sites (chlorinated pesticides, chlorinated solvents, heavy metals, and aromatic compounds respectively). Some preliminary studies have suggested that prematurity, low birth weight, birth defects and possibly learning deficits in children are a common denominator among families at such sites who have been exposed to one or more of these agents or their congeners.[50] Given the heightened sensitivity of infants and fetuses *in utero* to low doses of toxic chemicals (more on this in the next chapter), these findings deserve significant attention.

One of the caveats of low-dose studies conducted in test animal species is the possibility that some of the findings will prove not to be extrapolatable to humans. This appears to have been the case with the dioxins. One form of dioxin is the 2,3,7,8-tetrachlorodibenzo-*p*-dioxin, the major contaminant of Agent Orange. (Recall that dioxins are formed during the incineration of municipal and possibly hospital wastes, largely as the result of the contamination of such wastes with chlorinated compounds such as polyvinyl chloride plastics.) They are a significant contaminant of paper manufacturing and of some chemicals, such as the wood preservative, pentachlorophenol.

Corporate responsibility for high residual levels of dioxins in Agent Orange used in Vietnam has been a particularly contentious issue. Based on animal tests, particularly on the guinea pig, which succumbed to dietary levels measured in the parts per trillion range, researchers voiced grave concern about the health of veterans. At the Fourth National Environmental Health Conference held in San Antonio, Texas, in late June 1989, Centers for Disease Control researchers presented data from studies conducted on Missouri residents, Vietnam veterans, and citizens living around the town of Seveso, Italy, the site of a chemical explosion that released appreciable amounts of dioxins into the surroundings. Data were also presented on Operation Ranch Hand veterans (the group that supplied and loaded spray planes with Agent Orange in Vietnam) and on industrial plant workers exposed to 2,3,7,8-tetrachloro dioxins. These studies failed to reveal any consistent pattern of disease except for chloracne, a disfiguring cluster of comedoes (blackheads) on the face and other parts of the body.

Of course, it still remains to be seen if some adverse effects, such as soft tissue sarcomas and lymphomas, may in fact be increased. Other problems alleged to occur from dioxin exposure, namely, liver toxicity, neurological toxicity, and other organ damage were appreciably downplayed by recent studies performed by the Centers for Disease Control and several academic institutions.[51]

It is precisely this lulling effect of still incomplete investigations that concerns William Farland, director of the EPA's Office of Health and Environmental Assessment. At the conference, Farland stated that the EPA still calls dioxin a *probable* human carcinogen because of its positive activity in animal studies.[52] He concluded that these activities are consistent with the likelihood that dioxin is solely a "promoter" of carcinogenesis in that it stimulates already initiated precancerous cells to proliferate and thereby to develop into clinically visible lesions.

This conclusion is at variance with the observed toxicity and complete carcinogenicity of extremely low levels of dioxins in experimental animals.[53] Part of the explanation for the major discrepancy between the lethal and carcinogenic effects of dioxins and their related compounds in comparing humans and test animals may be different retention rates. Guinea pigs retain these chemicals for protracted periods. For tetrachloro-dibenzofurans, half of an ingested dose is still present forty days after feeding in guinea pigs — and as little as 4 micrograms per kilogram results in death for about a third of the treated animals.[54] Humans may retain less, and much higher amounts are probably needed for lethality. More research is clearly needed.

HORMESIS

In retaining toxicity down to such low concentrations, dioxins appear to be an exception. Most other toxic chemicals lose their toxicity with decreasing doses — and many appear to acquire new properties at the levels where dioxins retain toxicity. This *beneficial* but highly controversial property of chemicals (and ionizing radiation) is called hormesis.

That is, hormesis is the paradoxical ability of very low doses of toxic substances, including ionizing radiation, to produce net benefits instead of harm. The concept of low-dose stimulation was developed in the late 1800s by a team of German biologists, Hugo Arndt and Rudolph Schultz. Arndt and Schultz observed the growth-stimulating effects of low doses of a constellation of chemical agents among several different phyla. Their research was widely regarded as definitive in its day and led to the incorporation of the so-called Arndt-Schultz law into many pharmacology and biology texts.

Hormesis entered the vocabulary of biologists around 1940, and it was widely cited as a term that described the Arndt-Schultz phenomenon. But researchers considered that hormesis involved more than the simple stimulatory effect that precedes a more toxic response (much like the effect of the first one or two drinks of an alcoholic beverage). They took hormesis to mean the enhancement of longevity of the organism as a whole. In the 1950s, scientists offered often divergent explanations for this remarkable activity. Some postulated that this hypothetical enhancement might be due to protections afforded cells againsty aging–inducing substances (for example, free radicals); others to a reduction of the frequency of aging "lesions" or injuries; or just to some nonspecific protection against systemic deterioration or disease. By the early 1960s, enough data about low–dose effects of otherwise toxic chemicals had appeared to lead a major textbook on aging to incorporate a chapter that advanced the hormesis concept among competing theories of longevity.[55] In the late 1960s, the possibility that substances actually existed that could literally slow the rate of aging by decreasing the intrinsic rate by which cells aged and died was seriously proposed for the first time.[56] Hormesis had come of age.

But by the 1970s, only two phenomena had been charted that clearly had "hormetic" effects: one was the age–retarding effect of limiting animals' caloric consumption; the other was the increased life span observed in cold–blooded animals intentionally kept at lower temperatures. Since both of these observations are hardly revolutionary, the world still awaited the first true demonstration of life prolongation.

Advocates of hormesis acknowledge that the theoretical foundation is still incompletely formed. One hypothetical mechanism is that hormesis somehow causes a reduction in the rate of normal accumulation of intracellular and organismic injury and acts independently of the toxic effects of chemicals. A corollary is that hormesis is reversible. Upon cessation of low–dose treatments, for instance, the hormetic effect is presumed to dissipate at a constant rate. According to this model, toxicity and hormesis are always overlayed: where toxic effects dominate, the hormetic effect is hidden but nonetheless present. Only when the benefits from hormesis are greater than the disadvantages from the toxic effects of the chemical in question does the organism show a net benefit in terms of increased longevity. (One research team has calculated the doses beyond which toxic detriments can be expected to exceed the hormetic benefit of various chemicals.[57]) One of the convenient corollaries to this theory is that for some toxic substances (for example dioxins or DDT), the toxicity effects nearly always nullify the so-called hormetic benefit.[58]

Chemical Hormesis

In 1988, a team of U.S. researchers returned to Arndt and Schultz's initial work and extended the studies on radiation-induced hormesis to embrace toxic substances.[59] This team reinforced the concept that low doses of toxic substances that were injurious at high doses were *beneficial* at low doses. That is, the concept of hormesis was used to describe the benefits that purportedly accrue from low doses of radiation or toxic chemicals. This data, from carcinogenesis assays, appears to demonstrate that many carcinogens, while noxious to animals at high doses, actually appear to extend the life span of animals at the lowermost dose tested.

However, these ideas are confounded by observations that some chemicals exert their hormetic effect at virtually *all* the toxic dose levels tested. And some chemicals show a stimulatory effect on the proliferation of cells (considered to be part of the hormetic effect) *only* at doses near the level at which half of the treated animals are expected to die.[60]

One of the chemicals studied by the P. J. Neafsey team did appear to directly enhance longevity. The research team reviewed a study of inhalation exposure of female Syrian golden hamsters to methylene chloride. The hamsters were given up to 3,500 parts per million of methylene chloride (over 100 times the occupational limit) for six hours a day, five days a week. Astonishingly, given the highly toxic and carcinogenic nature of this chemical, *all* groups of animals showed a statistically significant extension of their life span compared to controls. How can scientists explain this? For one thing, it may be that the metabolism of methylene chloride at these extremely high doses is somehow protective of the animals from intrinsic aging factors. It is also possible that either the blocking of the protective enzyme system or the depletion of glutathione production protects against chemical damage.[61] (Recall that methylene chloride requires glutathione to be toxic.) A similar model could explain the paradoxical hormesis effect observed with a structurally related chemical, chloroform.[62]

A much more simplistic, but equally plausible model, has the longevity effect due entirely to the reduction of food consumption that occurs with many high-dose exposures to toxic substances. Animals exposed to the toxic and near-toxic levels of chemicals "on test" for their carcinogenicity commonly eat less and gain less weight than do controls. As we have seen, reduced caloric intake itself increases life span. Many researchers also consider caloric intake the best explanation for many of the apparent hormetic effects of low-dose radiation.[63] It is self-evident that "hormesis" applies only to animals that escape the tumorigenic or toxic effects of chemicals. Adaptation to the continuous, precisely metered amounts of chemicals or radiation given in the laboratory can hardly be said to mirror the lives of individuals in the real world.

The idea of hormesis, while heuristically attractive, is thus a dangerous notion. If put into practice, it could permit policymakers (or, more likely, those individuals with corporate or vested interests) to tolerate low-level contamination of the environment with toxic chemicals on the grounds that "a little toxicity is good for you." At another extreme, the short-term compensatory responses of organisms to environmental stress,[64] might be cited to downplay the long-term deleterious effects of low doses of toxic chemicals. It is worth noting that as of early 1991, no one has established unequivocally the existence of a beneficial effect on people of low-level exposure to *any* toxic substance — with the possible exception of radiation.

Radiation Hormesis

By the mid-1950s, research scientists had accumulated a number of observations that seemed to suggest that radiation could have hormetic effects. As a young precollege student at the Jackson Laboratory in Bar Harbor, Maine, in 1959, I vividly remember a talk by Dr. Sheldon Bernstein in which he discussed his own paradoxical observations of low-dose stimulation of red blood cells by radiation. Bernstein was struck by how long scientists had observed such phenomena and yet were reluctant to publish their data for fear of violating the dogma of the times that radiation was universally harmful. Twenty years later, hormesis could not be ignored: by 1979, more than .

1,200 studies could be cited to support a hormetic effect of low-dose radiation.[65]

By 1990, many research programs had shown that animals exposed to low-level radiation *outlive* their unexposed control populations.[66] A reasonable model for this effect can be found by analogy to the toxicity-protecting effects of microdoses of metals cited previously. That is, small doses of radiation may induce the DNA repair enzymes needed for recovery from genetic damage from *any* life-shortening encounters with chemicals or radiation. The persistence of this "activated" or heightened state of resistance may then provide protection to an animal exposed to further radiation doses.

Another schema proposes a system that blunts the consequences of the release of so-called free radicals (not the politico type) by toxic substances or radiation. Such radicals, made up predominantly of highly reactive molecules of free oxygen or hydroxyl groups, cause much of the damage from toxic exposures. Following low-dose radiation, free-radical-scavenging molecules commonly increase, which can protect the host from further toxic or radiation-mediated insults.

A final mechanism, cited by Leonard Sagan, an Electric Power Institute scientist, is the possibility that small cellular-damaging doses work like pruning shears, killing back a few cells but stimulating a compensatory (and thereby healthy) outgrowth of undamaged ones.[67]

While this viewpoint might seem somewhat self-serving (after all, the EPI is heavily committed to nuclear power), in fact there is substantial experimental evidence that such pruning effects exist. Among this data are studies that support a theory originally put forward by Dr. Richmond T. Prehn and myself that weak immune reactions stimulate rather than kill cells.[68] Independent data suggest a possible linkage between this theory of immunostimulation and radiation hormesis. Under some experimental conditions, low-dose radiation actually increases the number of immune cells and their activities, including increases in the cells of the thymus (a central organ in developing cell-mediated immunity); increased synthesis of DNA in spleen cells; and an increase in antibody-producing cells in the spleen.[69]

A final model has been proposed by radiation researcher S. Kondo. Kondo believes that low-dose radiation can cause what he calls "altruistic cell suicide." In this model, radiation-injured, undifferentiated primordial cells encourage uninjured cells to replace them, in the process effectively removing the likelihood of perpetuating the injured cell and possibly hurting the organism as a whole.[70]

Sagan points out that data from low-dose radiation exposure of humans is neutral in answering the question of hormesis. Chinese living at naturally high background levels of radiation fail to show any observable increase in cancer mortality expected from low-dose effects.[71] In India the rates of cancer are consistently *lower* in areas where environmental radiation levels are highest (and vice versa).[72]

At first blush, these data are unsettling — where are the tumors expected from low-dose exposure? Closer examination provides a partial answer. First, the exposed populations show other evidence of radiation damage, such as chromosome breakage.[73] Second, the Chinese population ingested considerable amounts of cancer-protective foods (see Chapter 10), and environmental carcinogens also vary in concentration throughout India. Among the *survivors* of the Hiroshima and Nagasaki bombings, radiation-related increases in cancers of breast, thyroid, leukemia, and skin have been recorded, although overall longevity does not seem to be affected. Nonetheless, low-level radiation has produced less damage than expected. Why might this be?

Recently, theoretical arguments about the resilience of DNA to radiation damage, the existence of multiple copies of enzymes that might be radiation damaged, and the compensatory replacement of damaged gametes (especially in males) have all been invoked to "explain" why radiation at low doses appears to stimulate cell survival or to be without effect. One plausible model is based on the observation that in the presence of above-normal levels of free radicals (such as those provoked by low doses of radiation), the cell "freezes" its DNA synthesis mechanisms, thereby effectively preventing the exposure of highly sensitive replicating strands of DNA to further radiation damage.[74] There is also evidence that at low energies, certain forms of ionizing radiation are less tumorigenic.[75]

The most parsimonious explanation for the apparent absence of radiation effects is the inability of the epidemiological studies to reveal actual adverse effects because of the limitations posed by the size of the population being studied or the sensitivity of the markers being followed. For instance, where such limitations probably do not apply, such as the atomic bomb survivor studies that involved literally tens of thousands of births, very different findings from those predicted by hormesis were made. William J. Schull and his Japanese colleagues recently conducted a careful scrutiny of all possible pathology in A-bomb survivors (confined to doses below 50 rads). Contrary to the predictions of hormesis, the Schull team found declining but continuous adverse effects as the radiation level decreased for incidences of cancer, chromosome aberrations, mental retardation, and cancer death.[76]

There is almost universal agreement that radiation causes mutations and that this effect extends down to the lowest radiation levels tested. Since mutations are almost always deleterious, the long-term intergenerational effects of low-dose radiation cannot be anything but harmful irrespective of any apparent enhancement of survival of present-generation individuals.[77]

Implications of the Hormesis Argument. Obviously, the debate over the existence of beneficial effects of low doses of radiation has profound public policy implications. If we were to believe the still hypothetical proposition of the enhancing effects of low-dose radiation (or even the absence of biological effects produced by such exposures), we might adopt entirely different policies with regard to protection from nuclear wastes, nuclear energy, or radon—even public policy regarding nuclear weapons. An example of the dangerously misleading use of this concept is the report by B. L. Cohen that purported to find that exposure to radon (an almost universally recognized lung-cancer-producing alpha particle) could afford *protection* to people in the United States against lung cancer.[78] (His data on the alleged hormetic effect of radon on lung cancer relied erroneously on cancer incidence data for the whole country, uncorrected for confounding factors.) Even if hormesis from low-dose radiation were a reproducible phenomenon in human populations (a far-from-established conclusion), researchers have pointed out that the same low-level effects that appear to benefit healthy tissues (vis-à-vis longevity) might very well stimulate tumor cells and other pathological proliferative responses.[79]

From all of the available evidence, it is at the minimum premature to conclude that low-dose radiation (or low doses of chemical carcinogens) is "safe," much less beneficial.

PARADOXICAL MICRODOSE EFFECTS (HOMEOPATHY)

The ability of profoundly toxic substances (or even those that are only mildly so) to cure disease when given at extremely low doses is a plausible if not controversial extension of the related themes of hormesis and low-dose effects.

The medical discipline that relies on ultralow dilutions of chemicals or extracts in treating disease is called homeopathy. Developed in the late 1800s in the United States by Samuel Hahneman and his followers, it is an extension of the doctrine of signatures, which holds that like should be used to treat like. Homeopathy is based on the observation that exposure to extremely low doses of agitated or "potentised" dilutions of chemicals can evoke specific toxic reactions in otherwise healthy persons. These reactions are taken by practitioners as a "proving" that the homeopathic dose of the chemical may cure a person who manifests similar symptoms as a result of disease processes, irrespective of the underlying causes of the illness. This form of medicine reached its greatest popularity in Europe and the United States during the mid-1800s. During this period, homeopathic medicines were widely prescribed — with reported success — in treating infectious diseases such as typhoid fever, yellow fever, scarlet fever, cholera, and pneumonia.[80]

While the exact mechanism of homeopathic remedies remains unknown, it is tempting to interpret "provings" as signs of the activation of host defences. This hypothesis is particularly attractive in light of what we now know about the close relation between *symptoms* of disease and the host reaction to invasive organisms and cancer. Many of the chemicals released during the immune response, such as interleukin-2, cause much of the symptoms of illness while helping to rid the body of offending organisms or cells.

The empirical demonstration of the efficacy of some of the homeopathic remedies was unestablished until the 1980s, when several studies published in reputable journals offered verification for some of the claims of homeopaths — and controversial findings about others. A review in 1990 cites twenty-four controlled studies, most of which successfully demonstrated some form of a homeopathic effect.[81]

A classic homeopathic medicine is known as Oscillococcinum. When diluted 1:100 two hundred times, very little if any of the original molecules of the remedy would be expected to persist. Yet a carefully designed "quadruple-blind" study (that is, one in which neither the investigators nor the patients knew whether the medicine being used was homeopathic or placebo) was recently done with rather remarkable results. Four hundred and eighty-seven patients with symptoms of influenza were randomly assigned to the homeopathic remedy or to a placebo. When the labeling code was broken and the patients were divided into placebo and homeopathic remedy groups, the researchers (some 149 French physicians) found that the symptoms were resolved within forty-eight hours in almost twice as many patients on the homeopathic remedy than in the placebo group.[82]

A more controversial experiment conducted by an international group of researchers at six laboratories in four universities claimed that the histamine release that accompanies the degranulation of a certain type of blood cell (the basophil) could be impeded by almost 60 percent by exposing the cells to antibodies (the IgE antibody) that normally *trigger* the degranulation.[83] In this study, the IgE antiserum was diluted 1:10 up to 120 times. Because the dilution was again sufficient to virtually ensure the exclusion of any remaining IgE molecules, this finding was greeted with much skepticism in the scientific world. In an accompanying editorial, the editor of *Nature,* John Maddux, expressed his profound reservations regarding the plausibility of the study, and he later joined magician James Randi and NIH scientist and fraud exposer Walter Stewart in a trip to the Paris laboratory of one of the major collaborators. After duplicating the conditions of the initial experiment and ensuring that the technicians did not know which slides were being analyzed for basophil degranulation, the trio claimed to have failed to replicate the findings and to have exposed a pattern of self-deception in the manner in which the studies were performed.[84]

However, in parallel studies, in which extracts of bees (*Apis mellifica*) and lung histamine were used in homeopathic dilutions, researchers successfully blocked the release of histamine and subsequent skin reddening by bee sting mediators or ultraviolet radiation.[85] The pharmacological basis for these findings has been well recognized for more than forty years. Called "pharmacological inversions," the ability of low doses to produce a physiological effect opposite to those produced by high doses is akin to the Arndt-Schulz phenomenon discussed earlier. Examples from substances as diverse as alcohols, anesthetic gases, barbiturates, tranquilizers, and toxic metals are all known to produce paradoxical effects at low doses.[86]

One classic example is the ability of heavy metals to cause degranulation of histamine-containing mast cells in rats. When diluted 1:10 some twelve times, zinc preparations produce the degranulation, even though at this dilution only a few atoms per milliliter of solution would be available.[87] A possible explanation for the ability of dilute solutions to cause degranulation is the hair trigger with which cells such as the basophil and mast cell are set to respond to antigenic or other substances. In order to assist the body in a timely way during an early acute attack by bacteria or other foreign agents, these cells appear poised to release their contained mediators of inflammation at the slightest provocation.

Several research studies also demonstrate classic homeopathic effects of high dilutions of heavy metals.[88] One showed that a combined cadmium-metallothionein complex, which is normally highly toxic for the kidney (which must excrete such heavy metals), becomes much less so after a first exposure at a very low dose. In this model experiment, the authors found that a first dose (which itself is mildly toxic) appears to protect the kidneys against further damage by subsequent doses.[89] Other studies also suggest that low-dose metal exposure has a beneficial effect. A week of exposure to very low doses of cadmium (0.05 to 0.1 mg/liter) in the water of the fish *Fundulus heteroclitus,* for example, actually enhanced their ability to regenerate an amputated fin over that of untreated controls when they were subsequently placed in cadmium-contaminated water.[90] Low levels of metals such as lead, copper, or tin have also been shown to stimulate the growth of hydra.[91]

Homologous effects across species lines have also been seen with low doses of lead. For example, rats exposed in utero to only 1 microgram of lead per gram of brain weight grew much faster after birth than did control animals.[92] Studies using homeopathic doses of lead *therapeutically* to stimulate the excretion of the same heavy metal proved inconclusive: an earlier study was positive[93] while a subsequent one was negative.[94] In contrast, French researchers have clearly shown that arsenic, in low concentration in rats, will accelerate the elimination of previously administerd doses of this classic poison.[95]

It is provocative to link studies on silica to homeopathic responses of the body. Apparently extremely dilute preparations of silica can stimulate macrophage activity in a manner strongly reminiscent of the macrophage response to silicone gels.[96] (More on this in Chapter 6.) If such small doses can set in motion a cascade of reactions that leads to an immunological overresponse, it is not unreasonable to consider if microdoses of immune-stimulating substances might be used to prod the immune system to take another direction. At least one recently published article suggests that something along these lines is plausible. One of the major groups of substances that regulates the nature and intensity of the responses of several components of the immune system are the interferons. When given in microdoses, interferons retain some of these modulating effects, shifting the proportions of antibody–producing cells and the resulting cytotoxicity in a beneficial direction.[97]

This hypothesis could be tested by using homeopathic regimes similar to those that have apparently resolved the symptoms of joint pain and discomfort in a majority of rheumatoid arthritic patients.[98] (It should be noted, however, that not all homeopathic remedies have proven successful in treating rheumatoid arthritic symptoms.)[99]

Commentary. While many of the hormetic and homeopathic findings discussed in this chapter can be explained by evoking the abilities of the body to *magnify* the effects of small doses of otherwise toxic or biologically active molecules, for example by releasing highly reactive "cytokines" or mediators, it is difficult to account for the activity of homeopathic remedies in high dilution. Because of the repeated reduction in total number of molecules by 10 (or 100, depending on the dilution factor) with each successive dilution, and the presence of no more than 10^{20} to 10^{25} molecules in any given starting solution of the chemical in question, any dilution of 1/10 made more than about twenty-five to thirty times will have in theory exhausted the total number of available molecules. (An aqueous dilution of 1/100 done nine times will leave in 1 milliliter approximately four hundred molecules of a 100% solution of a chemical the size of phenobarbitol; four more dilutions will in theory reduce the likelihood of one molecule being present to near zero.)

This theoretical observation may not hold true under certain conditions. For instance, even if the dilutions are made accurately and thoroughly (usually the case for homeopathic remedies, which are subjected to vigorous shaking between dilutions), the distribution of the molecules present in the later dilutents will be a function of the chance distribution of the molecules in solution (a phenomenon described by a Poisson distribution). This means that later dilutions may still contain a small number of molecules even as the theoretical limit is approached.

Another theoretical possibility is that the process of vigorous shaking (or *succussion* as it is termed by homeopaths) leaves in the aqueous solutions a "molecular memory" of the shape or configuration of the starting chemical which is perpetuated somehow. No known physical model of water suggests how such a reaction is likely, but the idea that a chemical somehow leaves its electromagnetic "signature" in the solution is a provocative one. Biophysicist Beverly Rubik has in fact suggested that such a signature may "manifest itself as a 'field effect' over the entire organism rather than as local molecular signals propagated molecule by molecule."[100]

Of course, any theory of the mode of action of a certain remedy presumes that the remedy in question works. While dilute solution data are quite convincing, especially for the release of pre-stored, potent biomolecules like histamine, or the induction of enzyme systems by trace levels of certain microsomal enzyme-stimulating substances, the literature demonstrating *true* homeopathic effects at micro-dose dilutions is still incomplete.

SUMMARY

All of these data speak to the question of when and if low doses of toxic chemicals cease being offensive to the organism. The central dogma of toxicology challenged in this chapter is that every toxic chemical shows a dose-response relationship of one sort or another that leads to complete inertness long before the chemical's concentration is exhausted in the body's fluids. Toxic substances are also predicted to exhibit a "threshold" below which absolutely no toxic effects will occur. However, these generalizations present an incomplete picture of toxicity.

Many classic poisons continue to be poisonous right down to a single molecule or so per cell. And while it is true that virtually every chemical shows a dose-response relationship for any *given biological effect,* many chemicals exhibit different biological effects as their dose is diminished. As we saw for gossypol, for some chemicals the transition from one toxic effect (for example, lethality) to another (for example, suppression of sperm production) may be abrupt. Pharmacologists are particularly well attuned to this and describe the ratio between the dose producing undesirable and that producing desirable effects as the "therapeutic index."

As for thresholds, more and more data are being developed that show this idea to be a dangerous red herring. Substances such as lead, which used to be considered threshold-acting, produce often irreversible damage to the developing brain down to extremely low doses. For many observers, the only prudent position is to assume that lead lacks a threshold altogether for its nerve-damaging effects. For other chemicals that interact directly with the cell's genetic material, there may be no threshold at all. Small doses, even infinitesimal ones, can in theory start a cascade of heritable changes in a single cell that can lead to cancer.

These observations have important ethical and policy implications. If, contrary to the general industry line, people exposed to even very low doses of neurotoxic substances (such as lead) or carcinogenic substances (such as benzene) *are* put at risk for neurological damage or cancer, manufacturers and waste haulers bear considerable responsibility for where their hazardous substances go. The no-threshold model means we must pay considerable attention to the toxic waste sites where thousands of persons are continually exposed to low-level carcinogenic contaminants. (Fortunately, this is currently the general posture of the EPA.) Note that "no threshold" does not mean that every person so exposed *will* get cancer. A dose-response relationship will probably still hold for virtually all carcinogens. Extremely low-dose exposures to carcinogens will thus produce an effect, but one that may take an extremely long time to become manifest—and then in only a small fraction of the population exposed.

As we have seen, some toxic chemicals also acquire different properties from one dose range to another. Chemicals that suppress a given system at high doses may stimulate it at lower ones. This may either be good or bad for the organism. And, as in the case of the organophosphorous pesticides cited at the beginning of Chapter 5, we do not know how this bimodal response will play out in terms of pathology for the host. For other chemicals, the new reactions that appear at low doses (for example, allergic reactions) may be less dramatic than the ones at high doses, but nonetheless disturbing to the host's equilibrium. (For example, as cited in the introduction, in foundry workers, high-dose chromate can erode the mucosa and cartilage in the nose to cause a perforated septum and may produce cancer, while at extremely low doses it will "only" produce contact dermatitis.)

Hormesis phenomena, in which low doses of chemicals or radiation actually appear to improve the viability of organisms, may also be misconstrued as evidence that we should ignore low doses—or even encourage them. The vast body of literature on chemical toxicity is inconsistent with the predictions of hormesis: At low doses, we are still negatively affected by highly potent toxins and other toxic agents. Animals eat less and slow down their metabolism under "hormetic environments," certainly not our everyday idea of the sybaritic conditions produced by the fountain of youth.

The so-called hormesis effects of radiation may also only be masking subclinical damage since cells so exposed either freeze their metabolic activities or begin to spend a lot more of their scarce chemical energies preparing for further damage. Even the data most often cited in favor of hormesis are suspect. Human populations exposed to low-dose radiation do exhibit "normal" cancer rates but have higher than expected rates of chromosome breakage. The idea that low doses of either radiation or chemicals are "good" for us—perpetuated by some adherents of hormesis—fails to recognize that the only time that so-called beneficial responses occur from low-dose exposures is when researchers study populations that are already compromised, sick, or about to get zapped with another round of radiation. (Recall that in healthy persons, homeopathic doses of chemicals *provoke* symptoms of illness.)

While it does appear true that very low doses of some chemicals can activate defense mechanisms in the host, such activation is not without its own deleterious consequences. When the host's defense system is engaged, it commonly elicits the full spectrum of inflammation-generating and immune responses irrespective of the size of the provocation. This means that many non-specific biomediators may be unnecessarily produced and others, surprisingly noxious in and of themselves, may also be elaborated. Many of the interleukins and interferons — among the likely mediators of low dose effects — produce fever, headaches, and "flu-like" symptoms. In a normal person, such reactions are clearly undesirable and constitute a toxic response.

Low concentrations of other substances or elements can trigger or induce a strong defensive response without producing overt damage. The prealerted host animal (or person) can be "primed" — much in the same way as the immune system can be activated by a vaccination — to respond more vigorously and effectively against what would otherwise be toxic doses of similar chemicals. The metallothionein system is a case in point. Here very low doses of metals start a very valuable host response in anticipation of further heavy metal or other toxic element exposure. In this way, very low doses of toxic chemicals can have paradoxical beneficial effects.

Observations of this sort demonstrate the existence of a subterranean world of toxicology at the lower levels of the dosage range that has been virtually ignored in the classic texts of toxicology and pharmacology (the Arndt-Schulz law excepted). Because so many human exposures to toxic substances are occurring at precisely these ranges of micro-doses, it is imperative that we renew our examination of the complexity of host responses to toxic substances.

And the place where low-dose effects certainly warrant our closest scrutiny is during development, where doses of chemicals that have minimal effects in the adult can wreak havoc n the developing organ systems of the embryo or fetus.

CHAPTER SEVEN

Myth 5:

The fetus develops out of reach of toxic danger

PARADOXICALLY, THE SITE WHERE LOW DOSES OF TOXIC CHEMICALS are most likely to affect persons is the place many researchers used to believe was best protected from environmental toxicants — the uterus. In the mid-1900s, it was not uncommon to read descriptions of the fetus as if it developed in the confines of a hothouse. Many researchers equated the fetus to the brain, believing that, like this central organ, it, too, was hidden "safely" behind a blood barrier.[1] This belief that the fetus is buffered from the trials and tribulations of a chemical world has proven disastrous in this century.

The fetus has actually proved to be extraordinarily vulnerable to many toxic substances. This vulnerability results from the embryo's accessibility to toxic chemicals during the first trimester of pregnancy; the embryo's and fetus's ability to concentrate certain harmful chemicals from its mother; and the existence of many rapidly developing tissues. Relatively small molecules (those with molecular weights of 100 or less) derived from maternally metabolized chemicals readily pass through the placenta along with vital nutrients and other complex molecules. Some fat-soluble chemicals may actually accumulate in fetal tissues, especially the brain. The fetus's constantly dividing cells are substantially more vulnerable to damage than are the more quiescent cells typical of most adult organs. Such characteristics help to explain why the fetus is adversely affected by many toxic insults that an adult endures with impunity. And this vulnerability is enhanced by the fetus's immaturity. The fetus lacks a fully developed detoxification system for many chemicals (see Chapter 4) and is thereby at risk for direct toxic effects.

Furthermore, for other chemicals, notably those that require activation to become carcinogens, the placenta serves as a veritable chemical factory, with some of the richest enzyme-based systems for biotransforming chemicals into active carcinogens ever found.[2] Sometimes, toxic chemicals strike at selected inadequately protected organ systems, for instance, the fetal lungs or liver,[3] or the developing nervous system.[4]

This only recently recognized sensitivity of rapidly dividing and differentiating cells in the fetus has led in the past to disastrous errors in prescribing. Numerous physicians have mistakenly prescribed drugs during pregnancy that have not been absolutely essential only to find that while treating the mother they poisoned her developing baby.

While many regulators are now aware of the cross-placental effects of chemicals such as thalidomide and diethylstilbestrol (DES), few have incorporated these general findings into their policy-making. A case in point is Valium, the most commonly used drug in the United States. Valium (diazepam) has been found in both maternal and cord blood, indicating that it crosses the placenta into the developing fetus. It is widely recognized as a potential teratogen since it has been associated with an increased risk of congenital malformations in infants of mothers who used Valium during the first trimester of pregnancy. (In animals, it can also depress the immune system of the offspring of treated mothers.) Yet its use in pregnancy is not contraindicated. The manufacturer (Roche Pharmaceuticals) notes in its 1982 *Physicians' Desk Reference* entry only that "use of these drugs is rarely a matter of urgency" and reminds the physician that "their use during this period should almost always be avoided." But it goes on to offer only this faint admonition against use in early pregnancy: "if [patients] become pregnant during therapy or intend to become pregnant they should communicate with their physicians about the desirability of discontinuing the drug."[5] Clearly, this drug, along with other minor tranquilizers, should be disallowed during pregnancy by virtue of the manufacturer's own acknowledgement of their dispensability and potential risk.

The classic example of the error of giving potent drugs during pregnancy occurred in the 1940s and 1950s. Synthetic estrogens were given early in gestation in the mistaken belief that they would prevent miscarriages. Physicians eager to assist women who appeared to be "habitual aborters" gave diethylstilbestrol (DES) to literally hundreds of pregnant women in Chicago and Boston. This potent nonsteroidal estrogen was thought to offset threatened miscarriages, even though no evidence was available that the treatment would work. We now know that a large percentage of early conceptions are normally miscarried.[6] DES is now recognized as a remarkably potent — and carcinogenic — estrogen. And it may even produce miscarriages rather than prevent them.[7]

DES also proved to be disastrously disruptive of the normal differentiation of the sex organs of both male and female fetuses. As many as 66 percent of DES-exposed daughters subsequently developed abnormal sex organ anatomy, as did a smaller percentage of DES-exposed sons.[8] Many of the young men whose mothers had taken these estrogen analogs are now suspected of being at high risk of testicular cancer.[9] Within two decades of their mothers' mistaken treatment, it was also apparent that the "DES daughters" were developing an unusual tumor known as clear cell vaginal adenocarcinoma at far above the background incidence.[10] (More about this in Chapter 9.) To better understand just how the developing embryo is at risk for such catastrophic events, it is important to understand the basic mechanisms of development.

THE DEVELOPING EMBRYO

After fertilization and the implantation of the developing ball of cells known as the blastocyst, the young embryo begins receiving its nourishment from the mother's circulation. Blood flow begins at the end of the second week after conception, marking the onset of embryonic vulnerability to chemicals or hormonal fluctuations. About two weeks later, the window of vulnerability opens fully, as the embryo's tissues organize themselves into specific groups called primordia that will become the major organs of the body. During this same time, the leg and arm buds form—small paddlelike plates of cells that will grow into the bones and digits of the limbs.

Along with the specialization that comes with these new functions, the primordia acquire different metabolic requirements and undergo rapid and dramatic cell divisions as they expand into their respective organs. It is during this period of organogenesis that the tissues of the fetus-to-be are most sensitive to disruption. Any chemical insult or breakdown in the coordination of the activities of the cells during this time can be catastrophic, leading to malformation, loss of structures, or complete failure of development. In the case of an arm/hand structure, there can be a foreshortening of the whole arm and hand (brachydactyly), absent digits or bones in the arm or wrist and/or loss of most of the arm structure altogether (amelia).

In addition to this organ-system damage, when the embryo is exposed to a teratogenic insult, it may die, experience nonspecific retardation of its growth, or develop with latent damage. Such damage may become visible only years after birth when the behavioral repertoire of the infant develops. Some only marginally toxic agents can produce neurological damage that shows up as a behavioral deficit in the adult. Others may interfere with the immune system. In a sense, the most injurious compounds can be the most sparing, since early embryonic or fetal loss is less traumatic than are injuries to a live-born infant that persist for a lifetime.

Something like this "sparing" effect may explain the curious results of radiation on atomic bomb survivors who were exposed while they were in utero. While a significant number of these survivors experienced a clear and dramatic increase in microcephaly and mental retardation, very few gross malformations were observed.[11] Similarly, no increased risk of leukemia was observed in children exposed to atomic radiation as embryos.[12] This was not so for those exposed as children and adults: they had a dramatic increase in leukemia risk, averaging from twenty to twenty-five times the expected norms.[13]

This type of data may reflect the hormesis phenomenon discussed in the last chapter or (as I believe) the dramatically increased mortality of children who received A-bomb radiation while they were in utero.[14] Recall that a massive period of social dislocation, starvation, and stress accompanied the bombings of Hiroshima and Nagasaki. We now know that embryos exposed in utero to diagnostic X radiation *are* at increased risk of developing leukemia compared to unirradiated offspring,[15] even though the X radiation used in such procedures is miniscule compared to that received by A-bomb mothers. It is findings such as these that underscore the vulnerability of developing embryonic systems to chemical and radiation disturbance.

THE CASE OF THE CHILD WITH NO ARMS OR LEGS

About ten years ago, I saw a migrant farmworker who had a son who lacked legs and arms entirely, except for tiny vestigial digits that jutted out directly from his shoulders. This wrenching defect, known as tetramelia (from the Greek for absence of four limbs), had previously been seen in infants whose mothers had taken the tranquilizer thalidomide during pregnancy. I was asked to review the condition and the boy's mother's work experience to determine if it was possible that any of the chemicals to which she was exposed could have caused the defect.

I found that the mother, who worked in a raisin grape operation in the Central Valley of California had had ample opportunity to be exposed to hazardous chemicals. The raisin grapes were routinely treated with sulfur and fungicidal chemicals intended to reduce rot. Among the fungicides she had been exposed to were captan and benomyl, two chemicals that were widely used at this time throughout California.

Captan bears a striking resemblance to thalidomide. It has the same phthalimide nucleus and many of the same structural features. But it had supposedly been tested for its teratogenicity (capacity to produce birth defects) by the manufacturer, Chevron Corporation, and found to be negative. A careful review of the literature — and a personal visit to Chevron's toxicology unit—convinced me that the "negative" findings were misinterpreted. In fact, the data showed that captan could produce birth defects in hamsters and was clearly capable of doing the same in rabbits and rats.

The literature on benomyl was noticeably deficient in this country. Although the chemical was a suspect teratogen, no published findings appeared in a literature search. However, a review of the world literature showed that Russian researchers were quite concerned about the possibility that benomyl was teratogenic for workers. They had found clear evidence of teratogenicity in their own studies, and issued warnings and reduced worker exposures accordingly.

The Environmental Protection Agency (EPA) as well as California's Department of Food and Agriculture had full files on both of these chemicals, but they are off limits to everyone except government personnel—and then only under conditions of strict confidentiality. What I did learn from these agencies is that both chemicals were under a "Rebuttable Presumption Against Registration" (RPAR), which meant that someone else was reviewing the data on toxicity. In 1988, captan was recalled—its toxicity was such that the EPA determined it could not be used safely. Among the most damning features was captan's genetic toxicity—and the data that showed it was an animal carcinogen.

This information came too late to help the farmworkers in California who had handled these chemicals daily. And it was little solace for the mother of the boy without arms or legs. The only hope for him was long-term care in an institution caring for people with major birth defects. Without resources of any kind, the mother asked for help first from the grower and then from the manufacturer. When none was forthcoming, she turned to the United Farmworkers Union (UFW). They advised her to sue.

What remained for me to do was to determine if the mother had been exposed to either or both of these chemicals and if that exposure could have caused the birth defects. A review of permits showed that substantial amounts of these chemicals had been used in the fields where she worked. She described how her clothes became caked with the dust and dirt from the fields and how she had had to wear a bandana to keep from breathing the dust. Since there wasn't water or any normal hygienic facilities, she got her liquid from eating the newly dusted grapes (even though that made her nauseous) and used the grape leaves for personal hygiene when she relieved herself. (The use of both captan and benomyl involves critical "reentry" rules that supposedly keep workers out of newly dusted fields for at least forty-eight hours. The field records in this case show that the workers went in the very next day after application.)

Then came the critical question: was this woman exposed during the critical period of development for her son's limb buds? The defense maintained that it was not possible that the limb abnormalities were caused by her exposure since she had stopped work early in her pregnancy because of morning sickness. But when I reviewed her work history, I found that she *had* worked during the first month of her pregnancy — in fact, through day 31. The limb buds for arms and legs start to form at the end of the third week of gestation. Their critical period is from about day 26 or so to the end of the seventh week. There was no doubt that she had been exposed.

Once this evidence was presented to the defense, the case was settled out of court. We cannot know if the farmworker got enough money to cover the institutional care for her child, or any for her own distress and devastation.

This child is one of the unfortunate victims of a system that has allowed literally thousands of mothers to be exposed to reproductive toxins. The extent of this exposure is presently unknown. What is known is that of the 70,000 plus chemicals currently in commerce, only 1,600 have been tested for their teratogenic capabilities. Nearly *half* have been found to be active in animal tests although less than fifty compounds have been found to be teratogenic or toxic to the developing human embryo.[16]

THE THALIDOMIDE TRAGEDY

Given the veritable sea of chemicals to which we are all potentially exposed, it is remarkable that more substances affecting mothers have not been found. The history of thalidomide provides a striking example of how even *one* mistake in letting such a chemical through the regulatory net can be tragically costly.

The tragedy of thalidomide was largely confined to Europe and Australia, thanks almost entirely to the efforts of Frances O. Kelsey, the science officer at the FDA who reviewed its application for use in the United States. Thalidomide had been marketed in Germany, England, and Australia in the late 1950s as a sedative to be used in the *last* trimester of pregnancy. It was a popular drug, because of its effectiveness in inducing sleep and its tranquilizing effects. Some women (estimates go as high as 100,000 or more) took the drug early in pregnancy because of its unproven effects as an antiemetic agent.

On September 12, 1960, the drug was submitted to the FDA for approval in the United States. At that time, any new drug could be cleared for marketing solely on the basis of safety claims. The agency had only sixty days to review the product and to notify the manufacturer if any deficiencies were found. Should the FDA fail to notify the applicant in time, the drug was automatically approved.

Kelsey's suspicions about thalidomide were piqued from the outset. She noted a multitude of deficiencies in the submitted safety records.[17] She asked for more information before allowing the approval process to go forward. By early 1961, it was evident that one of the side effects was potentially serious. In Britain, thalidomide had been found to cause a painful inflammation of the nerves of the legs and hands (peripheral neuritis) in some patients. The FDA recommended changes in the drug's warning label: it was to state that peripheral neuritis could occur — and that data were unavailable indicating the safety of its use in pregnancy.

While these side effects might have been glossed over by someone less scrupulous, Kelsey sent the materials back to the sponsor saying that the FDA could not approve the drug without further evidence of its safety. In mid-1961, all that stood between the U.S. public and a potential catastrophe were a handful of words on a warning label. Kelsey's problems with the warning label led to a series of communications with the sponsor that fortuitously delayed thalidomide's approval until its profound toxicity to the developing fetus was clear.

On November 30, 1961, the sponsor notified the FDA that the drug had been withdrawn from the market — but only in Germany — because of as yet unsubstantiated reports of birth defects. German researcher Wilhelm Lenz had just reported on more than *ninety* cases of limb abnormalities in Germany (another group was being uncovered in Australia) that appeared to be associated with maternal ingestion of thalidomide.[18] But other reports came into the agency, offering positive accounts of the experience of patients who had gotten relief from the drug — and had not had deformed children. (We now know that partial explanation for this discrepancy is that only a percentage of the women who took the drug between days 34 and 50 of gestation had offspring with some or all of the malformations associated with it.)

It was not until Kelsey and her colleague Dr. John Nestor received a letter from a concerned U.S. physician who had witnessed the German experience firsthand that action was taken to halt the introduction of thalidomide into the United States. The letter was from Dr. Helen Taussig, then a professor of pediatrics at Johns Hopkins University School of Medicine. Taussig had just returned from Germany and graphically described what really was happening. Thalidomide, it was clear, had diabolical potential as a teratogenic agent. On the strength of these findings,[19] Kelsey cancelled the registration proceedings for thalidomide.

In spite of the timely action of the FDA in suspending the permit for marketing the drug in the United States, it had permitted sixty investigators to have access to the drug for testing (presumably for its effectiveness in conditions other than pregnancy). Each had been warned in early December 1961 that thalidomide was associated with birth defects. Astonishingly, the FDA learned in early 1962 that the manufacturer had continued to distribute thalidomide to more than 1,200 physicians in the United States *without* approval. Also, according to Kelsey, the drug's sponsor (the manufacturer) made no effort to notify these physicians about possible birth defects until March 1962 when the FDA intervened, nor did the sponsor make any effort to recall the product from use.

Upon learning of this massive leak of thalidomide in the United States, the FDA sent investigators to visit virtually every one of the 1,200 physicians who had received thalidomide. According to Kelsey, many had incomplete records on patients who had received the drug. Some denied seeing or signing any agreement to use the drug only for investigational purposes or of being told that careful recordkeeping was mandatory for such investigational drugs.

As a result of this investigation, at least ten cases of birth defects were found among offspring of U.S. women who had been given thalidomide illegally, and seven more were found in children of mothers who obtained the drug abroad. This final tragedy revealed the manufacturer's duplicity and underscored the glaring loopholes in the FDA's regulatory machinery. Many thousands of additional cases were undoubtedly avoided by Kelsey's prompt and prudent action, but what if there had not been an alert official at the FDA?

The major impact of this saga was to provoke such public outrage that Congress mandated a wholesale review of the regulatory process that had come so close to passively acquiescing to the sale of this dangerous drug in the United States. This review led to reworking the laws governing the development and marketing of drugs in the United States. In 1962, Congress passed a spate of legislation that amended the Kefauver-Harris Food and Drug Act. In part, these amendments required the consent of human subjects in investigational use trials, mandated that all drugs be adequately tested in animals before being used in humans, and required that any drug shown to be a health hazard be removed immediately from the market. Prodded by the revelations in a series of hearings on the inadequacies of existing regulations, the FDA also modified its own regulations to require that all manufacturers compile and provide the FDA with accurate records of their experience with the product and that they report any and all adverse reactions promptly.

The thalidomide episode also pointed up the need for guidelines to assure that drugs were adequately tested for their safety during pregnancy. These guidelines were put in place in 1966 and require a three-tiered testing regime that includes (1) a study of general effects on reproductive performance and fertility, (2) a teratology study, and (3) a study that spans the period at the end of pregnancy and the early postnatal life of the newborn.

DRUG TERATOGENICITY

Of course, this system applied originally only to drugs that were developed for human, not veterinary use. And, even there, a positive teratogenicity test was not necessarily an impediment to marketing the product. All that was required was that the drug be categorized along a continuum (from grade A to D) of increasing teratogenicity. A separate category, identified as X, was set aside for drugs that had such high teratogenicity that the risk / benefit ratio exceeded even their prudent use. Thus isoniazid, which is critical for treating refractory cases of tuberculosis, is in use even though it has caused teratogenic reactions in some animal assays.[20]

Other drugs in commerce today, such as anticonvulsants such as phenobarbitol and the retin-A preparation for treating cystic acne, are on the border between D and X since they are potent teratogens. Drugs that are toxic to the fetus or are teratogenic are shown in Table 7-1.

Tretinoin (retin-A) in particular causes central nervous system defects in a high percentage (80 percent) of the affected offspring whose mothers take the drug during the first trimester. This product is so hazardous that the major manufacturer (Hoffmann-La Roche) has required that the treating physician not only ensure that the patient is not pregnant but that she is using an effective birth control agent. Nonetheless, the warnings for this anti–acne product have failed to stem fully the tide of serious birth defects in often young mothers.

Other drugs may be toxic to the developing fetus but not produce a specific morphologic change that qualifies it as a teratogen. For example, pyrrolizidine-containing drugs (the same chemical found in the plant genus *Senecio* that poisons cattle) are highly toxic to the developing liver.[22] Even simple aspirin is toxic to the blood–clotting system of the developing fetus and is contraindicated during the third trimester of pregnancy.

Teratology testing has now been extended to encompass pesticides that may be used on food products so that highly teratogenic agents may be identified before workers received undue exposure or there is a major consumer problem. One such pesticide was the ether-based pesticide manufactured by Rohm and Haas known as nitrofen. This pesticide proved to be so teratogenic (down to doses as low as 1 mg/kg) in animals that it cannot be used in California.

Other pesticides, such as chlordane, are remarkably toxic to fetuses. Even at low doses, chlordane interferes with lymphocyte function in mice exposed in utero.[23] This persistent

Compound	Adverse Effects	Likelihood of Adverse Effects from Typical Dosages
Alcohol	Fetal alcohol syndrome	Variable, depending on dose and intensity (e.g., binge drinking)
Alkylating agents such as cyclo-phosphomide and other anti-neoplastic drugs	Growth retardation; cleft palate; kidney malformations; heart defects; eye defects	10–50%
Antimetabolites (anticancer agents)	Neural tube defects; under-development of cerebrum; mal-formed extremities and digits; eye and ear malformations; malformed skull	7–75%
Cocaine	Central nervous sys-tem and gastro and genital-urinary de-formities; low birth weight and small head circumference	High; third trimester exposure highest
Coumadins (anticoagulants)	Cartilage deformi-ties; skeletal abnor-malities; atrophy of eyes; skull defects; CNS malformations; short arms; spasticity	15%
Diethylstilbestrol (DES) (antimis-carriage [sic] agent)	Clear cell vaginocar-cinoma; irregular menses; reduced pregnancy rates; increased preterm delivery; increased perinatal mortality and spontaneous abortion	0.1–0.14%

Table 7-1. Drugs Known to Be Teratogenic in Humans[21]

Compound	Adverse Effects	Likelihood of Adverse Effects from Typical Dosages
Disulfuram (antifungal)	Clubfoot; phoco- melia; loss of radial bones; fusion of vertebrae; tracheo- esophageal fistula	Unknown
Heparin (anticoagulant)	Bleeding	12.5%
Lithium car- bonate (bipolar depression; anticonvulsant)	Heart and vessel abnormalities; hydrocephalus; spina bifida and meningomyelocele; strabismus; wide mouth; large fon- tanels; abnormal ears; finger and nail abnormalities; microcephaly and mental retardation; growth deficiency; cleft lip and/or palate; heart abnor- malities; neuro- blastoma	10%
Tetracycline (antibiotic)	Yellow, gray- brown, or brown- stained teeth	50%
Thalidomide (sedative)	Limb phocomelia; amelia; congenital heart defects; kid- ney and testes ab- normality; deafness; absent or small ears	2–40%

Table 7-1 cont'd. Drugs Known to Be Teratogenic in Humans[21]

Compound	Adverse Effects	Likelihood of Adverse Effects from Typical Dosages
Toxidone (trimethadione) (anti-inflam-matory)	Growth retardation; heart abnormalities; cleft palate and/or lip; dysmorphic face and/or ears; mental retardation; tracheo-esophageal fistula	83%
Tretinoin (retinoic acid) (anti-acne drug)	Deformities of skull, ears, heart, limbs, liver; hydro- and microcephalus; heart defects; spon-taneous abortion	45%
Valproic acid (antiseizure)	Lumbrosacral spina bifida; CNS defects; microcephaly; heart defects	1.2%

Table 7-1 cont'd. Drugs Known to Be Teratogenic in Humans[21]

pesticide is also highly cytotoxic to the "natural killer" cells responsible for front-line defense against cancer cells.

The testing programs, of course, do not encompass drugs that are illegal or are intentionally abused, such as cocaine, heroin, alcohol, caffeine, nicotine, and marijuana. Some of these agents, notably cocaine, have disastrous effects on the developing fetus. Prematurity, bleeding into the brain, disturbed neural development, low-head circumference, and hyperactivity are all consequences of cocaine or "crack" abuse. Marijuana use, on the other hand, has either been found to have no adverse effect on fetal development or to cause only minor delays in development and/or lower than average birth weights. But heavy exposure to virtually any drug during pregnancy (for instance, as a result of attempted suicide) has been associated with higher than expected incidences of stillbirths, mild growth retardation, and modest increments in behavioral abnormalities.[24]

A real villain, however, is tobacco smoke. Long associated with low birth weight, tobacco smoke has recently received increasing attention as a possible teratogen and transplacental carcinogen. Researchers who exposed pregnant mice to tobacco smoke for as little as one hour have found that the exposed fetuses had dramatically higher rates of chromosome breaks than the controls.[25] Even smokeless tobacco has been found to inhibit the critical steps in bone formation in experimental studies of the mouse,[26] suggesting that any tobacco use in pregnancy could cause fetal malformations or developmental delay.

INDUSTRIAL TERATOGENESIS

Unfortunately, such testing does not apply equally to industrial chemicals or metals. In a review I did in the late 1970s, I found that there was evidence that many metals were teratogenic.[27] Some of those in widest commerce include mercury, lead, arsenic, cadmium, aluminum, selenium, and lithium. Many of these metals plus others that are teratogenic are found in the electronics industry, which uses rare earths such as indium and gallium arsenide to manufacture microchips.

Among the industrial metals, lead stands out because of its

remarkable toxicity for the central nervous system. At low levels of lead in the environment, social class appears to further aggravate its adverse effects. By the time lower-socio-economic-class infants with even modestly low levels of lead in their blood (6 to 7 micrograms per 100 milliliters) reach the age of 2, they are behind their higher socioeconomic counterparts with comparable levels of lead exposure. By the time blood lead levels reach 10 micrograms per deciliter (well below the figure currently permissible), even advantaged children start showing deficits in performance.[28] Early on, much of this blood lead reflects the transplacental movement of lead from the mother to her developing fetus. Only later, after the age of 1, does environmental exposure through pica (eating chips of paint with lead in them) or other behaviors become important.

The most intensive studies of teratogenic effects of heavy metals have been conducted in Scandinavia. Researchers in Sweden found adverse effects on the reproductive ability of women who lived close to or worked in smelters using arsenic and lead.[29] These effects included increases in spontaneous abortions, low birth weight and birth defects. However, similar studies performed among women who lived near petrochemical industries in Sweden did not find similar adverse effects, although a group of women who worked in one of the plants had six times the normal miscarriage rate.[30]

Heavy metals such as lead and cadmium may only cross the placenta with difficulty, but once across they can disrupt the normal balance of minerals needed for normal growth and development. When the mother is exposed to high levels of these metals, serious impairment of fetal development often leading to miscarriage, can occur. At lower levels, experimental findings indicate that cadmium is a behavioral teratogen.[31]

Solvents can also traverse the placenta and disrupt the developing nervous system. Finnish mothers who had children with central nervous system defects such as open spinal cord (spina bifida) were four times more likely to have been exposed to low levels of solvents during their pregnancies than were mothers of infants who were free of such defects.[32] A similar ratio was observed for the development of a complication of pregnancy called preeclampsia. U.S. women with solvent exposure roughly analogous to those of their Finnish counterparts were four times as likely to have a hypertension-associated disorder of pregnancy than were those without such exposure.[33]

Findings such as these underscore the likelihood that the most severe reproductive effects are likely to be found among women who work with industrial metals, solvents, or other chemicals or pesticides with potent teratogenicity since teratogens, unlike most (if not all) carcinogens, act above a certain threshold dose. Below that dose, no teratogenic effects are to be expected, although subteratogenic effects such as behavioral damage may be seen.

Consider, for example, alcohol as a model. Fetal exposure to alcohol can produce overt birth defects (dysmorphology) as well as profound developmental disturbances and behavioral disorders at high doses (more than four to six drinks per day).[34] At lower doses (down to even one or two drinks daily), alcohol or any of its metabolites that reach the fetus can cause deficits in attention span and neurological and motor development.[35] Reflex times in particular appear to be delayed by experimental alcohol exposure during pregnancy in mice. These and the observed defects in humans are best explained by alcohol's direct inhibition of DNA synthesis in the developing nerve cells in the brain.[36] These effects appear to be highly specific for ethanol alcohol.

Parallel studies that have looked for neurobehavioral effects in the offspring of mothers exposed in their workplaces to a wide range of solvents such as methyl ethyl ketone, trichloroethylene, or toluene have generally come up empty-handed.[37] In spite of these largely negative results, many industrial chemicals remain untested for their reproductive toxicity, particularly in the area of neurotoxicity. The glycol ethers are strong candidates as reproductive toxins that could affect the normal development of the fetal brain. The sulfanilamide tragedy of the 1930s, which resulted in neurological damage to more than a hundred children, was the result of putting this potent antibiotic in a solution of diethyl glycol and feeding it to infants. Perhaps surprisingly in view of its profound toxicity to the reproductive organs, derivatives of ethylene glycol have been found to have little overt malformation-inducing potential.[38]

POLYCHLORINATED BIPHENYLS
AS POTENT DEVELOPMENTAL TOXINS

As we have seen, Polychlorinated biphenyls (PCBs) were the chemicals that precipitated the environmental concerns that led to the Toxic Substance Control Act of 1976. Their virtual global use as transformer fluids, dye ingredients, and ink components ensured their widespread contamination potential. I remember a prophetic meeting in 1968 with University of California scientist Robert Riesborough after he returned from a pioneering trip to the Antarctic. I had just finished testifying at the California legislature about the dangers of DDT, and Riesborough wanted to let me in on what was then a brand new discovery. "PCBs are going to make DDT look like pablum," he said. "They're in every penguin egg in the Antarctic — and they're just tearing up the ecosystem." In fact, PCBs are much more persistent in ocean water than was the earlier contaminant, DDT.[39] Riesborough has been among the first to discover the phenomenon of eggshell thinning as a result of the reproductive toxicity of PCBs and to document the global reach of its impact on wildlife.[40] From the California pelican to the Antarctic skua, the predatory birds of the world were being slowly poisoned into oblivion. According to a recent review, by 1972, PCBs had been found in at least trace quantities "in virtually every living species and in every stretch of land and water examined."[41]

What we did not realize then was the almost universal reproductive toxicity of PCBs. PCBs proved capable of widespread damage to ecosystems because of their persistence, fat solubility, and ability to "bioaccumulate" as they entered the food chain. As one species preys upon another, the molecules contained in the "lower" prey animal tend to accumulate in the "higher" predator. Thus, the livers of insect-eating birds may contain only 1 ppm, while meat-eating kestrels, which feed higher on the food chain, have an average of 9 ppm.[42] The point at which reproductive toxicity occurs in the wild is about 10 ppm, although primates are more sensitive.[43] For birds, deformities in surviving chicks begin to occur when PCBs reach 10 to 15 ppm.[44] These data, unfortunately, came too late to forestall the first human tragedies with PCB contamination.

While the very first data on wildlife damage and malformations in birds were being accumulated, some 1,600 people in Kyushu in northern Japan consumed rice oil that was contaminated during its refining process with PCBs at a level of at least 1,000 ppm. (As little as 5 ppm of PCBs in the diet for seven months virtually obliterated the reproductive capacity of Rhesus monkeys.[45]) The rice oil apparently became contaminated when a heat transfer pipe containing kanechlor 400 leaked directly into the rice oil preparation. Among 1,200 patients followed prospectively, twenty-two died within five years and several infants were stillborn. Many adults developed severe acne and liver damage, nine died of cancer, and virtually all children had serious acne-like lesions and cysts.[46]

The most dramatic effects of the contamination were seen in offspring of women who had used the rice oil. The disease syndrome seen in the infants was called Yusho or rice oil disease. Infants characteristically were growth retarded and showed a dark brown pigmentation of the skin and mucosal membranes. Many newborns already had erupted teeth, and their gums were swollen and disfigured. PCBs were found in the skin and fat of the most severely affected newborns, clear-cut evidence of the transplacental movement of PCBs from the mother.

Unfortunately, the warnings of this tragic episode were lost for almost a decade. It took an even more extensive toxic epidemic in 1979 to demonstrate the extent of human health damage that could be caused by PCBs. The second incident occurred in Taiwan in a fashion that eerily mirrored the first episode. Beginning in May 1979, first 122 pupils and staff at a school for the blind and then 85 workers at a shoe factory developed florid skin eruptions and acne. Then, in late 1979, within a few weeks of each other, babies were born with hyperpigmentation and fully erupted teeth. Again, mothers were found to have ingested PCB-contaminated oil, this time from an adulterated rice bran extract. Twenty-one percent of their offspring died as a result of pneumonia, bronchitis, sepsis, and prematurity.[47] These severe effects have been attributed in part to the heavier contamination of the Taiwanese oil with PCBs and more toxic furans. (Some of the furans involved in the Taiwan contamination have appreciably more developmental toxicity than do the PCBs, dose for dose).[48] Of the 2,060 people exposed to the oil, twenty-four died within four years. Again, many of those who died had symptoms of liver damage.

It was clear from these episodes, if not from the "experiments" conducted on literally thousands of organisms in the wild, that PCBs have potent toxicity for the developing embryo. In humans, virtually every child begins life after having been exposed to PCBs in utero.[49] While these effects are rarely visible except in circumstances as extreme as those in Japan and Taiwan, no one can discount subtle effects of this potent toxic substance on our developing immune systems and liver function. In instances where workers have been exposed to higher amounts (measured in the hundreds of parts per million), immunological abnormalities[50] and raised serum enzymes indicative of liver damage have been seen.[51]

For the rest of us, the danger is that we will continue to underestimate the toxicity of PCBs for the most sensitive members of our population — pregnant women and their fetuses. This is likely because the acute toxicity of PCBs is in fact remarkably low. Common environmental exposures do not give rise to symptoms, and most healthy adults who had body burdens of PCBs at background levels have little or no visible signs of intoxication.

This halcyon picture blurs quickly when careful toxicological studies are made of populations with known exposure to PCBs. People with higher than normal levels of PCBs have had dramatic reproductive problems: men have lower sperm motility; women have higher than expected miscarriage rates; infants are delivered prematurely; and toxemia of pregnancy is elevated.[52] In other instances of high PCB exposure (usually among workers), researchers commonly find that the workers' microsomal detoxification systems have been stimulated into working overtime.[53]

If this reaction were to occur at lower levels of PCB exposure, it would have potentially far-reaching effects. A high level of microsomal enzyme activity would not only throw off all of the predicted rates at which we break down prescription drugs, but would put many of us at higher risk of carcinogenesis since we would be activating more carcinogens (see Chapter 4).

Given the enormous load of PCBs already in the ecosystem, and our inability to rapidly dispose of the millions of pounds of residual PCB compounds either in storage or in use, this chemical still casts a specter over our lives — and over those of our children.

TRANSPLACENTAL CARCINOGENESIS

At the extreme of chemical-induced damage are childhood tumors that result from parental exposure to carcinogenic chemicals. As we have already seen with DES, movement of carcinogenic chemicals across the placental barrier is both possible and potentially highly disruptive of normal organogenesis. DES was both a teratogen and a transplacental carcinogen, with the fetus converting this potent estrogenic chemical into a potent carcinogen.[54] Other teratogens, however, lack carcinogenic activity, and it is likely that the two properties (teratogenicity and carcinogenicity) are biologically distinct.

A partial listing of carcinogens that can reach the human embryo and fetus transplacentally includes at least the following chemicals and viral agents:

Chemical Group	Examples
Polycyclic hydrocarbons	7,12-dimethylbenz(a)anthracene; benzo(a)pyrene; 3-methylcholanthrene
Cytotoxic drugs	Antitumor alkylating agents; urethan; methyl and ethyl methansulfonate
Toxins	Aflatoxins
N-nitroso compounds	14-C-dimethylnitrosamine; 14-C-N-nitrosomethyl urea; nitrosohexamethyleneimine; diprophylnitrosamine; dibutylnitrosamine
Miscellaneous compounds	3-hydroxyxanthene; O-aminazotoluene; methylazoxy methanol
Viruses	HTLV-1; hepatitis B

Table 7-2. Carcinogens that Can Reach the Developing Human Fetus Transplacentally.[55]

Other chemicals not listed here, however, are converted to their active forms by the mother and then transmitted to the fetus. Ethylnitrosourea (ENU), a chemical intermediate, is a classic example. After maternal exposure (in rats especially), the molecule is metabolized and transmitted across the placenta. If exposure takes place late in pregnancy, when substantial cell division and growth are occurring in the central nervous system, even minute amounts of this chemical given to the mother in a single intravenous injection can result in nervous system tumors in the offspring.[56]

Genetic factors influence the carcinogenicity of ENU dramatically. In mice, a group of genes (the H-2 complex) associated with tissue compatibility, immune responsiveness, and glucose metabolism has a major effect on the number of tumors produced after pregnant mice are given ENU. When the mice have a particular genetic makeup, they are at increased risk of developing tumors of the intestine and lungs—an effect that was duplicated by injecting the mice with stress hormones.[57]

Some agents that induce cancer in adults appear to be less effective when delivered across the placenta.[58] These include chemicals (such as vinyl chloride and nitrosomethylurethane) that require activation to their final potent form, a step the fetus may be incapable of doing.

Viruses can also traverse the placenta. This is a tragic reality for the AIDS virus where about 40 percent of infected mothers show up with the virus in their own blood—and is also true for the hepatitis B virus. Hepatitus B virus was found in the mothers of more than 96 percent of children who developed an otherwise rare childhood liver cancer in Taiwan.[59] (The remaining 4 percent of the children had fathers who were infected with this virus.) We now recognize the hepatitus B virus as the first proven human transplacental carcinogen.

These data provide strong evidence for the vulnerability of children to chemically and virally transmitted carcinogenesis and may yet explain the proportion of childhood cancers that to date has eluded our best epidemiological minds. At least one of the conundrums is the uncertainty of latency effects since tumors may appear decades after childhood exposure (as with radiation of the thymus). In the case of chemical carcinogenesis, it is also likely that one or more of the events associated with sexual maturation serves as a biochemical trigger for latent cancer cells induced transplacentally. This certainly appears to be the case for DES carcinogenesis. One cancer type in particular, namely, osteogenic sarcoma, occurs mainly between the ages of 15 and 25. This tumor is considered to be a likely result of a transplacental carcinogen.[60]

COMMENT

The fetus has been revealed to us as an exquisitely vulnerable being in a chemical world. Metals such as lead and cadmium, carcinogens such as ethylnitrosurea and DES, and viruses such as hepatitis B find the fetus an easy target. The placenta did not evolve as a gating system that can distinguish between toxic and nontoxic synthetic products. In fact, the form of placenta on which primates rely (called hemochorial) provides the least separation of maternal and fetal systems of any among placental mammals. It is no surprise that cigarette smoke components traverse this thin barrier, nor that the chemicals that contaminate urban air and water do the same. What is most remarkable is that with all of the attention to the status of the embryo as an entity worthy of our protection — and I am thinking here especially of the right-to-life groups — no one has spoken out for the wanted embryos and fetuses that are destined to run a chemical gauntlet throughout development. This gauntlet is likely to be particularly taxing for those among us who are most heavily exposed to chemical contaminants: the farmworker exposed to pesticides, the poor mother exposed to lead-contaminated water, the families exposed to industrial wastes from a Superfund site. *Their* embryos and fetuses deserve our protection from such contamination. The more we know, the more we realize how much of developmental opportunity can be compromised, or, in the case of miscarriage and fatal forms of childhood cancer, truncated entirely, by mothers' exposure during pregnancy to hazardous chemicals.

While our founding fathers could not have conceived how far their revolution would take us toward degradation of our environment, the inference that any intelligent person draws from the "equal protection clause" of the Fourteenth Amendment is that all persons (and persons to be) are deserving of equal protection from harms. In the late twentieth century United States, the most pervasive of such harms must certainly be those that emanate from an unclean environment. Protecting our children, and the embryos and fetuses that precede them, from contaminants is a minimal claim that all members of the next generation can make on each of us.

To accomplish this successfully may also require a new understanding of "biocompatibility" and the assumptions that go with it. "Biocompatible" substances have long been sought among chemicals that could be used for prosthetic devices. The underlying system of thought that drove this search was the belief that chemical nonreactivity could be equated with biological nonreactivity. However, even some of the most presumptively biocompatible substances, such as the silicones, have been reported to have deleterious effects on the developing fetus.[61]

To fully understand how seemingly nonreactive chemicals may exert toxic effects, it is necessary to review the history and use of a representative class of such substances.

CHAPTER EIGHT

Myth 6:

"Nonreactive" chemicals lack adverse effects

IN CHAPTER 4 WE EXPLORED CIRCUMSTANCES IN WHICH THE BODY can be its own worst enemy. One way it subverts its own well-being is by occasionally converting toxic substances into more potent toxicants or carcinogens. This capacity also exists for chemicals that are virtually nontoxic substances. The body usually copes with natural chemicals well, but some, such as the extract from poison oak or ivy, cause damage only *because* the body reacts to them.

IMMUNOLOGICAL REACTIVITY

There is another way the body subverts its own well-being. In reacting to foreign substances, the body's defenses some-times *overreact*, engaging in futile attempts to engulf and de-stroy invading organisms or responding so aggressively that

149

the response itself is dangerous. The latter circumstances can occur during the immune response to some invading organisms or antigens, giving rise to states of hypersensitivity that can be just annoying or can generate organ damage or systemic imbalance. (Anyone with a sensitivity to poison oak or ivy can attest to the disturbing effects of "contact hypersensitivity" from misdirected immunity.) Allergies are another form of this reaction. So is the reaction to certain chemicals such as penicillin. In this case, the overreaction (called anaphylactic shock) can sometimes be fatal.

This observation is critical in distinguishing "nontoxic" from "nonreactive": penicillin is an extremely nontoxic chemical. It will not produce cancer even when given in amounts at or above 2 percent of body weight—grams of the stuff can be given without adverse effect in most persons. But if a person has developed an immunological sensitivity to penicillin, even a trace amount of this highly antigenic material injected into a muscle can produce a lethal immunologic reaction.[1]

If the body is repeatedly stimulated by a substance, a state of chronic overstimulation of the immune system can occur. When there are no invaders, the immune system may attack the body's own organs, leading to autoimmune diseases.

The Immune System

To understand these diverse reactions, it is necessary to have a basic understanding of the functions of the immune system. When bacteria, viruses, or certain chemicals enter the body, they encounter a system of "first-line defenders" in the form of cells that scavenge the offending agent. In normal circumstances, this scavenging operation is conducted by specialized cells in the blood and tissues called macrophages (Greek for "large eaters").

The macrophages break down the agent into antigenic chemical forms that specialized white blood cells can deal with. In the case of bacteria or other pathogens, these cells are usually B lymphocytes which can make antibodies. In rarer circumstances, where tissue or viral antigens are involved, they may be T lymphocytes, which can carry out cell-mediated killing actions. Cell-mediated immunity destroys incompatible tissue grafts. It is part of the system that is thought to defend the body against tumor cells. Other cells may assist the immune functions of T cells (so-called helper cells) or suppress them (so-called suppressor cells). A final cadre of cells termed natural killer or NK cells appear to patrol the body and can carry out more nonspecific cell-killing activities without having first to be activated by macrophage processing.

Under normal circumstances, so-called cytotoxic or cell-killing T cells tolerate the body's own cells, leading to a state of peaceful coexistence. However, sometimes this self-recognition system fails, and T cells attack the body's own constituents. This reaction is called autoimmunity.

In addition to this simplified scheme of classical immunity, an inflammatory reaction involving other white blood cells can occur. After a first wave of attack by a kind of white blood cell called the polymorphonuclear leukocyte (because of its multilobed nucleus), a chronic reaction can set in, in which a second team of white blood cells that includes macrophages, lymphocytes, and plasma cells, plus fibroblast cells that make the collagen and elastin components of scar tissue. This second tier of defenders attempts to wall off or contain a site of irritation, often forming a near-impervious capsule in the process.

When this whole system works, it is a commando's dream of a coordinated search-and-destroy operation, with the macrophages seeking out the offending substance and the backup white blood cells pouring on the fire power with destructive enzymes and antibodies that mop up and decimate the presumed enemy. But what happens when the targeted "enemy" is literally indestructible?

Such a circumstance occurs when macrophages encounter an organism such as the bacterium that causes tuberculosis: The outer membrane of the tubercle bacillus has a waxy coat that defies digestion by intracellular enzymes. When confronted with these bacteria, the macrophage goes a little berserk. First one, then many macrophages fuse together, forming a "giant cell" or epithelioid cell that may eventually contain the nuclei of as many as fifty to a hundred macrophages. In turn, the fibroblasts proliferate around the growing epicenter of failed containment as if to wall in the whole mass of giant cells and white blood cells with their ingested (but indigestible) contents. This lesion, known to pathologists as a granuloma, resembles an ancient walled city, with layer upon layer of protective cells.

Some granulomas can grow unchecked until they cause serious tissue damage by displacing normal tissue and releasing destructive enzymes into the surrounding body cavities. For diseases such as TB and a form of viral inflammation of the brain in rodents called lymphochoriomeningitis (or LCM), chronic inflammatory and immunological reactions cause most of the damage—not the organisms themselves. Experiments in mice have shown that if the mice are stripped of their immune systems before being infected with the LCM virus, the virus grows in their brains—but the mice stay well. If the immune system is reinstated, the mice sicken and die!

AUTOIMMUNE DISORDERS

Chronic insults can set off false alarms in the immune system throughout the body, activating immune responses to real or imagined enemies in a kind of cellular paranoia. These exaggerated reactions can lead to the self-destructive disease processes of an autoimmune reaction. Autoimmune diseases can be activated by chemicals called *adjuvants* in concert with antigens that mimic similar substances in the body. Adjuvants are any chemical that resists the body's efforts to tear antigens down and take them away, thereby providing a constant stimulus to the immune system's response.

Many human diseases arise because of such a self-directed immunologic attack against the body's own cells. A common group of these autoimmune diseases are called collagen-vascular diseases because the targets of the misguided immune system cells are the body's connective tissue and/or the blood vessels that course through it. (These disorders are also called immune diseases of connective tissue or mixed connective tissue disease.)

Rheumatoid arthritis is one such disorder that has a clear-cut autoimmune basis. So does the mixed connective tissue disease known as scleroderma. In scleroderma, the skin becomes almost rock hard as the result of contractures and collagen tightening. Other disorders in this class are Sjögren's syndrome, polymyositis, and dermatomyositis. Almost all of the symptoms of these diseases can be created by combining suitable antigens with adjuvants and injecting the mixture into a spot (such as the foot pads of rodents or guinea pigs) where the mixture becomes a chronic stimulus to the immune system.

All of these disease complexes share a common origin in the overreaction of the immune system. Since an exaggerated response can be provoked by any chemical that the immune response defines as an antigen, such chemicals need not be toxic in and of themselves. Other chemicals need only serve as *adjuvants* (without being antigenic themselves) to goad the body into mounting a profoundly damaging reaction. And some chemicals may provoke such a reaction by binding with other chemicals, such as blood proteins, and thereby altering their antigenicity; or by serving as haptens whereby they become antigenic by linking with surface proteins.

This certainly suggests that some otherwise nontoxic chemicals or agents may produce magnified or unpredictable pathological effects. To the extent that the body magnifies and hyperreacts to the substance in question, the response can appear to be out of synch with the maxims of the dose-response relationship or the *apparent* nontoxicity of a substance as measured in isolated laboratory experiments.

A classic example is a protein purified from egg white called ovalbumin. At very low doses this otherwise innocuous chemical (it is, after all, part of many morning breakfasts) can provoke an immune reaction in rabbits. If even smaller doses of the chemical are then injected directly into the space between the rabbit's joints, it will develop full-blown arthritis that mimics human rheumatoid arthritis.[2] No arthritis occurs in rabbits with joint injections but no prior sensitization.

DOCTRINE AND DOGMA

As noted, the body's unexpected and unpredictable reactions to some substances bely some of the traditional maxims of toxicology. Among these are the conviction that toxicity only occurs where there are highly reactive chemical constituents that interact directly with the body's proteins or genetic material. Another corollary is that one can predict toxicity from the structure of the molecule in question. It may be that some of these maxims have taken on the aura of dogma, limiting appreciation of the more subtle forms of toxic responses.

As I will attempt to illustrate in this chapter, a full appreciation of toxicological principles must include an understanding of how the body can intensify the toxicity of certain chemicals. (We have already seen how the body can convert otherwise innocuous appearing chemicals into extremely hazardous substances.)

SILICONES AS A CASE STUDY

The silicones may well be one such group of chemicals. Silicone was developed in the early 1940s as a kind of laboratory artifact with no initial use. It is made from the element silicon, which has the same electron configuration as carbon. This means that silicon has four sites available for linking with other molecules such as hydrogen, oxygen, and carbon itself. Like carbon, silicon can be used to make long chains of end-to-end bonded molecules. Silicone is constructed as one such molecule. It is a polymer (a long-chain molecule of repeating units with the same structures) of silicon dioxide (SiO_2). It is flanked by two methyl groups that also form the terminus of the long chain (see Figure 8–1).

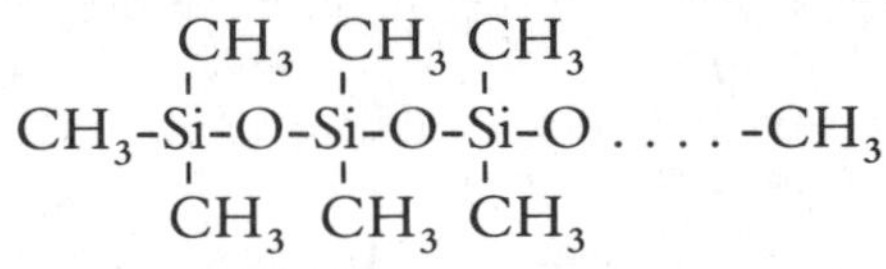

$$CH_3\text{-}Si\text{-}O\text{-}Si\text{-}O\text{-}Si\text{-}O \ldots \text{-}CH_3$$

with CH_3 groups above and below each Si.

Figure 8–1. Dimethylpolysiloxane

One of the more remarkable things about silicone is that it has very little chemical reactivity since all of the potential reaction sites on the silicon atom are conveniently occupied by stable atoms. This lack of reactivity is all the more remarkable since the backbone of the long polymer chain is silicon dioxide, which forms the nucleus for silica. Silica forms highly toxic irritating and lung-damaging crystals and may combine with other minerals to form silicates. Like crystalline silica, the

154

silicates can cause chronic inflammation that can produce nodules and fibrosis in the lungs.[3]

By the 1930s, no one would dream of *intentionally* putting raw silica into the human body because silica dust had been shown to cause acute illness and death or a chronic lung-damaging disease known as silicosis when the dust was breathed.[4] When inhaled into the body, its effects can last almost indefinitely.[5] When silicon dioxide in the form of crystalline silicon is injected into the body, it stimulates a florid inflammatory response. It is so potent an inflammatory agent that many laboratories use it as a "booster" or adjuvant to provoke the most massive immunologic response possible in test animals.

But in silicone, the reasoning apparently went, all of the potentially toxic atoms of silicon dioxide (SiO_2) would be shielded from any biological—and most chemical—activity by the presence of the two methyl (CH_3) groups. It was believed that any silica that might be produced would require the unlikely biological activity of macrophages that could convert silicone back into its monomeric state. But it proved unnecessary to invoke a remote biological phenomenon to explain the silicalike reactions of some recipients of breast implants. The Food and Drug Administration (FDA) has since found that silicone breast implants were intentionally adulterated with silica that was added as a filler in the envelope to change the properties of the silicone in the eslastomer envelope.[6]

When first developed, silicone was remarkable for its ability to withstand strong acids and other highly reactive chemicals. In spite of these chemical properties, researchers saw no immediate medical applications. In the 1940s, Dow Chemical Company acquired the patent rights and gave them to an independent subsidiary formed between Dow and the Corning Glass Corporation, the Dow-Corning Corporation of Midland, Michigan. (Corning had the most expertise in the world in dealing with silica, the basic ingredient of glass.)

In the early 1950s, Dow-Corning looked for industrial applications for silicone. It found widespread use as a caulking material (bathtub caulk is commonly made from silicone), glue, defoamer, lubricant, and oil for high-performance machinery and optical equipment. (Today, almost all syringe needles are given a thin coating of silicone to ease the delivery of inject-able drugs such as insulin.)

Silicones have been created as thin, transparent oils; as vis-cous fluids; as greases; and as rubberlike solids (feats obtained by proprietary chemical tricks of cross-linking and polymeri-zation). Some of the silicones that are widely used in industry for their defoaming action have entered our pharmacopeia as Dimethicone, the antigas ingredient in Di-Gel and other ant-acid combination products.

Infant pacifiers and even some children's toys have silicone parts. Its most famous incarnation may have been Silly Putty, an oozing, semisolid opaque material sold in a plastic egg. (Silly Putty has been the bane of many a household for its tendency to lodge in hair and hard-to-reach places where it mysteriously assumes its liquid form.)

This property of silicone, to be at one time a solid and at another a fluid, is what chemists call a gel-sol mixture. Under pressure, gels become more fluid. And, as anyone who has made Jello can attest, when cooled, gel—sols become more solid. This remarkable property of silicone gels was not lost on the medical profession. It meant that even highly viscous silicone oils that were nearly completely "gelled" would be fluid enough to be injected when put under the pressure of a hypo-dermic needle. Once injected into the body, such oils would be expected to assume a quasi-solid consistency at body tem-perature and yet stay in place where injected because of the coherence of the gel.

These early observations led to appreciable interest in the medical community in applications that might benefit patients with serious malformations or diseases. In 1958, in part as a response to these concerns, Dow-Corning established a Center for Aid to Medical Research.

Although silicone oils were high on the list of possible ap-plications, they were not initially what the center took on. Un-der the direction of Dow-Corning researcher John Holden, the first medical applications involved silicone tubing. Holden was powerfully motivated to find a solution to what was then a fatal and intractable medical problem—hydrocephaly, the ac-cumulation of fluid on the brains of infants born with a form of open spine known as spina bifida. Without a means to drain the constantly produced spinal fluid, the brain of such infants was progressively compressed by the fluid, until it lost all function. As the father of such an infant, Holden took on as the center's first task the construction of a special tubing and valve that would shunt the spinal fluid that accumulated in the brain cavity of hydrocephalic infants into the spinal canal (where it normally flows).

While the first hydrocephalic shunt was developed too late to save his own child, Holden's invention has become a mainstay of the pediatric community's travails in dealing with hydrocephalic infants. And Dow-Corning scientists have since found a plethora of uses for the semisolid form of silicone. Among those that have been tried are silicone rubber tubing for blood and dialysis equipment and solid rubber silicone prostheses for joints and cartilage replacements. Unfortunately, not all of these applications have been fully successful: hydrocephalic shunts routinely become clogged and fail; patients on dialysis tubing have developed unusual systemic complications; and rubber silicone prostheses fragment and provoke mysterious systemic illnesses.

By the early 1960s, Dow-Corning realized the monetary potential for silicone in medicine and started a Medical Products Division. One of its earliest ventures—and probably its most catastrophic—was in response to the medical community's demand for an inert, biocompatible injectable fluid that could be used in plastic surgery.

For part of this period, silicone was used as an injectable fluid to replace or fill in damaged or aged tissue. The results were so uncertain, and the few adverse reactions so catastrophic, that one state (Nevada) banned injectible silicone outright in 1975, as the FDA did a year later (see below). Nonetheless, attempts to use this seemingly miraculous fluid for medical purposes continued unabated throughout its history.

Artificial Breasts

During the late 1950s and early 1960s, the idea for making a breast prosthesis with totally enclosed silicone fluid arose. The concept of a material that mimicked the softness, contour, and feel of a true breast appears to have veritably "lit up" in the mind of a Dow-Corning chemist. According to a personal contact who worked during those years in the Dow-Corning division that was devising little silicone socks to diffuse the glare of light bulbs, he was asked if he could build a seamless, balloonlike membrane that would be big enough to hold 200 or even 400 cubic centimeters, about the size of a flood lamp. Without initially knowing what this membrane was to be used for, he consented and used his metal molds to construct the first full-sized human breast prosthesis. Designs for the first implants were filed in 1963 and patented three years later by Dr. Thomas D. Cronin, who assigned the rights to Dow-Corning. Early versions of this breast implant were promoted in 1964 by the Storz Instrument Company in St. Louis, Missouri, as being designed "to approximate the softness, contour, and fluidlike mobility of the normal breast."

Ten years later, Dow-Corning moved to improve the feel of its prosthesis. According to my contact, if the fluid had to really mimic human breast tissue, it would be much too thin and might transfer mechanical stresses to the rim of the prosthesis, causing rupture. He warned Dow-Corning against marketing such a fluid, arguing instead for a thicker, more viscous one. He stressed that the thicker material would also be safer because it would not migrate between planes of tissue nor disperse throughout the body if the prosthesis happened to rupture. Unfortunately, his pleas fell on deaf ears, and he was reassigned to another division.[7]

According to the *New York Times,* an average of some 356 U.S. women receive a silicone implant *each day,* amounting to 2–3,000,000 U.S. women in the past three decades.[8] Named after their inventor, the Cronin implants used in the earliest years of silicone prostheses (from about 1963 to 1968) were designed to provide a means of implanting otherwise semifluid silicone in an enclosing bag or envelope. Although the original 1966 patent described these implants as being a totally implantable, nonreactive device to be placed within the human body, adequate safety testing or formal trials of the new device were never conducted. That is, neither the degree of nonreactivity nor the adequacy of the containment of the silicone had been established prior to its marketing. In fact, according to Tom Talcott, the scientist who helped design the first envelopes, they were never designed to hold *and retain* silicone. (The slow oozing of silicone gel from breast prostheses manufactured in the early 1970s is evident to any person who has held them in his hands: they are greasy to the touch. Yet, the company has maintained that it could not have known that a "bleed problem" existed in their product until after researchers outside their laboratories tested them. See below.)

You might well ask how such a potentially catastrophic omission could have occurred. First, the U.S. Patent Office which approved the first Cronin implant design in 1966 did not (and was not legally required to) test the safety of the device.[9] Second, as long as silicone was treated as a medical *device* and not a drug, it did not have to pass as rigorous a review as did pharmaceutical products that are intended to be absorbed into the human body. Never mind that silicone *would* be absorbed into the human body as an inevitable consequence of its passive flow through the prosthesis's surrounding envelope.

The first implants made during 1964–66 routinely had a Dacron net on the back wall "to permit tissue fixation and assure firm chest wall attachment."[10] This porous material sometimes generated an intense inflammatory response of its own. Often the reaction was so intense that scar tissue formed, making complete removal of the implant, should problems arise, a sometimes insurmountable surgical problem. And problems, such as rupture of the implant, a chronic inflammation leading to capsule formation around the prosthesis, or mysterious oozing of silicone into the body, occurred with disturbing regularity. So many serious difficulties plagued the early versions of the implant that the Dacron patches were removed in the early 70s and more resilient implants were sought in the early 80s.

Until 1978, no one outside Dow-Corning had reason to know (although many surgeons who handled the implants must have guessed) that the envelope "containing" the silicone of the breast prostheses was in fact *permeable* to the silicone fluid within it, allowing free silicone to enter the human body. In that year, three researchers reported finding free silicone molecules in the fibrous capsules that formed outside the walls of intact prostheses.[11]

The editors of the prestigious journal *Science* considered this finding sufficiently novel and important to warrant publication among other studies announcing new developments to the scientific world. It took another year before plastic surgeons were alerted to this development by two disgruntled fellow practitioners who noted that new breast implants left on a shelf covered with papers routinely stained the documents with an oily fluid. The fluid was silicone.[12]

During 1978 and 1979, a flood of articles appeared documenting that breast prostheses customarily and uniformly bled silicone through their envelopes.[13] This free silicone appeared to be associated with complications previously ascribed to chance, idiosyncratic reactions of the body. For example, some of these reactions included the formation of a hard, cellular capsule around the implant[14] and swelling of the lymph nodes that drained the areas in which the implants were made.[15] At about the same time as these articles were appearing, reports that solid silicone rubber prostheses could generate similar problems began to appear. In one, a patient who had received a silicone finger joint prosthesis had lymph nodes swell in his armpit.[16] In another instance, a patient nearly died after developing a high fever, diffuse arthritis, kidney failure, and infiltrates in her lungs following the leakage of silicone from a breast prosthesis.[17] When both of her breast prostheses were removed, the patient improved dramatically.

These apparent pathological reactions to what had previously been considered by the manufacturer to be a virtually nonreactive substance were cause for concern. This was especially so since the surgical community had devised its own means of resolving the problems of hard-capsule formation, a complication that in the early years afflicted an estimated 20 to 25 percent of patients (and still affects some 5 to 10 percent). This technique, euphemistically called closed capsulotomy, entailed applying firm pressure with both palms over the breast of a supine patient and rupturing the fibrous capsule — without, hopefully, bursting the sac of silicone within it at the same time. Unfortunately, this brute-force solution was not always successful and also caused the implant to rupture in many cases.[18] The abrupt spillage of silicone into the breast tissue was an immediate consequence.[19] Further migration of the fluid gel to regional lymph nodes was the inevitable secondary effect.[20]

In the following years, a plethora of reports appeared that documented the unanticipated movement of the gel through the tissue planes within the body. (Recall that at least one design engineer at Dow-Corning had unsuccessfully urged his superiors to redesign the gel to a firmer consistency so that it could not migrate should implant failure occur. According to biomedical products engineer Tom Talcott, his concerns were first voiced in 1974–75 and were overridden by his superiors at Dow-Corning in 1975–76, leading to his resignation in protest.)[21]

Were silicone the biologically inert and virtually nonreactive material touted by Dow-Corning scientists,[22] even the physical movement of the gel after a prosthesis failure — or plain leakage — might be tolerable. But something else was clearly happening. The body was *reacting* to the gel in surprising and disturbing ways.

As early as 1965, Israeli researchers had noted that the injection of dimethylpolysiloxane (a silicone gel) produced a so-called siliconoma.[23] These lumps of tissue contained the telltale "giant cells" of a chronic inflammatory reaction. The possibility that these lesions were, in fact, granulomas (masses of chronically inflamed tissue) was vehemently denied by researchers who worked closely with Dow-Corning.[24] By the early 1970s, the fact that silicone did produce granulomas in animals and in humans was indisputable[25] — leaving uncertainty as to the basis for Dow-Corning's continuing claims to the contrary. (At least a partial explanation was the Dow-Corning scientists' continuing disbelief that it was *their* silicone that was producing the problems — in spite of the fact that they were virtually the sole manufacturer of medical-grade silicones.)

The systemic reactions to the spills of silicone gel from failed implants[26] were remarkably similar to the occasionally disastrous consequences previously observed in women (and men) who received injections of pure or adulterated silicone oils. (No technique exists to remove silicone in its entirety once it escapes — or is intentionally placed — into the body.) Florid inflammatory reactions in topless waitresses receiving such injections were recorded as early as 1968,[27] and inflammation of the lungs was seen some fifteen years later.[28] The FDA Medical Device Panel believes that as many as 20,000 women (mostly in Nevada) have had such injections. The pathological consequences were considered so alarming to some members of the medical community and Nevada state legislators that Nevada promulgated a special statute in its Crimes Against Public Health and Safety statutes in 1975 expressly forbidding the injection of liquid silicone.[29]

However, the fact that a ruptured breast implant was *tanta-mount* to an injection appeared to have passed unnoticed until 1982 when the FDA declared that silicone breast prostheses posed "a potential unreasonable risk for injury"[30] and reclassified silicone-based mammary implants into a category of medical devices that required premarket testing prior to approval.

In 1983, the previously cited report appeared in the animal literature linking the presence of silicone implants in the uterus of animals to birth defects.[31] By 1984, it was evident that something very serious can happen when free silicone enters the body.[32]

Adverse Reactions to Silicone

We now know that in some persons the body responds to free silicone with an outpouring of cells and fibrous tissue indistinguishable from the granuloma inflammatory response described at the beginning of the chapter. When this reaction occurs in response to an implanted object, it is commonly called a foreign-body response. A foreign-body response was once thought to be a nonspecific reaction to any "indigestible" substance. Many researchers now believe that the foreign-body reaction is a kind of immunological defense marked by the appearance of the so-called giant cells that develop from the macrophages.

The recognition that a foreign-body granuloma might form from spilled silicone raised the alarming possibility that the body might develop an ongoing inflammatory response to the silicone that could lead to systemic organ damage and/or auto-immune reactions. Granulomas proved to be a catastrophic occurrence in some patients receiving dialysis carried in silicone tubing,[33] and appeared to be a serious complication of ruptured silicone breast implants particularly in nearby or distant lymph nodes.[34]

But why does silicone apparently elicit such a reaction in some people and not others? A possible answer is suggested by the apparent linkage between the natural history of silicosis and that of rheumatoid arthritis. Silicosis has long been the bane of miners whose work entailed boring through granitic rocks. Silicosis involves the proliferation of fibroblast cells in the lungs after exposure to silica-containing dusts. These cells then form collagen-containing nodules or granulomas of functionally useless tissue. Although recognized as early as 1700 by Bernardino Ramazzini (1633–1714),[35] workers were knowingly put at risk of developing this chronic and often fatal destruction of lung tissue as recently as the 1930s. The sandblasting that took place during the construction of the infamous Gauley Bridge tunnel in West Virginia between 1932 and 1934 eventually killed four hundred workers.

In 1970, a Japanese researcher noted a relationship between silicosis and rheumatoid arthritis.[36] Approximately 4 percent of silicotic patients also had this joint disease. Most interestingly, this association also works the other way: about 5 percent of patients who have rheumatoid arthritis show signs on X rays of lung fibrosis.[37] Evidence is now available that shows that these two diseases may have a common genetic predilection.[38] Is it possible that persons who have a propensity to hyperreact to silica are the ones at risk for developing chronic inflammation — and autoimmune disease?

This idea is reinforced by the observation made more than twenty years ago that some coal miners who develop forms of silicosis also develop scleroderma, the same type of autoimmune disease exhibited by some patients who are exposed to silicone.[39] The linkage between silica and silicone appears too real to be dismissed. At least this is the view of some researchers on the continent: a German researcher team believes it is plausible if not likely that some silicone is degraded to raw silicon dioxide (the basic component of silica) within the macrophages.[40] Of course, such an elaborate and difficult metabolic feat would not be necessary if some silica were present in breast implants, a fact acknowledged publicly by the FDA in 1988.[41] Still, we needed to understand how *pure* silicone elastomer can produce such profound immunological disturbances.

This understanding was provided by Nir Kossovsky, a biomaterials specialist at UCLA. Kossovsky showed that silicone interacts with blood proteins to form novel antigenic materials that could serve as the breeding place for a powerful immunological stimulus.[42] Through his experiments on guinea pigs and his observations of human patients and pathology material, Kossovsky believes that an autoimmune reaction can be set in motion by silicone-protein complexes, a reaction that is augmented by the adjuvant-like activity of silicone gel itself.[43]

"Human Adjuvant Disease"

The major ethical issue is whether this potentially disastrous reaction could have been anticipated and curtailed by appropriate regulatory actions. A related question hinges on the duty of the manufacturer to disclose these reactions as among the risks of its product. (This last duty was not fully exercised until 1985, when Dow Corning added immunological reactions to its list of adverse responses disclosed on the package insert.)

The adjuvant-like activity of silicone had been noted by Japanese researchers who followed the consequences of injections of often impure preparations of oils for cosmetic purposes. In 1964, H. Miyoshi and his colleagues described a form of chronic stimulation of the immune system after breast augmentation.[44] Within the next decade, additional reports appeared in the Japanese literature, each documenting cases in which injections of oils (most of them silicone based) led to the appearance of a syndrome that looked very much like an autoimmune mixed connective tissue disease. Because of its association with silicone, the Japanese called it an "adjuvant disease" in recipients. By 1976, researchers had begun to publish in the Western literature, documenting that breast augmentation with silicone-based fluids could cause autoimmune-like phenomena.[45]

Thereafter, researchers in the United States came across increasing numbers of cases where breast implant failures had led to the appearance of severe connective tissue disorders such as scleroderma and severe systemic illnesses that were highly reminiscent of autoimmune disorders.[46] Of course, with several hundred thousand breast implantations, it might just be coincidental that the cases of scleroderma or other connective tissue disorders occurred in patients who also received breast implants.

However, further reports from Japan documented a full spate of autoimmune phenomena occurring after injection of silicone oil, including gall bladder and liver disease; scleroderma; and Sjögren's syndrome, a classic autoimmune syndrome involving most of the major organs and connective tissue.[47]

It is now clear that regulatory action was forestalled by the lack of disclosure of data that could have linked silicone to adverse immunological reactions. The case that broke open this story was reported in 1983. This study describes a patient with the major hallmarks of human adjuvant disease: namely, severe weight loss, hair loss, liver dysfunction, swelling of the lymph nodes, granuloma formation, infiltrating lymphocytes in sensitive organs such as the thyroid, and generalized malaise and weakness.[48] What made this particular case dramatic was not only the time course of the appearance of symptoms shortly after the rupture of one of two implants, but the partial resolution of the most severe immune reactions almost immediately after the accessible silicone was removed from the patient's body.

This case is also remarkable because the patient took her case to court. As a result of the trial proceedings in federal court in San Francisco (I was an expert witness for the plaintiff), the jury concluded not only that the plaintiff's symptoms and disease state were most likely attributable to silicone, but found Dow-Corning Corporation guilty of fraud. Dow-Corning appealed and lost, and then appealed again. Before the final ruling could be reached by the superior court, Dow-Corning offered a settlement that locked in the reasons for the verdict and included a stipulation that experts who appeared in the trial could not reveal the basis for the initial verdict, including the rationale for the decision that Dow-Corning was guilty of fraud in marketing a defective product. The protective order that binds witnesses to secrecy is presently under congressional review.

In early 1989, the FDA acted to restrict the marketing of breast prostheses. Fully seven years after indicating its intention to reclassify silicone-based breast prostheses, the FDA completed its 1982 ruling and determined that the existence of "general controls" (that is, industry filing requirements and quality control methods) were inadequate to protect the public from possible health risks and formally reclassified breast implants based on silicone as a product that requires "premarket approval" (class III).[49] Ironically, the product that requires such approval is still being marketed while the "approval" process awaits the submission of adequate data demonstrating long-term safety. In early 1992, the FDA classified silicone breast implants as experimental devices and strictly limited their use.

Commentary

It is now evident that silicone and silica materials can stimulate the immune system to go after body constituents that are normally isolated from immunologic assault. The very inertness of the silicone may constitute the basis for this paradoxical toxicity: because of silicone's chemical stability, the body's detoxification system is unable to metabolize or excrete it. As a result, silicone remains as a chronic source of immune stimulation, probably both because of the complexes it forms with normal protein components of the blood and tissues and because of its adjuvant-like property.

This property had been recognized for years in the experimental medicine community. Researchers had shown that related oils were capable of provoking full-blown autoimmune disease including rheumatoid arthritis-like symptoms in animals who were injected with adjuvants containing appropriate antigens. The Japanese had warned the medical community beginning in the mid-1960s that humans were also vulnerable to developing adjuvant-induced autoimmune symptomatology after injections of oils that included some silicone preparations. But the Western medical community was lulled into complacency by the assurances of Dow-Corning and some of their own colleagues that U.S.-made silicones were a "pure," totally biocompatible product that could not and did not provoke immune or chronic inflammatory reactions. These assurances were clearly mistaken. To the extent that such reactions presage further immunological damage in some women, failing to disclose these risks was a clear oversight on the part of the manufacturers. The FDA was also negligent in delaying review and action on the implants' makeup, design and marketing. Instead, changes in mammary implant design were driven by internal corporate considerations, leading to a generation of first high and then "low bleed" implants. As a result, an indeterminate portion of some 2 million U.S. women carry implants of a material that in some genetically susceptible or otherwise reactive hosts may enter the body and provoke a life-limiting and debilitating illness.

Ironically, the standard toxicological testing required by the FDA failed to identify the constellation of adverse effects characteristic of an adjuvant-like substance. Unless initial pathology reports are carefully scrutinized for evidence of granulomas and related phenomena, a relatively inert substance such as silicone could *still* easily pass the battery of short-term and medium-range toxicity tests required under law. (More serious concerns about the possible carcinogenicity of silicone are still being reviewed.)

The lessons of the silicone story are still being pieced together. At a minimum they suggest that our understanding of toxicity must embrace immunologically provocative reactions, and that we pay attention not only to the structure of the material in question but to its reactivity in the human body.

CHAPTER NINE

Myth 7:

The body's own chemicals are safe

THE AXIOM OF TOXICOLOGY THAT EVERY SUBSTANCE CAN BE TOXIC if given in high enough amounts obscures a more subtle observation: some substances causing little or no intrinsic toxicity in the body can produce pathological effects when they are only slightly out of balance with their normal concentrations. Of even greater concern is the observation that some of the body's own chemicals have carcinogenic effects when given in or stimulated to higher than normal levels.

These unsettling facts have been known for several decades for one class of chemicals, the hormones. These chemical messengers in the blood are designed to stimulate a whole range of biological reactions in target tissues carrying appropriate receptors. Hormones carry out these functions at extremly low concentrations (measured in the parts per million). They do so in a dynamic state of chemical balance that is delicately maintained by feedback loops of hormone releasing, stimulating, or other chemical mediators working directly within the brain. Disturbing this exquisite balance can lead to disease (a plethora of out-of-control hormonal conditions exist, including Addison's disease and acromegaly, or gigantism). Recognizing the tremendous physiological power of hormones, major pharmaceutical companies have been developing analogs and synthetic versions in an attempt to influence the body's internal milieu. These efforts are not without risk, since (as we will see) virtually all hormones require a precise balance point to assure the well-being of their hosts.

When hormonal levels are disturbed, a cascade of physiological reactions commonly ensues. Among the most important are those that trigger cell division. When such division is prolonged, as can occur during hormonal stimulation, cancerous changes are a risk.

We have already seen that dioxins and other carcinogens owe much of their potent activity to their interaction with other biological molecules. One of these molecules is a hormone. For some species, only the female develops cancer following carcinogen exposure. For example, female rats rapidly develop liver cancer after being injected with dioxin although at similar doses males are unaffected. The evidence points to a female hormone, because if the ovary is removed, the carcinogenic effect in females disappears.[1] This phenomenon is now attributed to the cell-stimulating effects of estrogens: dioxin-induced tumors invariably occur in tissues that have estrogen receptors. Studies of this kind have linked carcinogenicity to cell proliferation in and of itself, since dividing cells are most at risk of making genetic mistakes.

This linkage is critical for understanding both the dynamics of cell systems in the body and comparable proliferative impacts on ecosystems. The core maxim here is that while a certain level of cell- or growth-stimulating substances is "good," and even necessary for tissues or ecosystems, when such substances are present in higher than normal amounts they may be hazardous.

Because so many new drugs are replicates of naturally occurring biological chemicals, understanding how hormones or other stimulating chemicals work is critical in planning their wise use. This has proven especially important in our understanding of androgenic steroids such as testosterone and estrogens.

This latter group, epitomized by the development of oral estrogens, is the focus of this chapter.

ESTROGENS AS A CASE STUDY

Even "natural" growth-stimulating substances can disrupt normal homeostasis and cause cancer. One substance currently undergoing intense scrutiny is estrogen. Although estrogens today are commonly given to post-menopausal women, the major vehicle for its entry into the human body has been birth control pills.

Historical Perspectives

In 1957, the first three-year field study of an oral prototype of modern-day contraceptives was started in Humacao, Puerto Rico.[2] Puerto Rico had been chosen since its population pressure was considered a "public health problem." Two groups of women were selected: the first 1,107 women were chosen because they resided in crowded urban areas with presumably high reproductive rates. A second group was "recruited" from women who came to an outpatient clinic for contraceptive aid and were comparably poor. The earliest patients were seen immediately after they had given birth when contraception was routinely offered. At no time were any of the women told they were part of an experiment or that the long-term effects of the use of this powerful hormonal preparation had not been established. No informed consent appears to have been solicited along with the recruitment other than to let word of mouth spread that a new pill was available that promised instant control of fertility.

The experiment was patently unethical, even by 1957 standards. (Today it would be impermissible to have even selected the population in the manner described, since federal guidelines require that any research risks or benefits be distributed equitably among demographic, racial, and income groups.[3])

The research team began testing with doses six to nine times higher than are used in modern birth control pills.[4] Part of the rationale was to approximate the hormone levels of the highest dose pill supplied by G. D. Searle, the manufacturer of Enovid, an early contraceptive preparation. Two years into the study, the doses were halved, corresponding to Searle's 5 milligram Enovid pill. (It is noteworthy that when birth control pills were tested in a developed country (Birmingham, England, in 1961) a 2.5 milligram preparation with only 50 micrograms of estrogen was used.[5])

Not surprisingly, given the massive hormonal exposure, *no* Puerto Rican woman who followed the research team's instructions became pregnant during 518 woman-years of use. The researchers lauded their own success by declaring that the pill's *"physiological* effectiveness is complete, *clinical* effectiveness great and *demographic* effectiveness [presumably referring to the suppression of fertility in this urban, poor population]   marked" [emphasis in the original].[6]

Ominously, the research team noted that "Popular rumor had it that this procedure caused cancer."[7] The research team downplayed this possibility but acknowledged that three years was too short a time to know if cancer might occur. Many women experienced nausea, headaches, and mood disorders. Given the incomplete follow-up, the team brazenly concluded that the Pill in Puerto Rico proved to be safe as well as effective.

A second study supported by G. D. Searle also began in 1957. It was undertaken by Edris Rice-Wray, the director of health services in the small Puerto Rican community of Rio Pedras, under the auspices of the Family Planning Association of Puerto Rico. Rice-Wray explained her methods in a report presented at a symposium under the auspices of G. D. Searle. What was important, she said, was "how to handle the patients, how you present the project [sic] and what you say to them so they take it."[8] Ethical problems were compounded when Rice-Wray identified herself as a health official and expressly avoided mention of the Family Planning Association for fear of dissuading otherwise-willing participants.

As in the former study, the researchers noted that some 17 to 18 percent of the Pill-takers had acute symptoms of malaise, including vomiting, nausea, dizziness, headache, and gastralgia. Long-term effects were not known. In the discussion of Rice-Wray's paper, Dr. Warren O. Nelson pointedly observed that women were being encouraged to take the pills for as long as twenty-five years — a period during which the possible effects of the Pill were unknown.[9]

In spite of the almost total lack of data on safety, physicians greeted the Pill with almost universal enthusiasm. But public health advocate and author Morton Mintz noted in an opinion piece in the *Washington Post* that women who use birth control pills "have had an almost unquestioning trust that the pills pose no serious dangers."[10] Mintz quoted Dr. James A. Shannon, then director of the National Institutes of Health, as saying "I believe so" when asked if he believed women were "really taking a chance" when they took the Pill. Shannon concurred that "exploration" of the human response to taking the Pill had been inadequate through 1965.[11] In that year, according to the Food and Drug Administration's (FDA's) Advisory Committee on Obstetrics and Gynecology, some 5 million U.S. women were on the Pill. In 1970, the FDA estimated that 8.5 million U.S. women were on the Pill. Today, the number is about 20 to 22 million. (Note that the major continuing risk of these early formulations in encouraging blood clotting is not addressed in this chapter.)

The Cancer Link

Early in its review, evidence was available to the FDA from animal tests done by industry scientists that the hormones in the Pill could contribute to heightened risks of tumorigenesis. In 1966, the FDA's Advisory Committee on Obstetrics and Gynecology issued a *Report on Oral Contraceptives* that emphasized:

Sex steroids, particularly estrogens, have been shown to produce malignant lesions and to affect adversely the existing tumors in the mouse, rat, rabbit, hamster and dog . . . these agents [progesterone or progestogens] alone and in combination with other sex steroids have promoted neoplasia or metastatic growth in a few instances. . . . There is, nevertheless, a warning that an altered endocrine environment in human tissues might result in an abnormal expression or potentiation of growth, as [it has] in experimental animals.[12]

Three years later, in a second report, the committee observed again that steroids generally and estrogens in particular "may be carcinogenic in man [sic]."[13] While reaching no definitive conclusions regarding the existence of documentable malignant changes or metabolic disorders, the committee members concluded that "the systemic effects of the drugs are so fundamental and widespread, however, that continued medical surveillance and investigation is required."[14] This viewpoint was apparently either not taken seriously by the major pharmaceuticals or intentionally underplayed in their promotional material. At Senate hearings held in 1970, Senator Gaylord Nelson read from a drug company's pamphlet entitled "So Close to Nature" that its Pill was: "So close to your natural feminine patterns. . . . Unlike others available for the same purpose, this preparation follows the principles and system of nature itself. Its actions closely resemble those of your natural menstrual pattern, and it works without [sic!] upsetting the delicate balance of your normal body function."[15] (Note that the Pill only works to the extent that it *does* disrupt hormonal balances.)

Of course, this is the ideal, not the reality. In 1970, Dr. Hugh J. Davis, of the School of Medicine at Johns Hopkins University, testified before the Senate Select Committee on Monopoly that the uniqueness of the formulations of most of the ingredients of oral contraceptive pills made this distinctly unnatural for the body. Davis warned the Senate committee that "in using these agents, we are in fact embarked on a massive endocrinologic experiment with millions of healthy women. . . . If the oral contraceptives were an article of food there would be sufficient evidence on the basis of animal experiments to consider seriously removing them from the market."[16]

Anticipating the data of tumor risks in long-term users, Davis presciently noted that it was the chronic use beyond two to three years that concerned him most.

Actually, the story of estrogens and cancer goes back to the 1930s when investigators were first testing the newly synthesized human hormones 17-beta-estradiol and progesterone. One of these researchers, Michael Shimkin, was interested in the possible role that estrogens might play in generating cancer. Between 1941 and 1946, Shimkin tested a newly synthesized estrogen called stilbestrol (known later as DES) and natural estrogens for their cancer-promoting activity. He demonstrated that rather than being the panacea that many other scientists visualized, excess estrogens could accelerate the formation of tumors in mice.[17]

Instead of heeding these dramatic findings, scientists and regulators alike interpreted the studies as being "unnatural."

Since normal levels of estrogens never reached those used in the animal studies—even in estrogen-treated women—the findings of growth stimulation (hyperplasia), accelerated breast cancer development, and abnormal reproduction were dismissed as examples of normal physiological processes gone awry.

Diethylstilbestrol (DES). It took the human tragedy of an estrogen analog given to mothers during pregnancy to wake the scientific community out of its state of complacency. In 1971, thirty years after Shimkin showed its carcinogenicity for animals, Dr. Arthur Herbst and two colleagues at the University of Chicago reported on a startling finding. The first seven of eight young women who presented a remarkable and rare tumor of the vagina (known as clear-cell adenocarcinoma) had one factor in common: all had been exposed while in the womb some eighteen to twenty-six years earlier to tiny amounts of diethylstilbestrol, a synthetic estrogen developed in Germany in 1938.[18] The largest number of cases in any given year was seen in 1975, when thirty-one women were found with clear-cell adenocarcinomas. While further studies have shown that only 311 women had developed this tumor by 1987 (an incidence of about 1 in 1,000 women exposed in utero to DES), an indeterminate number of others—perhaps as many as 1 percent of the almost 0.5 million female fetuses exposed to DES while in the womb (that is, 5,000 women)—will have serious problems with reproduction.[19] (See p. 127.)

Some of these problems include formation of abnormal tissue near the cervix (called adenosis) and gross disturbance of development of the uterus, leading to a T-shaped or undersized organ incapable of carrying a pregnancy to term.[20] The disorganization of the tissue that forms at the junction of the cervix and vagina and the disruption of the normal circular composition of the uterine muscles apparently combine to thwart successful sperm transport and implantation of the fertilized ovum in many of the affected women.[21]

Much of the concern about the developmental disorganizing (teratogenic) and carcinogenic effects of DES shifted attention away from so-called natural estrogens. The unique configuration of DES's molecule allows DES to fold into a shape that fools the body into believing it is encountering a true steroidal hormone. Even after DES was shown to be a carcinogen and teratogen, few thought that natural estrogens would have similar properties. Unlike natural estrogens, DES was metabolized directly into potent carcinogenic molecules.[22] DES also behaves like a "non-genotoxic" carcinogen. That is, when normal cells are exposed to DES, they undergo transformation into tumorous cells without observable genetic changes.[23]

The myth that a natural chemical could not cause pathological changes persisted until the end of the 1970s. It was then that researchers working at the University of California at Berkeley's Department of Zoology showed that natural estrogens themselves could have properties previously attributed to DES alone. Until 1979, researchers believed that production of adenosis—the hallmark of DES's activity—was uniquely attributable to that chemical. In that year, however, the Berkeley team showed that mice exposed to "normal" estrogens could develop adenosis-like lesions near the cervix.[24]

The idea that naturally occurring estrogens could cause pathological changes was a difficult concept for the endocrinology community to accept. Estrogens, after all, were a key part of the body's natural repertoire. They were an essential part of the hormones necessary for assuring proper development and sexual maturation as well as ovulation and pregnancy. What a few researchers recognized, however, was that estrogens, like all other hormones, exist in a constant state of flux. The balance of any one hormone depends on signals from central glands in the brain. For example, the pituitary tells major hormone-producing organs such as the ovary to secrete estrogens by releasing stimulating hormones into the bloodstream. If the pituitary gland or hypothalamus discover that estrogens are already present—and in great quantity—they stop signaling. Apparently some such action is responsible for the paradoxical effects of estrogens given early in the development of experimental animals: sexual maturation is dampened, immune functions (which estrogens normally stimulate) are suppressed, and estrogen-responsive tissues overdevelop prematurely.

By using newborn rodents, which develop very slowly (their early postpartum organ system development matches that of human fetuses in the late stages of pregnancy), scientists can approximate the human effects of giving controlled amounts of any estrogenic compound.[25] While such hormones normally stimulate parts of the uterus to produce more cells, an unnatural burst of an estrogen at the wrong time can disrupt development and limit the number of cells that form in certain parts of the uterus. That these changes can be produced by natural estrogens, and not only by synthetic ones like DES, is strongly supported by data that show that 17-beta-estradiol ("natural" estrogen) and ethinylestradiol work as effectively as DES to reduce the amount of uterine tissues that develop in neonatally treated rats.[26] Paradoxically, the impact of the estrogens with the strongest deleterious effects on uterine growth (ethinylestradiol and DES) was analogous to those produced by denying rats *any* estrogen during development by castrating them just after birth.[27] This suggests that DES may lock onto estrogen receptors on hormone-sensitive cells and deny them normal stimulation by estrogens.

This counter-intuitive result can also be explained by a "blitzing" effect of externally administered estrogens on the sensitive control organs in the brain. The result is a long-lasting and apparently irreversible effect on the normal relationship among the hypothalamus, pituitary, and ovary.[28]

Birth Control Hormones and Cancer. After the dramatic and disturbing revelations about human cancer following intrauterine exposure to DES, one would think that there would be an international reappraisal of the use of estrogenic hormones in birth control pills. Although estrogen-based oral contraceptives were in widescale use in the 1960s, it took two more decades for studies to be done that carefully and systematically showed that birth control estrogens *themselves* could specifically aid and abet the cancer process.[29]

By 1986, some 150 million women around the world had been exposed to oral contraceptives. Most of these contraceptives contain estrogens that mimic those normally found in the female body. Currently (circa 1991), an estimated 22 million women in the United States use oral contraceptives, many with estrogens in the high-dose formulations (50 micrograms or more) that have been discouraged for the last twenty years. In England and Wales, estrogen-and-progestin pills are the most common form of contraception among women: some 7.3 million women (including a large but uncounted number of very young women under the age of 16) are currently pre-scribed oral contraceptives.[30]

The first ominous rumblings that something was amiss came during the period when the higher dose pills were in wide use. In 1971 and 1972, first one and then many researchers reported that administration of one or both birth control hormones were associated with the appearance of liver adenomas or carci-nomas.[31] Where did this data come from? Was it reliable? If real, why hadn't we heard about this effect sooner? The an-swer is that the first harbinger of untoward effects from es-trogens had tried to present her findings but had been stymied by a skeptical medical editor and his advisors.

In 1970, Dr. Janet Baum, a young Michigan physician, sub-mitted a report to the *Journal of the American Medical Associa-tion.* She had just seen the third of a group of young female patients with a remarkable history: each had been in good health until experiencing a sudden bout of abdominal pain. When taken to the emergency room, all had required immediate sur-gical intervention for serious bleeding. The source in each case: a ruptured liver adenoma. Baum believed it highly significant that the three had all been taking oral contraceptives for several years. However, her concerned letter was rejected out of hand. According to Baum's account, at least one reviewer termed her study "ridiculous."[32]

Over the next three years, Baum and her colleagues accumu-lated four more cases of liver tumors among women in Michi-gan. None of the women had any of the classic predisposing traits for liver cancer: none drank, nor had hepatitis, nor had any congenital problems of the liver. The tumors themselves were remarkable for two reasons: they were all the same type of liver adenoma, and they behaved differently than did any liver adenomas reported before in the literature. Each of the tumors was enormous as adenomas go and was so blood-filled that surgery was complicated by hemorrhaging.

What could have caused such a phenomenon? Baum again found one feature in common: all the women had been on the Pill for six months to seven years. Baum now knew that she was on to something. A review of all of the records at her hospital, the St. Joseph Mercy Hospital in Ann Arbor, Michigan, turned up only eight other "benign hepatomas" since 1913. Five of the eight were associated with cirrhosis. She and her colleagues also knew that the animal literature had begun to show links between steroids and cancer in other parts of the body. Could it be that certain steroids in the Pill could cause liver tumors?[33] This hypothesis was vigorously presented in 1974, but received little attention.[34]

Some scientists were sufficiently concerned about a Pill-cancer link to have begun testing the major steroids for their cancer-causing activity. Unbeknownst to the Baum team, a panel of researchers in England had begun a study of possible risks of cancer from the Pill two years before she submitted her first findings. Astonishingly, the British team found that the hormones *were* carcinogenic, but stated that no action need be taken since women were not then (in 1972) showing any signs of cancer after having taken the Pill for up to eight years.[35] It seems as if the British team lacked the advantage of seeing Baum's work, just as she missed theirs!

However, within two years, Baum's work stimulated a flood tide of correspondence and research. In 1973, the *Lancet* printed a letter from the medical examiner's office in Philadelphia. A pathologist there had autopsied a woman who had died from the rupture of an abdominal mass and had uncovered a ruptured "benign" liver tumor. The woman had taken an oral contraceptive. The pathologist believed the findings required "an urgent reappraisal of the effects of these [contraceptive] hormones."[36]

Thereafter, the first of literally dozens of confirmatory articles and letters appeared—all pointing to a sudden upsurge in the appearance of what previously had been an exceedingly rare tumor type. All were in the British literature.

Soon the data became unavoidable. Numerous articles began to appear that associated estrogens and estrogenic drugs with human liver cancer.[37] A second type of liver lesion (focal nodular hyperplasia) reported in animals given estrogens was also reported in women on the Pill.[38] As the number and variety of liver tumor types expanded, so did the roster of hormones implicated as causative agents. In 1975, a report appeared linking androgenic steroids (such as those currently used by weight lifters and athletes) and liver tumors.[39] As with Baum's first findings, the authors of this Australian report noted that the three patients in their care had no other factors that could predispose to liver tumors.

Epidemiological Studies.   The epidemiologic story was coming together as well. By 1976–77, it was clear that the longer women took the Pill, the greater was their risk of developing an adenoma. Epidemiologists who were used to citing relative risks of two and three (where the exposed group was two or three times more likely to be affected than were unexposed but otherwise similar controls) must have stood up when a research team published its findings on women who used the Pill for five to seven years. The researchers found these long-term Pill-users to be five times more likely to develop liver tumors (nine-year users were twenty-five times more likely) than were demographically similar women who practiced other means of contraception.[40]

Even the normally conservative *Journal of the National Cancer Institute* took note. In 1977 it published a review of the first hundred cases of liver tumors in women on oral contraceptives. The authors noted grimly that for the more than 35 million women who had by that year either taken or were taking the Pill, "the potential [for developing liver tumors] is evident."[41] Still, Pill use and its promotion continued unabated. (While some companies, notably Ortho Pharmaceuticals, began to experiment with "low dose" pills, no one pulled the higher dose pills from the market until 1982!)

By 1977, it was also clear to some researchers that these tumors tended to be "hormone dependent," that is, their growth and possibly progression were stimulated by the presence of the Pill's hormones (singly or in combination). This dependency extended to the focal nodular hyperplasias as well as the adenomas. Careful histological review by a Scandinavian team picked up dramatic signs of this stimulation when they compared the nodules in women on the Pill with those that appeared in non-Pill users or in men.[42] The role of hormones in stimulating the outgrowth of adenomas was also vividly drawn this same year. A group of Los Angeles physicians reported that in three cases in which early adenomas had been diagnosed, simply withdrawing the Pill had caused the tumors to regress.[43] A team of physicians from Wisconsin warned in unequivocal terms that "all patients should be strongly advised to permanently discontinue oral contraceptives" once a primary liver tumor was diagnosed.[44]

The most convincing study of this period came from a team

179

of researchers at the U.S. Centers for Disease Control in Atlanta. Their review of five hundred or so cases of liver adenomas through the end of 1976 revealed that the risks of developing liver tumors increased exponentially with increasing duration of exposure: "Compared to the risk in women with no more than a year's use, the risk of developing HCA [hepatocellular adenoma] was estimated to be 9, 120, and 500 times higher, respectively, for women with less than 4, 4–7 and for seven or more years of oral contraceptive use."[45] However, it took three more years for a warning to appear in the *Physician's Desk Reference* (PDR) that commented only that "Two studies relate risk with duration of use of oral contraceptives" and noted that the risk was greater after four or more years of use.

The Centers for Disease Control team also noted two additional factors that they believed were responsible for the upsurge in tumor incidence: the availability of high-potency pills (those with 50 or more micrograms of estrogen) and the use of such pills by women older than 26. This observation postdates the 1970 advisory issued by the FDA to physicians urging them to use the lowest effective dose in prescribing the Pill. A warning that high hormonal potency pills were associated with higher risks of adenomas than were low-potency ones did not appear in the PDR until 1982.

Firm epidemiological support for the causal linkage between use of the Pill with liver tumors finally appeared in 1983 with the publication of the first of several articles by a team of renowned British epidemiologists.[46] The team found the interval between the introduction of the Pill in England and Wales and the first appearance of liver tumors (approximately ten to fifteen years) as well as the association of oral contraceptive use almost exclusively with at least one tumor type (adenomas) to be convincing evidence.

Taking their lead from this new spate of articles, the editors of the *Lancet* provided its readers with suggestions about how women should be told about the risk of cancer from the Pill.[47]

Between 1984 and 1988 the credibility of the linkage between benign and malignant tumors and the Pill increased. Malignant liver tumors in Pill-takers were found to be qualitatively different than those that occurred in non–Pill-takers. In particular, the malignant tumor in Pill-takers, like its benign adenoma counterpart, was more susceptible to bleeding and rupture.[48] Other studies buttressed the now growing suspicion that malignant tumors were unequivocally linked to long-term oral contraceptive use.[49]

The penultimate report forging this linkage appeared in 1986, when the prestigious epidemiological team of D. Forman, T. J. Vincent, and R. L. Doll concluded that steroidal hormones do in fact interact with liver cells in a way that can lead to cancer. The team concluded that a substantial portion of all liver cancers in nonalcoholic women was due to oral contraceptives.[50] The British Committee on Safety of Medicines (but not its U.S. counterpart at the FDA) took note of this conclusion and recommended that the data sheets from all manufacturers of oral contraceptives carry warnings about the possible occurrence of malignant tumors of the liver.[51]

In the United States, the Planned Parenthood Federation downplayed these findings. Based on a cursory review of the available literature in the United States, Planned Parenthood attributed virtually all of the increase in tumor incident to high-dose preparations of the Pill, downplaying any risk associated with the lower doses in use in the late 1980s.[52] While risks were certainly higher from large-dose pills, long-term use of lower doses has never been proven safe.

By the end of the decade, however, the medical community *had* to be aware of the association between long-term oral contraceptive use and liver tumors. Both estrogens and progestins were documented as inducers (not merely promoters or enhancers) of liver tumor development.[53] Finally, in 1989, the direct transformation of an oral-contraceptive-caused adenoma to a hepatocellular carcinoma was observed.[54]

Where Was the FDA?   One would expect this wave of increasingly incriminating data to have an impact on the FDA, the agency charged to protect public health. Initially, the information linking steroids to tumors appeared to make an impact. In 1970, the commissioner of the Food and Drug Administration, Charles C. Edwards responded to a Senate committee inquiry concerning the quality of the data his agency had received when it approved the first oral contraceptive for sale in the United States in 1960. Edwards observed that "much of the data submitted in support of this oral contraceptive seem to be rather superficial in content in the light of our present state of knowledge."[55] Among the deficiencies Edwards noted were data on metabolism and liver function, as well as long-term studies both in humans and animals. In spite of these concerns, the FDA let go unchallenged the statement by G. D. Searle in 1964 that "few drugs in any category have ever been subjected to clinical tests as exhaustive as those already undergone by Enovid."[56]

Commissioner Edwards also told the Senate committee that his agency was sufficiently concerned about the risks of the Pill that it had drafted a leaflet that was intended to go to each patient using the Pill. In it, the FDA recommended in a section entitled "Note about Cancer: Scientists know the hormones in the Pill (estrogen and progesterone) have caused cancer in animals, but they have no proof that the Pill causes cancer in humans. Because your doctor knows this, he will want to examine you regularly."[57] The leaflet, however, was never published.[58] It was not until the end of 1970 that the FDA succeeded in getting a much watered-down patient insert included in the Pill's packaging.

In 1972, the FDA asked the major manufacturers of the Pill to issue a warning that their drug should not be taken by anyone whose liver function was seriously impaired. Such warnings appeared in due course—but were surprisingly dropped after two years.

During the 1973–75 period, cautionary voices appeared both within the FDA and the medical community at large downplaying the association that appeared to exist between Pill-takers and the burgeoning incidence of liver tumors. The authors of one such article concluded that "we believe that an association between focal nodular hyperplasia and oral contraceptive use may be merely coincidental."[59]

By way of background, liver cancer itself is rare in most communities, except where hepatitis, heavy alcohol use, or fungal contaminants are present. In a world survey conducted in 1944, some twenty years before the first widespread use of oral contraceptives, a researcher could find only sixty-seven cases of the particular tumor type called hepatic cell adenoma.[60] The rarity of this tumor prior to the mid-1970s was further reinforced by other studies.[61]

The pre-Pill era male-to-female ratio of primary liver cancers was dramatically high: more than 6 to 1 in some studies. But beginning in 1970, something clearly changed. These previously rare tumors began to appear—in droves. Examining the tumor registries from some 477 hospitals, the American College of Surgeons' Commission on Cancer found 378 primary liver tumors in women and only 165 in men aged 15 to 45 between the years 1970 and 1975. This woman-dominated prevalence not only reversed the normal sex ratio of malignant tumors, but was found to peak for women between the years of 26 and 30, the period of greatest contraceptive use.[62] Coupled with the increasing flood tide of human clinical studies, this prevalence study served as a capstone to the theory that most liver tumors in women (especially adenomas and focal nodular hyperplasias) were hormone related.

Warnings.   So what, you might easily ask, did the pharmaceutical companies do to alert consumers about this state of affairs? The answer is virtually nothing. By 1975–77, at least five relevant facts were known about the cancer related benefit-risk ratio of the Pill:

1. The medical research community had reached a near consensus that almost all liver adenomas in young women were attributable to oral contraceptive use.
2. Research had shown that the duration of the Pill's use increased the risk.[63]
3. Many analogs of the steroids used in oral contraceptives— and some of the major steroids themselves—had been found to either promote or induce liver cancer in animals.[64]
4. There was suggestive evidence that oral contraceptives use led to *malignant* tumors, not merely the benign tumors previously seen.[65]
5. By 1976, there was evidence that "benign" tumors such as adenomas and focal nodular hyperplasias could themselves progress to malignant ones.[66]

It took until 1982 for the pharmaceutical companies to acknowledge that malignant tumors were associated with Pill use. In that year, an Ortho entry appeared in the PDR that noted that "A few cases of hepatocellular carcinoma have been reported in women taking oral contraceptives." However, this "warning" went on to state: "The relationship of these drugs to this type of malignancy is not known at this time." Ironically, the contraindication section of the same warning contained the statement that if benign or malignant liver tumors developed during use of oral contraceptives or other estrogen-containing products, Pill use should stop.

Toward the end of the 1980s, most Pill manufacturers had added a patient insert as required by the FDA. A typical package insert is that supplied for the Ortho Pharmaceutical product Ortho-Novum 7/7/7 (the numbers refer to the days when each of three different formulations should be taken). The insert explains what is in each tablet, but does not mention that use of oral contraceptives requires physician supervision. It does list the often fatal adverse reaction observed by Baum almost three decades earlier as a form of liver rupture that can lead to severe bleeding. No allusion to the prospect of death is made. In spite of more than 120 studies that show a link between Pill use and liver tumors,[67] the insert ends with the notation that "However, studies to date in women taking currently marketed OCs [oral contraceptives] have not confirmed that OCs cause cancer in humans" (copyright 1989, Ortho Pharmaceutical Corporation). Seale's package insert, by comparison, does acknowledge the cancer risk.

While strict legalistic proof of causation with *new* Pills with lower dose formulations may be lacking, this statement implies that contemporary pills are somehow free of carcinogenic effect. This view ignores the problem of latency, namely, that as dosages of oral contraceptives are reduced, any tumors that might be promoted or caused would take longer to appear. Early studies of this population would thus not show dramatic cancer increases.

Ortho's formulation of its package insert differs graphically from that of its smaller competitors. A case in point is the 1989 insert from the manufacturers of the DeMulen 1/35. Under a listing of the dangers of oral contraceptives, the DeMulen insert mentions liver tumors as the second item. It also acknowledges that studies of animals with long-term exposure to estrogens showed increased cancer risks at such sites as the breast, cervix, vagina, liver, womb, ovary, and pituitary gland. The insert concludes that "These findings suggest that OCs may cause cancer in humans." While hedging that the evidence does not confirm that oral contraceptives cause human cancer, the insert adds "but it remains possible they will be discovered to do so in the future."

The Ethics of the Situation. The failure of most of the major pharmaceutical companies to acknowledge the association of liver adenomas with oral contraceptives much less to begin to withdraw the more potent formulations from market must be considered a major deception. At the very least, their statements were the most conservative reading of the data legally possible. But what a warning should do is evaluate risks, not dismiss or understate them.

Also remember that U.S. companies had tested the Pill (at often outrageously large doses) "offshore" in Puerto Rico where constraints on testing are much weaker than in the continental United States. By 1978, the earliest data from Puerto Rico had been in print for a year. The researchers were clearly convinced that at least the "benign" form of adenoma was linked to oral contraceptive use in the Puerto Rican women who participated in the trial.[68]

An ethical approach calls for erring on the side of safety. As early as 1977, one team from the University of California at Irvine declared straightforwardly that "Until substantive research at the biocellular level can be achieved, it is imperative that the syndrome of oral contraceptive use and liver tumors be recognized.[69] Subsequent research, as we have seen, *confirmed* the association, even as major manufacturers continued to downplay the risk.

Commentary

The overall pattern of an increase in the incidence of liver cancer after taking oral contraceptives or other steroids is a provocative example of the consequences of disturbing the normal hormonal homeostasis of the body. It also dramatically illustrates the failure of the producers of these powerful biologic agents to anticipate and monitor the consequences of their promotion of hormonal products. Instead of intensively researching the possibilities of major disturbances in endocrine function and/or neoplasia, it is evident from the record that the manufacturers continued their marketing practices as usual long after they could have known and warned about such serious and often tragic consequences of high-dose formulations and protracted use.

As early as 1965, Gregory Pincus, the pioneer in isolating and synthesizing sex hormones, warned about the bad mix that comes from combining social imperatives (controlling the population explosion) with unsophisticated and shortsighted use of powerful hormones. Pincus wrote that

The modern-day investigator cannot be satisfied with the invention of a "cunning device." The present accumulated knowledge concerning reproductive processes indicates that the production of gametes, their transport and mating, their fusion, and the fate of the fertilized egg, involves an intricate and delicately balanced set of sequential events. Interfering with this sequence at any of a large number of stages may have physiologic consequences that are not apparent on the surface.[70]

This admonition apparently fell on deaf ears. The full-scale development of the Pill went forward with breakneck speed, in spite of early warnings that disruption of the normal hormonal milieu was not totally innocent. Pincus himself observed that the effects of administering high doses of progesterone were not confined to the ovary, as he had predicted. Many women experienced "escape bleeding" and a buildup of the effects of continued progesterone on the ovary in later menstrual cycles. Pincus reminded his colleagues that their overall objective in developing any contraceptive pill was "to disrupt them [the hormonal relationships] in such a way that no physiological cost to the organism is involved."[71]

Somewhere along the line, this paramount ethical principle of "not harming" went by the wayside. All of the evidence points to the premature use of oral contraceptive preparations. High-dose preparations were used in the first studies in Puerto Rico to guarantee "favorable" results (that is, to ensure virtually no pregnancies) and carried no safeguards for that generation of human guinea pigs.

Certainly, by the late 1970s, enough data were available about the consequences of excessive steroid use to have sounded the alarm for women who might be entering their second decade of use of the Pill. Similar data were available about the ability of male hormone analogs and anabolic steroids to produce liver (and kidney) cancer.[72] In the ensuing years, evidence accumulated that progesterone and related hormones could induce liver enzymes to activate classical carcinogens and produce neoplastic changes in tissue culture. By 1983, it was clear that disturbances of the normal steroid milieu of the body could precipitate the occurrence of liver tumors.[73]

What was happening in this organ to incite cancer? We have already seen that the liver, especially in women, is usually quite resistant to carcinogenesis. A low density of hormone receptors on liver cells ensures that this organ responds to background levels of circulating steroids with only modest rises in enzyme function, and rarely with cell turnover or division. However, under the barrage of excessive steroids (as with carcinogenic substances), certain liver cells apparently proliferate to form nodules or clusters of cells with a new enzymatic makeup and shape. If the stimulation continues, the liver's entire "architecture" can change. These initially isolated islands of nodules can grow and fuse until virtually the entire liver is made up of new, usually more highly toxin-resistant cells.[74] While this response may be adaptive (that is, "good" for the organism in the short run), the dividing cells are at heightened risk of further neoplastic events.[75] The final transformation of the cells to malignancies can be caused by the continued stimulation by synthetic estrogens, which have carcinogenic activity.

What is clear is that a wave of liver neoplasms in several hundred women occurred over the past two decades. This trend is particularly evident in the developed countries that have used the Pill. So, will we thus see the eventual denouement of the Pill? Probably not. Drug manufacturers have introduced lower dose formulations with the expectation that the major side effects will be minimized. Some are even asserting that the Pill is "good" for women since it reduces other cancer rates.[76] But unless truly physiologic "low dose" estrogen-containing Pills are made universal, the distortions in the announcements of "all safe" bulletins from these companies will continue to ring false while more and more women who still take high-dose estrogen pills face the cancerous consequences of the pharmaceutical industry's chemical deception.

CHAPTER TEN

Myth 8:

Naturally occurring substances cause most cancer

CANCER ATTRIBUTION

In the past few years, a fierce debate has been raging over the causes of cancer. Since 1987, a dominant thesis in the scientific community has been that the risks to the public from synthetic industrial carcinogens and pesticides pale in comparison to the cancer risks posed by naturally occurring carcinogens found mostly in food. If true, this new concept represents a radical departure from previous positions. Between 1960 and 1970, it was common to find cancer biologists who asserted that virtually all human cancers were the result of environmental factors. Synthetic chemicals topped the list, with a large percentage of cancers attributed to such exposure. It was not uncommon to find responsible and authoritative cancer researchers writing articles in the popular press warning us of the dangers of life in the presence of a veritable "sea of carcinogens."[1] The often ambiguous basis for such declarations was recently reviewed by Michigan Cancer Foundation researcher G. Marie Swanson.[2] Swanson found most of the early studies of the contribution of industrial carcinogens to human cancer to be flawed or incomplete. In her analysis, researchers in the late 1960s and 1970s took great license with the word *environment*. Some invoked the term to embrace life-style (tobacco use, diet, and such factors), others meant general environmental factors such as air and water pollution, food additives, and pesticides. Swanson concludes that "environmental exposures" should be reinterpreted as being limited to outdoor air pollution, water contamination, or exposures resulting from pesticide residues.

Using this new definition, environmental data demonstrate the global reach of pollution since carcinogens can be found in virtually all the world's oceans and large freshwater lakes. But do these often "trace" levels of pollutants actually cause cancer? While the jury is still out, the circumstantial evidence is impressive. Animals and fish with tumors are often found in proximity to waste discharge points or living in contaminated rivers, estuaries, or embayments. Many environmentalists cite the correlation between concentrations of synthetic pollutants and such cancers as justifying the concern over contamination of watersheds and ocean bottoms with carcinogenic chemicals.[3]

But others disagree, citing natural factors other than industrial pollutants as explanations for where and why cancer occurs. One researcher, for example, found that fish in rivers seemingly free of industrial effluent had just as much precancerous genetic damage as did those from industrially polluted waterways.[4] While it is tempting to conclude that this and related findings absolve synthetic pollutants from blame, such studies often ignore the fact that carcinogenic pollution is global. That is, even seemingly pristine waterways can be contaminated with carcinogens from distant sources, such as diesel engine exhaust particulates, fly ash, and water-borne pollutants. Some of the pollutants increase the acidity of the water and leach other potentially toxic chemicals from river sediments. When researchers at the Environmental Protection

Agency (EPA) analyzed fish from areas free of known dioxin sources, for example, they still found significantly elevated residues in the fish tissue.[5] Other water-borne chemicals appear responsible for genetic damage in fish eggs, a finding which can explain later carcinogenesis.[6]

Such findings should at least raise the possibility that some "natural" cancer is, in fact, induced by products of human activity. This is not to deny that cancer does not arise from spontaneous genetic damage. We already know of some twenty or so genetic conditions in humans—and many more in animals—that predispose to malignant change, often with little or no external provocation. These and other vexing observations have led scientists to infer the existence within all of us of so-called oncogenes (or tumor genes). Such naturally occurring tumor genes have been documented in many tumorous conditions in humans as well as in experimental animals.

These discoveries appear to challenge the traditional treatment of cancer as an "externally" caused disease. But cancer researchers have never claimed that a chemical agent carries some specific "imprint" of itself into a cancer. What a chemical may well do is simply uncover a nascent oncogene or accelerate the sequence of genetic changes needed to set a cell on a course toward malignancy.

Of course, the industrial setting is a source of such chemicals. We have already seen how chemicals used in the manufacture of dyes, tar products, and machining oils can cause cancer among workers. What is at issue is how much of the cancer we see in the *general population* is caused by similar chemicals. Occupational cancers may be the proverbial "canaries in the mine," signaling a new wave of industrial-based carcinogenesis in the general population. In the past, factory walls held industrial carcinogens in check, but they inevitably escaped and confronted the population at large with carcinogenic risks, first at toxic waste sites, and now more universally.

Many claim such a cancer wave did not occur, even after dioxins, PCBs, and pesticide exposures became commonplace, prompting scientists to begin to look elsewhere for the cancer bogeyman. A few outspoken scientists have urged the public to turn elsewhere to look for the major source of chemically caused cancer.

THE RISE OF DIETARY EXPLANATIONS

Within the past decade, dietary factors have been singled out as the prime culprits in chemical carcinogenesis. Led by University of California at Berkeley biochemist Bruce Ames, some scientists have openly declared that diet is a much more compelling explanation for human cancer than are any of the industrial or pesticide candidates. Ames and his colleagues emphasize that chemicals that can be found in everyday market-basket items such as mushrooms (hydrazines) and celery (safroles) and in "natural" molds (aflatoxins) that contaminate foodstuffs are much more potent carcinogens than virtually any synthetic chemical.[7] Ames and his colleagues have further asserted that "It is probable that almost every plant product in the supermarket contains natural carcinogens."[8]

What is the truth? Is there a foundation for what appears (to those of us raised on the chemical-cancer link) to be a startling new claim? First, let us recognize the stakes that are involved. If most cancers are due to dietary factors, then cancer must be considered an opportunistic disease in which we are our own worst enemies. If it is not, and industrial activities remain the major culprits, cancer prevention must begin at the source of production.

At first, the news from the front seems to support Ames's position. The National Cancer Institute (NCI) says, "The good news is . . . a healthy diet may reduce cancer risk."[9] Its education booklet on diet and cancer identifies high-fiber and low-fat foods as dietary elements "that may help to reduce the risk of cancer."[10] But note that this advisory pamphlet never states that cancer is "caused" by any of the foods we eat, only that risks may be reduced by altering the composition of our diet.

Let's take a closer look at the details of the "cancer attribution" debate.

For Ames, the major extrinsic causes of cancer can be found entirely within the human diet.[11] He concludes that industrial chemicals are trivial causes of cancer when compared to their "natural" counterparts. That is, naturally occurring carcinogens not only contribute vastly more to the cancer burden that afflicts humankind, but they are also more potent than synthetic chemicals (by a factor of as much as 10,000) as a group in inducing cancer.[12]

However, this finding has been contested by a team of Columbia University School of Public Health researchers. Frederica Perera and Paolo Boffetta point out that Ames's team was biased in their selection of chemicals (many, such as DDT and PCBs, have by now been so well regulated that daily exposures are infinitesimal) and failed to compare reasonable daily exposures to natural versus synthetic chemical carcinogens.[13] For instance, Ames contrasted daily portions of exotic foods such as brown mustard, sake, dried squid, and comfrey-pepsin tablets with drinking water contaminated with an industrial carcinogen (chloroform). Perera and Boffetta reasonably ask how many Americans eat dried squid daily, while daily water intake may be well in excess of the two liters Ames allowed.

When the average daily exposure figures were corrected for likely ingestion, the Perera and Boffetta team found that the projected cancer-causing potencies of synthetic chemicals were *at least* as important as the so-called natural ones in contributing to human cancer in the United States. Nonetheless, Ames continues to assert that diet is preeminent as a cancer cause. Given these often confusing positions, how do we approach the truth?

An obvious way through the conflicting claims is to examine new patterns of cancer incidence to see if the likely causes implicate dietary over environmental factors or vice versa.. The most recent statistics are illuminating. From the period 1973 to 1987 (see Figure 10-1), the fastest rising rates of cancer in the United States included such sites as the skin (melanoma), lymphatic tissues (non-Hodgkins lymphoma), prostate gland, testis, lung, kidney, breast, central nervous system (especially the brain), liver, and bladder. With the exception of the prostate gland, in which elevated incidence rates appear to be largely artificial as a result of early surgical discovery of hidden lesions,[14] virtually all of the other sites have shown dramatic and real increases of at least 12 percent over the 14-year period.

Most of these sites are precisely the ones for which good data exist that implicate environmental factors in tumor formation. As we have seen, melanomas are associated with exposure to ultraviolet light and some industrial chemicals; non-Hodgkin's lymphoma with exposure to solvents and chlorinated phenolic

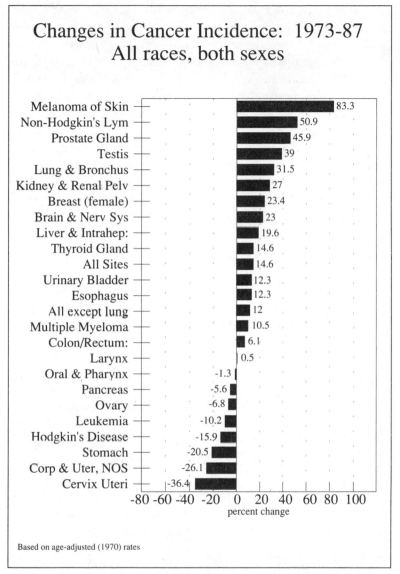

Changes in Cancer Incidence: 1973-87
All races, both sexes

Cancer Site	Percent Change
Melanoma of Skin	83.3
Non-Hodgkin's Lym	50.9
Prostate Gland	45.9
Testis	39
Lung & Bronchus	31.5
Kidney & Renal Pelv	27
Breast (female)	23.4
Brain & Nerv Sys	23
Liver & Intrahep:	19.6
Thyroid Gland	14.6
All Sites	14.6
Urinary Bladder	12.3
Esophagus	12.3
All except lung	12
Multiple Myeloma	10.5
Colon/Rectum:	6.1
Larynx	0.5
Oral & Pharynx	-1.3
Pancreas	-5.6
Ovary	-6.8
Leukemia	-10.2
Hodgkin's Disease	-15.9
Stomach	-20.5
Corp & Uter, NOS	-26.1
Cervix Uteri	-36.4

percent change

Based on age-adjusted (1970) rates

Figure 10-1. Changing cancer statistics over a fourteen-year period. Source: "Cancer Statistics Review 1973–1987," *Journal of the National Cancer Institute* 82(1990): 1238

chemicals; testicular cancer with heavy metals and solvents; cancers of the lung with smoking and possibly with air-borne pollutants; kidney cancer with hydrocarbon exposure; brain tumors with work in chemical industries; liver cancer with industrial chemicals and synthetic hormones; and bladder cancer with dyes and pesticides.[15] Some tumor types, such as melanoma show no association at all with diet,[16] while others, such as non-Hodgkin's lymphoma and cancer of the breast (see below), have only modest associations with milk products or fat intake and alcohol consumption, respectively.[17] In contrast, organ cancer sites within the digestive tract that have the closest proximity to food have shown either only modest increases (esophagus) or major declines (stomach).

This is not to say that diet cannot influence tumorigenesis at many of the sites that have shown rising incidence of cancer. But dietary factors that might have influenced these changes (for example, intake of moldy food, increased consumption of spices, and so on) simply have not changed that much over the past three decades to account for the observed shifts. For some tumors, such as brain tumors, the rate of increase in certain age groups has been so dramatic that only an environmental explanation makes sense. Among the elderly, for instance, the incidence of brain cancer has risen 187 percent for 75- to 79-year-olds, 395 percent for 80- to 84-year-olds, and 501 percent for people older than 85 in the ten years since 1973–74[18] This dramatic increase is particularly striking since it is occurring in an organ site that is "protected" by a blood-brain barrier. Could solvent chemicals, radiation, or some other barrier-traversing agent (for example, a virus) be the cause? Only further study will reveal the culprits but, in the meantime, chemical toxicants top the list of suspects.

These new patterns of cancer occurrence are telling us something important about causation. They are indicators that our total environment in the past two to three decades has been conducive to certain tumors and not others. Those in the relatively stationary or declining minority *do* have dietary factors in their genesis: colon cancer, stomach cancer, and oral and pharyngeal cancer—all of which can be modified by diet as the discussion below will show.[19] But the tumors we have most to fear (both in terms of their increasing mortality *and* incidence— notably melanomas, lung and brain cancers, and non-Hodgkin's lymphoma) are also those with major environmental factors in their origins.

DIET AND CANCER

Given this highly suggestive picture of the link of at least some major cancers to synthetic chemicals in the environment, where *does* diet come into play? Is there still room for dietary factors in the overall story? The answer is clearly yes. Diet certainly plays a major role in establishing the baseline incidence of certain cancers and is involved in setting the pace at which they emerge. But the dietary elements of greatest concern are *not* the naturally occurring chemicals cited by Ames but rather chemicals introduced into foodstuffs during their growth (pesticides), preparation, preservation, processing, and cooking. While it is true that many plants contain carcinogenic "natural pesticides" that ward off predators or pathogens, these plants (such as peppers, mustard, cloves, and other spices) make up a very small part of the U.S. diet.

More commonly ingested foods, such as celery, do contain weak carcinogens which increase in concentration when and if the plants are attacked by insect pests. Since damaged produce rarely makes it to the supermarket shelves, the cancer threat is likely overblown by Ames. Where diet is strongly linked with cancer types, the foods ingested are often exotic, for most Americans, consisting of salted, pickled, or smoked food. However, fats and alcohol, more common in the American diet, also play a role.

Much of this data on food was assembled and reviewed in 1982 by the National Academy of Sciences' National Research Council.[20] In reviewing the geographic distribution of cancers worldwide, the Committee on Diet, Nutrition and Cancer noted that regions with high incidence of cancer of the esophagus, stomach, and intestinal tract often have populations with dietary habits that include eating salt-cured, pickled, or smoked foods.

The committee also singled out such "nonnutritive" constituents of foods as chemicals produced by molds and other natural, chemical, or inadvertent additives as being potentially carcinogenic for humans. (We now know that fungal byproducts such as patulin and aflatoxin are bona fide carcinogens, see below.)

A final area of the committee's concern focused on alcohol, especially as it augmented the cancer risk of cigarette smoking. (Ames, too, cites alcohol as one of the major "natural" foodstuff carcinogens.)

It is worth reviewing the experimental literature on each of these elements that has appeared since the 1982 publication of *Diet, Nutrition and Cancer.*

Fat, High Caloric Intake, and Cancer

The National Academy of Sciences' Committee on Diet, Nutrition and Cancer cited numerous studies that appeared to implicate high fat consumption and high caloric intake with cancer risk. These findings were buttressed by animal research that showed that increased tumor rates in rats or mice were directly associated with high intakes of carbohydrates and proteins. Notable among these studies were epidemiologic analyses that showed a significant correlation between caloric intake and incidence of leukemia in men and breast cancer in women. One of the strongest models for this latter hypothesis has been the association of dietary fat and breast cancer.

The link between dietary fat and breast cancer was strongly supported by data available in 1982. Since then, however, the evidence supporting this link has been greatly attenuated. A recent reviewer found that while dietary fat might still be an important factor in colon cancer, studies supporting its role in breast tumorigenesis were inconsistent.[21] The best evidence for such an effect is limited to extreme caloric excess and not fat per se. That is, only when women gain twenty-two pounds or more after reaching adulthood, has their breast cancer risk been found to be higher (approximately double) than that of nonobese or slightly overweight controls.[22] A common factor in many obese women is that they have higher levels of a key estrogen than do women on a low-fat diet.[23] Indeed, women on a low-fat, low-calorie diet (especially vegetarians) have lower rates of breast cancer overall.[24] But these observations can be interpreted in two ways: that high fat intake increases cancer, or that low-fat or low-calorie diets decrease cancer (of course, a combination of the two might also be occurring.)

The Committee on Diet, Nutrition and Cancer opted for the latter model and advocated reducing caloric intake to lower cancer risk. Indeed, some animal studies appeared to support such a proposal. The most dramatic evidence of a role for reduced caloric intake and inhibition of cancer outgrowth was a classic study in which intentional underfeeding limited the incidence of a particular cancer, radiation-induced leukemia.[25] However, this and many other studies have yet to clarify the role of generalized malnutrition—in which all cell types are impaired—or the selective role of undernutrition in preferentially impairing tumor-cell proliferation. And whatever the explanation in animals, the committee overlooked the most likely explanation for a protective effect of dietary change in humans— something in the new low-fat/low-calorie diet was *preventing* cancer.

Protective Effects of Dietary Substances

New data have shown that diets rich in a substance found in cruciferous vegetables—the ones like cauliflower, broccoli, and brussel sprouts that we always turned our noses up at when we sat down at the dinner table—encourages the metabolism of estrogens (including those elevated in high-risk obese women) and possibly reduces their levels in the bloodstream.[26] Such an effect would reduce the cancer risk generated by high levels of this cancer-associated hormone.

The public has also come to believe that dietary fiber is a panacea against cancer, especially cancer of the colon. This idea has received widespread attention since the publication of *Diet, Nutrition and Cancer*. However, the data on the preventive effect of *all* fiber sources on colon cancer is ambiguous.

Fiber derived from some sources (for example, wheat bran and cellulose) *has* proven to be protective against colon tumors, while other sources (pectin, corn bran, undegraded carageenan, agar, Metamucil and alfalfa) actually *enhance* tumor growth in experimental animals.[27] Thus, contemporary researchers are reluctant to conclude that protection against colon cancer can be conferred simply by adding fiber to the diet.[28] In fact, taken in aggregate, these studies belie the aphorism that "an apple a day [a rich source of fiber] keeps the doctor away." And the notion that low-fiber diets *in and of themselves* contribute to high cancer rates in parts of the world has little or no epidemiological support. High-fat diets and sedentary life-style are at least as important, accounting for as much as 40 to 60 percent of colon cancer in some ethnic groups.[29]

Other dietary components have been shown to play a significant role in inhibiting tumor formation or growth. As we have seen, these include the cruciferous vegetables. Other potentially cancer-protective substances have only become known since the Academy of Sciences' report. Protective chemicals have been isolated from Chinese green tea,[30] plant seeds and cereal grains (inositol hexaphosphate),[31] extracts of green coffee beans (kahweol palmitate),[32] and grapefruit (citrus limonoids).[33] Plant phenols, such as ellagic acid, have shown particularly potent protective effects against chemically induced cancers in experimental animals.[34]

Certain common dietary ingredients, such as calcium glucarate,[35] vitamin E,[36] and beta carotene[37] also have remarkable and sometimes (as in the case of beta carotene) well-characterized antitumorigenic effects. Most recently, the alpha form of carotene, which is found in yellow, orange, and green vegetables (and in that much-maligned substance, palm oil), has been found to be a potent tumor inhibitor. In one study, researchers found this vitamin A precursor to be as much as ten times more inhibitory of tumor cell division than beta carotene.[38] Other naturally occurring carotenoids can be found in algae such as *Spirulina dunaliella.*[39] Like alpha carotene, these chemicals appear to exhibit antitumor effects without converting to vitamin A, a step that occurs readily for beta carotene.

Contributions of Pickled, Smoked, or Preserved Foodstuffs to Cancer

Populations that traditionally eat large amounts of smoked or pickled food have been shown to have an extraordinarily high incidence of certain tumors of the gastrointestinal tract or oropharynx (the region connecting the mouth and the nose). Otherwise rare tumors such as gastric cancer and nasopharyngeal cancer (a tumor of the region where the soft palate at the roof of the mouth joins with the nasal epithelium) also occur in high numbers in these parts of the world.

For example, in Guangdon province in southeastern China, nasopharyngeal cancer accounts for 15 percent of all cancer deaths.[40] (For comparison, in the United States, nasopharyngeal cancer accounts for a fraction of 1 percent of cancer deaths.) A common denominator among residents in Guangdon and other parts of Asia who develop this tumor at high rates is the consumption of salted fish. In Hong Kong, Malaysia, and Canton, where this tumor is endemic, salted fish are a staple in the diet among the poor. The earlier in life the fish are eaten, the greater the risk factor. (Unbelievably, babies are *weaned* on salted fish in these areas!)

Many other preserved foods, including dried fish, salted duck eggs, salted mustard greens and roots, and fermented soy-bean paste have also been found to be factors in nasopharyngeal cancer.[41]

Role of Additives in Cancer

The major additives that have come into question have been the antioxidants, butylated hydroxyanisole (BHA) and butylated hydroxytoluene (BHT). Although both chemicals have been implicated as promoters of carcinogenesis in some studies (BHA more clearly than BHT),[42] under some circumstances they show an ability to retard tumorigenesis.[43]

Other additives, too numerous to mention here, have been among the most carefully screened chemicals for possible carcinogenic effects.[44] That is not to say that all cancer-producing additives have been eliminated. While a few of the very worst offenders, notably certain food dyes such as butter yellow and several red dyes have been eliminated, many others are still in use. The Food and Drug Administration (FDA) has been less than aggressive in eliminating such agents from our diet. In 1960, Congress gave industry two and a half years to submit safety test results to the FDA. The FDA in turn gave industry one extension after another (twenty to date).[45] Between 1983 and 1985, red dye number 3 was found to be an animal carcinogen. Blue number 2 and yellow number 5 and 6 gave conflicting evidence of carcinogenicity. Between 1950 and 1984, per capita consumption of dyes tripled. In 1986, the FDA tried unsuccessfully to get an exemption from its regulatory responsibility to permit the continued use of a number of such weakly carcinogenic food colors.[46] But as of 1991, all four of the controversial dyes are still being used.

Molds and Dietary Carcinogenesis

The major concern about so-called natural carcinogenesis has focused on a single group of chemicals, the aflatoxins. This group of related compounds is recognized by the FDA as "an unavoidable natural toxicant" that contaminates food and feed.[47] (The role of aflatoxins in liver carcinogenesis is discussed at length in "Interactive Models of Carcinogenesis," below.)

Molds also produce patulin, a contaminant found in apples, and tricothecene toxins, which can contribute to the carcinogenicity of contaminated food. Fortunately, natural fermentation of apple juice can destroy patulin.

The Role of Alcohol in Cancer

Alcohol has been associated with several tumor types, in particular with liver cancer. However, since those who use alcohol almost always smoke more, weigh less, are more sexually active, and tend to abuse other drugs more than the general population, it is often difficult to determine the actual contribution of alcohol to cancer origins. Some researchers nonetheless believe that alcohol per se is a major cause of human cancer. In his widely publicized *Science* article, "Ranking Possible Carcinogenic Hazards," B. M. Ames and his colleagues called alcohol one of the two "largest identified sources of neoplastic death in the United States."[48] In spite of such strong assertions and the stand of the National Academy of Sciences that alcohol is a major factor in causing cancer of the digestive tract and other sites, the data supporting the view that alcohol per se is a carcinogen is inconsistent and weak.

A recent editorial in the *New England Journal of Medicine* urged readers to consider the plausibility of data supporting alcohol ingestion and breast cancer rates.[49] But Bengt Lindegård, a University of Gothenburg researcher and head of a team investigating the relationship of alcohol ingestion and breast cancer in Sweden, pointed out that the coassociation of both alcohol ingestion *and* breast cancer incidence with high socioeconomic status potentially skews the data. According to Linde-gård, his own findings in 1,123 women with breast cancer from a socioeconomically and ethnically homogeneous population in Sweden clearly showed no association of this cancer with any disease associated with alcohol ingestion or with alcoholism.[50]

Based on animal studies, Ames equates the carcinogenic effects of a daily glass of wine to that of a worker's "average" daily exposure to formaldehyde, a nasopharyngeal carcinogen in the rat. Writing a Technical Comment in rebuttal (a letter I edited and cosigned), Samuel Epstein of the University of Illinois and Joel Swartz of the University of Quebec point out that in four of the five studies that Ames cites to generate his data, alcohol was, in fact, noncarcinogenic. They conclude that while alcohol has been incriminated in causing tumors of the upper digestive tract, particularly in conjunction with tobacco smoke, and in setting the stage for liver cancer by producing cirrhosis, "there is no evidence incriminating alcohol per se as a potent carcinogen for the general population, particularly nonsmokers."[51] Others concur that the key linkage is between smoking and alcohol and have challenged the notion that alcohol by itself is carcinogenic.[52]

A closer look at the data shows that both parties in this dispute are in a sense "right." Pure ethanol can enhance the cancer-causing potency of other chemicals, particularly in animals whose diets are deficient in methylcholine.[53] Consumption of alcoholic beverages (as distinct from pure ethanol) is unequivocably linked with heightened cancer risks.[54] In fact, drinking certain alcoholic beverages is associated with higher risks of cancer of the larynx,[55] pharynx,[56] and mouth.[57]

However, a recent study casts a different light on these associations. By separating out "light" from "dark" liquors (that is, gin, vodka, and light rum as opposed to whiskeys, scotch, and bourbons), a research team headed by long-time alcohol researcher Kenneth J. Rothman at the Boston University Medical Center found that dark liquors were appreciably more carcinogenic for cancers of the mouth and throat than were light ones (although this effect was less striking for cancer of the larynx). These findings are consistent with the method by which the darker liquors are commonly produced, and the finding that some alcoholic beverages contain urethan, a potent carcinogen. Many of these drinks, notably whiskey and brandy, are left in contact with charred or smoked wood or are left in oaken barrels in which tannins (also carcinogens) permeate the drink.

Based on these findings, the Rothman team concluded that it is the nonalcoholic content of distilled alcoholic beverages that is responsible for most of the carcinogenic risk, and that alcohol itself acts primarily as a solvent for other carcinogens.[58] Again, this view supports the notion that while "natural" substances can contribute to cancer causation, they are mainly those that result from human processing and not necessarily an intrinsic property of the starting material.

The Role of Food Preparation in Cancer

Cancer risks are also added to otherwise benign foods by the manner of their preparation. Recent data show that a large variety of mutagens and carcinogens, which did not previously exist in the foods, rapidly appear as the foods are cooked.[59] The appearance of novel substances with potent gene-damaging activity occurs most often in fried, browned, seared, or smoked food and is independent of the means of preserving them (which itself may be an additional source of carcinogens).[60]

At least a dozen chemicals, many containing NH_2 groups, have been isolated from broiled or fried meat or fish that have potent mutagenicity in tissue culture tests. Many of the active chemicals can be found in the urine or feces of test animals where they maintain potent gene-damaging and presumptive carcinogenic activity. What would make the linkage between such substances and cancer plausible are (1) where the substances occur (they are found almost exclusively in the browned "crust" of meats and fish), (2) the association of eating such burned or crusted foods and cancer, and (3) the demonstration that the newly formed substances induce cancer in humans. While points 1 and 2 appear well established, the third point is still unproven.

What is clear, though, is that the association between eating heavily cooked or seared meat and fish products and cancer of the digestive tract is suggestive, but not as conclusive as is the association of preserved meats and fish with digestive tract cancers.

Interplay of Factors in Carcinogenesis

Such cancers, notably those of the esophagus, stomach, small intestine, and colon, have traditionally been associated with dietary patterns. Esophageal cancer may be associated with micronutrient deficiencies or imbalances.[61] Colon cancer, as we have seen, has been linked to a diet low in bulk and high in fat and a sedentary life-style.[62] Genetic factors also play a key role in colon cancer since the polyps that serve as precursors to most colon cancers have a clear-cut genetic basis. A single dominant gene puts an individual at risk of developing polyps beginning in middle age.[63]

I will concentrate on only three tumor types to illustrate the complex role that diet, synthetic, and "natural" substances play in promoting their appearance.

Stomach Cancer.　Stomach cancer is an example of a tumor type that has been attributed almost exclusively to diet, but that has other contributing factors as well. As shown in Figure 10-1 (see page 193), carcinoma of the stomach has been undergoing a rapid decline in the United States over the past two decades. The decline is widely attributed to improvements in the diet, but no one knows the full explanation. This tumor's incidence pattern shows a dramatic geographic distribution that suggests that one or more factors in the environment may be associated with its origins. For example, in the province of Narino in Columbia, South America, stomach cancer is more than four times more prevalent than in Columbia as a whole. In this region, stomach cancer may be associated with eating fava beans and the conversion of some of its chemical constituents to N-nitroso compounds.[64]

In the United States, the pattern of stomach cancer suggests other factors may be at work. For instance, Figure 10-2[65] shows a striking distribution of stomach cancer among urban areas and areas characterized by low socioeconomic class. (The map from 1950–69 is shown because less geographic mobility in the population permits a clearer depiction of clustering than do more recent maps.)

The death rates from cancer of the stomach are elevated in rural counties in Pennsylvania, Kentucky, and in the northern states of Wisconsin, Michigan, Minnesota, and the Dakotas.

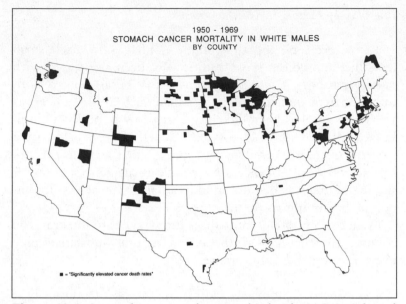

Figure 10-2. Stomach cancer and geographic locale, U.S.A. Adapted from *Atlas of Cancer Mortality for United States Counties 1950–1969,* T. J. Mason, et al., eds., Department of Health, Education and Welfare.

An additional cluster of high-risk areas can be seen in New Mexico and Colorado. Parallel atlases constructed for Japan show that stomach cancer is highly prevalent in the rural northwest areas of Honshu and is low on the more heavily populated island of Kyushu in the south. In Columbia and Chile, both countries with high rates of stomach cancer, the highest incidences are in agricultural provinces. In Iceland, the disease is most common on the rural, northwestern part of the island; in Yugoslavia, it is highest in the mountainous areas.[66]

What happens when the affected populations move to other regions of the world? Migrants as a rule have stomach cancer rates that are intermediate between their country of origin and their host country. With longer residence in areas of low cancer rates, the rates of the migrant population tend to decrease as well. This pattern is shown in Figure 10-2: regions of Minnesota, Wisconsin, and the Dakotas with high cancer rates also have relatively high populations of people from Scandinavia, the Soviet Union, and central Europe where stomach cancer is more common than in the United States generally. This association is particularly striking for Minnesota, which has one of the highest overall stomach cancer rates in the United States and also has a high proportion of individuals with the foreign ancestry described above.[67] Whether dietary habits brought over from the "old country" or genetic predisposition best explains this pattern of cancer remains to be determined.

Chinese in the United States have lower rates of stomach cancer than do native Chinese who reside in Taiwan, Hong Kong, and Singapore.[68] And Chinese born in the United States have almost the same rate as do their U.S. Caucasian counterparts. Japanese immigrants show a similar, though not as striking a pattern. Among U.S.-born Japanese, stomach cancer rates remain somewhat higher than for U.S. Caucasians as a group.[69] The most revealing study has been a case-control investigation from Hawaii in which new Japanese immigrants from high incidence areas in Japan were found to retain their high rates while their children tended to assume the rates of Caucasian Hawaiian Islanders.[70]

These latter findings have been interpreted as evidence of a strong dietary factor in stomach cancer.[71] Ingestion of salted foods, including soybean paste and salted fish, are directly linked with stomach cancer gradients on the Japanese Islands. Other foods, notably singed and charred meat, have been linked to high stomach cancer rates in areas of Iceland in which there is also a high consumption of smoked fish and meat. According to a British research team, the introduction of new methods of food preservation, notably refrigeration, may account for the dramatic declines of stomach cancer in the last century in countries such as Iceland.[72]

The chemical culprit in stomach cancer, however, is likely to be the same type of N-nitroso compound previously associated with cutting oil cancer (see Chapter 2). Nitrosamines (which can cause stomach cancer in animals) are formed in the stomach from nitrates that may be ingested from contaminated drinking water or from food preservatives. Since 1969, it has been known that nitrates can be reduced to nitrites by bacterial action in the saliva and gastric juice. The nitrites then react with dietary amines (present in many different foods, especially certain cheeses such as gorgonzola) to form N-nitroso compounds. While this hypothesis is still being tested, it does indicate that synthetic chemicals (the nitrates) may be just as significant in causing stomach cancer as certain foods. (In 1978, armed with data from research showing nitrites to be carcinogenic, the FDA and the Department of Agriculture planned to ban them. The FDA, however, subsequently rescinded its decision, and nitrites remain in use, especially in processed meats.)

In fact, it is becoming clear that a multitude of factors comes into play in stomach cancer. One unifying theory invokes injury to the mucosal lining of the stomach, which is then more subject to bacterial colonization. Such colonization means more nitrates can be reduced, leading to more N-nitroso compounds.[73]

Nasopharyngeal Cancer. Some of the thinking about stomach cancer also fits the natural history of nasopharyngeal cancer. Certainly, as we have seen, diet, especially smoked or charred meat, plays a role in inciting this unusual tumor. But a closer examination of the contributing factors among the highest risk population — southern Chinese — is revealing. Researchers who expanded their ecological studies to encompass other environmental factors besides diet found that three and possibly four elements come into play in shaping the epidemiology of this cancer. The first is diet, as we know. But the second turns out to be a ubiquitous agent known as the Epstein-Barr virus. A third is the genetic makeup of the population — only certain individuals (identified by their unusual makeup of human leukocyte antigen or HLA genes) appear to be at highest risk.[74] Still other researchers have implicated a fourth factor, the inhalation of certain chemicals found in the environment, particularly in wood smoke.[75]

Given that this rare tumor type is also strongly linked to certain occupations such as furniture making, the designation of nasopharyngeal carcinoma as *either* a purely "naturally" caused *or* a purely synthetic-chemical-associated tumor is clearly wrong. Again, a concatenation of factors comes into play in shaping the origins and development of these and almost all other tumors — including the genetics; innate resistance to carcinogenesis; immune system integrity; and environmental factors that span diet, synthetic chemicals, and substances that may be ingested or inhaled. What is clear is that synthetic substances generated either through food preparation or wood burning contribute far more to this tumor than does any unadulterated "natural" substance.

Liver Cancer.　Widespread geographic variations in liver cancer rates, as with those for stomach cancer, point to environmental factors in shaping this complex disease. As mentioned in Chapter 4, the highest rates are found in some parts of Africa (notably Maputo, Mozambique, Bulawayo, and Zimbabwe) and in Taiwan. In these regions, liver tumors rank as the number one cause of cancer death, having an incidence in men of more than 1 in 1,000.[76] (In the United States, by comparison, the rate in men is less than 4 per 100,000.[77])

As with stomach cancer, the rates for primary liver tumors in a given population tend to decrease when residents of high incidence areas move to lower incidence ones. This pattern obviously suggests that factors in the environment are significant contributing factors to the origins of the disease.

In 1965, a South African researcher suggested that mycotoxins (poisons derived from molds or fungi) were the major cause of liver cancer in Africa.[78] His evidence was simple and straightforward. In those areas with the highest rates of liver cancer, the inhabitants ingested grains or ground nuts that were commonly moldy, while in low-rate areas or tribes, the diet lacked moldy food. By 1969, this idea had found widespread acceptance.[79]

The age distribution of mold-associated liver cancer in Africa is unusual. Instead of the sharply increasing curve of incidence with age seen for all other epithelial tumors, liver cancers in the high-risk areas peak early (between the ages of 20 and 50) and then *decrease* with age.[80] But, as we saw in the discussion of transplacental carcinogenesis and childhood cancers (see Chapter 7), this incidence pattern (especially the shortened latency) strongly suggests a strong carcinogenic insult occurring either very early in life or in the uterus itself. The most likely culprit in utero is hepatitis B virus; thereafter, aflatoxin from molds is likely the major causative factor. Hence, mold-associated cancer may have at least two causes: a chemical carcinogen and a virus.

The clearest link of moldy foods and liver cancer was developed in the mid-1960s. Several catastrophic outbreaks of liver disease and cancer in poultry and hatchery-raised rainbow trout were traced to feed and fishmeal made from moldy peanuts. On analysis of the feeds, high levels of aflatoxins were found. Once aflatoxin was implicated, researchers conducted surveys of markets, home-stored goods, and even food on the dinner table in geographical "hot spots" of liver cancer in Swaziland, Uganda, Kenya, Mozambique, and Thailand. The finding of high aflatoxin contamination of foods in these areas corresponded remarkably with the regions that had the highest liver cancer rates in each country.[81]

However, in spite of these impressive patterns and statistics, recent data make it clear that hormones (see Chapter 9), alcohol,[82] cigarette smoking,[83] work in certain occupations (for example, dry-cleaning and gas station operations),[84] as well as infection with hepatitis B virus[85] are also associated with liver cancer.

INTERACTIVE MODELS OF CARCINOGENESIS

These studies taken in aggregate demonstrate the limited utility of thinking of cancer as being caused by any single factor. That is, the pattern of causation that best explains cancer is that of *interaction.* Let's, for example, consider all of the factors identified that contribute to carcinogenesis: we've seen that high-fat diets may exaggerate the carcinogenic effects of the estrogens described in the last chapter, especially if exposure to the fats occurs prenatally.[86] The major role of diet, as we've also seen, seems to be to modify or blunt the cancer-causing actions of contaminants, environmental carcinogens, or other synthetic substances. This is especially true for chemicals that are potent mutagens or liver carcinogens. The mutagenic (and, by inference, the cancer-causing) properties of aflatoxins, for example, can be blunted by the presence of other foodstuffs that contain a group of substances called flavonoids.[87] And naturally occurring antioxidants such as vitamins C and E are just being examined for their anticancer effects.[88]

Other epidemiologic factors only appear to be significant risk factors in combination with other factors. While cigarette smoking has been strongly associated with risk of lung cancer and less strongly with liver cancer, its effects are most dramatic in smokers who drink or who also have a hepatitis B infection.[89] Similarly, the cirrhosis that normally precedes liver cancer in alcoholics (hepatocellular carcinoma) is greatly exacerbated by the concurrent infection with hepatitis B virus.[90]

The predominant evidence suggests that, like the other tumors mentioned here, the initiator of primary liver cancer is *not dietary*. Rather, hepatitis B infection appears to be the principal factor, with aflatoxins, cigarette smoke, industrial or agricultural chemicals, hormones, and/or alcohol serving as cofactors or as promoting agents (even though some of these factors are carcinogens in their own right).

The data for this hypothesis is strong. For example, researchers P. Cook-Mozaffari and S. Van Rensburg, while supporting the aflatoxin hypothesis, believe that "a history of HBV infection may be an initiating factor in the development of most cases of PLC [primary liver cancer]."[91] The prevalence of persons with hepatitis B viral infections is also highest in those countries that have high liver cancer rates; the correlation of hepatitis B antigen prevalence and liver cancer holds up even down to the district level; the DNA from hepatitis B virus can be found in liver tumors; and prospective studies of persons who are either hepatitis B positive or negative show that almost all of the former (and virtually none of the latter) are at risk for liver cancer.

Human liver cells tested in tissue culture are, in fact, highly resistant to aflatoxin-provoked carcinogenesis.[92] But even where aflatoxins are not found because of climatic factors, the correlation of liver cancer and hepatitis B virus infection remains strong.[93]

It is also becoming clearer that Americans may be more resistant to aflatoxin-related liver damage than are Africans, independent of their antigenic status and hepatitis B virus. Diets high in protein appear to be highly protective of aflatoxin-mediated liver carcinogenesis at least in animals.[94] Thus, while the role of aflatoxins in promoting or contributing to liver cancer is clear in the developing world, its role in producing liver tumors in developed societies is not nearly as clear. In contrast, a causative role for hepatitis B is much clearer.

A person infected with the hepatitis B virus in the United States carries the same risk of developing liver cancer as does a person infected with hepatitis B in the countries with the highest liver cancer rates.[95] In fact, hepatitis B virus infection *alone* may be sufficient to induce liver cancer.

Policy Implications

These data not only provide evidence for a primary role of nonnutritive factors in the genesis of cancer, but have strong policy implications. To suggest (as does Bruce Ames) that diet in general and aflatoxins in particular be considered the major concern for carcinogenesis in Americans is at the least misleading. While there is little doubt that some chemical contaminants of moldy foodstuffs are both potent animal carcinogens and affect carcinogenesis in malnourished populations in developing countries, there is little evidence that they play a significant role in producing many cancers in developed countries such as the United States. This is partly because most of these tumors, such as nasopharyngeal, stomach, and liver cancer are so rare in almost all developed countries.

In fact, by the late 1970s, the evidence was compelling that hepatitis B—and not aflatoxins—is the etiological agent of greatest concern for liver carcinogenesis worldwide.[96] What is needed is a program of vaccination, not dietary advice, to minimize the risk of liver cancer. This idea, first proposed by Barry Blumberg of the Fox Chase Institute for Cancer Research in Pennsylvania,[97] is underscored by recent data that suggest that hepatitis B virus infection changes the liver in a way that makes it more susceptible to chemical carcinogens. For example, in virally infected woodchucks, which are the only other animal besides humans to be naturally susceptible to hepatitis viruses, metabolic activation of carcinogens is significantly increased in the liver.[98]

These data, coupled with the observation that chemical carcinogens are more potent in virally infected animals—and thus perhaps in similarly infected humans—support the conclusion that cancer cannot be neatly bifurcated into "natural" and "synthetic." Diet alone is hardly the answer, since foodstuffs must almost always interact with environmental factors *before* they become carcinogens!

DIET FOR A TOXIC PLANET

Let us then reconsider the role of dietary factors in cancer. While it is true that some components of the diet can contribute to increased cancer risk, they are likely to operate only when taken in excess (as in breast cancer and obesity). In fact, the levels of carcinogens in most unprocessed food is generally remarkably low. With the exception of some fungi, roots, and molds, the major conclusion of this review is that only when foods are *cooked, smoked, or preserved in certain ways* do new mutagens and carcinogens appear in significant levels.

It may nonetheless be wise to adjust our diets so that we avoid certain foods that do increase cancer risk. Reducing the amount of smoked, processed, heavily charred or seared meats and "dark" alcoholic beverages would be a first step since these are not only linked to higher cancer risks in some populations but contain most of the nitrosamines in a typical diet in a developed country.[99] Dietary additives that are new to our larder may be more dangerous than even the supposedly "potent" carcinogens found in molds and other foods. Fructose is a case in point. Introduced as a naturally sweeter sweetner, fructose is now being consumed in amounts that were previously impossible on a "natural" diet. With the advent of high-fructose corn syrups in the 1970s, more and more of the sugar content of our diet is being amplified by this "sweeter than cane sugar" sugar. The addition of substantial amounts of fructose to the diets of rats (12 percent of their drinking water) was shown to *double* the cancer incidence after the fructose-saturated animals were fed a liver carcinogen.[100] Furthermore, a genetic factor affecting the metabolism of glucose may also predispose to liver cancer.[101] These data certainly suggest reducing the amount of simple sugars in the diet generally, and processed sugars particularly.

It is also desirable to reduce or eliminate our reliance on smoked, pickled, or preserved food since many constituents of these products are proven carcinogens. However, it may not be necessary to abandon all such products. If the carcinogenic ingredients can be identified, certain preserved foods may be acceptable. For instance, the principal carcinogenic ingredient in Chinese pickled vegetables has been identified and could in theory be eliminated.[102] It is also possible to choose cooking methods that avoid—possibly completely—the formation of carcinogenic chemicals.

Avoiding tinctures, infusions, or extracts of roots would also appear to be sound advice (and here Ames and I agree).

Sassafras (the original "root" beer) and extracts of tansy ragwort and members of the *Senecio* genus are to be avoided. Similar advice to avoid rotted or moldy foods is almost self-evident
since some chemical constituents (such as patulin) can be both
carcinogenic *and* immunity suppressing.[103]

Avoiding excessive use of spices and some natural oils is
also good advice. Oils from plants such as star anise, cinna-
mon, camphor, and sassafras as well as such spices as mace,
ginger, and bay leaf contain trace amounts of weak carcinogens.[104] Fresh as compared to dried spices (particularly among
chilies) are also less likely to be contaminated with carcinogens such as the N-nitrosamines.[105]

It is obviously a good idea to eat cruciferous vegetables.
Chemicals found in these vegetables have been the first anti-
cancer-initiating agents discovered among foodstuffs in our
natural diet.[106] Adding broccoli and cabbage to rodent diets
(amounts equivalent to a little more than half a pound a day
for a 132-pound woman) greatly reduced the incidence of
chemically induced breast cancer.[107] Extracts of these same
vegetables also dramatically inhibited the cancer-causing properties of aflatoxins given to fish[108] and the formation of carcinogenic adducts between DNA and benzo(*a*)pyrene.[109]

Adding even modest amounts of garlic oil extracts to the
diet can dramatically (in animals) reduce colon cancer.[110] Green
tea appears to be an antimutagen and anticancer agent.[111] It
also suppresses the cell-damaging properties of aflatoxins.[112]

Other foods may contain *both* natural mutagens and antimutagens, so that caution in advocating their inclusion (or exclusion) from the diet would appear warranted. For instance,
some fermented soybean products are potent antimutagens but
also contain dangerous chemicals that can cause genetic
damage.[113] Another product with suspect chemical constituents as well as beneficial ones is yogurt. Recent studies have
shown that some cultures used to make yogurt at home can
favor the growth of some fungi that generate aflatoxins.[114]

RETHINKING THE CONTRIBUTIONS OF NATURAL
VERSUS SYNTHETIC CHEMICALS TO CANCER

In the end, even our best estimates for the role of workplace
and environmental factors in causing human cancers are still

woefully inaccurate. Even the most recent estimates place the figure for environmental causes as a broad range rather than an exact figure. The problem is not in our quantitation, but in our methods of parsing out the contribution of chemicals, be they from Mother Nature, our own internal chemical factories, the microsomal systems, or the chemical factory down the road.

The best thinking is that cancer is a *multifactorial* phenomenon, comprised of multiple steps, each of which can have multiple factors. A clear example of this complexity can be seen in the models that have attempted to induce respiratory tract cancer in experimental animals. For years, pure chemicals or even complex mixes such as those found in cigarette smoke condensates were remarkably unsuccessful in inducing tumors. (This fact was long cited by the tobacco industry as evidence that their products were not responsible for lung cancer in humans.)

It was not until cigarette smoke components were adsorbed onto iron or carbon particles and instilled into the lungs of experimental animals that an analog to human lung cancer was developed. As a result of the most recent studies, it is evident that factors such as damage to the mucosal lining of the throat and lungs, iron particles, and carcinogen exposure all interact to produce the highest risk of lung cancer.[115] As with hepatitis B and chemical carcinogens in the liver, the presence of viruses that can damage mucosal surfaces also appears to heighten the impact of the chemical carcinogens in tobacco. Mice latently infected with herpes simplex virus were much more vulnerable to the early carcinogenic effects of tar condensates of smoking tobacco than were noninfected controls.[116]

CONCLUSION: DISTILLING A KERNEL OF TRUTH

At the hub of the problem of attribution of cancer causation is thus the tendency to consider factors in isolation. Taking cancer causes one chemical at a time, as Bruce Ames and his colleagues do, is to miss the strong likelihood that a complex interplay among and between natural and synthetic chemicals is as important in cancer causation as are the individual chemicals themselves. Most critically, such a reductionist viewpoint restricts the global viewpoint necessary in the 1990s to "see" the concatenation of forces that mold our health and well-being.

Take, for example, chlorofluorocarbons. Only one of the synthetic chlorofluorocarbons has ever been shown to be carcinogenic. But in depleting the ozone layer, they have permitted a vastly increased flux of high-energy "natural" ultraviolet light to hit the planet and have thereby increased the likelihood of many more skin cancers and perhaps other malignancies. By the year 2010, one in seventy Americans will probably get melanoma—no dietary factors here!

Similarly, Ames's argument that nature makes the most potent carcinogens is flawed: synthetic chemicals such as DES are much more carcinogenic molecule for molecule than are almost all "dietary" carcinogens. The dichotomy between natural and synthetic can also be artificial. "Naturally" occurring botanical estrogens in yams are the starting point for synthesizing the estrogens in birth control pills. Such estrogens are as carcinogenic and as "unnatural" to the human body as are natural estrogens.

And the history of liver cancer adds other insights to the full picture of human carcinogenesis. While it is true that so-called natural mold contaminants like the aflatoxins are potent liver toxins and carcinogens, we have seen that they may not produce liver cancer by acting alone. Recent investigations have shown that the ability of one particularly potent aflatoxin group (aflatoxin B) to induce liver cancer may depend on background hormonal stimulation by estrogens.[117] Other studies have shown that to be an effective cancer-causing agent, the aflatoxins must act on a virally damaged liver, or one in a semi-starved animal.

Studies of this sort underscore that synthetic chemicals often interact with natural ones as well as with the individual makeup of each person in causing cancer. A premalignant cell goes through many steps in the progression from a genetically altered clone of cells to a clinically evident tumor. The factors that shape this evolution include overall diet, immunologic strength, genetic background, and the coexistence of chemical exposures.[118] Over time, evolutionary mechanisms have generally assured that people will be resistant to the rapid carcinogenic insults of most dietary ingredients. But a similar largess is not evident for synthetic ones.

What we do know is that the existence of "resistance" genes, antioxidants, host defenses, and dietary cancer protectants and antimutagens together comprise an "antirisk" group of factors that some scientists have intentionally or unintentionally ignored. While only passingly mentioned by Ames and his colleagues in their *Science* article,[119] the powerful role of such risk-reducing factors — most of which are dietary — in limiting the occurrence of cancer has been grossly neglected.

Policy Implications

Knowing what causes cancer or accelerates its appearance allows us to design prevention strategies. This knowledge is also freighted with political weight, since different strategies will have widely divergent economic, ethical, and practical impacts.

Given the multiplicity of factors that contribute to cancer causation, it is prudent to act on many fronts at once. If individual action can shift the conditions in favor of health, so much the better. Because dietary exposure largely is voluntary, it is most controllable by individual action.

But the responsibility for assuring that the human environment is not plagued with *more* carcinogens than occur by chance or natural means falls squarely on the *industrial sector*. As a result of the sweeping environmental legislation introduced in the last two decades, corporations are legally and morally bound not to knowingly release chemicals that pose carcinogenic risks either by their mode of manufacture or their use. The freedom to produce any and all chemical creations is also circumscribed by a higher law, which recognizes the need for assuring that the environment is vouchsafed for future generations. But until recently few if any corporations selected products by anticipating their environmental fate or chose their feedstocks to avoid creating carcinogenic risks.

Some countries have taken a first and significant step toward reducing indirect carcinogenesis by urging major cutbacks in the production of ozone-depleting chlorofluorocarbons. But to continue the noisome attack about cancer arising from supermarket baskets as if homemakers are responsible for polluting their family's dinner table is to miss the point of all the evidence assembled here. Modern diets can be reasonably modified to reduce the likelihood of forming carcinogenic by-products by avoiding smoked, preserved, or moldy foods and by keeping cooking temperatures low. Additional safeguards include eating whole grains, fruits, and cruciferous vegetables, and drinking green teas and other products that have natural "anticarcinogens" in them.

In the meantime, the lion's share of the responsibility for mitigating the onslaught of cancer lies with those who profit by adding chemicals to the environment or foods that induce or promote cancer. By assuring that corporations and public health agencies fulfill their promises and duties to protect the outside world, parents and homemakers can go a long way toward ensuring the safety of their internal ones. A key interface of these two worlds is the water we drink.

CHAPTER ELEVEN

Myth 9:

If it comes out of the tap, it's safe to drink

MOST DEVELOPED COUNTRIES TAKE IT AS A MEASURE OF THEIR advancement that they have conquered the water-borne diseases that have plagued civilizations since the time of the pharaohs. Many historians agree with British epidemiologist Thomas McKeown that more progress in combatting ill health was achieved in the eighteenth and early nineteenth centuries through *hygienic* measures that assured a modicum of clean water than by all of the previous advancements of medicine combined.[1]

This is not to say that we have fully triumphed in assuring a pure and clean water supply to our population. A critical step in this direction was taken in 1974 when Congress passed the Safe Drinking Water Act (PL 93-523). This act mandated the Environmental Protection Agency (EPA) to set standards that would protect all citizens from harmful contaminants in drinking water and assure the continued purity of the underground aquifers on which most of the water in the United

States depends. Data developed by the National Academy of Sciences (NAS) and recent reports from the EPA itself have shown that this goal has not been achieved.

Beginning in 1977, in a series of reports submitted under the mandate of the Safe Drinking Water Act, the NAS reported a wide spectrum of problems that could be expected if water levels of certain organic, inorganic, and chemical contaminants were not abated.[2] Presumably, this abatement is assured by water treatment of potentially contaminated surface water supplies. Unfortunately, this common assumption may be flawed. As the NAS observed in 1982, "the quality of a public water supply, although quite acceptable when it leaves the treatment plant, may deteriorate before it reaches the user."[3] And in 1983, in a seminal report from the University of Pennsylvania Press, two researchers documented the growing extent of contamination of the one water source that had been assumed to be largely protected from contamination — deep lying groundwater.[4]

Groundwater provides about half of all the drinking water in the United States. By the early 1980s, it was clear that this source was the primary vehicle for human exposure to chemical pollutants.[5] In 1984, the EPA estimated that toxic contamination of groundwater was occurring from migration of wastes from three-quarters of the 30,000 to 50,000 hazardous waste sites across the United States as well as from other stationary sources such as electronics plants and gasoline stations that stored hazardous materials in underground tanks.[6]

Other sources of contamination include the intentional application of pesticides to control outbreaks of "undesirable" insects in forested ecosystems or to limit the growth of certain plants or underbrush. Most often, pesticide contamination of drinking water stems from agricultural activities. Herbicides in particular have both a direct and indirect impact on the quality of water within whole watersheds, and on the deep water reserves in the ground below. Herbicides such as 2,4-D, picloram, paraquat, and atrazine have been routinely applied to croplands, and less often to forests, with little or no understanding of their geological fate or ecological consequences. According to water expert D. G. Neary, we know virtually nothing about the potential impacts of such chemicals on the quality of our water supplies.[7]

The EPA has since identified an increasing number of polluted aquifers as it tightens its water standards to keep apace of current epidemiological and cancer bioassay data. As of 1989, some seven hundred different substances had been uncovered in drinking water supplies. Only forty have been thoroughly evaluated for their health effects, and only fourteen to thirty organic compounds (depending on the state) are currently monitored in public community water systems.

THE PROBLEMS OF DISINFECTION

Chlorination

Not the least of the problems facing the country is the belated realization that virtually all of the techniques that water districts rely on to sanitize their drinking water simultaneously create other problems. To purify drinking water, communities have traditionally relied on the disinfecting properties of chlorine. By 1978, the existence of potent mutagenic substances in chlorinated water supplies was well established.[8] Hypochlorite, the major form of chlorine found in most municipal water systems, has itself been shown to produce damage in sperm assays.[9] These findings strongly suggest that chlorination itself may be mutagenic, a disturbing conclusion given that it is the most widely used disinfectant in the United States.

Researchers have since discovered that a constellation of compounds are formed each time a water supply is disinfected. This problem is particularly severe in water systems that rely on surface water with a high organic content, such as rivers. For example, in one study performed on water obtained from the Katsura River, which serves approximately 10 million people near Kyoto, Japan, researchers found that the weak background mutagenicity of the river water was greatly enhanced by chlorination.[10] Parallel studies performed on water samples taken from a river flowing by Des Moines, Iowa also demonstrated the formation of direct-acting mutagenic substances following chlorination.[11] The major significance of these findings is twofold: first, excess cancer rates have been observed in areas along the contaminated riverways; and second, it is unlikely that the standard methods of water treatment used after chlorination will remove the mutagenic substances that are formed during chlorination.[12]

Trihalomethanes. The major by-products of chlorine-based disinfection (from free chlorine gas, chlorine oxide, or any of the other chlorinated compounds that have been used) are the trihalomethanes (THMs). These are single methane molecules (one carbon plus four hydrogens) in which three of the hydrogen atoms are replaced with a halogen, either chlorine or bromine.

Cl	Br	Br	Br	Cl	Cl
H-C-Cl	H-C-Br	H-C-Cl	H-C-Cl	H-C-Br	H-C-Br
Cl	Br	Cl	Br	Cl	Br
Chloroform	**Bromoform**	**Other Trihalomethanes**			

Figure 11-1. The trihalomethanes

The THMs are produced because of the presence of organic molecules in surface water and to a lesser extent, in groundwater. Among the most common THMs are chloroform ($CHCl_3$) and bromoform ($CHBr_3$), both of which are potent carcinogens. Chloroform has been shown to produce liver cancer in all of the test animals in which it has been assayed.[13] And bromoform, while less thoroughly tested, has potent kidney and liver toxicity of its own.[14] These disturbing realizations led belatedly to the issuance of a standard for combined THMs in 1979 by the EPA of 100 parts per billion (ppb), a level that is far from protective at the standard risk level of one cancer death per million persons exposed to this water over a lifetime.

Systematic studies of populations whose drinking water has unusually high levels of THMs have since suggested that this standard is too low to afford the same protection given for other potential carcinogenic chemicals. The NAS has estimated that at 100 ppb, the cancer risk from chloroform (were it to be the sole chemical ingredient in the THMs) is one in 100,000.[15]

While data from earlier studies (circa 1970s) gave conflicting results regarding the association of THM contaminants in drinking water and cancer in exposed populations,[16] by 1982 it was clear that a pattern linking high levels of THMs to increased cancer deaths was emerging.[17] Ecologic studies of the late 1970s had shown that cancer mortality rates were higher than expected in regions with poor water quality, especially where chlorination had led to high THM levels. These data — albeit too insensitive to permit quantitative estimates — were interpreted as being useful in formulating a hypothesis of association.[18] Then, in 1981, case-control studies began to appear that relied on death certificate data to show a clear-cut relationship between exposure to chlorine-treated municipal water supplies and an increased incident of bladder, rectal, and colon cancer.[19] These data were particularly striking in municipalities that drew their water from surface or shallow aquifers, strongly suggesting that it was the high organic content typical of such supplies that contributed to the increased risk.

Not all of the epidemiological findings linking THMs with particular cancer sites such as the colon have proven reproducible.[20] Nonetheless, sufficient evidence is available to have led Kenneth Cantor of the National Cancer Institute to believe that the chlorinated organic molecules that form in drinking water from chlorination coupled with those that are unintentionally added combine to create a carcinogenic risk.[21] Others have been more cautious, citing only a "modest" increase in cancer risk.[22]

Of course, what comprises a contaminated water system is often difficult to determine — especially since the risk actually exists along a continuum proportional to the dose of the chemicals actually received by each affected population. However, in a penultimate study involving tens of thousands of people at risk from contaminated water systems, Cantor has shown a convincing dose-response relationship between the levels of halogenated contaminants (estimated from the amount of contaminated drinking water ingested) and the occurrence of bladder cancer.[23]

What makes Cantor's findings all the more disturbing is that the communities he studied were all on drinking water that had been treated "according to the rules," that is, the water met federal drinking water standards.

Other Chlorinated Molecules. Numerous epidemiologic studies published later in the 1980s have found a close correlation between water levels of THMs and other small chlorinated molecules such as 1,2-dichloroethane, trichloroethylene, and

1,1-dichloroethylene and the incidence of certain cancers of the digestive and urinary tracts.[24] Even in 1983, the NAS found data that implicated each of these three chemicals as possible carcinogens, but declined to recommend standards at that time.[25] Ironically, the existence of community records indicating elevated levels of these three chemicals in drinking water led to New Brighton, Minnesota, being the last of six towns selected by the Agency for Toxic Substance Disease Registry (ATSDR) of the Centers for Disease Control for inclusion in a study to record adverse health events.[26]

The first such community selected was Woburn, Massachusetts—the site of a cancer cluster of childhood leukemia. Study of the two wells of greatest concern (wells G and H) found 267 ppb of trichloroethylene, 21 ppb of perchloroethylene, and 12 ppb of chloroform. Subsequently, levels of trichlorotrifluoroethane (a chlorofluorocarbon) and 1,1-dichloroethylene between 20 and 30 ppb were also found. A team of epidemiologists from Harvard who studied the water distribution systems found a statistical association between the water from wells G and H and the occurrence of leukemia in the children of mothers who drank water from these two sources.[27]

Although some critics believe that the association between these chemicals and childhood leukemia is spurious, a larger study triggered by the Woburn experience developed surprisingly similar data. In an ecologic study conducted in New Jersey in 1984–85, state epidemiologists demonstrated a higher leukemia risk among females (but not males) in regions of the state in which high levels of volatile organic contaminants were found in the drinking water.[28] Taken alone, the New Jersey study does not provide conclusive evidence of a causal association. But in concert with other studies that showed a higher cancer mortality rate among drinkers of contaminated water, it is strongly suggestive that such a linkage exists in townships where leukemia rates are unexpectedly high. Although the researchers were unwilling to speculate publicly why only women showed an excess risk, Jerald Fagliano, the team leader, believes it may be because women were more likely to drink water at home during the day than were their husbands who worked outside the home.[29]

A closer look at the raw data shows that the rates of leukemia among females was highest in the townships in which significant chlorinated solvent contamination of the water had occurred (see Table 11-1). The excess observed among the 164 cases of leukemia was concentrated in the two highest exposure groups. In conjunction with the stepwise increase seen between dose of solvents and number of excess leukemias, these data suggest a linkage with exposure to drinking water-borne solvents.

Chlorinated Solvent* Level	Excess No. Leukemias (observed minus expected)	Significant?
3 ppb or less	− 1.8	No
5–12 ppb	+ 5.7	No
37–72 ppb	+ 9.7	Yes

*Solvents included trichloroethylene; perchloroethylene; trichloroethane; and 1,1-dichloroethylene.

Table 11-1. Excess Leukemias for Females in New Jersey Townships with Chlorinated Solvents in the Drinking Water. Adapted from Fagliano, et al.[30]

REGULATION OF DISINFECTION

Given the reality that chlorination creates hazardous molecules, the EPA and water officials have sought alternative forms of disinfection that might not create such a Mephistophelian trade-off between short-term risks from bacterial or viral disease and long-term risks from cancer. Unfortunately, the solution to this dilemma is rendered difficult by the ubiquitous nature of the chemical reactions that generate hazardous chemicals in the presence of strong oxidizers or other disinfectants. For instance, ozone has been proposed as a sanitizing agent. But after ozonation, haloacetic acids are formed that have their own carcinogenic properties. Chloramines, which appear to produce fewer hazardous by-products, simply have not proven their worth in disinfection systems. The main reason for their failure appears to be the necessity of having long contact times with infectious organisms to achieve disinfection.[31] A modest compromise of combining a little ozone with chloramine appears to be one of several possible solutions. However, regulators are uncertain if this alternative will reduce the presently unacceptably high level of THMs to one that is within the range of acceptable risk.

In 1989, few researchers or people involved with health would deny that the presently permissible levels of THMs (100 ppb) is too high. In fact, it has been regarded as "too high" for as long as I have reviewed water level standards as a health official and now as a professor of health policy (that is, since at least 1978). By 1984, at least one country had already set its THM standard at a quarter of this level,[32] closer to the World Health Organization recommendation that no more than 30 ppb of chloroform should be allowed in drinking water.[33] The permissible level of THMs still in use in the United States today represents a disproportionate and unacceptable risk of cancer for millions of persons whose drinking water approaches or exceeds this figure. I say disproportionate because the level of "acceptable risk" set for virtually all of the other contaminants for which standards are set is at or near one cancer death per million from lifetime exposure, while a 100-ppb level generates ten or more times that risk, depending on which THMs are included in the mix. I say unacceptable simply because no mechanism has been in place to either inform the public of this continuing hazard or to ask for its consent to its continuation.

Were the levels of chloroform present in typical disinfected water systems to be *introduced* by a manufacturer, it would undoubtedly be fined. (To take an analogous situation, when the Norelco Company distributed a "Clean Water Machine" for purifying water that actually *contaminated* drinking water with methylene chloride, it was fined and penalized heavily.)

Currently, in 1989, the EPA is attempting to decide what is possible for reducing the risk levels closer to acceptable norms. Unfortunately this process is snaggled in the normal snail's pace of bureaucratic machinations, having been in the Criteria and Standards Division of the Office of Drinking Water for at least three years. According to Dr. Richard Miltner of the EPA's Cincinnati office, THMs currently head a so-called Drinking Water Priority List of some twenty to thirty compounds.[34] Until completion of a review by a Science Advisory Board, the new recommended standard for THMs (of 20 to 50 ppb) remains a paper estimate. Miltner's view—that reaching this level is well within the feasibility of existing methodologies that combine ozonation with chloramine treatments—is not held by all officials—and certainly not by the purveyors of water systems whose disinfection processes will have to comply with this much more technically rigorous standard. Each purveyor may be required to have a gas chromatograph installed on line with the purifying water stream to assure this level of contaminants will not be breached.

Part of the problem is that more and more of the water on which we will rely will be drawn either from surface waters that have high organic content or from so-called recharged aquifers in which treated sewage effluent is passed back through the ground to reach underground water reserves. Both of these water supplies will have large quantities of organic carbon compounds that will convert readily to THMs and thereby make any disinfection process exceedingly problematic.

A further difficulty is that the microorganisms that once were readily disinfected have been replaced by hardier breeds. Still other problems are created by the discovery of a new constellation of bacteria that live *inside* other microorganisms such as paramecia. Since the paramecium is a much hardier organism than the bacteria it harbors, adequately disinfecting water teeming with "harmless" paramecia can be a daunting task indeed.

Regulation of Inorganic Chemicals

Inorganic substances that are controlled include such metals as arsenic, barium, lead, chromium, and mercury. Recently, some states have added aluminum to this list, in part because of recent concerns that this element may have neurotoxic properties (aluminum has been associated with the "tangles" in the brains of Alzheimer's patients and has contributed to the toxicity observed in long-term dialysis users). Table 11-2 is a complete list of the currently regulated metals and the most stringent permissible levels currently in force in the United States (in California).

Mercury is the most heavily controlled substance primarily because it can be converted by bacterial action to an organic molecule (methyl mercury) that can readily traverse the placenta and cause serious neurological problems. The standard for lead, which is a well-known neurotoxic agent, is

225

Chemical	Maximum Contaminant Level
Aluminum	1.0 mg/liter (ppm)
Arsenic	0.05 mg/liter
Asbestos	7 million fibers/liter
Barium	1.0 mg/liter*
Cadmium	0.005 mg/liter
Chromium	0.10 mg/liter
Lead	0.05 mg/liter
Mercury	0.002 mg/liter
Nitrate (as NO_3)	10.0 mg/liter
Nitrite	1.0 mg/liter
Selenium	0.05 mg/liter
Silver	0.05 mg/liter

Table 11-2. Maximum Permissible Contaminant Levels of Inorganic Chemicals Allowed in California Drinking Water. Source: US EPA Region 5, Water Division, 1-3-91.
*reproposed 1/91 for 2.0 mg/liter

presently under review since many researchers believe that the present level is insufficiently protective for children. A final standard for lead between 10 and 20 ppb (0.01–0.02 mg/liter) is due in the spring of 1991.

California also leads the nation in requiring identification and control of many pesticides and organic molecules (see Table 11-3).

The chemicals with the most rigorous standards, namely, ethylene dibromide and vinyl chloride, are both small halogenated molecules that have either proven to be human carcinogens (vinyl chloride) or are strongly suspected to be so (ethylene dibromide). Fortunately, both molecules are highly volatile and are only sparingly soluble in water. This saving grace is particularly important to health officials concerned about human carcinogenesis from drinking water. The reason is that vinyl chloride is part of the chain of chlorinated molecules that can form from the bacterial breakdown of solvents such as trichloroethylene and dichloroethylene in the soil. Nonetheless, EPA

Organic Chemicals	Maximum Contaminant Level
Benzene	0.001 mg/liter
Carbon tetrachloride	0.0005 mg/liter
O-dichlorobenzene	0.60 mg/liter
1,4-dichlorobenzene	0.005 mg/liter†
1,2-dichloroethane	0.0005 mg/liter†
1,2-dichloropropanel	0.005 mg/liter
1,3-dichloropropene	0.0005 mg/liter†
1,1-dichloroethylene	0.006 mg/liter
cis-1,2-dichloroethylene	0.07 mg/liter
trans-1,2-dichloroethylene	0.10 mg/liter
Ethylbenzene	1.70 mg/liter
Ethylene dibromide	0.00002 mg/liter†
Monochlorobenzene	0.030 mg/liter
Styrene	0.10 mg/liter
1,1,2,2-tetrachloroethane	0.001 mg/liter
Tetrachloroethylene	0.005 mg/liter
Tolvene	11.0 mg/liter
1,1,1-trichloroethane	0.200 mg/liter†
1,1,2-trichloroethane	0.032 mg/liter†
Trichloroethylene	0.005 mg/liter
Vinyl chloride	0.0005 mg/liter
Xylenes	10.0 mg/liter

Pesticides	Maximum Contaminant Level
Alachlor	0.002 mg/liter
Aldicarb	0.003 mg/liter*
Atrazine	0.003 mg/liter
Bentazon	0.018 mg/liter
Carbofurans	0.04 mg/liter
Chlordane	0.002 mg/liter

Table 11-3. Maximum Contaminant Levels of Organic Chemicals Allowed in Drinking Water. Source: US EPA Region 5, Water Division, 1-30-90.
†California values only
*Reproposed value

Pesticides	Maximum Contaminant Level
2,4-dichlorophenoxy acetic acid	0.07 mg/liter
Dibromochloropropane (DBCP)	0.0002 mg/liter
Ethylene dibromide	0.00005 mg/liter
Endrin	0.0002 mg/liter†
Heptachlor	0.0004 mg/liter
Lindane	0.004 mg/liter†
Methoxychlor	0.10 mg/liter
Molinate	0.02 mg/liter†
PCBs	0.0005 mg/liter
Pentachlorophenol	0.001 mg/liter
Simazine	0.01 mg/liter
Thiobencarb	0.07 mg/liter†
Toxaphene	0.003 mg/liter
2,4,5-trichlorophenoxy acetic acid	0.05 mg/liter

Table 11-3, cont'd. Maximum Contaminant Levels of Organic Chemicals Allowed in Drinking Water. Source: US EPA Region 5, Water Division, 1-30-90.
†California values only

studies at hazardous waste sites like the one in Hope, Maine (Union Chemical) show levels of vinyl chloride as high as 110 ppb in water on the site.[35]

Other molecules that have been recently regulated are unique because of their high mobility through soils and their relatively high water solubility. This proved to be the case for the triazine herbicides simazine and atrazine, both of which astonished California scientists in the late 1970s by their presence in deep aquifers, months or even years after soil applications. Similar findings have since been made in other states and in Europe.[36] The health effects from atrazine in particular remain a concern since it causes multiorgan genetic damage after exposure in animals.[37]

The phenoxyherbicides, 2,4-dichlorophenoxy acetic acid (2,4-D and its salts) and 2,4,5-trichlorophenoxyacetic acid (2,4,5-T or Silvex) are regulated primarily because of the risk of dioxin contamination. This risk is higher for 2,4,5-T than for 2,4-D, and the dioxin of greatest health concern, (2,3,7,8-dibenzodioxin) is only a contaminant of the former synthetic process.

Of all of the possible contaminants in drinking water, two — trichloroethylene (TCE) and benzene — stand out for particular notice. We have already noted that TCE has been linked to leukemia cases in the Woburn, Massachusetts, area and has been selected by ATSDR as its first molecule of concern for establishing a health registry of exposed persons.

Benzene, which is a proven human leukemogen, is the second molecule to be singled out by ATSDR for scrutiny. It, too, contaminates a large number of aquifers in the United States and poses at least a theoretical risk of cancer as great or greater than that posed by trichloroethylene. In the judgment of many toxicologists, benzene is a much more carcinogenic molecule than is TCE.

In October 1989, Barry L. Johnson, chief of the Exposure and Disease Registry Branch of ATSDR, provisionally approved the development of a subregistry for health effects that might be attributable to benzene. Benzene was found to have contaminated 468 of the 1,180 National Priority List waste sites and was found to be "ubiquitous in the environment."[38] According to ATSDR, there are at least 263 sites around the country in which underground water sources used for drinking water are contaminated with this chemical. Both private and public wells are implicated as potential sources of human exposure.

THE EFFECT OF SOLVENT
CONTAMINATION ON HUMAN HEALTH

Much of the contamination of drinking water dates back at least a decade if not longer. In New Brighton, Minnesota, for example, residents complained of off-taste water for six years before the city took their concerns seriously. It is possible that chemically contaminated water has been part of the diet of so many Americans for so long that it is likely that adverse health effects just now being recognized (for example, excess bladder, rectal, and colon cancer; leukemia and possibly learning disabilities in children) will be found to affect significant numbers of the population.

The likelihood of this eventuality is disputed by scientists hired in law cases. These scientists believe that the levels of contamination are far too low to support the claim of health damage. For example, they believe that the amounts of individual contaminants such as trichloroethylene in even the most highly contaminated water sources (for example, the 12,000 ppb uncovered at Dowagiac, Michigan)[39] are simply far too low to cause the metabolic or physiologic damage necessary to produce human illness. In one sense, these estimates are correct. Compared to occupational exposures, which can amount to a gram a day for trichloroethylene, the 12 milligrams that would be ingested with each liter of water simply does not add up to an "occupational" exposure. And since in the instance of trichloroethylene, these occupational exposures have yet to produce a completely convincing pattern of excess human cancers, it is reasonable to ask how experts can believe that TCE-contaminated drinking water comprises a health risk.

The answer hinges on two factors. The first is that all of the water that is ingested delivers its full dose of TCE to the body, while as much as 40 to 45 percent of an inhaled dose of TCE is promptly exhaled without interacting with the body. Second, the ingested TCE passes through a different metabolic pathway than does the inhaled TCE. After reaching the stomach, virtually all of the water-borne TCE is passed through the hepatic circulation to the liver, where it can be activated to its more potent molecular forms. After inhalation, the TCE is sent to the lungs and then through the body's arterial system before reaching the liver.

In specific instances in which damage has been alleged from TCE-contaminated water, two other elements come into play. For one thing, it is often children who receive the highest exposures proportional to their size. Mothers who drink TCE can be expected to transfer metabolites of this molecule (principally dichloro- and trichloroacetic acid) to their developing embryos with a higher likelihood of damage than if the same chemicals were given to adults. As we have seen in Chapter 6, these two chemicals have carcinogenic activity of their own. For another, the TCE is almost always mixed in with other mutagenic and/or carcinogenic chemicals that possibly add (synergistically) to its cancer-causing effect.

In drinking water, unlike most occupational situations, it is almost always true that exposures are multiple and complex. Typical chlorinated solvent–contaminated drinking water may have anywhere from four to twelve different chemicals present, all with different toxicological profiles. As yet, few studies exist that document how these chemicals might interact, or if their interactions are synergistic, additive, or inhibitory. Where studies have been done on combinations of structurally similar chemicals (such as trichloroethane and trichloroethylene[40]) or chlorinated molecules (carbon tetrachloride and trichloroethylene[41]), additive and synergistic properties have been found. It is reasonable to expect that similar interactive effects will be seen in drinking water.

The possibility that developmental defects will be seen following exposure of at-risk populations must be taken seriously, even though the studies done to date have been inconclusive. The offspring of women exposed to trichloroethylene at work have not been found to have measurable developmental problems,[42] although the women themselves were found to be at higher risk for preeclampsia,[43] a problem pregnancy characterized by high blood pressure and poor kidney function.

Populations exposed to water-borne contaminants that include heavy metals or chlorinated solvents have been shown to have higher than expected rates of miscarriage and/or birth defects. Elevated levels of mercury and arsenic were associated with miscarriages in one study.[44] Solvents were associated with birth defects in the study conducted by S. W. Lagakos and associates of the Woburn, Massachusetts, population, but others have raised methodological questions about the accuracy of this and other findings at Woburn.[45] In unpublished studies performed around a site of water contamination stemming from the Fairchild electronics plant in San Jose, California, the California Department of Health Services found excess rates of heart defects among children whose mothers lived in areas that included high levels of water contamination with trichlorethane. Subsequent studies have confirmed the excess, but questioned its association with solvent-contaminated drinking water.[46]

Follow-up studies of this same area showed a striking pattern of miscarriage rates for those on city water compared to bottled water. A similar finding has been reported by the California Department of Health Services for three independent areas. However, according to their analysis, it is more likely that some factor or factors in the bottled water may be protecting women against miscarriages, rather than the possible contaminants in the drinking water causing them.[47]

Water Conduit Contamination

A still more vexing problem is the tendency for some piping systems or fixtures to encourage the colonization of bacteria that can cause disease. Polyvinyl chloride (PVC) pipes permit the colonization of their interior surfaces with *Pseudomonads,* a genus that includes several highly pathogenic strains of bacteria. Even when PVC material is disinfected, it can become recontaminated during production.[48] Hospital outbreaks of mysterious infections from otherwise sterile surgical wounds have been traced to PVC pipe contamination. Plastic as well as metal hospital water fixtures, including faucets and shower heads, have also been found to encourage the growth of *Legionella* bacteria, the cause of Legionnaires' disease, an often fatal pneumonia.

As we have seen at the beginning of this chapter, even where water is processed adequately to eliminate the major bacterial, viral, and chemical contaminants, there remains the trip from the processing facility to the home. Safety standards do not factor in the pipes through which water must course to reach the home. Lead from brass fittings or solder and solvent and bacterial contaminants of PVC piping are some possible un- anticipated hazards from drinking water that was initially cleared as safe when it left the distribution point. En route, other unmeasured contaminants in the pipes and ducts that carry the water may contribute to health risks. Cement pipes lined with plastic can give off petroleum and chlorinated sol- vents such as tetrachloroethylene; asbestos-cement pipes can release asbestos fibers; and plastic pipes that are solvent-cemented may release lingering amounts of some of the solvents for weeks or months. Chlorinated water that stagnates for ten days or more in new plastic piping will be contaminated above EPA standards for some chlorinated solvents.[49]

While solvent contamination poses a small risk under nor- mal usage, asbestos has been singled out for attention because of the extent of its occurrence among water systems in the United States. In addition to asbestos-cement pipes, asbestos- cement roofing in Seattle and the natural erosion of serpen- tine rocks in the Bay Area of California contribute asbestos fibers to drinking water supplies. However, the National Acad- emy of Sciences' National Research Council concludes that the additional risk of gastrointestinal cancer that could accrue from swallowing asbestos fibers in drinking water is low for most of the water systems in the country. For those states that have water systems with more than 10 million asbestos fibers per liter of drinking water (approximately 11.2 percent of all sam- ples), the NRC estimate of additional risk predicts a dramatic 100 additional cancers for every 100,000 men exposed over a seventy-year lifetime.[50] No consistent pattern of elevated cancer of the gastrointestinal tract has been observed for cities with high contaminant levels, but a strong association between exposure and lung cancer has been reported.[51] (This finding was discounted by the NRC as being a statistical artifact, although migration of asbestos fibers to the lungs appears to be a plausible explanation for the observation of increased risk at this site.)

An additional problem is that piping systems may be perme- able to contaminants *outside* the conduit itself—even while the pipe remains watertight. I have found that near gasoline spills, chemicals such as benzene, toluene, and xylene can diffuse through the intact walls of certain plastic pipes (notably poly-ethylene and polybutylene) and into drinking water,[52] although the likelihood of this occurrence is downplayed by industry sources. Under "normal" environmental conditions, in which only trace amounts of gasoline or other contaminants are found, the amount of chemical contaminants that can diffuse into drinking water is likely to be low.

My own unpublished studies have shown that the gaskets and fittings of some of these piping systems can also contrib-ute contaminants. The acetal fittings of polybutylene pipes can release trioxanes into drinking water (especially hot water). Un-der the acid conditions of the human stomach, some of these trioxanes degrade into formaldehyde, a potent irritant and sus-pect carcinogen.[53]

COMMENT

Contaminated drinking water remains a central concern for people involved in limiting health risks from environmental toxics. The rationale is straightforward: water is a necessary component of the human diet. The EPA estimates that people drink an average of 2 liters of water per day. This value may be debated (the NAS has estimated that as little as 650 milli-liters of actual tap water may be consumed, and more recent estimates suggest that as much as 2.71 liters are ingested by a small subset of the population[54]); but toxic chemicals may also be absorbed from contaminated water via the skin (wash-ing) and may be inhaled as the water runs, providing addi-tional exposure to a given substance, depending on its volatility and absorption characteristics.

Because of the constancy of exposure — most of us bathe, brush our teeth, and ingest water daily — water is a major ve-hicle for exposure to toxic substances in our environment. There is a certain irony to the fact that just as we have suc-ceeded in reducing infectious diseases by successful disinfec-tion practices, we have discovered that we have created a second generation of bogeymen — toxic chemicals formed as the by-products of disinfection operations.

The potentially disastrous discovery of contamination of our purest water supplies—our underground aquifers—through carelessly constructed storage tanks, spills, and intentional dumping—should put us all on the alert for new problems ahead. The fact that bacterial degradation in the soil can make toxic chemicals more so (i.e., the conversion of chlorinated ethylenes to vinyl chloride), is just one example.

Chemical contaminants in drinking water may act in ways that our occupational experience with those chemicals does not adequately anticipate. By passing through the liver before entering the body generally, ingested substances that are absorbed through the gastrointestinal tract may be activated by the liver into more hazardous chemical by-products.

Water was once considered sacrosanct. We have now contaminated so many of our aquifers beyond repair (see Chapter 12) that we must consider treatment operations that repurify what nature had once thoroughly cleansed. But these treatment procedures generate problems of their own. In the worst case, we may see repetitions of the almost laughable tragedy of the water-cleaning product (the Clean Water Machine) that added an animal carcinogen to its treatment stream. And we still are ignorant of the biological properties of the most common and unavoidable by-products of disinfection, the chloroacetic acids, trihalomethanes, and related chemicals.

In time, we may find ways to accommodate to the unavoidable presence of pollutants in our aquifers while we devise ways to decontaminate them. This may mean supplying everyone with bacteria-resistant carbon filters or ensuring that our treatment plants have the best technology for assuring an adequate supply of pure drinking water.

In time, we may look to the natural bioindicators of our contamination of the waters of the planet for help. Just as some of the fish and other vertebrates along our shores and estuaries have revealed the presence of contaminants through the appearance of tumors, still others have found ways to seek purer water to live in by changing their life-styles and migratory habits.

But if we continue to contaminate the ultimate source of all water—the oceans themselves—in the profligate way we have seen in the Persian Gulf, no treatment solution will suffice, and oceanic life may run out of safe harbors. In the past, we have assumed all too readily that the natural processes by which water percolates to the water table ensures that harmful contaminants are effectively filtered out. We now know that this cleaning process does not always work. Indeed, the notion of self-cleansing processes at work on the planetary level is one of the most serious myths of all.

CHAPTER TWELVE

Myth 10:

The environment is resilient

THE EARTH HAS BEEN EMBRACED BY HUMANS AS AN EXTENSION
of ourselves. This notion of the planet as a macrocosm of the
human and of the human as a microcosm of the planet, in-
fuses many ancient cultures. Such a belief was once taken as
mystical, a form of magical thinking that helped us control nature. Today, this metaphor is a key to understanding the root
of our dilemma in sustaining a habitable planet. Our disregard
of human needs has been extended to the planet. As this chapter
will show, using the earth's vast resources as dumping grounds
for civilization's industrial detritus has jeopardized planetary
health in the same way as unhygienic conditions historically
precluded a modicum of human health. But this relationship
is more than metaphor. Ultimately, it is because planetary and
human health are so interconnected that understanding how
the planet works is critical.

A growing number of scientists believe that we must learn to see the earth's responses to environmental change as an integrated whole. And a small number believe that the best way to do this is to treat the earth as if it, too, were a living organism. For these scientists, planetary resilience is dependent on some of the same balancing mechanisms that are found in all living things.

If the metaphor is more than just that, if what we do to ourselves really *does* impact on the planet and vice versa, this contention bears close scrutiny. Some observations are in order: For one thing, human and planetary well-being are tightly interdependent today more than ever. By virtue of their prodigious scale, human activities have become so inextricably bound up in the natural cycles that govern the flow of food, energy, and waste on the planet that no global ecosystem escapes human impact. For another, many of the chemicals that we mistakenly developed to improve our own well-being (for example, pesticides, capacitor fluids, fossil fuels) have entered the environment in unprecedented amounts and thwart, stifle, and otherwise redirect the natural order of life.

The core question is whether the planet is sufficiently resilient to incorporate, neutralize, and rebound from these monolithic yet (in a geological time sense) transient events.

HOMEOSTASIS

The roots of this global view of resiliency can be found in medicine. French physician Claude Bernard (1813–1878) extolled the constancy of the body's "internal milieu" as the key element for sustaining existence in a changing environment.[1] Later, the U.S. physiologist Walter Cannon coined the word *homeostasis* to describe the balancing responses of the body to perturbations in living conditions. To Cannon, the essence of understanding the body's ability to withstand disturbance and disease involved learning how it constantly restored critical molecules and cells to optimal physiological levels. Cannon extolled this remarkable ability of the body to restore equilibrium as "the wisdom of the body."[2]

It is, however, one thing to know and describe such mechanisms for the closed system of the human body, where, for example, constant acid/base balance, temperature equilibrium, and precisely maintained ionic balances (sodium/potassium, calcium/phosphorous, and so on) are the norm. But it is quite another to ascribe the same properties to the open systems of the planet. Are there elaborate balancing, detoxifying, and repair mechanisms akin to human physiology operating on a planetary scale? We have seen that living organisms often lack adequate defenses against toxic insults. What about the planet?

THE WISDOM OF THE PLANET

According to a new generation of geophysicists and visionary evolutionary biologists, the earth exhibits a "wisdom" not unlike that of the body. Some of these scientists, notably University of Massachusetts at Amherst botanist Lynn Margulis and independent British scientist James E. Lovelock, perceive the planet itself as being alive. All of its living things interact to give the earth capacities of self-regulation remarkably similar to those of its individual organisms. (The countervailing view is that any appearance of self-regulation can be ascribed to geological forces alone.) This vision is coupled with an optimistic belief that since we share so much in common with the earth, we can harness some of the "know-how" of the planet to protect ourselves.[3]

The epicenter of this new thinking about the organismic nature of global evolution is embodied in the Gaia hypothesis. Developed first by Lovelock in the 1970s, this idea posits that the earth operates as a giant organism.[4] The scope of this hypothesis is conveyed by a description given by Margulis and her colleague J. F. Stolz, "Gaia, a single enormous system deriving from common ancestors . . . is connected through time (by ancestry) and space (through atmospheric chemical signals, ocean currents and the like) . . . the Gaian system persists in the face of changes (population expansions and extinction, sea-level changes and so forth)."[5] That is, the earth's massive cycles and elemental fluxes are governed by mechanisms directly analogous to those that operate in living things. Only in global systems, the so-called set points or environmental constants can change with time, while in warm-blooded animals most are held constant.[6] This means that the planet may adjust to a new global temperature profile over millennia and then keep the new temperature level constant, while warm–blooded animals are limited to keeping temperature set at a constant (for example, for humans, 98.6°F), irrespective of environmental fluxes.

A corollary to the Gaia hypothesis is that the earth's capacity to restore equilibrium confers an ability to heal itself through the collective biological activities of its mass of living things. The very first occasion for such an activity, according to Margulis, was when organisms evolved in the presence of toxic levels of gases such as oxygen and hydrogen sulfide and then rendered those atmospheric concentrations compatible with life through processes akin to photosynthesis.[7] The same system presently minimizes the concentration in the ocean of otherwise toxic ions such as sodium, manganese, and magnesium.[8]

We do know that many geological and biological cycles are interconnected. Geologic forces circulate elements like carbon and sulfur through volcanic activity, erosion, and leaching into molecular forms that are then incorporated into living things. The biomass on earth and in the seas, in turn, appears to interact to maintain these elements in relatively constant balance. Many of these systems, such as the cycle that moves carbon from deep within the earth to living things and back again to the sea where it becomes the calcium carbonate skeletons of plankton, shellfish, and coral, have kept the planet's carbon pool in a state of dynamic equilibrium over eons. (To appreciate the scale of this endeavor, you need only look at the white cliffs of Dover or the massive limestone formations that comprise most of Florida.) According to Margulis, these gigantic deposits of remnants of living creatures may even have influenced the movement of the giant tectonic plates that form and mold the continents.[9]

GAIA AND PLANETARY HEALTH

Can such systems cope with and neutralize our current atmospheric pollutants and carbon dioxide increase? Over the millennia, when extra amounts of carbon dioxide or other gases such as ammonia were present, they would stimulate more photosynthesis which would in turn trap more carbon and fix nitrogen, leaving these chemicals entombed in dead or dying plants and plankton. In this way, carbon and the other major elements of oxygen, sulfur, phosphorus, and nitrogren, which supported life on earth, were kept within reasonable bounds.

Today some of these elements, notably carbon dioxide, are being released again as we disinter fossil plants and burn them as coal or gasoline. As a result, the carbon cycle is seriously out of its traditional bounds. We know, of course, that living organisms continue to interact with the atmosphere and that they affect the quality and nutrient characteristics of bodies of water and rivers. But we do not know if they can restore homeostasis at a new set point. And we do not know if the massive releases of gases such as carbon dioxide and methane can be adequately assimilated into the ecosystem.

What about toxic substances? Are they being detoxified and digested as the Gaia hypothesis would predict? How adaptive will living things prove to be as they operate in the face of major human activities that threaten entire ecosystems and the atmosphere itself?

Five of our activities deserve special scrutiny in this regard: these include emissions of the greenhouse gases, production of acid rain, mining of minerals, pesticide use, and industrial contamination.

Turning Up the Thermostat?

Until recently, the earth appeared to keep its heat budget closely equilibrated, much as one does by setting a thermostat. In fact, over the past 100,000 years, the average temperature has fluctuated only 8° to 10° Fahrenheit. Yet even these fluctuations were of enormous moment for life on earth. A rise of only 5°F was sufficient to end the earth's last major Ice Age and caused a rise in the oceans of more than 300 feet. This elevation of temperature took place over approximately 10,000 years. Geophysicists have also found that global temperature and carbon dioxide levels have fluctuated together in slow wave patterns over the past 160,000 years.[10]

As we saw in Chapters 1 and 3, atmospheric modelers predict that the current flux in atmospheric gases, especially carbon dioxide but also methane, nitrous oxide, and chlorofluorocarbons, will lead to a comparable rise in global temperature, but this time within the next 30 to 50 years, not 10,000. Indeed, there are already reliable measurements suggesting that a greenhouse effect is occurring now.[11]

Most of this increase can be attributed to incremental changes in carbon dioxide, a gas that has been increasing steadily since the industrial revolution began in about 1800. The net effect of this rise is to trap about 1 percent more solar energy near the planetary surface, causing a net increase in the amount of energy retained by the earth of about 2 watts for every square meter of its surface (about equivalent to hanging two Christmas tree light bulbs over each square meter).[12]

It remains to be seen if the concomitant release of sunlight reflecting aerosols into the lower atmosphere by vast numbers of oceanic plankton will counteract this trend. Here is where Gaian activities *might* act to reverse the trend. That is, while some of these aerosols are made from sulfur dioxide, others are made from living things, such as the plankton *Phaeocystis,* which produces dimethylsulfide, a gas that is oxidized to form sulfates. According to the Gaia hypothesis, these sulfates *should* dampen the heat rise by forming condensation nuclei over the ocean that would increase the cloud cover.[13]

Would enough be formed? Should this 3° to 5°F temperature rise occur over the next forty years or so (and the evidence suggests that it is likely), the increase coupled with the projected doubling of carbon dioxide during the same period will greatly change the environment for plant growth. For planetary homeostasis to work, vastly more plankton and algae (and forests generally) would have to be generated than scientists now project as plausible.

While some researchers believe that the present climate will produce hothouse effects that in the main will be beneficial to plant life and thereby increase the "sink" for carbon,[14] this view is clearly in the minority. Desertification, now proceeding by as much as six miles a year in areas of the Sahel, may be accelerated. And once begun, the process of conversion of fertile soils to sand is largely irreversible.[15]

Carbon dioxide levels that favor the growth of some plants will stunt or dampen that of others. In fact, most researchers believe that the present climate changes will stress rather than aid plant ecosystems. Pollinators may be thrown off by changes in the flowering season; root-clinging bacteria, so essential to nitrogen fixation, may be disturbed; and herbivores may find their favorite plant extinguished, creating totally new evolutionary endgames.[16] The net effect may be a *lowering* in the biomass available to fix carbon dioxide and nitrogen, exactly the opposite effect of that predicted in the Gaia hypothesis.

So far, preliminary and still rudimentary plans for stabilizing any greenhouse-type effect have properly concentrated on reducing the load of greenhouse chemicals. However, another plan calls for the intentional seeding of the oceans with elemental nutrients that enhance the growth of oceanic plankton. Developed by the National Research Council, this innovation would seed the ocean with additional iron salts. By adding up to a quarter of a teaspoon of iron per football-sized area of ocean, the scientific team hopes to roughly halve the impending 23 percent increase in carbon dioxide anticipated by 2040.[17] (This increase will otherwise occur *even if* the present levels of carbon dioxide emissions are kept constant, in part because the oceans are at near saturation with dissolved carbon dioxide.)

The net conclusion is that in the short run (say, over the next hundred years), little of the predicted buffering of the greenhouse effect from Gaia's systems will operate. Planetary resilience here will simply not suffice to control atmospheric conditions unless they are greatly aided and abetted by human activities. What those activities should be is still a hotly contested issue, leaving the U.S. government (circa 1990) still reluctant to accede to global protections against a projected greenhouse phenomenon.

It remains to be seen if longer Gaian trends could in theory stabilize the present out-of-control pattern of carbon dioxide increase, an increase that itself is fueling the phenomenon of global heating. But by then, the damage to human life and well-being may make the outcome all but moot.

Acid Rain

Other gases produced during the industrial revolution have had more immediate and visible impacts on ecosystems than has carbon dioxide. Nitrogen and sulfur oxides have been generated in vast amounts as fossil fuels have been burned. These oxides form acids when they combine with water vapor in the atmosphere and also serve as condensation points when they form sulfates and nitrates. Together, these two phenomena have contributed to subtle increases in precipitation in some areas and to a dramatic increase in the acidity of the resulting rain.

In regions of the globe where industrial activities are concentrated, or where prevailing winds take these oxides, the net effect of this rain has been severely acidified lakes and rivers. The acidification has led to a kill-off of algae, paramecia, and other microorganisms at the base of the food chain, causing the decline of fish and other higher aquatic vertebrates. At pH levels below 4, fish reproduction is severely curtailed.

Such effects were particularly severe in early 1980s in the Adirondack region of New York State and the southwestern tip of Norway, where literally thousands of lakes were left bereft of larger life forms.[18] In both of these areas, a reduction in sulphate emissions from power plants is projected to allow the restoration of most lakes and rivers to their former acidity. The Norwegians also partially reversed some of the acidifying effects in lakes by dumping thousands of tons of alkaline mineral salts into them, a feat no natural system could have achieved.It remains to be seen if these adjustments will restore once fish-rich rivers and lakes to their previous abundance.

Acid rain is also a key element in an even more massive ecological disturbance. In the forests of Europe and the southeastern United States over the past two decades, massive declines in tree populations have occurred. By the late 1970s in northeastern Bavaria (home of the famous Black Forest), whole tracts of Norway spruce had needle damage and were dying. By the early 1980s, the damage spread: one-fifth to one-quarter of *all* of the forested regions in Europe were moderately or severely damaged.[19] Under such stresses, pines and other vulnerable species throughout Europe and the United States became stressed and vulnerable to diseases they would otherwise have resisted.

Damaged trees in turn were more susceptible to insect infestation, further compounding this ecological tragedy. A complex interplay of acid rain, nitrogenous gases, photo oxidants, and organic micropollutants seemed to be involved in the devastation.[20] The best theory is that a combination of atmospheric and geologic pollutants interacted directly and indirectly with the forest canopy and elements in the underlying soils to produce long-term changes in the makeup of the nutrients on which the trees depended.[21]

The breakthrough in understanding the composite effects of these factors came in a major article published in *Science*.[22] Professor E. D. Schulze of the University of Bayreuth demonstrated that a composite of ten factors impinged on German forests, beginning with a wave of acidification from massive burning of coal as fuel from 1870 to 1900. From 1900 to 1960, the now increased amounts of nitrates in the atmosphere were converted to ammonium by soil bacteria, "force-feeding" the acid-stressed trees.

However, even though the trees selectively increased their use of ammonium, excess nitrates remained in the soil. These residual nitrates dissolved in newly acidified rain water and produced nitrous acid, further acidifying the subsoil. As the soil became more acidic, the bacteria that normally convert nitrates into ammonium ions died, creating a vicious circle of more and more nitrates remaining behind in the soil.

Even the natural buffering that was expected in carbonate-rich soil did not occur. Acid rain precipitated salts in the soil, leading to high levels of inaccessible calcium ions. This excess calcium in turn blocked the uptake of potassium, further compromising the internal balance of ions in the trees.

The net result was that the roots could not take up critical stores of calcium and magnesium needed for needle and stem production. In the last stage, the trees died because of the increased permeability of their roots to aluminum in the soil (made available by the leaching of granitic soils by acid groundwater).

The whole process that led to such massive declines in Europe and the southern tip of Scandinavia is occurring now in the United States in the higher elevations of the Appalachians from southern North Carolina to the New England states. (These high-elevation soils are already nutrient-poor, accelerating the effects of acid rain.)

The lesson from this ongoing disaster is that the buffering effects of a Gaia-like system are simply not operating on the scale and with the speed necessary to stem the tide of either fish kills or tree destruction triggered by acid rain. On a more hopeful note, when the deficient nutrients in forest soils are known and the damage detected at an early stage, depleted nutrients can be replaced through fertilization, leading to the restoration of forest growth and well-being. Unfortunately, human and not natural activities are necessary to rescue acid-rain-damaged tree communities.

Mining the Planet

When astronaut Buzz Aldrin looked back at the earth from his vantage point above the moon, the only man-made geological feature he could see was the Kennecott Copper mine in Utah. Mining has taken place on such a massive scale that by the year 2000, large-scale global extraction of metals will have directly disturbed an area the size of Oregon. Copper mining by itself disrupts 1,600 square kilometers of land.[23]

In all, up to 70,000 metric tons of often highly toxic metals are added to the aquatic environment annually.[24] The mercury, copper, lead, arsenic, antimony, tin, cadmium, and silver impact in varying degrees on living things. Fish in particular are vulnerable to acidification and metal contamination from high concentrations of copper, zinc, cadmium, lead, and arsenic. By 1977, fisheries in more than 21,000 kilometers of waterways worldwide were found to be decimated by heavy metals contaminants.[25] And refinement of the mined ores, through smelting, adds further to the deposition of such hazardous metals by atmospheric transport. (Contamination of large areas in and around Tacoma, Washington, with arsenic from the ASARCO copper plant has been cause for much public health concern over the past decade.)

In the past twenty years, massive mining operations in developing countries such as Brazil and New Guinea have led to contamination of previously pristine waterways with mercury (from gold mining in the Amazon) and other heavy metals. In Papua New Guinea more than 600 million tons of tailings have been dumped into the previously pristine waters of the Kawerong River at a rate of 130,000 tons a day.[26]

The critical question is whether these perturbations of natural cycles of elements and the direct disturbance of the environment through mining are subject to remediation or control through natural, regenerative actions as predicted by the Gaia hypothesis.

We can begin by examining the constellation of problems at the Clark Fork River Basin area of Montana. More Super-fund sites are concentrated in this intensely mined region (covering an area about a fifth the size of Rhode Island) than anywhere else in this country. In a study to consider whether the extensive contamination of water, soil, and air had an impact on human health, researchers examined the vital statistics of surrounding cities and counties. Butte, Montana, which abuts the Clark complex, had the highest mortality rate of any city in the United States from 1950–51 and 1959–61.[27] Similarly grim statistics were obtained for the counties in and around the site.

A research team from the University of Montana and the U.S. Geological Survey concluded from examining the data on this mining site that "the near impossibility of attaining pre-development status in the Clark Fork Complex is a clear example of this unpleasant reality [of lack of remedial options for intensively mined sites]. In such cases, the only reasonable remediation response may be perpetual monitoring."[28]

One glimmer of hope is that microorganisms will eventually assimilate toxic metals and return soils to their pre-mined state. Unfortunately, mining engineers have turned this Gaia idea on its head, utilizing vast numbers of bacteria to oxidize ores or convert complex salts *to* pure metals. In Brigham Canyon, Utah, a massive experiment is under way in which thousands of pounds of bacteria are being used to oxidize iron ore. To achieve the desired extraction, over a billion *Thiobacillus* bacteria are being used to extract each kilogram of iron, contaminating a watershed with both live organisms of unknown pathogenic potential *and* toxic metal-bearing debris.[29]

It has become evident that any site restoration that depends on biogenic activities is virtually impossible for heavily contaminated old mining sites. And acidification of water by percolation through mine tailings, heavy-metal contamination, and topsoil loss through erosion combine to make many less severely damaged sites equally unrestorable. It may be that in the long run (measured in tens of thousands of years) the earth can heal such scars, but in the frame of importance for those of us presently alive, it is an affront to offer "natural regeneration" as a solution to mining damage.

Pesticides

We have already looked at massive pesticide contamination episodes that have led to wildlife and human death, notably the crises posed by DDT contamination in the 1950s and 1960s and the Bhopal explosion in 1984. We are left with two kinds of legacies: one is the persistent contamination from chlorinated pesticides (including DDT) and related chemicals (PCBs) that have been phased out of production. The second is the insidious infiltration of aquifers and waterways with widely used herbicides such as simazine and atrazine.

The first dilemma posed by nonbiodegradability is that ecosystems that have otherwise recovered from serious contamination episodes continue to bioconcentrate persistent pesticides. Bioconcentration in turn leads to extraordinarily high concentrations in many forms of wildlife that are at the top of their respective food chains. Heavily chlorinated pesticides such as dieldrin and DDT are concentrated tens of thousands of times higher in fish than in the seawater in which they are swimming.[30] And any higher organisms that ingest the contaminated fish will also retain and more often than not further bioconcentrate the offending chemicals. The greatest ecological damage is thus to the major predators (including humans) at the end of food chains. For example, dolphins have been found with extraordinarily high concentrations of chlorinated, multiple-ringed chemicals stored in their fat. (In the recent die-off of dolphins in the Mediterranean, levels of PCBs as high as 680 parts per million were found.) Such massive concentrations probably suppress the immune system and thereby contribute to both dolphin and seal mortality from virally caused pneumonia.

While no one can predict the long-term consequences of continued use of the persistent pesticides like chlordane still in commerce, bioconcentration carries with it a dire warning — continued use of persistent, chlorinated pesticides will eventually lead to their reaching biologically untenable levels somewhere at the upper reaches of the ecosystem. This occurred twenty years ago when DDT levels reached such extraordinary levels that the reproduction of birds of prey such as the peregrine falcon, brown pelican, and even Antarctic penguins were severely impaired and their survival jeopardized. The fact that most of the affected species have staged a remarkable comeback once the chemicals were strictly limited *is* a positive sign that balancing forces in the environment may limit the long-term consequences of bioaccumulation — if humans stop producing these chemicals.

This insight, however, has not daunted efforts to introduce and use comparably persistent pesticides such as dieldrin and heptachlor and related chemicals. (In the late 1970s, milk contaminated with heptachlor was found in Hawaii, and thousands of gallons and hundreds of cattle had to be destroyed.)

Whether the earth's resiliency will extend to the chronic introduction of persistent toxic pesticides is an open question. Is there some foundation organism deep in the base level of the ecosystem that has the ability to dechlorinate these persistent molecules? The opposite possibility, that microorganisms at lower trophic levels may be eliminated by these pollutants, is equally likely.

Something like this may be happening among the corals of the Caribbean. Sporadically over the decade of the 1980s (and only rarely before then), whole colonies of coral went through a pattern of "bleaching" or blanching in which the normal brownish-green color of the living coral became stark white. This whitening effect occurs when the coral polyps expel the zooplankton that live with them. (This relationship is described as a commensal one [literally, "living at the same table"].) But the corals can live for only one or perhaps two years without this plankton.

According to most experts, the most likely culprit is the dramatic warming of the surface levels of the Caribbean, which has been observed to accompany or precede the expulsion of the zooplankton. (Temperatures as high as 102° and 103°F are not uncommon among some shallow reefs.)

But another and still hypothetical linkage to this potentially catastrophic destruction of coral reefs is that plant-killing pesticides in the Mississippi may be reaching the Gulf of Mexico, contributing to the damage of the stressed ecosystems. Ten different pesticides have been detected in amounts greater than 10 parts per billion in the Mississippi and its tributaries. In particular, atrazine, metalochlor, and alochlor in amounts as high as several hundred metric tons a year enter the Gulf from the Mississippi.[31] Some of the pesticides (in particular atrazine) have the ability to interfere with photosynthesis and may thus be highly toxic to vulnerable plankton and zooplankton.

While the minimum concentrations of these pesticides that would shut down photosynthesis are *thought to be* higher than those currently reached in the Gulf, no one knows if there are vulnerable plankton species that may be poisoned at picogram concentrations of these potent herbicides. No one knows the full range of consequences of this continuing pesticide contamination, although at least one learned body has expressed grave concern that such chemicals designed to be toxic to living things are now threatening the environment in unprecedented amounts.[32]

So here the Gaia hypothesis is still untested, since the disturbances in plankton levels that would upset global climate have fortunately only been regional.

Industrial Activities

The many episodes of pollution highlighted in this book are the direct or indirect result of industrial activities. These activities have led to massive contamination of aquifers with industrial solvents. The worldwide consumption of hazardous chemicals that find their way into the environment is staggeringly high. From 1974 to 1985, in Western Europe alone, more than 10,000 kilotons of chlorinated solvents were consumed (and released), about half as much as in the United States during the same period.[33] Annual releases of the four most common chlorinated solvents (methylene chloride, perchloroethylene, trichloroethylene, and 1,1,1-trichloroethane) continues to average at or near 200 kilotons per year. The earth's detoxification mechanisms for these chemicals are limited to ultraviolet light and ozone-mediated destruction in the atmosphere and to microbial destruction and hydrolysis in water. Most of the chemicals in this group are so volatile that the atmosphere bears the brunt of contamination, except where deep groundwater is affected. All deplete the ozone layer.

We already know that contaminated aquifers—whether from pesticides or synthetic industrial chemicals—are both extensive and extremely resistant to clean-up. In fact, the authors of a recent study which examined four contaminated sites in depth concluded, "aquifer restoration is currently technically impossible."[34] Neither natural systems based on bacterial de-chlorination mechanisms, nor the pumping and treatment processes presently employed suffice to restore chemically contaminated aquifers. This means that the extensive contamination of ground water throughout the industrialized world and in the United States in particular represents an irremediable, permanent inroad on the purity of underground water.

The earth's natural propensity to trap contaminants in the organic matter in soils impedes rather than abets any clean-up process. The adherence of contaminants to soil particles drastically complicates restoration efforts. Moreover, many of the most prevalent contaminants, like trichloroethylene, are both denser than water and only partially water soluble. This means that much of the contamination is held back in what are known as the non-aqueous phases of the water-soil matrix. Even pumping for 100–200 *years* is estimated to be sufficient only for a reduction of contamination by a factor of 100, often way below that needed for assuring ideal water quality.[35]

It remains to be seen if the present atmospheric levels of these or similar chemicals (estimated to be in the range of 0.01 to 0.1 part per billion) pose a hazard to living things beyond their contribution to the breakdown of the ozone layer and to the greenhouse effect. What is known is that the breakdown is still continuing and that an equilibrium in the concentration of such gases as 1,1,1-trichloroethane has not yet been reached.[36]

In the world as a whole, most airborne pollutants such as the chlorinated solvents are still released by "stationary sources" and not by automobiles or refrigerators or appliances used by individuals. Control of these pollutants therefore depends on control of the industrial sector. In the United States, such controls have been written into the Clean Air Act. (Its provisions are discussed in the next chapter.)

CONCLUSIONS

One thing is evident: our predictions of the ability of the planet to restore homeostasis and heal itself have been woefully inadequate to date. We lack the data needed to make the critical predictions and extrapolations. For example, a U.S. expert group reviewing the minimum data base needed for preserving global ecosystems wrote: "We lack 10-year observations of the background physical, chemical, and ecological variations in fresh waters, oceans, and the atmosphere that are adequate to distinguish natural changes from perturbations attributable to human activities."[37]

But we do know that too many activities are occurring at rates that threaten the earth's ability to compensate for them. One lesson common to evolutionists and physiologists alike is that for life to persist, change must take place slowly. Organisms can adapt to minor perturbations in their environments on a seasonal or diurnal basis, but can only adapt to major changes in conditions as fast as their genes mutate to offer new possibilities. Today, human activities have disturbed so many of the earth's systems so radically that it is reasonable to ask if some forms of life may be able to keep up.

The argument that change has always occurred and life endured overlooks the fact that the rate of change today is unprecedented in geological time. In the words of one ecologist, "Extinctions have always occurred because change has always occurred, but the enormously accelerated rate of environmental change is causing an 'extinction crisis.'"[38]

At the crux of the problem is that we are using the same flawed toxicological estimates of risk to ecosystem health that we have applied to human health. For this reason, we have failed to anticipate many of the problems currently afflicting global ecosystems. Among the flawed assumptions we have made are:

- that thresholds exist below which toxic chemicals lose all effects on living things
- that most if not all toxins can be effectively detoxified
- that chemicals that appear innocuous in short-term tests will prove innocuous in the long run
- that all toxic insults are reversible

We have learned the hard way that many organisms in the natural environment are actually more susceptible to low concentrations of some toxic substances than we are.[39] Some chemicals, notably the PCBs, DDT, and dioxin, are extremely resistant to biodegradation. And chemicals that some organisms seem to tolerate either become more toxic to those on the next trophic level (as a result of biomagnification) or produce delayed effects on nervous or reproductive systems that were missed in the toxicity assays done to vouchsafe their use. Impacts on genes, both for the organism itself (cancer) or its descendants (heritable mutations), are by definition irreversible.

It should come as no surprise, then, that many of our "best" chemical solutions have irreversibly affected the natural world. There is no way to remove PCBs from wildlife such as the Atlantic bluefish or the Mediterranean dolphins, nor any way to assure that any of the large populations of fish and wildlife presently decimated by pesticides will recover.[40]

Solving the carbon dioxide problem is so complex that all of our efforts to date can be considered mere tinkerings with a system already out of control. If ecological management is to succeed, it must stem the tide of carbon dioxide release from massive forest burns. Replanting is an incomplete and inadequate solution since no amount of reforestation can create a sufficient carbon dioxide sink to hold all the excess carbon produced by burning fossil fuels and the forests themselves. Toxic substances are part of this pattern of ecosystem destruction. As ecologist George Woodwell has observed, "The spread of toxins as well as toxic effects simply speeds the demise of forests."[41]

All too often today, extreme reactions occur that escape the normal balancing mechanisms. These demand our immediate attention. This appears to be the case for carbon dioxide and methane gas production, both of which are presently so out of control that global warming appears inevitable. The constant regeneration of chlorine oxide from CFCs in the stratosphere is another instance crying out for cure. (As we have seen, the extraordinarily long half-life of these molecules ensures that damage to the fragile ozone layer will likely persist even if we are successful in reining in our production of chlorofluorocarbons.)

It is evident that the current rate of environmental change is unprecedented. Under the impact of human activities, the earth's homeostatic mechanisms are being increasingly thrown out of kilter. The shift in the carbon cycle, the depletion of ozone, the destruction of forests, and the loss of the earth's temperature set point describe a disturbed planet, not one in balance. Failure to heal human-damaged ecosystems like those in the Sahel in Africa or the mining fields of Montana belie the assurance that earth will endure because it is intrinsically resilient.

Oceanic systems that are the lifeblood of the planet are being stressed by extraordinary fluxes of ultraviolet light (in the Antarctic) and toxic chemical residues. Forests and lakes are being decimated by acid rainfall. And once these primary systems go, other terrestrial ecosystems will likely soon follow. Global warming may disrupt fragile ecosystems such as coral reefs that are the equivalent of tropical rain forests: together they are repositories of the greatest number of species of life on the planet. Deforestation (whether through burning or acidification) breaks the continuity of a host of geological and biological systems that permit the recycling of elements and water. Earth warming stresses some animal forms past the point of recovery. And elevated carbon dioxide differentially favors some species at the expense of others needed to maintain ecosystem integrity.

To understand the impact of our changes on the planet requires that we think through again our belief system about its characteristics — and our own.

The End of the Game

The thesis of this chapter is simple: at some deep subconscious level, the flawed belief in the earth's resilience (as in our own) has blocked inventive and essential solutions to control toxic substances. Unfortunately, the solutions that are needed are those that recognize that we require a wholesale shift in what we produce and how we dispose of our excess by-products.

By now we should know that the earth has no more or less capacity to perform acts of self-healing in the face of synthetic chemicals than does the body. It is more the luck of the draw than any divine plan that determines which synthetic molecules will be degraded to innocuous by-products and which rendered even more potent as they age. To count on the earth to heal itself is as foolhardy as counting on the body to process all toxic molecules into innocuous ones.

There *was* a time when products of human activity were completely "recyclable" both in the natural world and in the body. Human wastes would degrade completely to their common organic denominators, ammonia, carbon dioxide and water. Sulfur-containing compounds would be incorporated into innocuous sulfhydryl groups, and excess nitrogen would be released via the urea cycle. On the planet, excess carbon would be absorbed in "sinks" in the ocean or elsewhere, and free ammonia would be fixed by soil microorganisms. Equilibrium would be restored by the simple expedient of new growth and faster decay. But with the addition of synthetic chemicals, these cycles of metabolic and geologic degradation have been short-circuited.

We are now in an end game. How we play it will determine the survival of ourselves, and perhaps even that of the planet.

CHAPTER THIRTEEN

Conclusion

THIS BOOK HAS CHARTED BOTH HUMAN AND GLOBAL EPISODES OF toxicity and discussed the myths that have perpetuated them. Its theme has been simple: what we have done to our bodies we are now doing to the planet. The mistakes, failures, and oversights that have led to this century's worst cases of environmental contamination have their roots in our personal mistakes and those of the less than aggressive governmental agencies charged to protect the public from unsafe exposure to drugs and chemicals. On a larger scale, the blithe disregard by many industries — and governments — for the welfare of the environment has led to wholesale destruction of habitats and global contamination.

Many of the products responsible for global toxicity were developed with little or no regard to their environmental fate. Scientists overestimated the capacity of the planet to absorb or neutralize seemingly nontoxic chemicals — products such as chlorofluorocarbons or polychlorinated biphenyls which were mass produced and *assumed* to be largely nonreactive and hence nontoxic. Industry-based medical researchers likewise underestimated the body's response to presumptively nonreactive molecules such as silicone because they did not understand the complexities or nuances of the extraordinary ability of the immune system to recognize non-self molecules. Other scientists developed poisons against pests, and in the process caused more human suffering than did the organisms the chemicals were used to combat. At least some of this suffering resulted from the inaccurate extrapolation of expected toxicities to humans. And many deaths have been caused by chemicals whose warnings were inadequate, sometimes containing "instructions" written in a language the user did not speak.

The ability of the planet and persons to cope with toxic substances has been clearly overestimated. New and subtle toxic effects at low doses were erroneously ignored, first for radiation and later for lead and neurotoxic chemicals. Detoxifying mechanisms were presumed to work, when for some chemicals, such as benzopyrene or chlorinated solvents, they just made problems worse. Chemical breakdown products that were more hazardous than the original molecules were unanticipated. And long-term effects of chemicals resistant to biological digestion, such as DDT, dioxins, and PCBs, were just plain ignored.

CHEMICAL IRRESPONSIBILITY

In the 1940s and 1950s, many chemicals intended for environmental or human use were developed and marketed without any adequate testing. Carcinogenicity testing really did not begin until the late 1960s. By the 1970s, cancer bioassays had shown that a number of widely used chemicals were carcinogenic in animals. By the end of the decade, human studies of people dying from cancer were finding higher than expected levels of many of the same chemicals in body tissues.[1] In 1982, the International Agency for Research on Cancer reported sixty-one chemicals that were deemed "probably" carcinogenic to humans.[2] Even today, pesticides are still being put into service with virtually no testing for delayed neurotoxic effects and cancer-causing chemicals (for example, dyes) are still being permitted to be used as food additives and industrial materials.

Sometimes pure avarice led to toxic disasters. Chemicals that had been shown to be carcinogenic or extremely hazardous to workers were blindly used as precursors for pesticides (MIC), or plastics (vinyl chloride), as solvents, or as parts of drugs. Reproductively toxic glycol ethers, toxic alcohols, and carcinogenic chloroform were all used because of convenience as carriers for antibiotics, nonspecific "elixirs," and even in children's toothpaste, respectively. Silica, which proved disastrous for workers who mined rocks or drilled tunnels, was added as a "secret" ingredient to strengthen silicone-based medical devices. Only later did clinical researchers find that some women with breast implants developed many of the same secondary symptoms of silicosis as had their worker counterparts who got autoimmune disorders.

THE SCALE OF POLLUTION

Chemical production, which reached mammoth levels after World War II, led to the release of billions of pounds of wastes and by-products into the environment. By last count, 11,250 kilotons (22.5 billion pounds) of toxic chemicals were released to the environment by the United States alone.[3] Polychlorinated biphenyls were dumped or spilled into the environment for more than two decades, decimating bird populations and making large fish from the Great Lakes inedible. Chlorofluorocarbons were mass produced even after scientists predicted that their release could destroy the vital stratospheric ozone layer that protects life from DNA-damaging ultraviolet light and would contribute to global warming.

Not the least of our errors was the hubris that led to the use of new chemicals with untested or unexamined properties. It is true that after World War II many government agencies instituted testing regimes—as did industry itself—in an effort to anticipate adverse consequences of chemical production. However, these safeguards were all too often too little and too late. By the 1960s, tens of thousands had been exposed as a result of hundreds of major chemical plant explosions, railroad car derailments, and container truck accidents that spewed chemicals with unknown toxic properties into the surroundings. In the case of the Bhopal disaster in 1984, more than 200,000 persons were eventually reported injured.[4]

As our sophistication about toxicology and chemical synthesis increased at the level of manufacture, so did our failure to recognize the long-term consequences of mass release at the level of the environment. For some carcinogenic chemicals, production and use became so widespread that no community in the United States has been spared from contamination. This is especially true for benzene which is now adequately safeguarded at petroleum refineries, but has yet to be so in the environment at large. Air levels regularly reach 10 to 20 $\mu g/m^3$ in some major cities, concentrations that constitute a manifest public health hazard. Other chemicals, notably the trihalomethanes and some chlorinated solvents, are now near-ubiquitous contaminants of water supplies. This is especially true of communities that rely on surface water or that have the dubious distinction of being adjacent to one or more hazardous waste sites or industries that wantonly disposed their industrial solvents. These problems have become community-wide disasters as hazardous wastes contaminate soils, water, and air in a seemingly random pathwork of chemical contamination across the nation and around the world.

DRUG PROBLEMS

Our history of development and use of pharmaceutical products is no less checkered. Many highly potent drugs were developed without sufficient testing or were given in dosages that far exceeded the levels needed for efficacy and safety. This reality has proved especially painful for the millions of women who relied on the high-dose synthetic and semisynthetic estrogens in birth control pills. Other drugs, such as diethylstilbestrol, just should not have been used in people in the first place because of their overt tumor-producing qualities in test animals. Silicones were never adequately tested for long-term safety. Still others, such as thalidomide, were toxic time bombs waiting to go off. Improper or absent testing allowed these products a place on pharmacy shelves.

COMMUNICATING RISKS

When industrial producers knew of adverse effects, the record shows that they often failed to communicate them to an unwary public—or to their own workers. This was true for the glycol ethers, ethylene oxide, benzene, and lead. Still other commercially profitable chemicals required highly dangerous feed stocks, putting first workers and then the public in harm's way as accidents or disasters plagued production and toxic residuals such as vinyl chloride contaminated consumer products.

Some of these events were certainly simply the result of bad luck. Accidents by definition cannot be accurately predicted. But most of the contamination that plagues the United States in the 1990s is the result of anticipatable or intentional pollution. Rivers and streams are today's equivalent of Rome's *Cloaca maxima,* receiving almost 10 billion pounds of wastes in 1987, 43 percent of all our chemical effluvia.[5] Only our overweening pride in believing we can keep abreast of any problem generated by our vast synthetic capability has kept us from developing a more rational plan for recycling our often unnecessary waste — or limiting production in the first place.

As we have seen, though, there is little cause for optimism that such plans are being made. Time and again, commercial pressures and simple ignorance have led to the production, use, and/or release of substances that have proved harmful to ourselves and our environment. We misread the evidence of planetary organisms evolving with new genetic structures as evidence that they are adapting adequately to new selection pressures. We take the emergence of alien strains of gasoline- or PCB-tolerant microorganisms and pesticide-resistant insects as evidence that our planet is accomodating to toxic substances and integrating them into viable ecosystems. In fact, only the most robust organisms generally can make such adaptations, and then only at the expense of more vital genetic information.

Substituting chemical selection for natural selection is not good stewardship for the planet. The capacity of the earth to absorb our by-products is now at a critical juncture. Either we learn how to rein in our excesses or our deleterious impacts on living systems may well prove irreparable.

EARTH FIRST

For too long, we have relied on the same flawed toxicological principles used to establish "safe exposures" for people to determine what is safe for the planet. We have already examined some of these myths:

- that there is a "safe" threshold below which there are no health effects that warrant control or regulation
- that most if not all toxics will eventually be metabolized or safely assimilated
- that toxics are innocuous as long as concentrations are kept low enough

What is flawed about these beliefs is not merely that they fail as universal truths for humans; but that they cannot readily be extrapolated from humans to other life. This blind anthropomorphism underscores the major dilemma highlighted by this book: that even if we did a modestly effective job in protecting human life, planetary life would not necessarily be better off. By focusing solely on human well-being we are missing a chance to vouchsafe all life on the planet. This last truth underscores the message given by thoughtful persons who met under the auspices of the Council on Environmental Quality in 1984. These scientists advocated a regulatory system "that places a high priority on protection of the planet's biota."[6]

It is obviously difficult to change. The political and economic forces that have driven our planet and its people to the present state have their own long half-lives. As long as they appear to be generating benefits in the short run, it seems nearly impossible to stem the tide.

However, we must find a way to change the patterns that have led us to the brink of ecological catastrophe. As long as we have thought only of ourselves, interim solutions have been tragically short-sighted. Consider, for example, the cascade of chemical solutions used in the electronics industry to speed our computer revolution. Moving from water to chlorinated solvents such as TCE to trichloroethane, and then from these to CFCs to clean circuit boards and microchips was a pyrrhic victory over human toxicity. In the process, we eliminated chlorinated solvents with high human toxicity, only to replace them with a legacy of persistent chemicals that were globally toxic. How much better to have stayed with the water-based cleaning systems to which the electronics industry has now belatedly returned!

PROPOSED SOLUTIONS

We are now trying to reintroduce the idea of economic incentives to get major polluters to control their emissions and waste products. Richard J. Mahoney, the chairman and CEO of Monsanto Corporation, has urged an end to short-term "fixes" of environmental problems by giving industries incentives for voluntary, market-based initiatives to minimize their impact on the environment.[7] In exchange for a lifting of what he perceives as unduly prescriptive rules, Mahoney said industry would be willing to commit itself to the idea of "no significant impact on the environment." To this end, Monsanto and other major chemical producers would increase their efforts to eliminate, reuse, or recycle wastes on site rather than releasing them into the environment. These are not bad ideas, just limited ones. Indeed, Monsanto's work on recycling its own chemicals is a model of efficiency and wise stewardship.

Control at the source, where decisions are made about a chemical's persistence and degradation, is critical. We must learn to consider the effects of the feed stocks, breakdown chemicals, and secondary pollution in how much of a potentially toxic chemical is made, instead of simply controlling how the wastes in its production are dispersed. Most of the hazardous waste sites in the country are contaminated by spent chemicals, not their by-products. And most of the pollution we see is the result of primary use (such as that caused by internal combustion engines). Hence it is critical to meter out how much of any given chemical is allowed to be produced, not merely to control it after the fact. It may be just as dangerous to make a chemical that can only be destroyed by an incineration process that yields chlorinated dioxins as it is to make a dioxin-contaminated chemical in the first place. And virtually indestructible and superfluous plastics such as polystyrene can best be controlled by not making them rather than by the elaborate schemes presently being considered for recycling old styrene containers. Nonetheless, for some essential toxicant-generating industrial processes, control at the source makes good sense.

Source Reduction

The new proposals for clean air legislation are a useful focal point. The 1990 bill requires a 10 million ton reduction in emissions of sulfur dioxide and a 2 million ton reduction in nitrogen oxides (down from 4 million tons annually) from power plants by the year 2000. Both gases are acid rain precursors, and nitric oxide has recently been associated with ozone depletion. The new law also requires phasing out the major ozone depleters — the CFCs, carbon tetrachloride, and 1,1,1-trichloroethane, and the hydrochlorofluorocarbons (HCFCs). (The CFCs) by January 1, 2000; trichloroethane by January 1, 2002; and the HCFCs by 2030.) The new law also puts the onus on the Environmental Protection Agency to assure that the sources of some 250 categories of toxic pollutants have adequate controls on their emissions to ensure that the health effects of the aggregate are minimal. That is, the EPA is required to issue standards by *category of industry*. All major sources (with the exception of coke ovens) are required to install "maximum available control technology" over their emissions between 1995 and 2003 (coke ovens by 2020). These controls have to be good enough to assure that no one will experience more than a 1 in a 10,000 lifetime risk of cancer from exposure to the maximum likely amount of emissions. What is new in this concept is that the risk figure is based on the combined health effects of all emissions from any given source, thus requiring the regulatory body to measure additive and multiplicative effects of hazardous chemicals.

The new Clean Air Act amendments also require the establishment of a Chemical Safety Board to investigate chemical accidents. Other provisions control hydrocarbon and nitrogen oxide emissions from cars, reduce ozone levels by controlling sources and requires cities with air pollution problems to sell gasoline containing oxygen and to cut cancer risks by 75 percent.[8] While these are good first steps, a more radical solution to chemical pollution is, as I said above, to regulate which chemicals are produced — and for those that pass muster, to allow only a controlled amount into processes from which contamination is inevitable. This might involve reducing the amount of energy produced annually, a good primary control device for much contamination, or the overt elimination of certain chemicals altogether.

Chemical Elimination

We should certainly seriously consider eliminating each of the herbicides that has been consistently found to contaminate surface or ground water.[9] Often, the contamination level is above that permitted for drinking water. This problem is particularly acute for surface waters in states with heavy agricultural chemical use (in the Midwest, for example, forty-four streams were found to contain contaminants in excess of the EPA's proposed drinking water standards).[10] The most prevalent are the triazine herbicides, chemicals with a well-known proclivity for migration through sandy soils. (As we have seen, these herbicides, which include alachlor, simazine, atrazine, triazine, and cyanazine, have long been recognized as having potentially deleterious health effects.) Elimination of these herbicides from commerce would have a salubrious effect on the environment also since many of them are known to damage paramecia and other single cell organisms as well as some of those responsible for photosynthesis. Reducing reliance on agricultural chemicals is in principle a good idea.

This type of recommendation is reinforced by the findings of the National Academy of Sciences' National Research Council. Their recent report, *Alternative Agriculture,* documents that agricultural practices are the major nonpoint source of water pollution in many states. They urge a return to sustainable agricultural methods that avoid pesticides and lessen reliance on synthetic fertilizers and excessive nitrate use because they believed that such use contributed to environmental, occupational and health problems.[11]

The industry response is that such blanket prohibitions on production limit the discretionary judgment of farmers and violate the rules under which the Department of Food and Agriculture and the EPA permitted them to register pesticides in the first place (they were not responsible for end-use consequences). They also argue that eliminating some of the most toxic pesticides, for example, the fungicides, would have a deleterious impact on commerce in general. A study conducted under the direction of the industry trade organization responsible for continued support for such chemicals, the National Agricultural Chemicals Association, concluded that banning fungicides would lead to a 13 percent rise in consumer food prices and a 24 percent fall in the available supply of fruits, vegetables, and peanuts.[12] Others, notably Bruce Ames, have pointed to the protective role fungicides play in limiting exposure to mold and fungal toxins.[13]

So, we are told we would pay a stiff price for toxic-free food. But the industry calculation did not factor in the benefits of using toxic-free food or those that might accrue to an industry that refocused its chemical production away from often carcinogenic and highly toxic production processes. While it is true that some fungicides reduce the amount of mold (and hence mold-associated contaminants such as the aflatoxins), it is not inevitable that such products will form in properly stored foods. And it is also true that targeted pests and weeds are fast developing resistance to the major pesticides, driving a cycle of chemical dependency.

Costs

Yet, each of these proposals—the Clean Air Act, phasing out certain agricultural chemicals, and so on)—*is* costly, at least initially. Some estimates place the cost of the Act at $2 billion to $4 billion a year for carbon dioxide reduction alone.[14] But does it really matter so much what the short-term costs are of programs that promise to do away with chemicals that are intrinsically harmful to people and the environment? We are talking about the difference between a planet that will be habitable by our grandchildren and great-grandchildren and one habitable only for ourselves.

ETHICS AND TOXICS

Our chemical evolutionary adolescence has run its course. Like the 15-year-old who cannot get to his bed through the mess in his room, we have fouled our nest to the point where someone must clean it up. To date, we have "solved" this problem by locating the lion's share of our hazardous waste sites in proximity to the poorest in our population—and in the world at large—asking them to bear the brunt of our excesses.

Even a rudimentary understanding of ethics leads to the conclusion that there is something intrinsically immoral if not evil about this distribution. We ask the most disadvantaged to help provide the goods and services for our affluent society (goods that they can only purchase in limited amounts) and then ask them to live with the trash. For example, consider for a moment who has reaped the benefits and who the risks of excessive reliance on chlorofluorocarbons. How many of the working-class women who developed neurological damage after laboring at electronics plants that relied on solvents and CFCs in New Mexico and California went home in CFC–air conditioned cars or to CFC–air conditioned homes or dry cleaned their clothes with chlorinated solvents?[15] How many of their husbands who worked the fields in these same communities were put at risk for skin cancer after being exposed to excessive ultraviolet light because CFCs released wantonly from this plant and thousands of others depleted the ozone layer? And how many of their families used CFC-based aerosol spray cans of expensive hair dyes, perfumes, and processed cheese — or the high-tech electronic products that were the fruits of their labor?

Elementary ethics calls for some proportionality between who benefits and who gets hurt from use of toxic substances. At the moment, the balance is all out of proportion. Too few benefit and too many are — or will be — hurt from present excesses. Skin cancer and intergenerational harms are but two examples discussed in this book.

GUIDELINES FOR A TOXIC PLANET

It is long past time we cleaned up our act. The first step is to agree on some basic rules and principles. Foremost among them is that we apply some version of the traditional maxim of our native American forebearers: *No change can be allowed unless we can look ahead seven generations to the world of our children's children and say it is good.* This may mean foreswearing some of the most coveted short-term chemical solutions to our immediate needs. We may have to ask industry to reduce the amount of production of particularly hazardous chemicals whose environmental fate poses the most serious risks. (To its credit, Du Pont de Nemours has taken the initiative in this regard, promising to phase out all of its production of CFCs in the next few years.) Industry must also promise to keep its waste products right where they are produced and not burden the rest of us with the offal.

The second step is to integrate what has been discussed in this book into more general goals. And here, the principal action is to somehow shift our attention away from human-centered interests to those of the planet as a whole. If the primary goal of our regulatory actions is first to protect the biota of the planet, human life will be protected more than adequately. For almost every toxic substance, there are species that are more sensitive to its effects than are humans.

The third step is to recognize that our megalithic creations of cities and urban landscapes are ecosystems in and of themselves. One way is to assure that they contribute neither more nor less to environmental degradation than did their green predecessors. Imagine if Chicago added no more pollutants than the marsh it replaced! Such a balance would assure a continuity of life not now in evidence.

The fourth step is to assure that toxic-stressed environments be relieved and that self-sustaining, regenerative ecosystems be fostered. Some soil-depleting crops may need to be transformed into "renewable" resources. Marshes can be used to process human and animal wastes. And some severely shocked systems (such as coral reefs in Micronesia or Florida) should be simply left alone.

The fifth and final step is to assure that long-persisting, non-biodegradable, and fundamentally toxic substances not be released into the environment.

A list[16] of reasonable objectives to achieve these ends would look something like this:

1. No new carcinogenic fungicides or pesticides.

2. Elimination of all carcinogenic or reproductively hazardous agricultural chemicals by 1996.

3. No nondegradable plastics.

4. No CO_2-generating fossil fuels to be used in internal combustion engines after the year 2010.[17]

5. No long-term administration of hormones, drugs, or medical devices to people or animals without equally long-term analysis of their effects.

6. No environmental (nonagricultural) applications of any pesticide without an Environmental Impact Report that includes analysis of the pesticide's degradation and ultimate fate.

7. No reproductively hazardous products in commerce where human exposure is likely or inevitable.

8. Phase out all CFCs and ozone-depleting chemicals by 1997.

9. Reduction of CO_2 emissions by 20 percent by the year 2000 and 40 percent by the year 2010.

10. Inclusion of multiplicative and additive effects of combinations of chemicals into risk assessment methodologies.

The present system, which allows a "balancing" consideration to be given to chemicals that are effective as "economic poisons" (that wonderful bureaucratese for pesticides) but pose some risks, must be changed. Instead, there need to be hard and fast rules as to environmental safety so that no chemicals are released that persist, cause genetic damage and/or pose risks of reproductive and tumorigenic harm.

The present-day federal Environmental Impact Study and California's Environmental Impact Report are steps in the right direction. Both are "triggered" when any new program or project poses a scientifically credible possibility of harm, injury, or dislocation to the ecosystem or its human inhabitants. But both fall short of having the necessary tests for what constitutes a "significant" impact. Both concentrate on short-term effects and downgrade the weight to be given to future problems that might arise from nonbiodegradability or from the second-order breakdown of the chemicals into more hazardous molecules.

If the Environmental Impact Study model worked, it would have foreseen the impact of CFCs on the ozone layer. Both the chemistry of these molecules and the resulting impact of released chlorine were known prior to 1973 when the first intimations of an ozone-depleting phenomenon were uncovered.

This generation of scientists owes a better legacy to the future. But it is evident that its funders are unwilling or unable to produce the necessary studies to anticipate the problems that some chemicals may create for future generations. For this reason, change is needed. I have suggested some directions. The details and implementation are up to the forces in government. And these forces are ultimately responsible to one voice, yours.

In the end, it is up to us, members of the public whose dreams and aspirations for a good life are circumscribed by toxic emissions, contaminated housing tracts, and toxics in our drinking water. It is all of us who must take control over the fate of the earth.

Is it not time to take stock of what we are doing to ourselves and the rest of the living things on our planet? Can we not asume the enlightened stewardship that knowledge of the toxic by-products of our life-style demands?

It is only too late if we persist in our self-deception that chemicals will forever make "for better living." Chemicals can be whatever we want them to be. Now is the time to put them to the service of life instead of its destruction.

Notes

PREFACE

1. See, in particular, W. T. Brookes, "The global warming panic," *Forbes Magazine* 144 (25 December 1989): 96-102.

2. National Academy of Engineering, *Technology and environment* (Washington, DC: National Research Council, 1989).

CHAPTER ONE: TOXICOLOGICAL PERSPECTIVE

1. This perspective is developed in the many recent writings of Bruce Ames. See, in particular, B. N. Ames, "What are the major carcinogens in the etiology of human cancer? Environmental pollution, natural carcinogens, and the causes of human cancer: Six errors," in Vincent T. De Vita et al., eds., *Important advances in oncology* (Philadelphia: Lippincott, 1989), 237–47.

2. I wrote previously about such "successful" adaptations of microorganisms to our onslaught of antibiotics. See Marc Lappé, *When antibiotics fail* (Berkeley, CA: North Atlantic Books, 1986).

3. Chemicals with carcinogenic activity, according to Professor Dietrich Henschler, "pose an incalculable risk to future generations" and "comprise a new toxic risk." See D. Henschler, "Carcinogenicity testing—existing protocols are insufficient," in *Federation of European Societies of Toxicology (FEST), Supplement* (Amsterdam: Elsevier, 1985), 26–28.

4. R. A. Rinsky and his associates demonstrated that excess cancer deaths from leukemia can be plotted on a line that intersects at or near the origin, i.e., without an apparent threshold. See R. A. Rinsky et al., "Benzene and leukemia: An epidemiologic risk assessment," *New England Journal of Medicine* 316 (1987): 1044–50. P. F. Infante and M. C. White have shown that doses of benzene all the way down to 1 ppm and below produce a measurable increment in leukemia risk. See P. F. Infante and M. C. White, "Projections of leukemia risk associated with occupational exposure to benzene," *American Journal of Industrial Medicine*

7 (1985): 403–17. The "industrial level exposures" mentioned encompass levels of 0.6 to 32 ppm in air: see Table II in B. Holmber and P. Lundberg, "Benzene: Standards, occurrence and exposure," *American Journal of Industrial Medicine* 7 (1985): 375–83.

5. J. O. Nestor, a former U.S. Food and Drug Administration official, has documented the early catastrophes that accompanied using humans and animals concurrently as guinea pigs for testing new drugs. See J. O. Nestor, "Results of the failure to perform adequate preclinical studies before administering new drugs to humans," *South African Medical Journal* 49 (1975): 287–90.

6. These studies were reported by W. V. Ligon, Jr., S. B. Dorn, and R. J. May, "Chlorodibenzofuran and chlorodibenzo-*p*-dioxin levels in Chilean mummies dated to about 2800 years before the present," *Environmental Science and Technology* 23 (1989): 1286–90.

7. See L. Hardell, "Malignant lymphoma of histiocytic type and exposure to phenoxyacetic acids or chlorophenols," *Lancet* 1 (1975): 55–56.

8. See L. Hardell, "On the relation of soft tissue sarcoma, malignant lymphoma and colon cancer to phenoxy acids, chlorophenols and other agents," *Scandinavian Journal of Work and Environmental Health* 7 (1981): 119–30.

9. See, as an example of a retrospective study, K. Wilkund and L. E. Holm, "Soft tissue sarcoma risk in Swedish agricultural and forestry workers," *Journal of the National Cancer Institute* 76 (1986): 229–34.

10. See M. S. Gottlieb, J. K. Carr, and J. R. Clarkson, "Drinking water and cancer in Louisiana: A retrospective mortality study," *American Journal of Epidemiology* 116 (1982): 652–67.

11. See K. S. Crump and H. A. Guess, "Drinking water and cancer: Review of recent epidemiological findings and assessment of risks," *Annual Review of Public Health* 3 (1982): 339–57.

12. See L. Hardell et al., "Malignant lymphoma and exposure to chemicals, especially organic solvents, chlorophenols and phenoxy acids: A case-control study," *British Journal of Cancer* 43 (1981): 169–71. See also F. H. Zahm, "A case-control study of soft tissue sarcoma," *American Journal of Epidemiology* 130 (1989): 665–74. A full review of the use of epidemiological studies in this area can be found in Zahm, "Herbicides and cancer: Review and discussion of methodological issues," *Recent Results in Cancer Research* 120 (1990): 132–45.

13. See A. S. Whittemore et al., "Mycosis fungoides in relation to environmental exposures and immune response: A case-control study," *Journal of the National Cancer Institute* 20 (1989): 1560–67.

14. See W. J. Nicholson, "IARC evaluations in the light of limitations of human epidemiologic data," *Annals of the New York Academy of Sciences* 534 (1988): 44–61.

15. See K. Wilkund and L. E. Holm, "Soft tissue sarcoma risk in Swedish agricultural and forestry workers," *Journal of the National Cancer Institute* 76 (1986): 229–34; and S. K. Hoar et al., "Agricultural herbicide use and risk of lymphoma and soft tissue sarcoma," *Journal of the American Medical Association* 256 (1986): 1141–47.

16. See, especially, the work of N. E. Pearce in New Zealand: N. E. Pearce et al., "Leukemia among New Zealand agricultural workers," *American Journal of Epidemiology* 124 (1986): 402–9; and N. E. Pearce, A. H. Smith, and D. O. Fisher, "Malignant lymphoma and multiple myeloma linked with agricultural occupations in a New Zealand cancer registry–based study," *American Journal of Epidemiology* 121 (1985): 225–37.

17. See L. F. Burmeister et al., "Selected cancer mortality and farm practices in Iowa," *American Journal of Epidemiology* 118 (1983): 72–77; see also L. Brown, "Pesticide exposures and other agricultural risk factors for leukemia among men in Iowa and Minnesota," *Cancer Research* 50 (1990): 6585–91.

18. See D. T. Silverman, L. I. Levin, and R. N. Hoover, "Occupational risks of bladder cancer in the United States. II. Non-white men," *Journal of the National Cancer Institute* 81 (1989): 1480–83.

19. See, for instance, A. F. Olshan et al., "Childhood brain tumors and parental occupation in the aerospace industry," *Journal of the National Cancer Institute* 77 (1986): 17–19; H. A. VanSteensen-Moll, H.A. Valkenburg, and G. E. Van Zanen, "Childhood leukemia and parental occupation," *American Journal of Epidemiology* 121 (1985): 216–24; and M. Zack et al., "Cancer in children of parents exposed to hydrocarbon-related industries and occupations," *American Journal of Epidemiology* 122 (1980): 357–65.

20. The chemical releases associated with these events are discussed in J. Saxena, ed., *Hazard assessment of chemicals,* vol. 2 (New York: Academic Press, 1983). See, especially, J. Charlton, A. Chow, and H. D. Gesser, "Accidental release of vinyl chloride: The train derailment near MacGregor, Manitoba," pp. 245–67; and G. Reggiani, "Anatomy of a TCDD spill: The Seveso accident," pp. 269–335.

21. The Seveso accident occurred on July 10, 1976, and included three other townships in the communities just north of Milano, Italy: Meda, Cesano, and Desor. While some 81,131 animals died within three months of the accident, no human deaths have been directly attributed to the release of dioxins that accompanied the chemical reactor excursion. (See G. Reggiani, note 20.) In Bhopal, by contrast, some 2,000 people died within the first few days after the accident; another 1,500 died thereafter. Estimates of the number of injured range from the industry number of 5,000 to activists' estimate of 20,000.

22. The Indian lawyers cited a plant in Virginia that also made MIC and showed that it had much more elaborate safeguards. Inspection records of the Bhopal plant showed that it was a factory waiting for an accident to happen. We may never know the truth since the case has been settled out of court, although not a single victim has yet received compensation.

23. Indian activists estimate the number of injured at 20,000 or more: the more conservative number was presented by W. Lepkowski, "Bhopal settlement still on hold," *Chemical and Engineering News* 18 (September 1989): 15–16.

24. Ibid.

25. See M. D. Shelby et al., "Results of in vitro and in vivo toxicity tests on methyl isocyanate," *Environmental Health Perspectives* 72 (1987): 183–88. The likelihood of persistent cellular damage caused by methyl isocyanate is discussed in H. K. Goswami, "Cytogenetic effects of methyl isocyanate exposure in Bhopal," *Human Genetics* 74 (1986): 81–84.

26. See J. R. Bucher et al., "Carcinogenicity and pulmonary pathology associated with a single 2-hour exposure of laboratory rodents to methyl isocyanate," *Journal of the National Cancer Institute* 81 (1989): 1586–87.

27. Ibid.

28. These positions are discussed in T. Kuhn's famous treatise, *The structure of scientific revolutions,* 2nd ed. (Chicago: University of Chicago Press, 1970).

29. I have been an expert witness in several lawsuits where industrial files were found to contain incriminating evidence of past cover-ups of compromising data. Unfortunately, court "protective" orders, won as a concession to settlement, presently prevent me or other potential witnesses from discussing the particulars of individual cases.

30. The event earmarked the pharmaceutical industry instead for

sweeping legislative reform: The sulfanilamide crisis provoked the public outcry that led to the passage in 1938 of the Kefauver-Harris Amendments to the Food and Drug Act, which mandated pretesting of all drugs in animals.

31. See F. H. Wiley et al., "The formation of oxalic acid from ethylene glycol and related solvents," *Journal of Industrial Hygiene and Toxicology* 20 (1938): 269–77. Another contemporary study showing similar damage is H. J. Morris, A. A. Nelson, and H. O. Flavery, "Observations on the chronic toxicities of propylene glycol, ethylene glycol, diethylene glycol, ethylene glycol mono-ethyl-ether, and diethylene glycol mono-ethyl ether," *Journal of Pharmacology and Experimental Therapeutics* (1942): 266–73.

32. See N. A. Brown, D. Holt, and M. Webb, "The teratogenicity of methoxyacetic acid in the rat," *Toxicology Letters* 22 (1984): 93–100. For a review, see P. E. Berteau et al., "The toxicity of glycol ethers, with emphasis on genetic and reproductive effects." (Berkeley, CA: Hazard Evaluation and Information Service, California Department of Health Services, 1982).

33. These findings were made by two investigative reporters at the *Wall Street Journal:* see B. Meiere and A. Pasztor, "Risky business: Despite health threat, glycol ethers remain in use in some plants," *Wall Street Journal,* 26 June 1984, pp. 1, 15.

34. J. L. Welch, memo to K. D. Kover, Environmental Protection Agency, 29 April 1983, re Eastman Kodak's 2 March 1983, Section 8(e) submission on ethylene glycol butyl ether.

35. "Hazard alert on glycol ethers, update." Alert no. 8 (Berkeley, CA: Hazard Evaluation System and Information Service, California Department of Health Services, 1982).

36. See W. Hevelin, "Reproductive and hematopoietic toxicity of the glycol ethers: An update." (Berkeley, CA: Hazard Evaluation System and Information Service, California Departments of Health Services and Industrial Relations, 1989).

CHAPTER TWO: A CHRONOLOGY OF TOXIC ENCOUNTERS

1. P. Pott, *Chirurgical observations* (London: L. Hawkes, W. Clarke, and R. Collins, 1775).

2. Ibid., vol. 3, 177–83.

3. See H. J. Butlin, "Three lectures on cancer of the scrotum in chimney sweeps and others," *British Medical Journal* 1 (1892): 1341; 2: 1–6, 66–71.

4. See J. Bell, "Paraffin epithelioma of the scrotum," *Edinburgh Medical Journal* 33 (1876): 135–37.

5. See D. D. Rutstein et al., "Sentinel health events (SHEs) (Occupational): A basis for physician recognition and public health surveillance," *American Journal of Public Health* 73 (1983): 1054–62. Rutstein and her colleagues define SHEs as a "preventable disease, disability or untimely death whose occurrence serves as a warning signal that the quality of preventive and/or therapeutic medical care may need improvement" in D. D. Rutstein et al., "Measuring the quality of medical care: A clinical method," *New England Journal of Medicine* 294 (1976): 582–86.

6. See A. L. Weinstein, H. L. Howe, and W. S. Burnett, "Sentinel health event surveillance: Skin cancer of the scrotum in New York State," *American Journal of Public Health* 79 (1989): 1513–15.

7. See E. Bingham, "Carcinogenicity of mineral oils," *Annals of the New York Academy of Sciences* 534 (1988): 452–58.

8. See L. Rehn, "Blasengeschwülste bei Anilinarbeitern," *Archive für Klinische Chirugie* 50 (1895): 588–94.

9. See E. E. Evans, "Causative agents and protective measures in the aniline tumor of the bladder," *Journal of Urology* 39 (1937): 212–16; R. A. M. Case and J. T. Pearson, "Tumors of the urinary bladder in workmen engaged in the manufacture and use of certain dyestuff intermediates in the British chemical industry," *British Journal of Industrial Medicine* 11 (1954): 213–16; and P. Kirsch et al., "Auramine: Toxicology and occupational health," *Arbeitsmedizin Sozialmedizin und Präventivmedizin* 13 (1978): 1–28.

10. P. DeLore and C. Borgomono, "Acute leukemia following benzene poisoning: On the toxic origin of certain acute leukemias and the relationship to serious leukemias," *Journal de Médecin de Lyon* 9 (1928): 227–36.

11. Citations for pre-1980 carcinogens can be found in W. J. Nicholson, "Research issues in occupational and environmental health," *Archives of Environmental Health* 39 (1984): 190–92; citations for post-1980 carcinogens can be found in International Agency for Research on Cancer, *Monographs on the evaluation of the carcinogenic risk of chemicals to humans,* Supplement no. 4 (Lyon, France: I.A.R.C., 1982), 17–24.

12. See K. Yamagiwa and K. Ichikawa, "Experimental study of the pathogenesis of carcinoma," *Journal of Cancer Research* 3 (1918): 1–21.

13. See E. L. Kennaway, "Experiments on cancer-producing hydrocarbon from coal tar," *British Medical Journal* 2 (1925): 1–4.

14. See J. W. Cook, C. L. Hewett, and I. Hieger, "The isolation of cancer-producing hydrocarbon from coal tar," *Journal of the Chemical Society* 1 (1933): 395–405.

15. See C. Maltoni and I. Selikoff, Preface in "Living in a chemical world. Occupational and environmental significance of industrial pollution," *Annals of the New York Academy of Sciences* 534 (1988): xv–xvi.

16. See W. J. Nicholson, "IARC evaluations in the light of limitations of human epidemiologic data," *Annals of the New York Academy of Sciences* 534 (1988): 44–61.

17. See S. Li, "An epidemiological approach for the risk assessment of chemicals causing human cancer and other disorders," in M. L. Richardson, ed., *Risk assessment of chemicals in the environment* (London: Royal Chemical Society, 1988).

18. Ibid.

19. See S. Lagakos, B. J. Wesen, and M. Zelen, "An analysis of contaminated well water and health effects in Woburn, Massachusetts," *Journal of the American Statistical Association* 81 (1986): 583–96.

20. These and other criticisms may be found in three commentaries that accompanied the Lagakos, Wesen, and Zelen article (see note 19): B. MacMahon, pp. 597–99; R. L. Prentice, pp. 600–1; and W. J. Rogan, pp. 602–3.

21. See N. Sadamori et al., "Skin cancer among atom bomb survivors," *Lancet* 1 (1989): 1267.

22. See M. Lappé, "The role of immunologic surveillance in the production of skin tumors by 3-methychloranthrene in the mouse," Dissertation Microfilms (Ann Arbor, MI, 1968).

23. I conducted independent experiments in 1981 with a Sacramento, California, laboratory that uncovered this vulnerability in water piping. See Anlab Laboratory report, "Permeability of plastic piping," Sacramento, CA (December, 1981).

24. F. Poncelet et al., "Mutagenicity, carcinogenicity, and teratogenicity of industrially important monomers," in M. Kirsch-Volders, ed., *Mutagenicity, carcinogenicity and teratogenicity of industrial pollutants* (New York: Plenum Press, 1984) 205–81.

CHAPTER THREE: THE PROBLEM IS LOCALIZED

1. R. Carson, *Silent Spring* (New York: Fawcett Crest Books, 1962). Of course, most chemicals are not in and of themselves "con-

taminants": a chemical becomes a toxic contaminant when it is not naturally found in a specific locale; it is potentially harmful; and when its level exceeds a permissible threshold, usually set at or below a concentration where exposure can be expected to produce "no observable effect" on health. For chemicals that are carcinogens, this level is often set at the lowest concentration feasible or, preferably, zero.

2. See A. Hecht, "PCBs: Coping with the indestructible pollutant," *FDA Consumer* 10 (1977): 21–25.

3. See, for example, G. R. N. Jones, "Polychlorinated bipehenyls: Where do we stand now?" *Lancet* 2 (1989): 791–94.

4. See J. R. Hollis, "Plasma temperature incineration," *Environmental Progress* 2 (1983): 7–10.

5. See C. Schreiner, "Application of short-term tests to safety testing of industrial chemicals," in G. M. Williams, V. C. Dunkel, and V. A. Ray, eds., *Cellular systems for toxicity testing* (New York: New York Academy of Sciences, 1983), 367–73.

6. See I. Fishbein, *Potential industrial carcinogens and mutagens. Studies in environmental science* (New York: Elsevier, 1979), 2–4. It is a common misconception that only the most toxic chemicals have been tested. The test list includes chemicals as benign as carageenan (the algal derivative used in food and cosmetics products), penicillin, and common over-the-counter medicines like acetaminophen. None of these proved carcinogenic.

7. See "Production by the U.S. chemical industry," *Chemical and Engineering News* (19 June 1989): 38–50.

8. Cited in *New York Times,* 20 November 1989, p. A13.

9. See P. I. Landrigan, "Epidemiologic approaches to persons with exposures to waste chemicals," *Environmental Health Perspectives* 48 (1983): 93–97.

10. Ibid.

11. U.S. Environmental Protection Agency, *National priorities list. 786 current and proposed sites in order of ranking and by state,* HW-7.2, rev. ed. (Washington, DC: GPO, December 1984).

12. The Superfund Law is also known as the Comprehensive Environmental Response, Compensation, and Liability Act of 1980, Public Law 96-510.

13. The site ranking is done by estimating on a scale of 0 to 100 the human and environmental risks posed by the migration of hazardous chemicals from the site through groundwater, surface water, and the air. Key parameters are the methods of containment;

the likely or actual escape routes; the physical and biological properties of the entrained chemicals; and the size of the at-risk population. See the *Federal Register* (30 December 1982), 47 FR 58476.

14. B. Paigen, personal communication, 28 November 1989. Dr. Paigen is currently a senior scientist at the Jackson Laboratory in Bar Harbor, Maine.

15. These data were reviewed and summarized in a recent study by J. Griffith et al., "Cancer mortality in U.S. counties with hazardous waste sites and groundwater pollution," *Archives of Environmental Health* 44 (1989): 69–74.

16. This point is discussed at length in R. L. Dixon and C. H. Nadolney, "Problems in demonstrating disease causation following multiple exposures to toxic or hazardous substances," in S. Draggan, J. J. Cohrssen, and R. E. Morrison, eds., *Environmental impacts on human health* (New York: Praeger, 1987), 117–38.

17. Ralph Abascal, personal communication, 20 November 1989. Mr. Abascal is the General Counsel for the California Rural Legal Assistance group in San Francisco, CA.

18. Many of these studies are reviewed in an article by R. C. Brownson et al., "Cancer risks among Missouri farmers," *Cancer* 64 (1989): 2381–86.

19. Studies based on county-wide statistics are summarized by C. S. Stokes and K. D. Brace, "Agricultural chemical use and cancer mortality in selected rural counties in the U.S.A.," *Journal of Rural Studies* 4 (1988): 239–47.

20. See D. Whorton et al., "Testicular function in DBCP-exposed pesticide workers," *Journal of Occupational Medicine* 21 (1979): 161–68.

21. See L. I. Lipshulz et al., "Dibromochloropropane and its effect on testicular function in man," *Journal of Urology* 124 (1980): 464–68.

22. See T. R. Torkelson, S. E. Sadek, and V. K. Rowe, "Toxicologic investigations of 1,2–dibromo–3–chloropropane," *Toxicology and Applied Pharmacology* 3 (1961): 545–51. As revealed in trial testimony, unpublished work sponsored by Shell.Oil during this same period also found reduced testis weights in rats exposed to DBCP.

23. The technical reason given by Lyman to me was that the Department of Health Services would have allowed a water system to make a similar dilution to bring its finished water under the state

limit of 5 ppb. D. Lyman, personal communication, 13 June 1990. (Dr. Lyman is Chief of the Preventive Disease Section of the California Department of Health Services in Sacramento, CA) However, this step had been allowed as an emergency measure for communities that had no other recourse for potable water. And this was only done with water contaminated with trihalomethanes, such as chloroform, which form during disinfection. It had never been done for DBCP, which had been proven to be a potent animal carcinogen and mutagen. According to W. Crawford, Regional Administrator of the California Food and Drug Branch, Region 2, his staff had originally ordered all of the contaminated wine to be dumped. W. Crawford, personal communication, 13 June 1990.

24. See O. Wong et al., "An epidemiological investigation of the relationship between DBCP contamination in drinking water and birth rates in Fresno County, California, U.S.A.," *American Journal of Public Health* 78 (1988): 43–46.

25. See Section 429.11, Health and Safety Code, State of California.

26. For a statistical breakdown, see U.S. Surgeon General, "Health effects of toxic pollution: A report from the Surgeon General" (Washington, DC: GPO, 1980).

27. U.S. Department of Health, Education and Welfare, *Carcinogenesis bioassay of trichloroethylene,* Publication no. 79-01-6 (Washington, DC: GPO, 1976).

28. This estimate appeared in H. A. Tilson and C. L. Mitchell, "Neurobehavioral techniques to assess the effects of chemicals on the nervous system," *Annual Reviews of Pharmacology and Toxicology* 24 (1984): 425–50.

29. See J. E. Vena, "Air pollution as a risk factor in lung cancer," *American Journal of Epidemiology* 116 (1982): 42–56; and I. T. T. Higgins, "Epidemiologic evidence on the carcinogenic risk of air pollution," in *Environmental pollution and carcinogenic risk,* INSERM, no. 52 (1976): 371–78.

30. Cited in P. Passell, "Life's risks: Balancing fear against reality of statistics," *New York Times,* 8 May 1989, pp. 1, 9.

31. Ibid., p. 9.

32. Cited in A. Clymer, "Polls contrast U.S.'s and public's views," *New York Times,* 22 May 1989, p. 11.

33. Data in M. S. Reisch, "Top 50 chemical production slowed markedly last year," *Chemical and Engineering News* (9 April 1990), table, p. 12.

34. U.S. Congress. House Committee on Energy and Commerce. Subcommittee on Oversight and Investigations, *"Air pollution: EPA's strategy to control emissions of benzene and gasoline vapors.* Report to the chairman," Washington, DC GPO 1986.

35. See L. A. Wallace, "Major sources of benzene exposure," *Environmental Health Perspectives* 82 (1989): 165.

36. See A. W. Horton et al., "Carcinogenesis of the skin: The accelerating properties of aliphatic and related hydrocarbons," *Cancer Research* 17 (1957): 758–66.

37. See R. Lindquist et al., "Increased risk of developing acute leukemia after employment as a painter," *Cancer* 60 (1987): 1378–84.

38. Hansen v. Day et al., Case no. 831502, San Francisco Superior Court (1989). As of early 1991, the case is on appeal.

39. The EPA considers the risk for ecological damage from the greenhouse effect to be extremely high; by contrast, only 33 percent of the public construes the risk for ecological damage from exposure to a global warming effect to be very serious (see note 32).

40. Anonymous, "Health in the greenhouse," *Lancet* 1 (1989): 819–20.

41. See A. Leaf, "Potential effects of global climatic and environmental change," *New England Journal of Medicine* 321 (1989): 1577–83.

42. U.S. National Aeronautics and Space Administration, *Report of the Ozone Trends Panel* (Washington, DC: NASA, March 1988).

43. This observation has led to a more general hypothesis of carcinogenesis and its relationship to DNA repair: see K. H. Kraemer, M. M. Lee, and J. Scotto, "DNA repair protects against cutaneous and internal neoplasia: Evidence from Xeroderma pigmentosum," *Carcinogenesis* 5 (1984): 511–14.

44. D. Takebe, cited in M. M. Wick, "Proceedings of the United States—Japan melanoma and skin cancer seminar on the biology and comparative features in the United States and Japan," *Journal of Investigative Dermatology* 92 (Supplement, 1989): 201S.

45. See J. Scotto, T. R. Fears, and J. F. Fraumeni, Jr., *Incidence of nonmelanoma skin cancer in the United States.* National Institutes of Health Publication no. 83-2433 (Washington, DC: GPO, 1983).

46. See M. L. Kripke, "Impact of ozone depletion on skin cancers," *Journal of Dermatology and Surgical Oncology* 14 (1988): 853–57.

47. See J. S. Hoffman, ed., *An assessment of the risks of stratospheric modification* (Washington, DC: U.S. Environmental Protection Agency, March 1987).

48. See Kripke, note 46.

49. See J. M. Elwood, "Epidemiology and control of melanoma in white populations and in Japan," *Journal of Investigative Dermatology* 92 (Supplement, 1989): 214S–19S.

50. In the U.S. and New Zealand, melanoma is among the most common tumors in young adults. In New Zealand, it accounts for 23 percent of all tumors between the ages of 20 and 39. (See Elwood note 49.)

51. See K. Himbow et al., "Report on United States–Japan cooperative cancer research program: Melanoma and skin cancer — Biology and comparative features in the United States and Japan," *Journal of Investigative Dermatology* 92 (Supplement, 1989): 202S.

52. Ibid., p. 201S.

53. D. Austin, personal communication, 1 November 1989.

54. See T. J. Mason, et al., *Atlas of Cancer Mortality 1959–69,* NIH 75-780 (Washington, DC: National Institute of Health, DHEW, 1975).

55. Elwood, note 49, p. 214S.

56. Ibid., p. 219S.

57. See S. T. Robbins, R. S. Cotran, and V. Kumar, *Pathologic basis for disease* (Philadelphia: Saunders, 1984), 1280.

58. See T. Kimura et al., "Chemical induction of chromatophoromas in the croaker, *Niea mitsukurii,*" *National Cancer Institute Monographs* 65 (1984): 139–54.

59. See C. J. Sindermann et al., "The role of pathobiology in pollution-effect monitoring programs," in V. Rapp, ed., *Pathobiology panel report* (Washington, DC: GAO, 1980) 135–51.

60. J. J. Black, "Field and laboratory studies of environmental carcinogenesis in Niagara River fish," *Journal of Great Lakes Research* 9 (1983): 326–34.

61. Ibid.

62. See Kimura, note 48.

63. See, for example, M. Voytek, *Ominous future under the ozone hole: Assessing biological impacts in Antarctica* (Washington, DC: Environmental Defense Fund, 1989).

64. See E. C. McCoy, J. Hyman, and II. S. Rosenkranz, "Activation of polycyclic aromatic hydrocarbons to mutagens by visible light," *Biochemical and Biophysical Research Communications* 89 (1979): 729–34; and S. DeFlora and G. Badolati, "Activation of

mutagens by sunlight and ultraviolet light," *Proceedings of the International Cancer Congress* 13 (1982): 591.

65. See S. DeFlora et al., "Photoactivation of mutagens," *Carcinogenesis* 10 (1989): 1089–97.

66. These chemicals include aromatic amines, aflatoxins, polycyclic hydrocarbons, and 2-acetylaminofluorene. Ibid.

67. See W. D. Carpenter, "Insignificant risks must be balanced against great benefits," *Chemical and Engineering News* 69 (1991): 37–39.

CHAPTER FOUR: THE BODY'S DEFENSES ARE ADEQUATE

1. See V. O. Longo, L. Citti, and P. G. Gervasik, "Biotransformation enzymes in nasal mucosa and liver of Sprague-Dawley rats," *Toxicology Letters* 44 (1988): 289–97.

2. The microsomal enzymes (which include the so-called mixed-function oxidases) are associated with the cytochrome system, so called because of its colorful staining characteristics. These enzyme groups are often given numerical designations such as P-450 or P-448.

3. Benzene is eventually metabolized to benzoquinone and quinone, both of which can produce the same spectrum of toxicity as benzene itself. One other pathway of benzene also exists, which takes the benzene molecule through a series of reactions that bypass the spontaneous rearrangement of the epoxide to phenol. These reactions allow benzene to acquire sulfur or sulfhydryl groups that permit it to bind with a chemical called glutathione. Glutathione-bound benzene metabolites can be excreted through the kidneys.

4. These effects can be observed at doses as low as 10 ppm, and for only six to eight hours, in test animals, and have been seen in humans with past exposures to benzene. See A. Forni et al., "Chromosome changes and their evolution in subjects with past exposure to benzene," *Archives of Environmental Health* 23 (1971): 385–93.

5. For example, to 61 ppm or higher for two to four weeks: see W. Deichmann, W. Macdonald, and E. Bernal, "The hemapoietic tissue toxicity of benzene vapors," *Toxicology and Applied Pharmacology* 5 (1963): 201–4.

6. See P. Delore and C. Borgomano, "Leucemie alignée au cours

de l'intoxication benzenique: Sur l'origine toxique de certaines leucemies aigues et leur relation avec les anemies graves," *Journal de Médecin* (Lyons) 9 (1928): 227–36.

7. Indirect evidence for such an effect can be found in R. E. Kouri et al., "Positive correlation between high aryl hydrocarbon hydroxylase activity and primary lung cancer as analyzed in cryopreserved lymphocytes," *Cancer Research* 42 (1982): 5030–7.

8. See E. S. Bessell, "Pharmacogenetic perspectives on susceptibility to toxic industrial chemicals," *British Journal of Industrial Medicine* 44 (1987): 505–7.

9. Experimental confirmation of this likelihood was recently obtained by demonstrating that liver cells taken from fast acetylating rabbits convert a precarcinogen known as 2-AF (for 2-aminofluorene) into a potent bladder- and liver-cancer-causing chemical known as 2-AAF (2-acetylaminofluorene). The slow acetylating rabbits bound up the precarcinogen in a conjugated form, ready for rapid and presumably harmless excretion. See C. A. McQueen, M. J. Miller, B. M. Way, and G. M. Williams, "Extracellular metabolites of 2-aminofluorene in cultures of rapid and slow acetylator rabbit hepatocytes as a model for urinary and biliary metabolism," *Chemistry of Biological Interactions* 66 (1988): 71–83.

10. See A. J. Smith and J. K. Chipman, "Interindividual variation in the mutagenic activation of 2-acetylaminofluorene by human liver in relation to animal metabolic models," *Mutagenesis* 3 (1988): 323–28.

11. See the discussion in M. A. Lappé, "Ethical issues in genetic screening for susceptibility to chronic lung disease," *Journal of Occupational Medicine* 30 (1988): 493–501.

12. See M. F. W. Festing, "Genetic factors in toxicology: Implications for toxicological screening," *CRC Critical Reviews in Toxicology* 18 (1987): 1–26.

13. See G. R. Venning, "Identification of adverse reactions to new drugs. I. What have been the important adverse reactions since thalidomide?" *British Medical Journal* 286 (1983): 199–202.

14. Mammalian liver cells have detoxifying enzymes that are particularly well suited for working on the pyrene nucleus, a common molecular component of many carcinogens. See S. Snyder, I. C. Hsu, and B. F. Trump, "Comparison of metabolic activation of carcinogens in human, rat and hamster hepatocytes," *Mutation Research* 182 (1987): 31–39.

15. See M. Ukikusa et al., "Amino acid metabolism during hemoperfusion over biological materials," *Life Support Systems* 1 (1983): 78–81.

16. Most importantly, the decontamination includes potentially harmful industrial chemicals as diverse as styrene oxide and p-nitrobenzylchloride. See, for example, D. Tsikas and G. Bruneer, "Enzymatic detoxification using lipophilic hollow-fiber membranes: IV. Glutathione conjugation reactions," *International Journal of Artificial Organs* 12 (1989): 121–28.

17. See D. H. Monroe and D. L. Eaton, "Effects of modulation of hepatic glutathione on biotransformation and covalent binding of aflatoxin B1 to DNA in the mouse," *Toxicology and Applied Pharmacology* 94 (1988): 118–27.

18. See H. Yokota et al., "Enhancement of the UDP-glucuronyltransferase, UDP-glucose dehydrogenase, and glutathione S-transferase activities in rat liver by dietary administration of eugenol," *Biochemical Pharmacology* 37 (1988): 799–802.

19. See K. Nakashima et al., "Glutathione contents in rat livers after acute and chronic exposure to ethylene oxide," *Sangyo Ika Daigaku Zasshi* 9 (1987): 355–59.

20. See R. J. Rush et al., "Mechanisms of chloroform and carbon tetrachloride toxicity in primary cultured mouse hepatocytes," *Environmental Health Perspectives* 69 (1986): 301–5. As with most processes involved with detoxification, paradoxical results are also possible. Some substances, such as the solvent methylene chloride, achieve their toxicity only after binding with glutathione, so that for exposures to this chemical, depletion of glutathione reserves may actually protect against toxicity.

21. See V. Garry et al., "Ethylene oxide: Evidence of human chromosomal effects," *Environmental Mutagenesis* 1 (1979): 375–82.

22. See R. Carubelli and P. B. McCay, "Dietary butylated hydroxytoluene protects cytochrome P-450 in hepatic nuclear members of rats fed 2-acetylaminofluorene," *Nutrition and Cancer* 10 (1987): 145–49.

23. See K. L. Khanduja et al., "Effect of large doses of ascorbic acid on the hepatic and extra-hepatic drug-metabolizing enzymes in the guinea pig," *Biochemistry International* 13 (1986): 659–70.

24. See B. H. Lauterburg and J. R. Mitchell, "Therapeutic doses of acetaminophen stimulate the turnover of cysteine and glutathione in man," *Journal of Hepatology* 4 (1987): 206–11.

25. See E. C. To and P. G. Wells, "Biochemical changes associated with the potentiation of acetaminophen hepatoxicity by brief anesthesia with diethyl ether," *Biochemical Pharmacology* 35 (1986): 4139–52.

26. See L. K. Griffeth, G. M. Rosen, and E. J. Rauchman, "Effects of model traumatic injury on hepatic drug metabolism in the rat. VI. Major detoxification/toxification pathways," *Drug Metabolism and Disposition* 15 (1987): 749–59.

27. See B. I. Ghanayem et al., "Effect of age on the toxicity and metabolism of ethylene glycol monobutyl ether in rats," *Toxicology and Applied Pharmacology* 91 (1987): 222–34.

28. See J. Kapitulnik et al., "Fetal and adult human liver differ markedly in the fluidity and lipid composition of their microsomal membranes," *Hepatology* 7 (1987): 55–60.

29. See J. Ludwig and R. Axelson, "Drug effects on the liver," *Digestive Disease Science* 28 (1983): 651–63.

30. See T. D. Boyer and D. A. Vessey, "Inhibition of human cationic glutathione S-transferase by nonsubstrate ligands," *Hepatology* 7 (1987): 843–48.

31. Loss of carrier molecules, lecithin, or other key substances can also lead to the accumulation of trigyclerides and a fatty liver.

32. See J. L. Farber, "Xenobiotics, drug metabolism and liver injury," *Monographs in Pathology* 28 (1987): 43–53.

33. See E. Farber, "Biochemical pathology of liver cell injury," in M. Liakim, J. Eshchar, and H. J. Zimmerman, eds., *International symposium on hepatoxicity* (New York: Academic Press, 1974).

34. See P. E. Martino et al., "Studies on the mechanism of the acute and carcinogenic effects of N-nitrosodimethylamine on mink liver," *Journal of Toxicology and Environmental Health* 23 (1988): 183–92.

35. See I. Bremmer, "Involvement of metallothionein in the hepatic metabolism of copper," *Journal of Nutrition* 117 (1987): 19–29.

36. See J. M. Frazier and W. S. Din, "Role of metallothionein in induced resistance to cadmium toxicity in isolated rat hepatocytes," *Experientia* 52 (Supplement, 1987): 619–26.

37. One model has the promoting agent being selectively toxic for other liver cells. Another has it directly stimulating the initiated cells, for instance, by binding with cell surface receptors.

38. See S. DeFlora et al., "Metabolism of mutagens and carcinogens in woodchuck liver and its relationship with hepatitis virus infection," *Cancer Research* 47 (1987): 4052–58.

CHAPTER FIVE: TOXIC EFFECTS NOT SEEN WILL NOT OCCUR

1. According to one critic, such testing systems "depend on a systematic approach that focuses on a traditional definition of acute lethal toxicity," see M. G. Cherniack, "Toxicological screening for organophosphorus-induced delayed neurototoxicity: Complications in toxicity testing," *NeuroToxicology* 9 (1988): 249–72. *Acute* usually refers to short-term exposures lasting hours or days and their immediate aftereffects.

2. See R. J. Molyneux, A. E. Johnson, and L. D. Stuart, "Delayed manifestation of Senecio-induced pyrrolizidine alkaloidosis in cattle: Case reports," *Veterinary and Human Toxicology* 30 (1988): 201–5.

3. See R. A. Roth and P. E. Ganey, "Platelets and the puzzles of pulmonary pyrrolizidine poisoning," *Toxicology and Applied Pharmacology* 93 (1988): 463–71.

4. See M. J. Hodgson et al., "Encephalopathy and vestibulopathy following short-term hydrocarbon exposure," *Journal of Occupational Medicine* 31 (1989): 51–54.

5. See E. Grandjean et al., "Investigations into the effects of exposure to trichloroethylene in mechanical engineering," *British Journal of Industrial Medicine* 12 (1955): 131–42.

6. See R. G. Feldman et al., "Long-term follow-up after single toxic exposure to trichloroethylene," *American Journal of Industrial Medicine* 8 (1985): 119–26.

7. See R. D. Stewart et al., "Accidental vapor exposure to anesthetic concentrations of a solvent containing tetrachloroethylene," *Industrial Medicine and Surgery* 30 (1961): 327–30.

8. See Y. Yamamura, "N-hexane polyneuropathy," *Folia Psychiatrica Neurologica Japan* 23 (1969): 45–57. Also in U.S. Department of Health, Education and Welfare, Public Health Service, *Criteria for a recommended standard: Occupational exposure to refined petroleum solvents* (Washington, DC: GPO, July 1977), p. 38.

9. See Y. Takeuchi, C. Mabuch, and S. Takagi, "Polyneuropathy caused by petroleum benzine," *Internationale Archives für Arbeitsmedicine* 34 (1975): 185–91. Also in *Criteria for a recommended standard,* note 8, pp. 40–41.

10. See, for example, M. E. Littorin et al., "Focal epilepsy and exposure to organic solvents: A case-referent study," *Journal of Occupational Medicine* 30 (1989): 805–9.

11. See, for example, W. A. Temple and D. G. Ferry, "Solvent exposure and risk assessment," in M. L. Richardson, ed., *Risk assessment of chemicals in the environment* (London: Royal Society of Chemistry, 1988).

12. See D. Mergler et al., "Neuropsychological impairment among former microelectronics assembly workers," *NeuroToxicology* (in press); see also D. Mergler, R. Bowler, and J. Cone, "Colour vision loss among disabled workers with neuropsychological impairment," *Neurotoxicology and Teratology* 12 (1990): 669–72.

13. Ibid.

14. See Temple and Ferry, note 11, p. 235.

15. Ibid.

16. See C. D. Drug, "The systemic neuronal affinity of triorthocresyl phosphate," *Brain* 65 (1962): 34–47; and J. P. Morgan, "The Jamaica Ginger paralysis," *Journal of the American Medical Association* 248 (1982):1 1864–67.

17. See J. P. Morgan and T. C. Tulloss, "The Jake Walk Blues," *Annals of Internal Medicine* 34 (1976): 402–3.

18. See J. P. Morgan and P. Renovich, "Jamaica ginger paralysis," *Archives of Neurology* (1978): 35–53.

19. See C. S. Davis and R. J. Richardson, "Organophosphorus compounds," in P. S. Spencer and H. H. Schaumberg, eds., *Experimental and clinical neurotoxicology* (Baltimore: Williams & Wilkins, 1980), 527–44.

20. See M. Pellin, J. L. Vicedo, and E. Vilanova, "Sensitivity to tri-o-cresyl phosphate in n-hexane exposed hens as a model of simultaneous hexacarbon and organophosphorous occupational intoxication," *Archives of Toxicology* 59 (1988): 311–18.

21. See N. Sennayake and J. Jeyaratnam, "Toxic polyneuropathy due to gingili contaminated with tri-cresyl phosphate affecting adolescent girls in Sri Lanka," *Lancet* 1 (1981): 88–89; and M. I. Smith and J. M. K. Spalding, "Outbreak of paralysis in Morocco due to orthocresyl phosphate poisoning," *Lancet* 1 (1959): 1019–21.

22. See M. G. Cherniack, "Toxicological screening for organophosphorous-induced delayed neurotoxicity: Complications in toxicity testing," *NeuroToxicology* 9 (1988): 249–72.

23. See R. L. Metcalf, "Historical perspective of organophosphorus ester induced delayed neurotoxicity," *NeuroToxicology* 3 (1982): 269–84.

24. See P. Bidstrup et al., "Paralysis following poisoning by a new

organic phosphorous insecticide (Mipafox)," *British Medical Journal* 1 (1953): 1068–70.

25. See N. Senanayake and L. Karalliedde, "Neurotoxic effects of organophosphorus insecticides: An intermediate syndrome," *New England Journal of Medicine* 316 (1987): 761–63.

26. See D. Tanaka, Jr., and S. J. Bursian, "Degeneration patterns in the chicken central nervous system induced by ingestion of the organophosphorus delayed neurotoxin, triorthotolyl phosphate," *Brain Research* 484 (1989): 240–56.

27. See C. M. Thompson, "Stereodependent intoxication by thiophosphorus esters," USDHHS Project Proposal no. CRISP/89/SO4434-01 (Bethesda, MD: National Institute of Environmental Health Sciences, Public Health Service, National Institutes of Health, 1989).

28. See C. Xintaras et al., "Occupational exposure to leptophos and other chemicals: NIOSH health survey of Velsicol pesticide workers," Publication no. (NIOSH) 78-136 (Washington, DC: GPO, March 1978).

29. See M. B. Abou-Donia, "Organophosphorus-induced delayed neurotoxicity," *Annual Reviews in Pharmacology and Toxicology* 21 (1981): 511–48.

30. See Cherniack, note 22, pp. 252–53.

31. See R. Singer, "Early recognition of toxicity by assessing nervous system function," *Biomedical and Environmental Science* 1 (1988): 356–62.

32. See T. H. Milby et al., *Potential health effects associated with the use of phenoxy herbicides: A summary of recent scientific literature* (Berkeley, CA: Environmental Health Associates, October 1980).

33. See N. G. Hildreth, R. E. Shore, and P. M. Dvoretsky, "The risk of breast cancer after irradiation of the thymus in infancy," *New England Journal of Medicine* 321 (1989): 1281–84.

34. See J. J. Broerse, D. W. Van Bekkum, and C. Zurcher, "Radiation carcinogenesis in experimental animals," *Experientia* 45 (1989): 60–69.

35. See M. A. Lappé and R. T. Prehn, "Immunologic surveillance at the macroscopic level: Non-selective elimination of premalignant skin papillomas," *Cancer Research* 29 (1969): 2374–78.

36. See B. R. Blakley, "The effect of cadmium on chemical- and viral-induced tumor production in mice," *Journal of Applied Toxicology* 6 (1986): 425–30.

37. See B. E. Walker, "Tumors in female offspring of control and diethylstilbestrol-exposed mice fed high-fat diets," *Journal of the National Cancer Institute* 82 (1990): 50–54.

38. See L. S. Kothari, "Influence of chronic melatonin on DMBA-induced mammary tumors in female Holtzman rats exposed to continuous light," *Oncology* 44 (1987): 64–66.

39. See W. Bednarz, "Primary and transplantable hepatomas induced by aflatoxin B1 in hypothyroid rats," *Neoplasma* 36 (1989): 113–26.

40. See R. Spirtas and R. Kamminski, "Angiosarcoma of the liver in vinyl chloride polyvinylchloride workers: 1977 update of the NIOSH register," *Journal of Occupational Medicine* 20 (1978): 427–31.

41. See R. D. Jones, D. M. Smith, and P. G. Thomas, "A mortality study of vinyl chloride monomer workers employed in the United Kingdom in 1940–1974," *Scandinavian Journal of Work and Environmental Health* 14 (1988): 153–60.

42. See K. W. Kizer and D. F. Austin, *Cancer in California,* Technical Report no. 2 (Berkeley, CA: California Department of Health Services, 1988).

43. See J. E. Vena and R. C. Fiedler, "Mortality of a municipal-worker cohort: IV. Fire fighters," *American Journal of Industrial Medicine* 11 (1987): 671–84.

44. See R. S. Koskela et al., "Mortality and disability among granite workers," *Scandinavian Journal of Work and Environmental Health* 13 (1987): 18–25.

45. See, in particular, the cancer policy of the State of California: *Guidelines for chemical carcinogen risk assessments and their scientific rationale* (Berkeley, CA: California Department of Health Services, November 1985).

46. See S. N. Yin et al., "Leukemia in benzene workers: A retrospective cohort study," *British Journal of Industrial Medicine* 44 (1987): 124–28.

47. See W. A. Anwar et al., "Enhancement of benzene clastocenicity by praziquantel in mice," *Mutation Research* 222 (1989): 283–90.

48. See L. R. Depass et al., "Influence of housing conditions for mice on the results of a dermal concogenicity bioassay," *Fundamental and Applied Toxicology* 7 (1986): 601–8.

49. See T. Lahiri and M. Banerjee, "Differential responses of carcinogen induced fibrosarcoma of mice to altered regimes of cold exposure," *Neoplasma* 33 (1986): 307–12.

50. The EPA estimates that 31,000 to 126,000 new cases of melanoma among individuals born before 2075 may arise as a result of depletion of the ozone layer is based on UV exposures alone. It is likely that even more will be produced: see L. R. Brown, ed., *State of the World, 1989: A Worldwatch Institute report on progress toward a sustainable society* (New York: Norton, 1989), p. 243.

CHAPTER SIX: ALL EFFECTS OF TOXICS
DISAPPEAR AS DOSES DIMINISH

1. The ability of some coal tar dyes such as Red dye no. 2 and Benzol violet to be toxic for developing embryos at *both* very high and very low doses was reported to the public in 1974. See L. Franks, "FDA approves a challenged food dye," *New York Times,* 14 December 1974, p. 1.

2. See R. E. Rodgers, M. L. Stern, and O. F. Ware, "Effects of Subacute administration of O, S, S-trimethyl phosphorodithioate on cellular and humoral immune response systems," *Toxicology* 54 (1989): 183–95.

3. See "Possible enhancement of carcinogenesis by selenium in an animal tumor model," *Nutrition Reviews* 47 (1989): 173–75.

4. See J. van Ulsen et al., "Chromate dermatitis from a homeopathic drug," *Contact Dermatitis* 18 (1988): 56–57.

5. See A. M. Fan, "Trichloroethylene: Water contamination and health risk assessment," *Reviews of Environmental Contamination and Toxicology* 101 (1988): 55–92.

6. See, for example, D. Ozonoff et al., "Health problems reported by residents of a neighborhood contaminated by a hazardous waste facility," *American Journal of Industrial Medicine* 11 (1987): 581–97.

7. These six lines of evidence have been adapted from a paper by former National Cancer Institute Director A. C. Upton: "Are there thresholds for carcinogenesis? The thorny problem of low level exposure," *Annals of the New York Academy of Sciences* 534 (1988): 863–84.

8. Some 50,000 mice were given AAF in graded doses: Liver tumors generally arose in a direct, linear fashion according to dose, while bladder cancers only began to appear after the mice received a critical minimal amount of carcinogen. See N. A. Littlefield, J. H. Farmer, and D. W. Taylor, "Effects of dose and time in a long-term, low-dose carcinogenic study," *Journal of Environmental Pathology and Toxicology* 3 (1979): 17–34.

9. See, for example, I. D. Boss et al., "A dosage response curve for the 1 rad range: Adult risks from diagnostic radiation," *American Journal of Public Health* 69 (1979): 130–35; and C. E. Land, "Estimating cancer risks from low doses of ionizing radiation," *Science* 209 (1980): 1197–99.

10. See, for example, A. C. Upton, "Biological basis for assessing carcinogenic risks of low level radiation," in E. Huberman and S. H. Barr, eds., *Carcinogenesis: A comprehensive survey,* vol. 10, *The role of chemicals and radiation in the ethiology of cancer* (New York: Raven Press, 1985), 381–401.

11. Ibid., p. 869.

12. See M. E. Wrenn and C. W. Mays, "Ionizing radiation," in W. N. Rom, ed., *Environmental occupational medicine* (Boston: Little, Brown, 1983), 667–85.

13. See *Carcinogen Policy,* State of California, Department of Health Services (Berkeley, CA, 1982), p. 20.

14. See, for example, F. D. Shaumberg, "Banning trichloroethylene: Responsible reaction or overkill?" *Environmental Science and Technology* 24 (1990): 17–22.

15. See S. Herren-Freund et al., "The carcinogenicity of trichloroethylene and its metabolites, trichloroacetic acid and dichloroacetic acid in mouse liver," *Proceedings of the American Association for Cancer Research* 27 (1986): 91–94.

16. William Goodman, the attorney of record in this case, personal communications.

17. This is true for the neurotoxicity produced by exposure to solvents such as n-hexane combined with TOCP, or methyl ketone with n-butyl ketone, or 1,1,1-trichloroethane plus trichloroethylene. See B. F. Craft, "Solvents and related compounds," in *Environmental occupational medicine,* note 12, pp. 511–53. It is also true for the dramatic enhancement of hepatoxicity due to carbon tetrachloride when preceded by exposure to hepane. See H. M. Mehendate, "Potentiation of halomethane hepatoxicity by chlordecone," *Medical Hypothesis* 33 (1990): 289–99.

18. This phenomenon is commonly due to a single drug or chemical simultaneously acting on more than one target (e.g., drugs that lower blood pressure will work on the heart, blood vessels, and nerve endings—all at different doses).

19. This phenomenon is due to the fact that larger molecules have more mass. However, a mole of any chemical contains the same number of molecules equal to Avogadro's constant: 6.022×10^{23}.

(A mole is technically the amount of substance that contains as many elementary entities as there are in 12 grams of carbon-12; or, in simple terms, a chemical's molecular weight expressed in grams.) Large molecules, such as the palytoxin produced by coral or the saxitoxin produced by red tide organisms, can have molecular weights as high as 140,000, while TCE has a molecular weight of about 131. This means that 1 picogram (or any unit weight) of TCE will have slightly more than a thousand times *more* molecules than will 1 picogram of palytoxin. The obvious significance for toxicity is that saxitoxin may appear to be 1,000 times more toxic than TCE on a dose basis (i.e., per pg/kg of chemical), but in reality be 1,000,000 times as toxic as TCE on a molecule by molecule basis. See *Quantities, Units and Symbols in Physical Chemistry* (Blackwell Scientific Publications, Oxford, England, 1988): 64 and 81.

20. See N. F. Cheville and R. B. Rimler, "A protein toxin from *Pasteurella mulocida* type D causes acute and chronic hepatic toxicity in rats," *Veterinarian Pathology* 26 (1989): 148–57.

21. See K. Sandberg, C. J. Berry, and T. B. Rogers, "Studies on the intoxication pathway of tetanus toxin in the rat pheochromocytoma cell line: Binding, internalization, and inhibition of acetylcholine release," *Journal of Biological Chemistry* 264 (1989): 5679–86.

22. See B. Eberspacher, F. Hugo, and S. Bhakdi, "Quantitative study of the binding and hemolytic efficiency of *Escherichia coli* hymolysin," *Infection and Immunity* 57 (1989): 983–88.

23. See D. FitzGerald and I. Pastan, "Targeted toxin therapy for the treatment of cancer," *Journal of the National Cancer Institute* 81 (1989): 1455–63.

24. See Y. Endo et al., "The mechanism of action of ricin and related toxic lecins on eukaryotic ribosomes," *Journal of Biological Chemistry* 262 (1987): 5908–12.

25. See C. S. Ramsden, M. T. Drayson, and E. B. Bell, "The toxicity, distribution and excretion of ricin holotoxin in rats," *Toxicology* 55 (1989): 161–71.

26. See M. Izquierdo et al., "High toxic efficiency of ricin immunotoxins specific for the T-cell antigen of a human leukemia T-cell line," *International Journal of Cancer* 43 (1989): 697–702.

27. See M. Bregni et al., "B-cell restricted saporin immunotoxins: Activity against B-cell lines and chronic lymphocytis leukemia cells," *Blood* 73 (1989): 753–62.

28. See K. D. Clinkenbeard, D. A. Mosier, A. L. Timko, and A. W. Confer, "Effects of *Pasteurella haemolytica* leukotoxin on cultured bovine lymphoma cells," *American Journal of Veterinary Research* 50 (1989): 271–75.

29. See J. N. Carlson and R. A. Rosellini, "Exposure to low doses of the environmental chemical dieldrin causes behavioral deficits in animals prevented from coping with stress," *Psychopharmacology* 91 (1987): 122–26.

30. Fetal and newborn mice exposed just before and just after birth to comparable doses (equivalent to 21.3 and 204.8 mg/kg/day) in their drinking water showed appreciable deficits in their ability to remember a previously learned avoidance exercise. See M. J. Kallman, G. L. Kaempf, and R. L. Balster, "Behavioral toxicity of chloral in mice; An approach to evaluation," *Neurobehavioral Toxicology and Teratology* 6 (1984): 137–46. Assuming humans are 10 times more sensitive and allowing another factor of 10 for interindividual variation, the equivalent human dose is .0213 and .2048 mg/kg/day, or approximately 21 and 204 µg/kg/day, respectively. Assuming one liter of tap water is ingested by a 10 kg (22 lb) infant, 200 ppb of TCE would give a dose of 200 µg or 20 µg/kg.

31. See I. J. Light and J. M. Sutherland, "What is the evidence that hexachlorophene is not effective," *Pediatrics* 51 (1973): 345–51.

32. See A. Curley et al., "Dermal absorption of hexachlorophene in infants," *Lancet* 2 (1971): 296–98.

33. See C. Jacquelin and D. Colomb, "Erythème fessier et coma. Diagnostic étiologie tardiff," *Revue d'E.E.G. et de Neurophysiologie Clinicale,* 2 (1972): 414–18.

34. See "Hexachlorophene and newborns," *FDA Drug Bulletin* (December 1971): 1; and W. I. Pines, "Hexachlorophene: Why FDA concluded that hexachlorophene was too potent and too dangerous to be used as it once was," *FDA Consumer* 6 (1972): 24–25.

35. See W. B. Herter, "Hexachlorophene poisoning," *Kaiser Foundation Medical Bulletin* 7 (1959): 228–36.

36. See, for example, R. D. Kimbrough, "Review of the toxicity of hexachlorophene," *Archives of Environmental Health* 23 (1971): 119–22.

37. See warning in M. F. Tripier et al., "Experimental hexachlorophene encephalopathy in mice and baboons: Light and electron microscopic study," *Acta Neutopathological Supplement* (Berlin) 7

(1981): 40–43. Similar recommendations can be found in nursing and toxicology textbooks printed in the late 1970s. See, for example, L. E. Govoni and J. E. Hayes, *Drugs and nursing implications,* 3rd ed. (New York: Appleton-Century-Crofts, 1978), 330; and see also J. M. Arena, *Poisoning,* 4th ed. (Springfield, IL: Charles C. Thomas, 1979), 628.

38. See R. Rabin, "Warnings unheeded: A history of child lead poisoning," *American Journal of Public Health* 79 (1989): 1668–74. Blood lead levels at and below 15 μg/dl (100 ml) are now regarded as being in the range capable of producing neurotoxicity in children.

39. See H. L. Needleman et al., "Deficits in psychologic and classroom performance of children with elevated dentine lead levels," *New England Journal of Medicine* 300 (1987): 689–95.

40. Cited in a summary of the Fourth National Environmental Health Conference in *Health and Environment Digest* 3 (1989): 3–4.

41. See R. M. Booze et al., "Neonatal triethyl lead neurotoxicity in rat pups: Initial behavioral observations and quantification," *Neurobehavioral Toxicology and Teratology* 5 (1983): 367–75.

42. See E. J. Ritter et al., "Teratogenicity of dimethoxyethyl phthalate and its metabolites methoxyethanol and methoxyacetic acid in the rat," *Teratology* 32 (1985): 25–31.

43. See D. J. Oudiz et al., "Male reproductive toxicity and recovery associated with acute ethoxyethanol exposure in rats," *Journal of Toxicology and Environmental Health* 13 (1984): 763–75.

44. California Hazard Evaluation System and Information Service, "Hazard alert for glycol ethers" (Berkeley: California Department of Health Services, 1984).

45. See M. Gafvels et al., "Toxic effects of the antifertility agent gossypol in male rats," *Toxicology* 32 (1984): 325–33. A dose of 1 mg/kg injected daily for five weeks has negligible effects, while 10 mg/kg depresses sperm production and killed 13 percent of the animals.

46. See C. C. Hsia et al., "Natural occurrence and clastogenic effects of nivalenol, 15–acetyl deoxynivalenol and zearalenone in corn from a high risk area of esophageal cancer," *Cancer Detection and Prevention* 13 (1988): 79–86.

47. This horrific episode of human and environmental contamination is spelled out in graphic detail in Ralph Nader's classic, *Who's poisoning America?* (San Francisco: Sierra Club Books, 1981).

48. EPA investigators at the W. R. Grace site found an unattended refuse pipe extending from the plant premises deep underground,

providing an invisible conduit from the plant to the aquifer below. TCE was allegedly dumped directly into this illegal pipe.

49. The substitution of benzene for lead antiknock compounds was a classic example of trading the devil we know for one we are just beginning to appreciate: benzene, too, has dramatic behavioral and motor effects at very low doses. See K. A. Paksy et al., "Comparative study on the acute effects of benzene, toluene and m-xylene in the rat," *Acta Physiologica of the Hungarian Academy of Sciences* 59 (1982): 317–24.

50. See B. Paigen et al., "Prevalence of health problems in children living near Love Canal," *Hazardous waste and hazardous materials* 2 (1985): 23–43; and L. R. Goldman et al., "Low birth weight, prematurity and birth defects in children living near the hazardous waste site, Love Canal," Ibid., 209–23.

51. See K. B. Webb et al., "Medical evaluation of subjects with known body levels of 2,3,7,8-TCDD," *Journal of Toxicology and Environmental Health* 28 (1989): 83–93. These studies are at variance with a series of papers that appeared the previous year: See review and commentary by M. Gochfeld, "New light on the health of Vietnam veterans," *Environmental Research* 47 (1988): 109–11.

52. Cited in "Setting Priorities: The Fourth National Environmental Health Conference," *Health and Environmental Digest* 3 (September/October 1989): 5. Farland stated that: "The Agency's current position is that the information on dioxin based on epidemiologic studies is inadequate for hazard evaluation. . . . Dioxin can act in a number of areas: it can affect populations of initiated cells, enzyme activities, xenobiotics, membranes. . . . Overall, it can act as a promoter of carcinogenesis."

53. See P. E. Lillienfeld et al., "2,4-D, 2,4,5-T and 2,3,7,8-TCDD: An overview," *Epidemiological Reviews* 11 (1989): 28–58.

54. See H.Y.M. Ionnou, L. S. Birnbaum, and H. B. Matthews, "Toxicity and distribution of 2,3,7,8-tetrachlorodibenzofuran in male guinea pigs," *Journal of Toxicology and Environmental Health* 12 (1983): 541–53.

55. See G. A. Sacher and E. Trucco in N. W. Shock, ed., *Biological Aspects of Aging* (New York: Columbia University Press, 1962), 244–51.

56. See P. J. Neafsey et al., "A Gompertz age-specific mortality rate model of aging, hormesis, and toxicity: Dose-response studies," *Drug Metabolism Reviews* 20 (1989): 111–50.

57. Ibid.

58. Ibid., p. 146.

59. See P. J. Neafsey et al., "A Gompertz age–specific mortality rate model of aging, hormesis, and toxicity: Fixed-dose studies," *Drug Metabolism Reviews* 19 (1988): 369–401.

60. An example of such activity is found with four different surfactants (chemicals that change the surface of cells to make them more water soluble), see J. Benoit, M. Cormier, and J. Wepierre, "Comparative effects of four surfactants on growth, contraction and adhesion of cultured human fibroblasts," *Cell Biology and Toxicology* (1988): 111–22.

61. Researchers using human and Syrian golden hamster tissues in tissue culture have found that this animal (like its rodent counterparts) uses two different pathways to break down methylene chloride. As the amount of methylene chloride goes up, the animals switch over from the system that relies on the mixed-function oxidases of the microsomes (see Chapter 4) to one that uses glutathione: See R. H. Reitz, A. L. Mendrala, and F. P. Guengerich, "In vitro metabolism of methylene chloride in human and animal tissues: Use in physiologically based pharmatokinetic models," *Toxicology and Applied Pharmacology* 97 (1989): 23–46.

62. See E. J. Calabrese, M. E. McCarthy, and E. Kenyon, "The occurrence of chemically induced hormesis," *Health Physics* 52 (1987): 531–41.

63. See J. R. Totter, "Physiology of the hormetic effect," *Health Physics* 52 (1987): 549–51.

64. See R. B. Laughlin, Jr., J. Ng, and H. E. Guard, "Hormesis: A response to low environmental concentrations of petroleum hydrocarbons," *Science* 211 (1981): 705–11; and J. E. Hose and H. W. Puffer, "Oxygen consumption rates of grunion (*Leuesthes tenuis*) embryos exposed to the petroleum hydrocarbon, benzo(*a*)-pyrene," *Environment Research* 35 (1985): 413–20.

65. See, for example, T. Luckey, *Hormesis with Ionizing Radiation,* (Boca Raton, FL: CRC Press, 1980).

66. Cited in L. A. Sagan, "On radiation, paradigms, and hormesis," *Science* 245 (1989): 574, 621.

67. Ibid., p. 574.

68. See R. T. Prehn and M. A. Lappé, "An immunostimulation theory of tumor development," *Transplantation Reviews* 7 (1971): 26–54.

69. See S. Z. Liu, W. H. Liu, and J. B. Sun, "Radiation hormesis:

Its expression in the immune system," *Health Physics* 52 (1987): 579–83.

70. See S. Kondo, "Altruistic cell suicide in relation to radiation hormesis," *International Journal of Radiation Biology* 53 (1988): 95–102.

71. See L. Wei et al., "Cancer mortality study in high background radiation areas of Yangjiang, China," in *Epidemiological investigations on the health effects of ionizing radiation* (Cologne, Germany: Institüt für Strahlenschutz, 1988): 7–25.

72. See K. S. Nambi and S. D. Soman, "Environmental radiation and cancer in India," *Health Physics* 52 (1987): 653–57.

73. See Z. Wang et al., "Thyroid nodularity and chromosome aberrations among women in areas of high background radiation in China," *Journal of the National Cancer Institute* 82 (1990): 478–85.

74. See L. E. Feinendegen et al., "Intracellular stimulation of biochemical control mechanisms by low-dose, low-LET (linear energy transfer) irradiation," *Health Physics* 52 (1987): 663–69.

75. See discussion in A. C. Upton, "Carcinogenic effects of low-level ionizing radiation," *Journal of the National Cancer Institute* 82 (1990): 448–49.

76. See H. Kato et al., "Dose-response analyses among atomic bomb survivors exposed to low-level radiation," *Health Physics* 52 (1987): 645–52.

77. Sheldon Wolff, in a companion piece to Leonard Sagan's *Science* article (see note 61), observes that the type of random mutational changes produced by radiation can only be expected to reduce an organism's fitness by disturbing the fine balance that exists between adaptations and the ecological niche in which the organism lives: see S. Wolff, "Are radiation-induced effects hormetic?" *Science* 245 (1989): 575, 621.

78. See B. L. Cohen, "Tests of the linear, no-threshold dose-response relationship for high LET radiation," *Health Physics* 52 (1987): 629–36.

79. See C. C. Congdon, "Radiation hormesis and nuclear safety," *Nuclear Safety* 29 (1988): 49–57.

80. See H. Coulter, *Divided Legacy,* vol. III (Berkeley, CA: North Atlantic Books, Berkeley, 1975).

81. See J. Horning, "Publications on controlled clinical trials in homeopathy," *Berlin Journal on Research in Homeopathy* 1 (1990): 16–18; see also B. Rubik, "Report on the status of research on

homeopathy with recommendations for future research," *British Homeopathic Journal* 78 (1989): 86–96.

82. See J. P. Ferley, D. Zmirous, D. D'Adhema, and P. Balducci, "A controlled evaluation of a homeopathic preparation in the treatment of influenza-like syndromes," *British Journal of Clinical Pharmacology* 27 (1989): 329–35.

83. See E. Davenas et al., "Human basophil degranulation triggered by very dilute antiserum against IgE," *Nature* 333 (1988): 816–18.

84. See J. Maddox, J. Randi, and W. Stewart, "High-dilution experiments a delusion," *Nature* 334 (1988): 287–90.

85. See B. Poiteven, E. D. Avenas, and J. Benveniste, "In vitro immunological degranulaton of human basophils is modulated by lung histamine and *Apis mellifica*," *British Journal of Clinical Pharmacology* 25 (1988): 439–44; see also J. Bildet et al., "Demonstrating the effects of *Apis mellifica* and apium virus dilutions on erythema induced by UV radiation in guinea pigs," *Berlin Journal on Research in Homoeopathy* 1 (1990): 28–33.

86. See A. Furst, "Hormetic effects in pharmacology: Pharmacological inversions as prototypes for hormesis," *Health Physics* 52 (1987): 527–30.

87. See G. Harisch and M. Kretschmer, "Smallest zinc quantities affect the histamine release from peritoneal mast cells of the rat," *Experientia* 44 (1986): 761–62.

88. See, for example, W. E. Boyd, "The action of microdoses of mercuric chloride on diastase," *British Homeopathic Journal* 31 (1941): 1–28.

89. See D. Holt, S. Sparrow, and M. Webb, "The chronic toxicity of equine cadmium metallothionein in the rat," *Archives of Toxicology* 57 (1985): 200–4.

90. See P. Weis and J. S. Weis, "Cadmium acclimation and hormesis in *Fundulus heteroclitus* fin regeneration," *Environmental Research* 39 (1986): 356–63.

91. See A. R. D. Stemming, "Hormesis: Stimulation of colony growth in *Campanularia fluxuosa* (Hydrozoa) by copper, cadmium and other toxicants," *Aquatic Toxicology* 1 (1981): 227–38.

92. See B. Cragg and S. Rees, "Increased body:brain weight ratio in developing rats after low exposure to organic lead," *Experimental Neurology* 86 (1984): 113–21.

93. See P. Fisher and I. Capel, "The treatment of lead intoxication in rats by Plumbum metallicum and penicillamine," *Proceedings*

of the 35th Congress of the Liga Homeopathica Internationalis, London, pp. 320–22.

94. See P. Fisher et al., "The influence of the homeopathic remedy Plumbum metallicum on the excretion kinetics of lead in rats," *Human Toxicology* 6 (1987): 321–24.

95. See J. Boiron et al., "A pharmacological study of the retention and mobilization of arsenic, as caused by Hahnemanian potencies of Arsenicum album," *Aspects of Research in Homeopathy* 1 (1983): 19–38.

96. See E. Davenas et al., "Effect on mouse periotoneal macrophages of orally administered very high dilutions of silica," *European Journal of Pharmacology* 135 (1987): 313–19.

97. See V. Daurat, P. Dorfman, and M. Bastide, "Immunomodulatory activity of low doses of interferon in mice," *Biomedicine and Pharmacotherapeutics* 42 (1988): 197–206.

98. See R. G. Gibson et al., "Homeopathic therapy in rheumatoid arthritis: Evaluation by double-blind clinical therapeutic trial," *British Journal of Clinical Pharmacology* 9 (1980): 453–59.

99. See M. Shipley et al., "Controlled trial of homeopathic treatment of osteroarthritis," *Lancet* 1 (1983): 97–98.

100. See Rubik, second part of note 81.

CHAPTER SEVEN: THE FETUS DEVELOPS
OUT OF REACH OF TOXIC DANGER

1. From an anatomical viewpoint, the concept of a "protected" site for fetal development *appears* to make sense: early in development, the placental thickness is more than 25,000 angstroms, which is ten to twenty times the normal thickness of cellular membranes. However, this thick cell wall quickly thins during pregnancy, and whole cells as well as larger molecular weight substances readily pass through the placenta as term approaches.

2. The placenta's markedly inducible P-450 enzyme system is discussed in M. R. Juchau, "Disposition of chemical contaminants in maternal/fetal systems," in J. Saxena, ed., *Hazard assessment of chemicals,* vol. 2, (New York: Academic Press, 1983), 126.

3. See M. S. Miller et al., "Differential induction of fetal mouse liver and lung cytochromes P-450 by beta-napththoflavone and 3-methylcholanthrene," *Carcinogenesis* 10 (1989): 875–91.

4. See T. Archer et al., "Hyperactivity and instrumental learning deficits in methylazoxymethanol-treated rat offspring," *Neurotoxicology and Teratology* 10 (1988): 341–47.

5. *Physicians' Desk Reference,* vol. 36 (Oradell, NJ: Medical Economics Company, 1982), 1623.

6. Accurate numbers are still unavailable for the spontaneous miscarriage rate, but a pregnancy loss of from 15 to 50 percent has been reported in numerous studies: see for instance, F. W. Byrn and M. Gibson, "Infectious causes of recurrent pregnancy loss," *Clinical Obstetrics and Gynecology* 29 (1986): 925–40.

7. A later analysis of the experiments cited in support of the protective effect of this potent estrogen showed that the women who took the drug had a *higher* than expected rate of fetal loss than did the controls. See Y. Brackbill et al., "Dangers of diethylstilbestrol: Review of a 1953 paper," *Lancet* 2 (1978): 520.

8. See M. Bibbo et al., "Follow-up study of male and female offspring of DES-exposed mothers," *Obstetrics and Gynecology* 49 (1977): 1–8.

9. See R. H. Depue, M. C. Pike, and B. E. Henderson, "Estrogen exposure during gestation and risk of testicular cancer," *Journal of the National Cancer Institute* 71 (1983): 1151–55.

10. The first reports of this rare tumor type were by A. L. Herbst and his coworkers: See A. L. Herbst and R. E. Scully, "Adenocarcinoma of the vagina. A report of seven cases including six clear-cell carcinomas (so-called mesonephromas)," *Cancer* 25 (1970): 745–57. The linkage of this tumor with DES was firmly made a year later: see A. L. Herbst, H. Ulfelder, and D. C. Poskanzer, "Adenocarcinoma of the vagina. Association of maternal stilbestrol therapy with tumor appearance in young women," *New England Journal of Medicine* 284 (1971): 878–81.

11. It is now clear that below 5 rads of radiation, no visible congenital malformations are seen. Between 5 and 15 rads, the risk of a major malformation goes up two- to threefold: see R. L. Brent and D. A. Beckman, *Clinics in perinatology,* vol. 13, no. 3 (Philadelphia: Saunders, 1986).

12. See Y. Yoshimoto, H. Kato, and W. J. Schull, "Risk of cancer among children exposed in utero to A-bomb radiation, 1950-4," *Lancet* 2 (1988): 665–69.

13. See A. Butturini and R. P. Gale, "Age of onset and type of leukemia," *Lancet* 2 (1989): 789–91.

14. See H. Kato, *Mortality of in utero children exposed to the A-bomb*

and of offspring of A-bomb survivors, (IAEA-SM224/603 Vienna: International Atomic Energy Agency, 1978), 49–60. Cited in Butturini and Gale, note 13.

15. See J. D. Boice and J. F. Fraumeni, *Radiation carcinogenesis: Epidemiology and biological significance* (New York: Raven Press, 1984).

16. See B. S. Shane, "Human reproductive hazards: Evaluation and chemical etiology," *Environmental Science and Technology* 23 (1989): 1187–94.

17. See F. O. Kelsey, "Thalidomide update: Regulatory aspects," *Teratology* 38 (1988): 221–26.

18. See W. Lenz, "Thalidomide embryopathy in Germany, 1959–61," in M. Marois, ed., *Prevention of physical and mental congenital defects. Part C: Basic and medical science, education and future strategies* (New York: Alan R. Liss, 1985), 77–83.

19. See H. B. Taussig, "A study of the German outbreak of phocomelia—The thalidomide syndrome," *Journal of the American Medical Association* 180 (1962): 1106–14.

20. See D. A. Dawson et al., "Developmental toxicity testing with FETAX: Evaluation of five compounds," *Drug and Chemical Toxicology* 12 (1989): 67–76.

21. Adapted from M. Bologna-Camaeanu et al., "Prenatal adverse effects of various drugs and chemicals," *Medical Toxicology* 3 (1988): 307–23.

22. See R. J. Huxtable, "Human embryotoxicity of pyrrolizidine-containing drugs," *Hepatology* 9 (1989): 510–11.

23. See B. L. Blaylock et al., "The effect of pre-postnatal exposure to chlordane on the body weight and lymphocyte activity of Balb/c mice," abstract of paper presented at the 73rd Annual Meeting of the Federation of American Societies for Experimental Biology, March 19–23, 1989, New Orleans, LA.

24. See A. Czeizel et al., "A study of adverse effects on the progeny after intoxication during pregnancy," *Archives of Toxicology* 62 (1988): 1–7.

25. See R. M. Balansky and P. M. Blagoeva, "Tobacco smoke-induced clastogenicity in mouse fetuses and in newborn mice," *Mutation Research* 223 (1989): 1–6.

26. See Y. Kim et al., "Effects of smokeless tobacco on femur ossification in the mouse," abstract of paper presented at the 18th Annual Session of the American Association for Dental Research, March 1989, San Francisco, CA.

27. See M. A. Lappé, "Trace metals and birth defects," in S. Rose, ed., *Trace elements and health* (London: Butterworth, 1979).

28. See D. Bellinger et al., "Low level lead exposure, social class, and infant development," *Neurotoxicology and Teratology* 10 (1988): 497–503.

29. See S. Nordstrom, L. Beckman, and I. Nordenson, "Occupational and environmental risks around a smelter in northern Sweden. I. Variations in birth weight," *Hereditas* 88 (1978): 43–46; "II. Frequencies of spontaneous abortion," *Hereditas* 88 (1978): 51–54; and "IV. Congenital malformation," *Hereditas* 90 (1979); 297–302.

30. See G. Axelsson and I. Molin, "Outcome of pregnancy among women living near petrochemical industries in Sweden," *International Journal of Epidemiology* 17 (1988): 363–69.

31. See W. R. Holloway, Jr., and D. H. Thor, "Cadmium exposure in infancy: Effects on activity and social behaviors of juvenile rats," *Neurotoxicology and Teratology* 10 (1988): 135–42.

32. See P. C. Homberg and M. Nurminen, "Congenital defects of the central nervous system and occupational factors during pregnancy, a case referent study," *American Journal of Industrial Medicine* 1 (1980): 167–76.

33. B. Eskenazi, "Exposure to organic solvents and hypersensitivity disorders of pregnancy," *American Journal of Industrial Medicine* 14 (1988): 177–88.

34. See K. L. Hones and D. W. Smith, "Recognition of the fetal alcohol syndrome in early infancy," *Lancet* 2 (1973): 999–1001.

35. See S. Landesman-Dwyer, S. Keller, and A. P. Streissguth, "Naturalistic observations of newborns: Effects of maternal alcohol intake," *Alcoholism Clinical and Experimental Research* 2 (1978): 171–77; and A. P. Streissguth et al., "Teratogenic effects of alcohol in humans and laboratory animals," *Science* 209 (1980): 353–61.

36. See A. A. Ciociola and R. F. Gautieri, "Teratogenic and behavioral anomalies induced by acute exposure of mice to ethanol and their possible relation to fetal brain DNA synthesis," *Pharmacology Research* 5 (1988): 447–52.

37. See B. Eskenazi et al., "In utero exposure to organic solvents and human neurodevelopment," *Developmental Medicine and Child Neurology* 30 (1988): 492–501.

38. See R. W. Tyl et al., "Evaluation of the developmental toxicity of ethylene glycol monohexyl ether vapor in Fischer 344 rats

and New Zealand white rabbits," *Fundamental and Applied Toxicology* 12 (1989): 269–80.

39. See G. R. Harvey, W. G. Steinhauer, and J. M. Teal, "Polychlorobiphenyls in North Atlantic ocean water," *Science* 180 (1972): 643–44.

40. See R. W. Riesborough et al., "Polychlorinated biphenyls in the global ecosystem," *Nature* 220 (1968): 1098–1102.

41. See J. R. N. Jones, "Polychlorinated biphenyls: Where do we stand now?," *Lancet* 2 (1989): 7691–94.

42. See I. Prescott, D. J. Jefferies, and N. W. Moore, "Polychlorinated biphenyls in wild birds in Britain and their avian toxicity," *Environmental Pollution* 1 (1970): 3–26.

43. See Jones, note 41.

44. See C. F. Tumasonis, B. Bush, and F. D. Baker, "PCB levels in egg yolks associated with embryonic mortality and deformity in hatched chicks," *Archives of Environmental Contamination and Toxicology* 1 (1973): 312–24.

45. See G. B. Fuller and W. C. Hobson, "Effect of PCBs on reproduction in mammals," in J. S. Waid, ed., *PCBs and the environment,* vol. 2 (Boca Raton, FL: CRC Press, 1986), 101–25.

46. See F. Yamashita and M. Hayashi, "Fetal PCB syndrome: Clinical features, intrauterine growth retardation and possible alteration in calcium metabolism," *Environmental Health Perspectives* 9 (1985): 41–45.

47. See P. H. Chen and S. T. Hsu, "PCB poisoning from toxic rice bran oil in Taiwan," in J. S. Waid, ed., *PCBs and the environment,* vol. 3 (Boca Raton, FL: CRC Press, 1986), 207–13.

48. See L. A. Couture, M. W. Harris, and L. S. Birnbaum, "Developmental toxicity of 2,3,4,7,8-pentachlorodibenzofuran in the Fischer 344 rat," *Fundamental and Applied Toxicology* 12 (1989): 358–66.

49. See J. Mes, "PCBs in human populations," in Waid, note 47, pp. 39–61.

50. See J. R. Wilkins and J. T. Nickel, "Adverse health effects and exposure to polychlorinated biphenyls," *Reviews in Environmental Health* 4 (1984): 269–86.

51. See A. B. Smith and D. P. Brown, "Polychlorinated biphenyls in the workplace," in Waid, note 47, pp. 63–82.

52. Reviewed in Jones, note 41.

53. See A. P. Alvares et al., "Alterations in drug metabolism in

workers exposed to chlorinated biphenyls," *Clinical Pharmacology and Therapeutics* 22 (1977): 140–46.

54. See M. Metzler and J. A. McLachlan, "Oxidative metabolites of diethylstilbestrol in the fetal, neonatal and adult mouse," *Biochemical Pharmacology* 27 (1978): 1087–94.

55. Adapted from C. L. Berry, "What's new in transplacental carcinogenesis," *Pathology Research and Practice* 181 (1986): 452–55.

56. See V. E. Walker and J. A. Swenberg, "Phenobarbital lacks promoting activity for neurogenic tumors in F 344 rats transplacentally exposed to ethylnitrosourea," *Journal of Neuropathology and Experimental Neurology* 48 (1989): 263–69.

57. See L. C. Oomen et al., "Glucocorticoid hormone effect on transplacental carcinogenesis and lung differentiation: Influence of H-2 complex," *Journal of the National Cancer Institute* 81 (1989): 512–17.

58. Cited in C. L. Berry et al., "Transplacental carcinogenesis with radioactive phosphorus," *Human Toxicology* 2 (1983): 49–62.

59. See A. H. Chang et al., "Maternal transmission of hepatitis B virus in childhood hepatocellular carcinoma," *Cancer* 64 (1989): 2377–80.

60. See Berry, note 58, p. 54.

61. Silicones, when injected into the uterus or peritoneal cavity, were reported by the FDA to disrupt normal fetal development in the rabbit. Since some of these products were intended for use in intrauterine devices, it became important to understand the range of biological responses to this chemical.

CHAPTER EIGHT: "NONREACTIVE"
CHEMICALS LACK ADVERSE EFFECTS

1. In anaphylactic shock the body's immune responses trigger vasolidation and shock stemming from a massive histamine release, that can lead to swelling of tissues and often fatal constriction of the larynx.

2. Even this immunologic effect has been found to be reducible to a classic dose-response relationship. When graded doses of ovalbumin, for example, are injected into the joints, the lowermost amounts produce a smoldering, low-level arthritis, while the higher doses produce a florid, aggressive arthritic response. See P. Howson, N. Shepard, and N. Mitchell, "The antigen induced arthritis model: The relevance of the method of induction to its

use as a model of human disease," *Journal of Rheumatology* 13 (1986): 379–90.

3. See I. Lemaire, P. G. Dionne, D. Nadeau, and J. Dunnigan, "Rat lung reactivity to natural and man-made fibrous silicates following short-term exposure," *Environmental Research* 48 (1989): 193–210.

4. This reaction is described in any classic pathology text: See, for example, S. L. Robbins, R. S. Cottran, and V. Kumar, *Pathologic Basis of Disease,* 3rd ed. (Philadelphia: Saunders, 1984), 435–37.

5. Rats that inhaled crystalline silicon dioxide for as short a time as eight days retained both the silica and the inflammatory response throughout the next year. See M. P. Absher et al., "Biphasic cellular and tissue response of rat lungs after eight-day aerosol exposure to the silicon dioxide cristobalite," *American Journal of Pathology* 134 (1989): 1243–47.

6. See U.S. Food and Drug Administration. Medical Device Division, FDA, *Risks and benefits of silicone gel-filled breast implants: A summary of findings in the literature* (Washington, DC: FDA, Medical Device Division, undated). Although kept secret by the manufacturer as part of the proprietary information about the composition of the gels and envelopes, these facts were revealed in the patents for the implants: see Van Aken Redinger et al., "Silicone gel filled prosthesis," U.S. Patent #4,455,691, June 26, 1984. Fabricated silicones can contain up to 30 percent by weight of fumed silica. See R. S. Ward et al., *Procurement of primary reference materials.* National Technical Information Service Report no. NO1-HV-9-2933-5 (Washington, DC: GPO, 1984).

7. Personal communication, Thomas Talcott, September 25, 1989.

8. See W. E. Leary, "Breast implants, a look at the record," *New York Times,* 13 November 1988, p. E9.

9. The duty to prove safety was established through several court rulings in the 1960s as the responsibility of the Food and Drug Administration, not the Patent Office. See B. Amernick, "Essentials of patent law," *Journal of the National Cancer Institute* 81 (1989): 1450–54.

10. This attribute was described in the original Cronin patent (No. 3,293,663: "Surgically implantable human breast prosthesis"; filed August 12, 1963; patented Dec. 27, 1966). It was further extolled as one of the virtues of the implant: see, for example, "Mammary prosthesis, Cronin technique," advertisement appearing in the *Journal of Plastic and Reconstructive Surgery,* 34 (1964).

11. See M. G. Wickham, R. Rudolph, and J. L. Abraham, "Silicon

identification in prosthesis-associated fibrous capsules," *Science* 199 (1978): 437–39.

12. See R. B. Bergman and A. W. van der Ende, "Exudation of silicone through the envelope of gel-filled breast prostheses: An in vitro study," *British Journal of Plastic Surgery* 32 (1979): 31–34.

13. See, for example, D. Barker, M. I. Retsky, and S. Schultz, "Bleeding of silicone from bag-gel breast implants and its clinical relation to fibrous capsule reaction," *Journal of Plastic and Reconstructive Surgery* 61 (1978): 836–38.

14. See J. Smahel, "Foreign materials in the capsules around breast prostheses and the cellular reaction to it," *British Journal of Plastic Surgery* 32 (1979): 35–42.

15. See R. Hausner et al., "Foreign-body reaction to silicone gel in axillary lymph nodes after an augmentation mammaplasty," *Plastic and Reconstructive Surgery* 62 (1978): 381–84.

16. See T. Kircher, "Silicone lymphadenopathy: A complication of silicone elastomer finger joint prostheses," *Human Pathology* 11 (1979): 240–44.

17. See B. F. Uretsky et al., "Augmentation mammoplasty associated with a severe systemic illness," *Annals of Plastic Surgery* 3 (1979): 445–49.

18. See G. Little and J. L. Baker, Jr., "Results of closed compression capsulotomy for treatment of contracted breast implant capsules," *Journal of Plastic and Reconstructive Surgery* 65 (1980): 30–33.

19. See L. C. Argenta, "Migration of silicone gel into breast parenchyma following mammary prosthesis rupture," *Aesthetic Plastic Surgery* 7 (1983): 253–54.

20. See W. K. Wintsch, J. Smahel, and L. Clodious, "Local and regional lymph node response to ruptured gel-filled mammary prostheses," *British Journal of Plastic Surgery* 31 (1978): 349–52.

21. See Talcott, note 7.

22. See G. Robertson and S. Braley, "Toxicologic studies, quality control and efficacy of the Silastic R mammary prosthesis," *Medical Instrumentation* 7 (1973): 100–6.

23. See N. Ben Hur and Z. Neuman, "Siliconoma — Another cutaneous response to dimethylpolysiloxane," *Journal of Plastic and Reconstructive Surgery* 36 (1965): 629–32.

24. T. Rees et al., "Visceral response to subcutaneous and intraperitoneal injections of silicone in mice," *Journal of Plastic and Reconstructive Surgery* 39 (1967): 402–6.

25. See C. Delage, J. J. Shane, and F. B. Johnson, "Mammary silicone granuloma," *Archives of Dermatology* 108 (1973): 104–7.

26. See R. P. Gruber and H. W. Jones, "Review of closed capsulotomy complications," *Annals of Plastic Surgery* 6 (1981): 271–76. See also B. M. Zilde, "Complications of closed capsulotomy after augmentation," *Journal of Plastic and Reconstructive Surgery* 67 (1981): 657.

27. See W. S. C. Symmers, "Silicone mastitis in 'topless' waitresses and some other varieties of foreign body mastitis," *British Medical Journal* 3 (1968): 19–21.

28. See J. M. Maresa and F. Maresa, "Silicone pneumonitis," *Lancet* 2 (1983): 1373–75.

29. See Nevada statutes, Crimes Against Public Health and Safety, 202.248 (1975), p. 120.

30. See *Federal Register* 47 2820–21 (19 January 1982). The FDA gave three reasons for its ruling: 1) migration of gel; 2) capsular contraction; and 3) long-term sequelae.

31. No explanation or replication of this effect has since been published. See S. M. Barlow and A. M. Knight, "Teratogenic effects of Silastic intrauterine devices in the rat with or without added medroxyprogesterone acetate," *Fertility and Sterility* 39 (1983): 224–30.

32. Some features of breast augmentation, notably contracture or capsule formation, were shown to be abetted by silicone, but not due to it. See J. Ferreira, "The various etiological factors of 'hard capsule' formation in breast augmentations," *Aesthetic Plastic Surgery* 8 (1984): 109–17.

33. See J. Bommer et al., "Silicone cell inclusions causing multiorgan foreign body reaction in dialysis patients," *Lancet* 1 (1981): 1101–13.

34. See Wintsch et al., note 20; and P. Wilfingseder, G. Hoikes, and G. Mikuz, "Tissue reactions from silicone implant in augmentation mammoplasties," *Minerva Chirugica* 38 (1983): 877–80.

35. B. Ramazzini, *De morbis artificum diatriba,* chap. xxv (Modena, Italy, 1700), cited in A. A. Bisetti, "Bernardino Ramazzini and occupational lung medicine," *Annals of the New York Academy of Sciences* 534 (1988): 1029–37.

36. See S. Suzuki, "Chest disorders and rheumatoid arthritis," *Ryumachi* 10 (1970): 20–26.

37. See P. Ellman and R. E. Ball, "Rheumatoid disease with joint and pulmonary manifestation," *British Medical Journal* 2 (1943): 816–20.

38. See K. Honda et al., "HLA and silicosis in Japan," *New England Journal of Medicine* 319 (1988).

39. See G. P. Rodnan et al., "The association of progressive systemic sclerosis (scleroderma) with coal miners' pneumoconiosis and other forms of silicosis," *Annals of Internal Medicine* 66 (1966): 323–28.

40. See W. Kaiser, G. Biesenbach, and J. Zazgornik, "Autoimmunphanomene nach silikonimplantation," *Deutsche medische Wochenschrift* 112 (1987): 1376–79.

41. See FDA hearings before the Medical Device Panel, 20 November 1988.

42. See N. Kossovsky, J. P. Heggers, and M. C. Robson, "Experimental demonstration of the immunogenicity of silicone-protein complexes," *Journal of Biomedical Materials Research* 21 (1987): 1125–33.

43. See N. Kossovsky, J. P. Heggers, and M. C. Robson, "The bioreactivity of silicone," *CRC Critical Reviews in Biocompatibility* 18 (1987): 81–128.

44. See H. Miyoshi et al., "Hypergammaglobulinemia by prolonged adjuvanticity in man: Disorders developed after augmentation mammaplasty," *Japanese Medical Journal* 212 (1964): 9–13.

45. See K. Yoshida, "Post mammaplasty disorder as an adjuvant disease of man," *Excerpta Medica,* Supplement 34: Plastic Surgery (1986): 229.

46. See B. Uretsky et al., "Augmentation mammaplasty associated with a severe systemic illness," *Annals of Plastic Surgery* 3 (1979): 445–49.

47. See Y. Kumagai et al., "Clinical spectrum of connective tissue disease after cosmetic surgery," *Arthritis and Rheumatism* 278 (1984): 1–12; see also Y. Okano, N. Nichiakai, and A. Sato, "Scleroderma, primary biliary cirrhosis, and Sjögren's syndrome after cosmetic breast augmentation with silicone injection. A case report of possible human adjuvant disease," *Annals of Rheumatic Disease* 43 (1984): 520–25. For a recent review, see H. Spiera, "Scleroderma after silicone augmentation mammaplasty," *Journal of the American Medical Association* 260 (1988): 236–38.

48. See C. M. Baldwin, Jr., and E. N. Kaplan, "Silicone-induced human adjuvant disease?" *Annals of Plastic Surgery* 10 (1983): 270–73.

49. The exact rationale used by the FDA was as follows: "FDA classified the silicone gel-filled breast prosthesis into class III because insufficient information exists to determine that general

controls would provide reasonable assurance of the safety and effectiveness of the device or to establish a performance standard to provide such assurance. FDA has weighed probable risks and benefits to the public from the use of the silicone gel-filled prosthesis and believes that the studies discussed above present evidence of significant risks associated with the use of the device," FDA, note 6, p. 21.

CHAPTER NINE: THE BODY'S OWN CHEMICALS ARE SAFE

1. Cited in M. Holloway, "A great poison," *Scientific American* 263 (1990): 16–20.

2. See H. H. Cook, C. J. Gamble, and A. P. Satterwaithe, "Oral contraception by norethynodrel — A 3-year field study," *American Journal of Obstetrics and Gynecology* 82 (1961): 442–45.

3. See "Research on human subjects," 45 Code of Federal Regulations, 46 (1982).

4. The test pills used 9.85 milligrams of a synthetic progesterone (norethynodrel) combined with 150 micrograms of a synthetic estrogen (ethinylestradiol-3-methyl ether). For comparison, modern-day minipills typically contain 1 milligram of a synthetic progesterone (progestagen) combined with 10 to 25 micrograms of synthetic estrogen.

5. See P. Eckstein et al., "The Birmingham oral contraceptive trial," *British Medical Journal,* Supplement (1961): 1172–73, 1178.

6. See P. Eckstein et al., "The Puerto Rico trial," *British Medical Journal,* Supplement (1961): 741.

7. Ibid.

8. See E. Rice-Wray, "Field study with Enovid as a contraceptive agent," in *Proceedings of a symposium on 19-nor progestational steroids* (Chicago: G. D. Searle & Company, 1957), 78–82.

9. W. O. Nelson, in *Proceedings,* above, p. 92.

10. See M. Mintz, "Are birth control pills safe? — Some doctors doubt that the drug has been tested well enough for possible side effects," *Washington Post,* 16 December 1965, section E.

11. Ibid.

12. See Food and Drug Administration, Advisory Committee on Obstetrics and Gynecology, *Report on Oral Contraceptives* (Washington, DC: FDA, 1966), 1–13.

13. See Food and Drug Administration, Advisory Committee on

Obstetrics and Gynecology, *Second Report on the Oral Contraceptives* (Washington, DC: FDA, 1969), 1–9.

14. Ibid., p. 8.

15. U.S. Congress, Senate Select Committee on Monopoly, *Hearings on oral contraceptives,* 91st Congress, 2nd session, testimony of 14 January 1970.

16. Ibid., p. 7.

17. See M. B. Shimkin and H. C. Grady, "Toxic and carcinogenic effects of stilbestrol in strain C3H mice," *Journal of the National Cancer Institute* 2 (1941): 55–60; and M. B. Shimkin and R. S. Wyman, "Mammary tumors in male mice implanted with estrogen-cholesterol pellets," *Journal of the National Cancer Institute* 7 (1946): 71–75.

18. See A. L. Herbst, H. Ulfelder, and D. C. Poskanzer, "Adenocarcinoma of the vagina: Association of maternal stilbestrol therapy with tumor appearance in young women," *New England Journal of Medicine* 284 (1971): 878–81.

19. See S. Melnick et al., "Rates and risks of diethylstilbestrol-related clear-cell adenocarcinoma of the vagina and cervix: An update," *New England Journal of Medicine* 316 (1987): 514–16.

20. See R. H. Kaufman et al., "Upper genital tract changes associated with exposure in utero to diethylstilbestrol," *American Journal of Obstetrics and Gynecology* 128 (1977): 51–59.

21. See R. H. Kaufman et al., "Upper genital tract changes and pregnancy outcome in offspring exposed in utero to diethylstilbestrol," *American Journal of Obstetrics* 137 (1980): 299–308.

22. See M. Metzler and J. A. McLachlan, "Oxidative metabolites of diethylstilbestrol in the fetal, neonatal and adult mouse," *Biochemical Pharmacology* 27 (1978): 1087–94.

23. See J. C. Barrett, A. Wong, and J. A. McLachlan, "Diethylstilbestrol induces neoplastic transformation without measurable gene mutation at two loci," *Science* 212 (1981): 1402–4.

24. See L. Plapinger and H. A. Bern, "Adenosis-like lesions and other cervicovaginal abnormalities in mice treated neonatally with estrogen," *Journal of the National Cancer Institute* 63 (1979): 507–18.

25. See H. A. Bern et al., "Use of the neonatal mouse in studying long-term effects of early exposure to hormones and other agents," *Journal of Toxicology and Environmental Health* 1 (1976): 103–16.

26. See W. S. Branham et al., "Alterations in developing rat uterine cell populations after neonatal exposure to estrogens and antiestrogens," *Teratology* 38 (1988): 271–79.

27. See F. D. Baker and C. L. Kragt, "Maturation of the hypo-thalamic–pituitary–gonadal negative feedback system," *Endocrinology* 85 (1969): 522–27.

28. See H. A. Bern and F. J. Talamantes, "Neonatal mouse models and their relation to disease in the human female," in A. L. Herbst and H. A. Bern, eds., *Developmental effects of diethylstilbestrol (DES) in pregnancy* (New York: Thieme Stratton, 1981), 129–41.

29. See J. J. Li and S. A. Li, "High incidence of hepatocellular carci-nomas after synthetic estrogen administration in Syrian golden hamsters fed alpha–naphthoflavone: A new tumor model," *Journal of the National Cancer Institute* 73 (1984): 543–47.

30. See W. Taylor, "Risk factors associated with the use of sex hor-mones," *Anticancer Research* 7 (1987): 943–48.

31. See M. S. Bernstein, R. L. Hunter, and S. Yachnin, "Hepatomas and oral contraceptives," *Lancet* 2 (1971): 349–50; and F. L. Hohnson et al., "Association of adrogenic-anabolic steroid ther-apy with development of hepatocellular carcinoma," *Lancet* 2 (1972): 1273 76.

32. See J. K. Baum, "Liver tumors and oral contraceptives story," *Journal of the American Medical Association* 232 (1975): 1329.

33. See J. K. Baum et al., "Possible association between benign hepa-tomas and oral contraceptives," *Lancet* 2 (1973): 926–29.

34. See J. P. N. Davies, "Liver tumors and steroid hormones," *Lancet* 2 (1974): 516–17.

35. In the first of a series of carcinogenicity tests on the hormones present in the Pill, a select Committee on the Safety of Medi-cines reported in 1972 that administration of the progesterone components of the Pill (norethynodrel or norethisterone), with or without estrogen (mestranol), produced a significant increase in both benign and malignant liver tumors in male rats. Even more provocatively, the panel found that the currently used ana-log of natural estrogen (ethinylestradiol) could increase the num-ber of malignant liver tumors in female rats. However, the committee concluded that there was little *human* evidence avail-able (circa 1972) that estrogens and progestogens were produc-ing benign or malignant hepatomas. See *Carcinogenicity tests of oral contraceptives: A report by the Committee on the Safety of Medi-cines* (London, Her Majesty's Stationery Office, 1972).

36. See O. L. Contostavlos, "Benign hepatomas and oral contracep-tives," *Lancet* 2 (1973): 1200.

37. Representative articles during this period include: "Liver tumours

311

and the Pill," *British Medical Journal* 3 (1974): 3–4; "Oral contraceptives and the liver," *British Medical Journal* 4 (1974): 430–31; R. Hooghie, "Benign hepatomas and oral contraceptives," *Lancet* 1 (1974): 630–31; D. R. Kelso, "Benign hepatomas and oral contraceptives," *Lancet* 1 (1974): 315–16; W. A. Knapp and B. H. Ruebner, "Hepatomas and oral contraceptives," *Lancet* 1 (1974): 270–71; and N. C. Thalassinos et al., "Liver cell carcinoma after long-term estrogen-like drugs," *Lancet* 1 (1974): 270.

38. See E. T. Mays, W. M. Christopherson, and G. H. Barrows, "Focal nodular hyperplasia of the liver," *American Journal of Clinical Pathology* 61 (1974): 735–46.

39. See G. C. Farrell et al., "Androgen-induced hepatoma," *Lancet* 1 (1975): 430–31.

40. See H. A. Edmondson, B. Henderson, and B. Benton, "Liver cell adenomas associated with use of oral contraceptives," *New England Journal of Medicine* 294 (1976): 470–73.

41. See W. M. Christopherson and E. T. Mays, "Liver tumors and contraceptive steroids: Experience with the first one hundred registry patients," *Journal of the National Cancer Institute* 58 (1977): 167–71.

42. See J. Moesner et al., "Focal nodular hyperplasia of the liver. Possible influence of female reproductive steroids on the histological picture," *Acta Pathological Microbiologica Scandinavia* 85A (1977): 113–21.

43. See H. A. Edmondson et al., "Regression of liver cell adenomas associated with oral contraceptives," *Annals of Internal Medicine* 86 (1977): 180–82.

44. See C. K. Chan and D. E. Detner, "Proper management of hepatic adenomas associated with oral contraceptives," *Surgery, Gynecology and Obstetrics* 144 (1977): 703–6.

45. See J. B. Rooks et al., "The association between oral contraception and hepatocellular adenoma — A preliminary report," *International Journal of Gynecology and Obstetrics* 15 (1977): 143–44.

46. See D. Forman, R. Doll, and R. Peto, "Trends in mortality from carcinomas of the liver and use of oral contraceptives," *British Journal of Cancer* 48 (1983): 349–54.

47. See "Oral contraceptives and neoplasia," *Lancet* 2 (1983): 947.

48. See J. Srigly and J. L. Murray, "Clinical and pathological comparison of young adult women with hepatocellular carcinoma with and without exposure to oral contraceptives," *American Journal of Gastroenterology* 80 (1985): 479–85.

49. See J. Drige and J. Guillebando, "Hormonal contraception and cancer," *British Journal of Hospital Medicine* (January 1986): 25–29; and J. Neuberger et al., "Oral contraceptives and hepatocellular carcinoma," *British Medical Journal* 292 (1986): 1355–57.

50. See D. Forman, T. J. Vincent, and R. L. Doll, "Cancer of the liver and the use of oral contraceptives," *British Medical Journal* 292 (1986): 1357–61.

51. See A. Goldberg, "Oral contraceptives and hepatocellular carcinoma," *British Medical Journal* 292 (1986): 1392.

52. See R. Stone, "U.S. data fails to uphold claims made in *British Medical Journal* showing a link between long-term oral contraceptive use and liver cancer," Planned Parenthood Federation of America News Release, 23 May 1986.

53. See L. E. Porter, D. H. Van Thiel, and P. K. Eagon, "Estrogens and progestins as tumor inducers," *Seminars in Liver Disease* 7 (1987): 24–31.

54. See E. J. Gyorffy, J. E. Bredfeldt, and W. C. Black, "Transformation of hepatic cell adenoma to hepatocellular carcinoma due to oral contraceptive use," *Annals of Internal Medicine* 110 (1989): 489–90.

55. See C. C. Edwards, letter, in U.S. Congress, Senate Select Committee on Small Business, Subcommittee on Monopoly, *Hearings on the present status of competition in the pharmaceutical industry*, 91st Congress, 2d session, 1970.

56. See G. D. Searle, *Enovid bulletin no. 20,* 1964.

57. See Edwards, note 55.

58. In fact, the version given to the Senate committee was itself greatly watered down from an earlier one: the proposed leaflet originally identified the association with blood clots as *definite,* noting that "The risk of this complication is six times higher for users than for nonusers." See "F.D.A. restricting warning on pill—A draft revision indicates original is toned down," *New York Times,* 24 March 1970.

59. See D. M. Knowles and M. Wolff, "Systemic oral contraceptives and the liver," *Annals of Internal Medicine* 83 (1975): 907.

60. See V. Warvi, "Primary neoplasms of the liver," *Archives of Pathology* 37 (1944): 3677–82.

61. A thorough review of all the patients seen at the world famous Mayo Clinic in Rochester, MN from 1907 to 1954 found only four liver adenomas: see S. W. Henson, Jr., H. K. Gray, and M. D. Dockerty, "Benign tumors of the liver," *Surgery, Gynecology &*

Obstetrics 103 (1956): 23–30. A half-million hospital admissions in Scandinavia yielded only six more cases of liver adenomas and three focal nodular hyperplasias. Other researchers checked the entire English, French, German, and Scandinavian literature published between 1923 and 1974 and found only 200 lesions of both these types: see T. A. Sorenson and H. Baden, "Benign hepatocellular tumours," *Scandinavian Journal of Gastroenterology* 10 (1975): 113–19.

62. See W. Holck, "Cancer and the pill," *World Health* (November 1987): 18–19.

63. This likelihood is underscored by studies which showed a high proportion of women with hepatocellular carcinoma were long-term Pill-users. In one such study, 18 of 26 women younger than 50 years with liver cancer were found to have used oral contraceptive for a median of 8 years: see J. Neuberger et al., note 49.

64. See S. Sherlock, "Progress report: Hepatic adenomas and oral contraceptives," *Gut* 16 (1975): 753–56.

65. Studies done as early as 1962 showed that exposure to the hormones in Ortho's contraceptive pill could produce *invasive* liver tumors in mice. But these tumors were reported as benign by the laboratory that conducted the studies (Huntington Research Laboratory in England).

66. See M. Davis et al., "Histological evidence of carcinoma in a hepatic tumour associated with oral contraceptives," *British Medical Journal* 4 (1975): 496–98.

67. Among the many studies were some that were sponsored by the drug companies themselves: see, for example, J. Vana et al., "Primary liver tumors and oral contraceptives," *Journal of the American Medical Association* 238 (1977): 2154–58.

68. Ibid.

69. See E. D. Nissen, D. R. Kent, and S. E. Nissen, "Etiologic factors in the pathogenesis of liver tumors associated with oral contraceptives," *American Journal of Obstetrics and Gynecology* 127 (1977): 61–66.

70. See G. Pincus, *The control of fertility* (New York: Academic Press, 1965), 5–8.

71. See G. Pincus, "Some effects of progesterone and related compounds upon reproduction and early development in mammals," in *Report of the proceedings of the Fifth International Conference on Planned Parenthood* (London: Planned Parenthood Federation, 1955), 175–82.

72. See D. J. Evans, "Liver tumors elicited by specific factors: Synthetic androgens and anabolic steroids," in H. Remmer et al., eds., *Primary liver tumors* (Baltimore: University Park Press, 1978), 213–16.

73. See R. A. Malt, J. J. Galdabini, and B. W. Jeppson, "Abnormal sex-steroid milieu in young adults with hepatocellular carcinoma," *World Journal of Surgery* 7 (1983): 247–52. See also T. Imai, "Studies on hepatocarcinogenesis by oral contraceptive, synthetic estrogen and progestogen. Sequential development of hyperplastic nodules and hepatocellular carcinomas and effect of withdrawal of hormone administration on the developed hyperplastic nodules," *Acta Hepatologica* (Japan) 24 (1983): 182–92.

74. See E. Farber, "Liver carcinogenesis and cell biology." Paper presented at the University of Illinois at Chicago, 1 June 1989.

75. See E. Cayama et al., "Initiation of chemical carcinogenesis requires cell proliferation," *Nature* 275 (1978): 60–61.

76. The claim that the net balance of cancer of women on the Pill is at or near the neutral point because Pill-takers have lower incidences of endometrial and ovarian cancer [see F. L. Coe et al., "The risks of oral contraceptives and estrogen replacement therapy," *Perspectives in Biology and Medicine* 33 (1989): 86–106] is undercut by the fact that in certain user groups, *both* liver and breast cancer rates are elevated. These data must also be measured against the uncounted number of cases of pill-associated adenomas, nodular hyperplasias, and other liver neoplasias, many of which have required urgent surgical intervention to rescue women from possible fatal complications. Note that long-term estrogen use *alone* is associated with a doubling of breast cancer rates and a tenfold increase in endometrial cancer: see B. E. Henderson, "The cancer question: An overview of recent epidemiologic and retrospective data," *American Journal of Obstetrics and Gynecology* 161 (1989): 1859–64. Combination-type Pills with *low* estrogen may now be safer than those described in this chapter.

CHAPTER TEN: NATURALLY OCCURRING
SUBSTANCES CAUSE MOST CANCER

1. See, especially, P. Shubik and V. Shubik, "Living in a sea of carcinogens," *Harper's* (June 1976), 46 ff.

2. See G. M. Swanson, "Cancer prevention in the workplace and natural environment: A review of etiology, research design and

methods of risk reduction," *Cancer,* Supplement 62 (1988): 1725–46.

3. See, for example, H. F. Kraybill, "Global distribution of carcinogenic pollutants in water," *Annals of the New York Academy of Sciences* 298 (1977): 80–89; and D. C. Malins, "Toxic chemicals in urban embayments: Effects on marine life and the consumer," in *Proceedings of the Puget Sound Water Quality Conference* (Seattle: Puget Sound Council of Governments, 1983), 35–50.

4. See B. Kurelec et al., "Natural environment surpasses polluted environment in inducing DNA damage in fish," *Carcinogenesis* 10 (1989): 1337–39.

5. See C. C. Travis, H. A. Hattenmeyer-Frey, and E. Silbergeld, "Dioxin, dioxin everywhere," *Environmental Science and Technology* 23 (1989): 1061–63.

6. See A. C. Longwell and J. B. Hughes, "Cytologic, cytogenic and developmental state of Atlantic mackerel eggs from sea surface waters of the New York Bight," *Rapports et Procés-verbaux des Réunions. Conseil International pour Exploration de la Mer* 179 (1980): 275–91.

7. See B. N. Ames, "Dietary carcinogens and anticarcinogens: Oxygen radicals and degenerative diseases," *Science* 221 (1983): 1256–64; and B. N. Ames, R. Magaw, and S. Gold, "Ranking possible carcinogenic hazards," *Science* 236 (1987): 271–79.

8. See B. N. Ames and L. Swirsky Gold, "Pesticides, risk, and applesauce," *Science* 244 (1989): 755–57.

9. Advertisement in the *Journal of the National Cancer Institute* 81 (1989): 1567.

10. See National Cancer Institute, *Diet, nutrition and cancer prevention: The good news* (Washington, DC: GPO, 1989).

11. See B. N. Ames, "Cancer and diet," *Science* 224 (1984): 668–70, 757–60.

12. See Ames, Magaw, and Gold, note 7.

13. See F. Perera and P. Boffetta, "Perspectives on comparing risks of environmental carcinogens," *Journal of the National Cancer Institute* 80 (1988): 1282–91.

14. See A. L. Potosky et al., "Rise in prostatic cancer incidence associated with increased use of trans-urethral resection," *Journal of the National Cancer Institute* 82 (1990): 1624–27.

15. For representative articles implicating these chemicals, see T. Berge, "Increase of cancer among vinyl chloride and polyvinyl chloride workers: Further evidence for an association with malignant melanoma," *British Journal of Industrial Medicine* 44 (1987): 718–19; H. Olsson et al., "Risk of non-Hodgkin's lym-

phoma among men occupationally exposed to organic solvents," *Scandinavian Journal of Work and Environmental Health* 14 (1988): 246–51; A. M. Ducatman, "Dimethylformamide, metal dyes and testicular cancer," *Lancet 1* (1989): 911; I.C.T. Nisbet et al., *Review and evaluation of evidence for cancer associated with air pollution* (Research Triangle Park, NC, EPA Publication no. 450/5-83-006R, 1983; S. Kadamani et al., *"Occupational hydrocarbon exposure and risk of renal cell cancer,"* *American Journal of Industrial Medicine* 15 (1989): 131–34; R. J. Waxweiler et al., "Neoplastic risk among workers exposed to vinyl chloride," *Annals of the New York Academy of Sciences* 271 (1976): 40–49; H. Austin et al., "Case-control study of hepatocellular carcinogenesis, occupation, and chemical exposures," *Journal of Occupational Medicine* 29 (1987): 665–69; P. Hartage et al., "Unexplained excess risk of bladder cancer in men," *Journal of the National Cancer Institute* 82 (1990): 1636–39. Also see R. Doll and R. Peto, *The causes of cancer* (London: Oxford University Press, 1981).

16. See A. Osterlind et al., "The Danish case-control study of cutaneous malignant melanoma. IV. No association with nutritional factors, alcohol, smoking and hair dyes," *International Journal of Cancer* 42 (1988): 825–28.

17. See S. Franceschi et al., "Dietary factors and non–Hodgkin's lymphoma: A case-control study in the northeastern part of Italy," *Nutrition and Cancer* 12 (1989): 333–41; and W. C. Willett et al., "Dietary fat and the risk of breast cancer," *New England Journal of Medicine* 316 (1987): 22–28.

18. See N. H. Grieg et al., "Increasing annual incidence of primary malignant brain tumors in the elderly," *Journal of the National Cancer Institute* 82 (1990): 621–24.

19. Although alcohol has traditionally been associated with these tumor types, recent data suggest that ingestion of maize (sweet or Indian corn) is correlated with risk of cancer of the upper digestive tract. See S. Franceschi et al., "Maize and risk of cancers of the oral cavity, pharynx, and esophagus in northeastern Italy," *Journal of the National Cancer Institute* 82 (1990): 1407–11.

20. See National Academy of Sciences, National Research Council, Committee on Diet, Nutrition and Cancer, *Diet, nutrition and cancer* (Washington, DC: National Academy Press, 1982).

21. See T. Byers, "Diet and cancer: Any progress in the interim?" *Cancer* 62 (1988): 1713–24.

22. See B. Ingram et al., "Obesity and breast disease," *Cancer* 64 (1989): 1049–53.

23. See C. Longcope et al., "The effect of a low-fat diet on estrogen metabolism," *Journal of Clinical Endocrinology and Metabolism* 64 (1987): 1246–50.

24. See J. L. Kesey, "A review of the epidemiology of breast cancer," *Epidemiological Reviews* 1 (1979): 74–109.

25. See L. Gross, "Inhibition of the development of tumors or leukemia in mice and rats after reduction of food intake: Possible implications for humans," *Cancer* 62 (1988): 1463–65.

26. See J. J. Michnowicz and H. L. Bradlow, "Induction of estradiol metabolism by dietary indol-3-carbinol in humans," *Journal of the National Cancer Institute* 82 (1990): 947–49.

27. See L. R. Jacobs, "Modification of experimental colon carcinogenesis by dietary fiber," in R. Poirrier et al., eds., *Essential nutrients in carcinogenesis* (New York: Plenum, 1986), 105–18.

28. See D. M. Klurfeld and D. Kritchevsky, "Dietary fiber and human cancer: Critique of the literature," in *Essential nutrients in carcinogenesis,* note 27, pp. 119–35.

29. See A. S. Whittemore et al., "Diet, physical activity, and colorectal cancer among Chinese in North America and China," *Journal of the National Cancer Institute* 82 (1990): 915–26.

30. See R. J. Ruch, S.-J. Cheng, and J. E. Klaunig, "Prevention of cytotoxicity and inhibition of intercellular communication by antioxidant catchins isolated from Chinese green tea," *Carcinogenesis* 10 (1989): 1003–8.

31. See A. M. Shamsuddin, A. Ullah, and A. K. Chakravarthy, "Inositol and inosital hexaphosphate suppress cell proliferation and tumor formation in CD-1 mice," *Carcinogenesis* 10 (1989): 1461–63.

32. See L. W. Wattenberg and L. K. T. Lam, "Protective effects of coffee constituents on carcinogenesis in experimental animals," *Banbury Report* 17 (1984): 137–45.

33. See E. G. Miller et al., "The effect of citrus limonoids on hamster buccal pouch carcinogenesis," *Carcinogenesis* 10 (1989): 1535–37.

34. See H. Mukhtar, M. Das, and D. R. Bickers, "Inhibition of 3-methylcholanthrene-induced skin tumorigenicity in BALB/c mice by chronic oral feeding of trace amounts of ellagic acid in drinking water," *Cancer Research* 46 (1986): 2262–65.

35. See D. Dwivedi et al., "Effects of the experimental chemopreventative agent, glucarate, on intestinal carcinogenesis in rats," *Carcinogenesis* 10 (1989): 1539–41.

36. See O. Ochukoya, F. Harwach, and G. Shidar, "Retardation of experimental oral cancer by topical vitamin E," *Nutrition and Cancer* 6 (1984): 98–104.

37. See D. Suda, J. Schwartz, and G. Shklar, "Inhibition of experimental oral carcinogenesis by topical beta carotene," *Carcinogenesis* 7 (1986): 711–15.

38. See M. Murakoshi et al., "Inhibitory effects of alpha carotene on proliferation of the human neuroblastoma cell line GOTO," *Journal of the National Cancer Institute* 81 (1989): 1649–52.

39. See J. Schwartz et al., "Prevention of experimental oral cancer by extracts of *Spirulina dunaliella* algae," *Nutrition and Cancer* 11 (1988): 127–34.

40. See "Salted fish and nasopharyngeal carcinoma," *Lancet* 2 (1989): 840–42.

41. See M. C. Yhu et al., "Preserved foods and nasopharyngeal carcinoma: A case control study in Guangxi, China," *Cancer Research* 49 (1988): 1954–59.

42. See T. Shirai et al., "Effects of butylated hydroxyanisole, butylated hydroxytoluene, and NaCl on gastric carcinogenesis initiated with N methyl N—nitro N nitrosoguanidine in F344 rats," *Journal of the National Cancer Institute* 72 (1984): 1189–98.

43. See K. Mizumoto et al., "Inhibitory effect of butylated hydroxyanisole administration on pancreatic carcinogenesis in Syrian hamsters initiated with N nitrosobis(2-oxypropyl)amine," *Carcinogenesis* 10 (1989): 1491–94.

44. See, for example, W. J. Curran, "Cancer-causing substances in food, drugs, and cosmetics: The *de minimus* rule versus the Delaney clause," *New England Journal of Medicine* 319 (1988): 1262–64.

45. See G. Kolata, "U.S. food regulation: Tales of a twilight zone," *New York Times,* 10 June 1987, pp. 1, 22.

46. See *Public Citizen v. Young,* No. 86-1548, District of Columbia Circuit Court (1987).

47. See D. L. Park and L. Stoloff, "Aflatoxin control—How a regulatory agency managed risk from an unavoidable natural toxicant in food and feed," *Regulatory Toxicology & Pharmacology* 9 (1989): 109–30.

48. Ames, note 7.

49. See S. Graham, "Alcohol and breast cancer," *New England Journal of Medicine* 316 (1987): 1211–13.

50. See B. Lindegård, "Survival and age at diagnosis in breast cancer," *New England Journal of Medicine* 316 (1987): 750–51.

51. See S. E. Epstein and J. B. Swartz, "Carcinogenic risk estimation," *Science* 240 (1988): 1043–45.

52. See D. G. McCoy and E. L. Wynder, "Etiological and preventive implications in alcohol carcinogenesis," *Career Research* 39 (1982): 2844–50.

53. See E. A. Porta, N. Markell, and R. D. Dorado, "Chronic alcoholism enhances hepatocarcinogenicity of diethylnitrosamine in rats fed a marginally methyl-deficient diet," *Hepatology* 5 (1985): 1120–25.

54. See K. J. Rothman, "The proportion of cancer attributable to alcohol," *Preventive Medicine* 9 (1980): 174–79.

55. See K. J. Rothman et al., "Epidemiology of laryngeal cancer," *Epidemiology Reviews* 2 (1980): 195–209.

56. See S. Graham et al., "Dentition, diet, tobacco and alcohol in the epidemiology of oral cancer," *Journal of the National Cancer Institute* 59 (1977): 1611–15.

57. See E. L. Wynder, I. J. Bross, and R. M. Feldman, "A study of the etiological factors in cancer of the mouth," *Cancer* 10 (1957): 1300–23.

58. See K. J. Rothman, C. I. Cann, and M. P. Fried, "Carcinogenicity of dark liquor," *American Journal of Public Health* 79 (1989): 1516–20.

59. See J. S. Felton et al., "Identification of the mutagens in cooked beef," *Environmental Health Perspectives* 67 (1986): 17–24; and T. Kato et al., "Carcinogenicity in rats of a mutagenic compound, 2-amino-3,8-dimethylimidazol [4,5-*f*] quinoxaline," *Carcinogenesis* 9 (1988): 71–73.

60. See H. Kasai et al., "Structure of a potent mutagen isolated from fried beef," *Chemical Letters* (1981): 485–88.

61. See N. E. Day, "The geographic pathology of cancer of the esophagus," *British Medical Bulletin* 40 (1984): 329–34.

62. See J. E. Vena et al., "Lifetime occupational exercise and colon cancer," *American Journal of Epidemiology* 122 (1985): 357–65; D. H. Garabrant et al., "Job activity and colon cancer risk," *American Journal of Epidemiology* 119 (1984): 1005–14; and A. S. Whittemore et al., see note 29.

63. See L. A. Cannon-Albright et al., "Common inheritance of sus-

ceptibility to colonic adenomatous polyps and colorectal cancers," *New England Journal of Medicine* 319 (1988): 533–37.

64. See W. G. Stillwell et al., "Urinary levels of nitrate, N-nitrosoproline, 7-methylguanine and 3-methyl adenine in a human population at elevated risk toward gastric cancer," *Proceedings of the American Association of Cancer Research* 30 (1989): A1257 (abstract).

65. From T. J. Mason et al., *Atlas of cancer mortality for U.S. counties: 1959–1969,* NIH 75-780 (Washington, DC: National Institutes of Health, Department of Health, Education and Welfare, 1975).

66. See D. Coggin and E. D. Acheson, "The geography of cancer of the stomach," *Medical Bulletin* 40 (1984): 335–41.

67. See R. Hoover, T. J. Mason, F. W. McKay, and J. F. Fraumeni, Jr., "Cancer by county: New resource for etiologic clues," *Science* 189 (1975): 1005–7.

68. See H. King and W. Haenszel, "Cancer mortality among foreign and native born Chinese in the United States," *Journal of Chronic Disease* 26 (1973): 623–46.

69. See Coggin and Acheson, note 66, p. 337.

70. See W. Haenszel et al., "Stomach cancer among Japanese in Hawaii," *Journal of the National Cancer Institute* 49 (1972): 969–88.

71. See Coggin and Acheson, note 66, p. 339.

72. Ibid. p. 340.

73. See P. Correa, W. Haenszel, and S. Tannenbaum, "Epidemiology of gastric carcinoma: Review and future prospects," *National Cancer Institute Monographs* 62 (1982): 129–34.

74. See J. H. C. Ho, "Nasopharyngeal carcinoma," *Advances in Cancer Research* 15 (1972): 547–82.

75. See R. W. Armstrong et al., "Salted fish and inhalants as risk factors for nasopharyngeal carcinoma in Malaysian Chinese," *Cancer Research* 43 (1983): 2967–70.

76. See P. Cook-Mozaffari and S. Van Rensburg, "Cancer of the liver," *British Medical Bulletin* 40 (1984): 342–45.

77. Ibid.

78. See A. G. Oettlé, "The aetiology of primary carcinoma of the liver in Africa: A critical appraisal of previous ideas with an outline of the mycotoxin hypothesis," *South African Medical Journal* 39 (1965): 817–25. Cited in Cook-Mozaffari and Van Rensburg, note 76.

79. See H. F. Kraybill and R. E. Shapiro, "Implications of fungal toxicity to human health," in L. Goldblatt, ed., *Aflatoxin* (New York: Academic Press, 1969), 401 ff.

80. See Cook-Mozaffari and Van Rensburg, note 76, p. 342.

81. See C. A. Linsell and F. G. Peers, "Aflatoxin and liver cell cancer," *Transactions of the Royal Society of Tropical Medicine and Hygiene* 71 (1977): 471–73.

82. See Cook-Mozaffari and Van Rensburg, note 76, p. 344.

83. See D. Trichopoulos, B. MacMahon, L. Sparros, and G. Merikas, "Smoking and hepatitis B negative primary hepatocellular carcinoma," *Journal of the National Cancer Institute* 65 (1980): 111–14.

84. See A. Stemhagen, J. Slade, R. Altman, and J. Bill, "Occupational risk factors and liver cancer," *American Journal of Epidemiology* 117 (1983): 443–54.

85. See D. A. Shafritz et al., "Integration of hepatitis B virus DNA into the genome of liver cells in chronic liver disease and hepatocellular carcinoma," *New England Journal of Medicine* 305 (1981): 1067–73.

86. See B. E. Walker, "Tumors in female offspring of control and diethylstibestrol-exposed mice fed high-fat diets," *Journal of the National Cancer Institute* 82 (1990): 50–54.

87. See A. R. Francis, T. K. Shetty, and R. K. Bhattacharya, "Modifying role of dietary factors on the mutagenicity of aflatoxin B1: In vitro effect of plant flavonoids," *Mutation Research* 222 (1989): 393–401.

88. See notes 10 and 36.

89. See K. C. Lam et al., "Hepatitis B virus and cigarette smoking: Risk factors for hepatocellular carcinoma in Hong Kong," *Cancer Research* 42 (1982): 5246–48.

90. See N. M. Pettigrew et al., "Evidence for a role of hepatitis virus B in chronic alcoholic liver disease," *Lancet 2* (1972): 724–25.

91. See Cook-Mozaffari and Van Rensburg, note 76, p. 343.

92. See H. Falk, "Liver," in D. Schottenfeld and J. F. Fraumeni, eds., *Cancer epidemiology and prevention* (Philadelphia: Saunders, 1982), 668–72.

93. See D. Trichopoulos et al., "Geographic correlation between mortality from primary hepatic carcinoma and prevalence of hepatitis B surface antigen in Greece," *British Journal of Cancer* 34 (1976): 83–87.

94. See note 76.

95. See L. I. Lutwick, "Relation between aflatoxin, hepatitis B virus and hepatocellular carcinoma," *Lancet 1* (1979): 755–57.

96. See B. S. Blumberg, "Australia antigen and the biology of hepatitis B," *Science* 197 (1977): 17–25; and W. Smuzness, "Hepatocellular carcinoma and hepatitis B virus: Evidence for a causal association," *Proceedings of the National Academy of Sciences* 24 (1978): 40–69.

97. See B. S. Blumberg and W. T. London, "Hepatitis B virus: Pathogenesis and prevention of primary cancer of the liver," *Cancer* 50 (1983): 2657–65.

98. See S. De Flora et al., "Enhanced metabolic activation of chemical hepatocarcinogens in woodchucks infected with hepatitis B virus," *Carcinogenesis* 10 (1989): 1099–1106.

99. See B. G. Osterdahl, "Volatile nitrosamines in foods on the Swedish market and estimation of their daily intake," *Food Additives and Contaminants* 5 (1988): 587–95.

100. See H. Enzman et al., "Enhancement of hepatocarcinogenesis in rats by dietary fructose," *Carcinogenesis* 10 (1989): 1247–52.

101. See J. Limmer et al., "Hepatocellular carcinoma in type I glycogen storage disease," *Hepatology* 8 (1988): 531–37.

102. See J. G. Liu and M. H. Li, "Roussin red methyl ester, a tumor promoter isolated from pickled vegetables," *Carcinogenesis* 10 (1989): 617–20.

103. See L. Escoula et al., "Patulin immunotoxicology: Effect on phagocyte activation and the cellular and humoral immune system of mice and rabbits," *International Journal of Immunopharmacology* 10 (1988): 983–89.

104. See G. N. Woogan, "Mycotoxins and other naturally occurring carcinogens," in H. F. Kraybill and M. A. Mehlman, eds., *Environmental cancer* (Washington, DC: Hemisphere, 1977), especially p. 283; and A. W. Archer, "Determination of safrole and myristicin in nutmeg and mace by high-performance liquid chromatography," *Journal of Chromostaography* 438 (1988): 117–21.

105. See A. R. Tricker, M. Siddiqi, and R. Presuumann, "Occurrence of volatile N-nitrosamine in dried chillies," *Cancer Letters* 38 (1988): 271–73.

106. See R. H. Dashwood et al., "Quantitative interrelationships between aflatoxin B1 carcinogen dose, idole-3-carbinol anticarcinogen dose, target organ DNA adduction and final tumor response," *Carcinogenesis* 10 (1989): 175–81.

107. See L. W. Wattenberg et al., "Inhibition of mammary tumor

formation by broccoli and cabbage," *Proceedings of the American Association of Cancer Research* 30 (1989): A719 (abstract).

108. See R. Dashwood et al., "Inhibitory vs. promotional potency, and timing of modulator treatment: Tumor dose-response studies with aflatoxin B1 and indole-3-carbinol," *Proceedings of the American Association for Cancer Research* 30 (1989): A712 (abstract).

109. See T. V. Reddy, F. C. Kopfler, and F. B. Daneil, "Modulation of benzo(a)pyrene adduction with cellular DNA and blood proteins by benzyl isothiocyanate," *Proceedings of the American Association for Cancer Research* 30 (1989): A663 (abstract).

110. See H. Sumiyuoshi and M. J. Wargovich, "Effect of organosulfur compounds on 1,2-dimethylhydrazine-induced nuclear toxicity and GST activity in mouse colon," *Proceedings of the American Association for Cancer Research* 30 (1989): A718 (abstract).

111. See Z. Y. Wang et al., "Protection against polycyclic aromatic hydrocarbon-induced skin tumor initiation in mice by green tea polyphenols," *Carcinogenesis* 10 (1989): 411–15.

112. See Y. Ita, S. Ohnishi, and K. Fuji, "Chromosome aberrations induced by aflatoxin B1 in rat bone marrow cells in vivo and their suppression by green tea," *Mutation Research* 222 (1989): 253–61.

113. See N. S. Rapp et al., "Mutagenic and anti-mutagenic properties of meju and other Korean food products from fermented soybeans," *Yonsei Medical Journal* 29 (1988): 117–23.

114. See J. L. Blanco et al., "Experimental aflatoxin production in home-made yoghurt," *Zeitschrift für Lensem. Undersuchen Forsch.* 186 (1986): 323–26.

115. See K. P. Keenea et al., "Multifactorial hamster respiratory carcinogenesis with interdependent effects of cannula-induced mucosal wounding, saline, ferric oxide, benzo(*a*)pyrene and N-methyl-N-nitrosourea," *Cancer Research* 49 (1989): 1528–40.

116. See N. H. Park, E. G. Herbosa, and J. P. Sapp, "Effect of tar condensate from smoking tobacco and water-extract of snuff on the oral mucosa of mice with latent herpes simplex virus," *Archives of Oral Biology* 32 (1987): 47–54.

117. In one study, forerunners of liver cell cancers were vastly more common when rats were treated with a continuous administration of estrogens like those in the Pill than when aflatoxins were given alone. See L. Kamdem et al., "Induced hepatotoxicity in female rats by aflatoxin B1 and ethynylestradiol interaction," *Toxicology and Applied Pharmacology* 67 (1983): 26–40.

118. See G. S. Omenn, "Ecogenetics and susceptibility to cancer," *Health and Environment Digest* 4 (1991): 1–3.

119. Ames, Magaw, and Gold, note 7.

CHAPTER ELEVEN: IF IT COMES OUT
OF THE TAP, IT'S SAFE TO DRINK

1. See T. McKeown, *The role of medicine: Dream, mirage or nemesis* (London: Nuffield Provincial Hospital Trust, 1976).

2. See National Research Council, Safe Drinking Water Committee, *Drinking water and health,* vol. 1 (Washington, DC: National Academy of Sciences, 1977).

3. Ibid., vol. 4 (1982), p. 1.

4. V. I. Pye, R. Patrick, and J. Quarles, *Groundwater contamination in the United States* (Philadelphia: University of Pennsylvania Press, 1983).

5. See T. H. Maugh, "Just how hazardous are dumps?" *Science* 215 (1982): 490–93.

6. See U.S. Environmental Protection Agency, *National priorities list. 786 current and proposed sites in order of ranking and by state, October 1984.* HW-7.2, revised (Washington, DC: GPO, 1984).

7. See D. G. Neary, "Effects of pesticide applications on forested watersheds," in W. T. Sward and D. A. Crosseley, Jr., eds., *Ecological studies, vol. 66: Forest hydrology and ecology at Coweeta* (New York: Springer-Verlag, 1988), 325–37.

8. See B. A. Glatz et al., "Examination of drinking water for mutagenic activity," *Journal of the American Water Works Association* 70 (1978): 465–68.

9. See J. R. Meier, "Evaluation of chemicals used for drinking water disinfection for production of chromosomal damage and sperm head abnormalities in mice," *Environmental Mutagenesis* 7 (1985): 201–11.

10. See S. Maruoka and S. Yamanaka, "Production of mutagenic substances by chlorination of waters," *Mutation Research* 79 (1980): 381–86.

11. See S. M. Grimm-Bibalo, B. A. Glatz, and J. S. Fritz, "Seasonal variation of mutagenic activity in drinking water," *Bulletin of Environmental Contamination and Toxicology* 26 (1981): 188–95.

12. See A. M. Cheh et al., "Nonvolatile mutagens in drinking

water: Production by chlorination and destruction by sulfite," *Science* 207 (1980): 90–92.

13. See T. A. Jorgenson et al., "Carcinogenicity of chloroform in drinking water to male Osborne-Mendel rats and female B6C3F1 mice," *Fundamental and Applied Toxicology* 5 (1985): 760–69.

14. See L. W. Condie et al., "Comparative renal and hepatotoxicity of halomethanes," *Drug Chemistry and Toxicology* 6 (1983): 563–78.

15. This figure assumes a 70-year-old man ingesting one liter of water per day. National Research Council, *Drinking Water and Health, Disinfectants and Disinfectant Byproducts,* vol. 7, (Washington, DC, National Academy Press, 1987).

16. See J. R. Wilkins et al., "Organic chemical contaminants in drinking water and cancer," *American Journal of Epidemiology* 110 (1979): 420–48.

17. See K. S. Crump and H. A. Guess, "Drinking water and cancer: Review of recent epidemiological findings and assessment of risks," *Annual Review of Public Health* 3 (1982): 339–57.

18. See W. A. Temple and D. G. Ferry, "Solvent exposures and risk assessment," in M. L. Richardson, ed., *Risk assessment of chemicals in the environment* (London: Royal Society of Chemistry, 1988), 222–41.

19. See T. B. Young, M. S. Kanarek, and A. A. Tsiatis, "Epidemiologic study of drinking water chlorination and Wisconsin female cancer mortality," *Journal of the National Cancer Institute* 67 (1981): 1191–98.

20. See T. Young, "Case control study on colon cancer and trihalomethanes," *International Journal of Epidemiology* 16 (1987): 190–97; and D. Cragle, "A case control study on colon cancer and water chlorination in North Carolina," *Water Chlorination* 5 (1987): 190.

21. See K. P. Cantor, "Epidemiological evidence of carcinogenicity of chlorinated organics in drinking water," *Environmental Health Perspectives* 46 (1982): 187–95.

22. See P. A. Murphy and G. F. Craun, "A review of recent epidemiologic studies reporting associations between drinking water disinfection and cancer," In: J. Condle et al., eds., *Water Chlorination Chemistry, Environmental Impact and Health Effects,* vol. 6 (Chelsea, MI, Lewis Pubs., Inc., 1990) pp. 361–72.

23. See K. P. Cantor, "Bladder cancer, drinking water source and tap water consumption," *Journal of the National Cancer Institute* 79 (1987): 1269–79.

24. See G. F. Craun, "Epidemiologic studies of organic micropollutants in drinking water," *Science of the Total Environment* 47 (1985): 461–72; and R. J. Bull, "Carcinogenic and mutagenic properties of chemicals in drinking water," *Science of the Total Environment* 47 (1985): 385–413.

25. See National Research Council, note 2, Vol. 5 (1983), pp. 28–39, 79–84.

26. JeAnne Burg, director, ATSDR, personal communication, 16 November 1989.

27. See S. W. Lagakos, B. J. Wessen, and M. Zelen, "An analysis of contaminated well water and health effects in Woburn, Massachusetts," *Journal of the American Statistical Association* 81 (1986): 583–96 (Applications).

28. See J. Fagliano et al., "Drinking water contamination and the incidence of leukemia: An ecologic study," *American Journal of Public Health* 80 (1990): 1209–12.

29. Jerald Fagliano, personal communication, 8 October 1988.

30. See note 28.

31. Robert Halquist, Department of Health Services, State of California, personal communication, 16 November 1989.

32. New Zealand, Wellington Department of Health, *Drinking water standards for New Zealand* (Wellington, New Zealand: Board of Health, 1984).

33. See "Setting environmental standards," in H. W. de Koning, ed., *Guidelines for decision-making* (Geneva: World Health Organization, 1987).

34. Richard Miltner, personal communication, 16 November 1989.

35. Unpublished data, EPA, October 1990.

36. See C. Howard, "Pesticides posing unknown risks," *Peoria Star Journal,* 6 March 1990, pp. 31–32; and E. Funari, "Extensive atrazine pollution of drinking water in the Lombardia region (Italy) and related health effects," *Biomedical and Environmental Science* 1 (1988): 350–55.

37. See A. Pino et al., "DNA damage in stomach, kidney, liver and lung of rats treated with atrazine," *Mutation Research* 209 (1988): 145–7.

38. See J. A. Burg, "Rationale for choosing benzene as a primary contaminant," memorandum dated 12 October 1989, to B. L. Johnson, Chief of the Exposure and Disease Registry Branch, Agency for Toxic Substances and Disease Registry.

39. Unpublished data supplied by Region V EPA.

40. See H. Savolainen et al., "Trichloroethylene and 1,1,1-trichloroethane: Effects on brain and liver after five days intermittent inhalation," *Archives of Toxicology* 38 (1977): 229–37.

41. See D. Pessayre et al., "Hepatoxicity of trichloroethylene–carbon tetrachloride mixtures in rats," *Gastroenterology* 83 (1982): 761–72.

42. See S. Tola et al., "A chohort study on workers exposed to trichloroethylene," *Journal of Occupational Medicine* 22 (1980): 737–40.

43. See B. Eskenazi, "Exposure to organic solvents and hypersensitivity disorders of pregnancy," *American Journal of Industrial Medicine* 14 (1988): 177–88.

44. See A. Aschengrau et al., "Quality of drinking water and the occurrence of spontaneous abortion," *Archives of Environmental Health* 44 (1989): 283–90.

45. See S. W. Lagakos, B. J. Essen, and M. Zelen, note 23. See also the rejoinder by these same authors to the criticisms (pp. 597–610) published in the same issue, pp. 611–14.

46. See M. Wrensch, "Pregnancy outcomes in women potentially exposed to solvent-contaminated drinking water," *American Journal of Epidemiology* 131 (1990): 283–300.

47. See California Department of Health Services, *Pregnancy outcomes in Santa Clara County 1980–1985* (Berkeley: Epidemiological Studies Section, 1987).

48. See R. L. Anderson et al., "Effect of disinfectants on pseudomonads colonized on the interior surface of PVC pipes," *American Journal of Public Health* 80 (1990): 17–21.

49. See M. Lappé et al., *Final report on potential health hazards associated with the use of plastic pipe in potable water systems,* Hazard Evaluation System, State of California Department of Health Services (Berkeley, CA), October 17, 1980.

50. The NRC risk estimate is based on the formula $1 + 0.05 \times \text{dose} \times 10^{-12}$. For men, this risk equates to 1 extra GI tract cancer per 100,000 exposed to 0.11×10^6 fibers/liter as seen in transmission electron microscopy. Since 10 fibers/liter is approximately 100 times this number, 100 deaths might be expected. See National Research Council, note 21, p. 143. High-risk areas of the United States include Duluth, Minnesota, where asbestos fibers reached 1 to 30 million/liter in 1973; Connecticut townships, where asbestos-cement pipes were in use between 1935 and 1973; and the San Francisco Bay Area, where "natural" asbestos comes from serpentine rock. Fiber levels here have reached as high as 180 million/liter.

51. See M. S. Kanarek et al., "Asbestos in drinking water and cancer incidence in the San Francisco Bay Area," *American Journal of Epidemiology* 112 (1980): 54–72.

52. See M. Lappé, "Permeation of gasoline through plastic pipe," unpublished studies (Anlab Laboratory, Sacramento, CA, December 1981).

53. See M. Lappé, "Aqueous extractives from acetal fittings of polybutane pipe," unpublished studies, Berkeley, CA, 1983.

54. See A. C. Ershow and K. P. Cantor, "Population based estimate of water intake," *Federation Proceedings* 45 (1986): 706.

CHAPTER TWELVE: THE ENVIRONMENT IS RESILIENT

1. See C. Bernard, *Introduction to the study of experimental medicine,* trans. by C. Green (New York: Dover, 1957). (Published originally in 1865.)

2. See W. B. Cannon, *The wisdom of the body* (New York. Norton, 1932), chap. 12.

3. See E. Sahtouris, *Gaia: The human journey from chaos to cosmos* (New York: Pocket Books, 1989), wherein she states: "In recognizing our planet as an experienced living system with a good deal of 'body wisdom' to teach us, we gain the perspective to see how we might apply some of that wisdom to our own human problems."

4. See J. E. Lovelock, *Gaia: A new look at life on earth* (London: Oxford University Press, 1987).

5. See L. Margulis and J. F. Stolz, Letter, *Scientific American,* March 1990, p. 12.

6. Ibid.

7. See L. Margulis, *Symposiosis in cell evolution: Life and its environment on the early earth* (San Francisco: Freeman, 1981).

8. See Margulis and Stolz, note 5.

9. See Margulis, note 7.

10. See D. A. Bromley, "The making of a greenhouse policy," *Issues in Science and Technology* 7 (Fall 1990): 55–61.

11. See A. Raval and V. Ramananthan, "Observational determination of the Greenhouse Effect," *Nature* 342 (1989): 758–61. See also R. A. Kerr, "Global temperature hits record again," *Science* 251 (1991): 274.

12. See J. Hansen, W. Rossow, and I. Fung, "The missing data on global climate change," *Issues in Science and Technology* 7 (1990): 62–69.

13. See L. Margulis and E. Dobb, "Untimely requiem," *The Sciences* (June 1990): 44–50.

14. Sherwood B. Idso, at the Department of Agriculture Laboratory in Phoenix, AZ, is one such person. See W. K. Stevens, "Carbon dioxide may alter plant life, researchers say," *New York Times,* 18 September 1990, Science Times, C1, C9.

15. See W. H. Schlesinger et al., "Biological feedbacks in global desertification," *Science* 247 (1990): 1043–48, wherein the roles of grazing, off-road vehicles, row crop agriculture, and global warming are cited as forces that lead to permanent desertification.

16. See Stevens, note 14, p. C1.

17. See "The Geritol solution," *Newsweek,* 5 November 1990, p. 67.

18. See B. O. Rosseland and A. Henriksen, "Acidification in Norway — Loss of fish populations and the 1,000 lake survey of 1986," *Science of the Total Environment* 96 (1990): 45–56.

19. See G. H. Tomlinson, ed., *Effects of acid deposition on the forests of Europe and North America* (Boca Raton, FL: CRC Press, 1990).

20. See N. Simmleit and H. R. Schulten, "Pattern recognition of spruce trees. An integrated, analytical approach to forest damage," *Environmental Science and Technology* 23 (1989): 1000–6.

21. See P. Pathy, ed., *Air pollution and ecosystems* (Dordrecht, Netherlands: D. Reidel, 1988).

22. See E. D. Schulze, "Air pollution and forest decline in a spruce (*Picea abies*) forest," *Science* 244 (1989): 776–82.

23. See W. Salomons in *Proceedings of the International Hydrology Programme* (Bangkok, Thailand: Asian Institute of Technology, 1989), 7.

24. See T. C. Hutchinson, in J. O. Nriagu, ed., *Copper in the environment* (New York: Wiley, 1979), 451.

25. See C. G. Downs and J. Stocks, *Environmental impact of mining* (New York: Wiley, 1977), 25.

26. See *Proceedings of the International Hydrology Programme,* note 23, p. 76.

27. See M. Feinleib et al., *Mortality from cardiovascular and noncardiovascular diseases for U.S. cities,* Publication no. (NIH) 79-1453 (Washington, DC: GPO, 1979).

28. See J. N. Moore and S. N. Luoma, "Hazardous wastes from

large-scale metal extraction," *Environmental Science and Technology* 24 (1990): 1278–85.

29. See A. L. Demain and N. A. Solomon, "Industrial microbiology," *Scientific American* 245 (1981): 67–75.

30. See C. C. Travis and H. A. Hattenmeyer-Drey, "Assessing the extent of human exposure to organics," in C. C. Travis, ed., *Carcinogen risk assessment* (Boca Raton, FL: Plenum, 1988), 61–75. Dieldrin's concentration gradient is 14,125; DDT's is 51,286.

31. The amounts of these three pesticides in 1989 were 429 kilotons (atrazine), 212 kilotons (metoloachlor), and 129 kilotons (alachlor). See W. E. Pereira and C. E. Rostad, "Occurrence, distributions, and transport of herbicides and their degradatio products in the lower Mississippi River and its tributaries," *Environmental Science and Technology* 24 (1990): 1400–6, Table III.

32. See British Medical Association, Board of Science and Education, *Pesticides, chemicals, and health* (London: British Medical Association, 1990). Cited in *The Lancet* 336 (1990): 999.

33. See P. Herbert et al., "The occurrence of chlorinated solvents in the environment," *Chemistry and Industry* (15 December 1986): 861–69. The solvents in question include methylene chloride, trichloroethylene, perchloroethylene, and 1,1,1-trichloroethane.

34. C. C. Travis and C. B. Duty, "Can contaminated aquifers at superfund sites be remediated?" *Environmental Science and Technology* 24 (1990): 1464–66.

35. See C. W. Hall, "Practical limits to pump and treat technology for aquifer remediation," Ground Water Quality Protection: Preconference workshop, Dallas, TX, 1988, cited in Travis and Duty, above.

36. See Herbert, note 33, p. 863.

37. See "Report of the Chairmen," in S. Draggan, J. J. Cohrssen, and R. E. Morrison, eds., *Preserving ecological systems* (New York: Praeger, 1987), xxi.

38. See E. A. Norse, "Habitat diversity and genetic variability," in *Preserving ecological systems,* note 37, p. 94.

39. See R. D. Harbison, "Chlorinated hydrocarbons: old fears new facts," unpublished manuscript (1991), Appendix B.

40. See G. M. Woodwell, "On toxins and toxic effects: Guarding life in a small world," in *Preserving ecological systems: The agenda for long-term research and development,* note 37, pp. 41–49.

41. Ibid., p. 43.

CHAPTER THIRTEEN: CONCLUSION

1. See M. Unger and J. Olsen, "Organochlorine compounds in the adipose tissue of deceased people with and without cancer," *Environmental Research* 23 (1980): 257–63.

2. See *International Agency for Research on Cancer Monographs on the evaluation of the carcinogenic risk of chemicals to humans,* Supplement 4 (Lyon, France: I.A.R.C., 1982), 15–17.

3. See J. W. Patterson, "Industrial wastes reduction," *Environmental Science and Technology* 23 (1989): 1032–38.

4. See "Pesticides here but where tomorrow?" *The Lancet* 336 (1990): 9990.

5. See Patterson, note 3, p. 1034.

6. From "Summary report of the expert panel meeting on environmental impacts and their mitigation," in S. Draggan, J. J. Cohrssen, and R. E. Morrison, eds., *Preserving ecological systems: The agenda for long-term research and development* (New York: Praeger, 1987), 4.

7. Mahoney spoke at the EPA Region III conference in Philadelphia in November 1989, as reported in *Chemical and Engineering News,* 27 November 1989, p. 34.

8. See Keith Schneider, "The Clean Air Act, immediate costs, long-term gains," *New York Times,* 23 October 1990, pp. A1, A12.

9. See J. Long, "EPA issues policy for groundwater protection," *Chemical and Engineering News,* 7 March 1990, p. 7.

10. Cited in *Chemical and Engineering News,* 27 November 1989, p. 34.

11. See G. Jones-Robbins, ed., *Alternative agriculture,* National Research Council, NAS (Washington, DC, 1989).

12. Cited in *Chemical and Engineering News,* 27 November 1989, p. 34.

13. According to Ames, eliminating fungicides such as ethylene dibromide, a carcinogenic and highly mutagenic compound, "might result in a regression of public health, not an advance, and would also greatly increase costs." See B. N. Ames, "What are the major carcinogens in the etiology of human cancer?" in B. N. Ames, *Important advances in oncology* (Philadelphia: Lippincott, 1989), 237–47, quote on p. 245.

14. See M. L. Wald, "Utilities call cleaner air feasible but expensive," *New York Times,* 23 October 1990, p. A12.

15. More than two hundred Hispanic women who worked at the

GTE–Lenkurt fabrication facility in Albuquerque developed serious and often irreversible neurological damage as a result of exposure to CFCs and other chlorinated solvents and chemicals at their worksite according to an extensive evaluation conducted by a team headed by Dr. Rosemarie Bowler of Berkeley, California. A report documenting these impacts is in press.

16. A related list was developed by George M. Woodwell, "On toxins and toxic effects: Guarding life in a small world," in *Preserving ecological systems,* note 6, pp. 41–49.

17. According to *Ethanol Report 3* (no. 1: 1989), a gallon of gasoline emits 21.54 pounds of CO_2 compared to 5.26 pounds released by combustion of a gallon of ethanol. In addition, gasoline combustion engines are a major source of benzopyrene and other carcinogens, particularly from spent oil. (The new Clean Air Act mandates that cleaner fuels be introduced by 1992.)

Index